The Va

Yevgeny Vakhtangov was the [...] or of fantastic realism, credited with reconciling Meyerhold's [...] experiments with Stanislavsky's naturalist technique. *The Va[...]gov Sourcebook* compiles new translations of his key writing[...] he art of theatre, making it the primary source of first-hand r[...]..l on this master of theatre in the English-speaking world.

Vakhtangov's essays and articles are accompanied by:

- unpublished diary and notebook excerpts
- his lectures to the Vakhtangov Studio
- in-depth accounts of Vakhtangov's methods in rehearsal
- production photographs and sketches
- extensive bibliographies
- director's notes on key performances.

An extensive introductory overview from editor Andrei Malaev-Babel explains Vakhtangov's creative life, his ground-breaking theatrical concepts and influential directorial works.

Andrei Malaev-Babel is Assistant Professor of Theatre at the Florida State University/Asolo Conservatory for Actor Training. He holds an MFA from the Vakhtangov Theatre Institute in Moscow, where he trained under Aleksandra Remizova. He is a member of the international faculty for the Michael Chekhov Association (MICHA).

Figure 1 Yevgeny Vakhtangov, 1918. © Moscow Art Theatre's Museum.

The Vakhtangov Sourcebook

Edited, translated and
with an introduction
by Andrei Malaev-Babel

Routledge
Taylor & Francis Group

LONDON AND NEW YORK

First published 2011
by Routledge
2 Park Square, Milton Park, Abingdon OX14 4RN

Simultaneously published in the USA and Canada
by Routledge
711 Third Avenue, New York, NY 10017

*Routledge is an imprint of the Taylor & Francis Group,
an informa business*

British Library Cataloguing in Publication Data
A catalogue record for this book is available from the British Library

Library of Congress Cataloging-in-Publication Data
A catalog record for this book has been requested

ISBN: 978-0-415-47268-5 (hbk)
ISBN: 978-0-415-48257-8 (pbk)
ISBN: 978-0-203-85291-0 (ebk)

Typeset in Sabon by
Bookcraft Ltd, Stroud, Gloucestershire

Printed and bound in Great Britain by
TJ International Ltd, Padstow, Cornwall

This publication was made possible by a generous grant from the Dolores Zohrab Liebmann Fund.

I would like to dedicate *The Vakhtangov Sourcebook* to the memory of my teacher, and Vakhtangov's student, Aleksandra Remizova. The youngest of Vakhtangov's disciples, Remizova acted in her teacher's productions of *The Miracle of Saint Anthony* and *Princess Turandot*. For over fifty years, she remained one of the leading directors of the Vakhtangov Theatre in Moscow. Through five years of close professional collaboration and personal contact with Aleksandra Remizova, I have been fortunate to be exposed to her wisdom and creative genius (see Figure 2).

Figure 2 Aleksandra Remizova as Zelima and Yuri Zavadsky as Calaf in Act 3, Scene 6, of *Princess Turandot*, 1922. © Vakhtangov Theatre's Museum.

Contents

x *Contents*

PART IX
Correspondence with Colleagues   309

List of Illustrations and Plates

Illustrations

Plates

Acknowledgements

There are quite a few people without whom this book would not have been possible. At Routledge, I would like to acknowledge Talia Rogers, Ben Piggott and Niall Slater; I would also like to thank Minh Ha Duong for seeing the book through in its early stages.

I am greatly indebted to Franc Chamberlain, whose insightful comments and suggestions helped me better express my thoughts and clarify my ideas.

Florida State University and its Council on Research and Creativity provided me with a generous award in support of my work on this book. I am thankful to them and to those people who supported my application: Dr. Sally McRorie, Dean of the College of Visual Arts, Theatre and Dance; Dr. C. Cameron Jackson, Director of the School of Theatre; Professors Terry Lynn Hogan and Martha Cooper, as well as School of Theatre's administrative associate Tanya Byrd. I would also like to thank Kirby Kemper, Vice President for Research and Jan Townsend of the Council on Research and Creativity.

The Dolores Zohrab Liebmann Fund gave a generous gift in support of *The Vakhtangov Sourcebook*. I would like to thank the Liebmann Fund, and especially Edward L. Jones and Mr. M. Haigentz, for their contribution to this pioneering Vakhtangov edition.

My wife, Lisa Eveland Malaev, proofread every word of my writings for the past eighteen years. I want to thank her, my son Nicholai, my mother Lidiya and my grandmother Antonina for their tremendous patience and support during my Vakhtangov saga. My deep gratitude goes to Steven Ross Evelend, who has patiently edited every word I have penned for the past fifteen years.

I am also indebted to Anna Brusser, Professor of the Vakhtangov Theatre Institute in Moscow (Schukin School) for her kind permission to publish her grandmother, Vera L'vova's, records of Vakhtangov's rehearsals and talks. I want to thank Roza Zaripova, the head of Arsis

Books, for her kind assistance in my research. I also want to thank Dr. Pavel Dmitriev of the St. Petersburg State Theatre Library, and noted St. Petersburg theatre scholar Margarita Laskina, for the unique opportunity they gave me to become acquainted with the theatrical heritage of Vakhtangov's contemporary, director and teacher Nikolai Demidov. Demidov's rare insight into the Stanislavsky System, and his own unique school of acting, allowed me a better understanding of Vakhtangov's heritage.

I am especially grateful to Galina Remizova, the Moscow actress and daughter of my teacher Aleksandra Remizova, for her selfless support of my work. I would also like to thank Geraldine Martin of Taylor & Francis Books, Elizabeth Hudson of the Little Red Pen and Nick Morgan of Bookcraft for seeing *The Vakhtangov Sourcebook* seamlessly through production.

Several generous and patient individuals were instrumental to helping me identify and secure illustrations for this collection. My deep gratitude goes to Marfa Bubnova, Director of the Moscow Art Theatre's Museum, for her invaluable help and advice. I would like to thank Mr. Dmitry Radionov, Director of the Bakhrushin State Central Theatre Museum in Moscow, for his understanding, and support of my work. Natalia Mashechkina, the museum's Academic Secretary, provided me with invaluable help in identifying Vakhtangov-related images both at the Bakhrushin Museum and in other collections. Elena Giritch of the museum's International Department was also important to the process of preparing and relaying unique materials, such as the audio recording of Michael Chekhov's lecture on Vakhtangov. At the Vakhtangov Theatre's Museum, I would like to thank the museum's curators Irina Sergeyeva and Margarita Litvin, for their generous support, and for the research they conducted on my behalf. At the St. Petersburg State Museum of Theatre and Music, I am grateful to the museum's Director Natalia Metelitsa, the museum's Academic Secretary, Evgenia Suzdaleva and Assistant to the Deputy Director for Development, Anna Fedotov. In Jerusalem, Israel, I would like to thank Polina Kapsheev of the Israeli State Radio REKA, as well as Nina and Natalia Mikhoels. I am deeply indebted to the Director of the Israel Goor Theatre Archives and Museum Luba Yuniverg, as well as to Leonid Yuniverg. Both Luba and Leonid were generous in sharing the Goor Archives' collection with me, and connecting me with other organizations in Israel. I also would like to thank the talented photographer Gregory Khatin, who is associated with the Goor Archives. My gratitude also goes to the Central Zionist Archives, and especially to the Head of the archive's Photograph Collection, Anat Banin.

I am forever indebted to the noted Russian scholar Vladislav Ivanov, who demonstrated an unprecedented generosity of spirit by sharing with me the manuscript of his fundamental two-volume edition, *Yevgeny Vakhtangov, Documents and Evidence*, prior to its Russian publication in February 2011. This groundbreaking Vakhtangov collection restored the Soviet-era censorship cuts to major Vakhtangov texts, and it introduced many new, previously unpublished materials by Vakhtangov and on Vakhtangov. Thanks to Mr. Ivanov and the Moscow Indrik publishers, *The Vakhtangov Sourcebook* translations appear uncensored and uncut, thus allowing English-language readers around the globe to appreciate Vakhtangov as a futuristic, highly spiritual thinker and artist.

Last but not least, I would like to thank my colleagues and students at the Florida State University/Asolo Conservatory for Actor Training and at the New College of Florida. I learn from them daily.

Special thanks to the Florida State University's Council on Research & Creativity for their support through the COFRS grant award.

Editor's Note

The Vakhtangov Sourcebook is the first book collection of Yevgeny Vakhtangov's writings, lectures, rehearsal records and talks to be published in the English-speaking world. Unless specified otherwise, materials in this volume first appeared in the original Russian as part of the pioneering Vakhtangov heritage collection printed in the Soviet Union (Vakhtangova et al. 1939). Other original Russian sources are identified in the sourcebook text and appear in the Bibliography. All publications mentioned or quoted by the editor are identified in the Introduction and featured in the Bibliography. All publications mentioned or quoted by Vakhtangov are identified in footnotes, in order not to break the flow of Vakhtangov's texts.

All Vakhtangov materials in the sourcebook appear in a new translation from the Russian by Andrei Malaev-Babel. This translation aims to bring Vakhtangov's unique voice to the reader. As part of this effort, the translator preserved Vakhtangov's original use of gender. According to the customs of Vakhtangov's period, words such as 'he', 'his', 'himself', etc., were often used conventionally and, in fact, implied both genders.

Unless otherwise noted, materials in Parts I, II, IV, and VII of the sourcebook appear in English for the first time. Previous English translations of Yevgeny Vakhtangov's texts include a free digest from Vakhtangov's diary notes and rehearsal talks, compiled by Vakhtangov's disciple Boris Zakhava (Zakhava 1927 and 1930). An unattributed translation of Zakhava's digest was printed in the USA as part of a Stanislavsky-system anthology (Cole 1947).[1] Another unattributed English translation of Vakhtangov's *Two Discussions with Students* was featured

---

1 Boris Zakhava (1896–1976), one of Vakhtangov's oldest students, a co-founder of the Vakhtangov Studio. Zakhava remained one of the leading Vakhtangov Theatre directors until 1959. He also headed the Vakhtangov Institute in Moscow (the Schukin School) for five decades.

in a US-published directing anthology (Cole and Chinoy (eds.) 1953). Unless otherwise noted, materials in Parts III, V, VI and VIII of the sourcebook previously appeared in Doris Bradbury's English translation (Vendrovskaya and Kaptereva 1982). This Soviet Union publication is currently out of print and was never widely available in the West.

Part I of *The Vakhtangov Sourcebook* features excerpts from talks given by Vakhtangov at the Vakhtangov Studio in Moscow between 1914 and 1921. Some of these talks were given at the training rehearsal sessions, conducted by Vakhtangov. Vakhtangov's talks did not narrowly apply to the scenes rehearsed. In his training practices, Vakhtangov separated general talks about art and the creative process from notes given to actors on their characters and scenes. For Vakhtangov, a talk on the fundamentals of the creative process was a step into different territory; it was meant to redirect the actors' **attention** (thus providing a needed rest to an actor in the middle of a rehearsal), to inspire them, to outline homework, etc.

The specific rehearsal notes, delivered by Vakhtangov, are featured in Part VI of the sourcebook. They provide an invaluable record of Vakhtangov's rehearsal work with the student-actors. For editorial purposes, however, general talks about theatre and an actor's creative process, even if delivered in the midst of a rehearsal, are featured in Part I, which is dedicated to the fundamentals of the Vakhtangov technique. An inquisitive reader wishing to know what play or scene was rehearsed on the day when a particular talk was given, can easily do so by comparing dates between Parts I and VI.

According to Michael Chekhov's memoir *The Path of the Actor* (Chekhov 2005), Chekhov encouraged Vakhtangov Studio members to take notes of their master's talks and rehearsals. Vera L'vova (1898–1985) followed Chekhov's advice. L'vova was a student of Vakhtangov, a Vakhtangov Theatre actress, and one of the leading professors of the Vakhtangov Theatre Institute in Moscow (Schukin Theatre School) for over sixty years. Her records were originally published in a book authored by her husband, Leonid Shikhmatov (1887–1970) (Shikhmatov 1970). Vera L'vova's records are reproduced in this volume by the gracious permission of L'vova and Shikhmatov's granddaughter, Anna Brusser, a professor at the Vakhtangov Theatre Institute.

Other Vakhtangov Studio rehearsal and class records featured in the sourcebook were originally published in the first Soviet Union collection of Vakhtangov's heritage (Vakhtangova et al. 1939). This book collection did not provide the names of students who took and compiled the Vakhtangov Studio class and rehearsal records.

Part I

Introduction

1   On Vakhtangov's Work and Writings

Prologue

Russian-Armenian director Yevgeny Bogrationovich Vakhtangov was born on February 13, 1883, in the Russian provincial city of Vladikavkaz (currently the capital of the Russian Republic of North Ossetia-Alania—the neighboring region of the ongoing Russian–Georgian and Chechen conflicts). Like Konstantin Treplev from Anton Chekhov's *The Seagull*, nineteen-year-old Vakhtangov arranged his first theatre outdoors; an open stage merged with the mountainous landscape of the Caucasus. Vakhtangov's production of Chekhov's short comedies "began before dark and ended by the time the sun set down" (Vakhtangova 1959: 334). It breathed in unison with the natural **rhythms**.

Vakhtangov's Heritage and Contemporary Theatrical Practices

In 1955, Michael Chekhov (1891–1955), an actor still considered as Russia's greatest twentieth-century talent, delivered one of his final lectures to a group of Hollywood actors. The subject of the lecture, entitled 'On Five Great Russian Directors', was personal to Chekhov. In it he spoke of his mentors, contemporaries, colleagues, and friends: Konstantin Stanislavsky (1863–1938), Vladimir Nemirovich-Danchenko (1858–1943), Alexander Tairov (1885–1950), Vsevolod Meyerhold (1874–1940), and Yevgeny Vakhtangov. He spoke of them in that particular order, saving Vakhtangov for last, thereby placing him at the top of the pyramid:

> Now, this combination of Nemirovich and Stanislavsky was also taken by Vakhtangov. He always found, very easily too [like Nemirovich],

this main line, this scaffolding [of the performance], and he took from Stanislavsky the human, warm-heart[ed] feelings, emotions, **atmosphere** – brought them together. Vakhtangov was, as it were, a vessel into which all the positive things came. Not that he robbed them [Nemirovich and Stanislavsky] of their good qualities. It was his genius, Vakhtangov's genius; he just quickly, naturally swallowed it, digested it. So, he was a kind of vessel, as I say, where all the positive things of this period of the Russian theatre of which I am talking were accumulated, amalgamated in his own way, in Vakhtangov's way.

... And these things, coming from Stanislavsky, Nemirovich, Tairov, Meyerhold, apparently can be combined. And Vakhtangov did combine them; he brought them together – these extreme and seemingly irreconcilable things – he brought them together ... Vakhtangov showed us that everything can be brought together, amalgamated and a new product – very beautiful, very wonderful, very deep, and very light, and very mathematically clever and humanly bright – it can be done.

(Vinyl audio record; Bakhrushin State Central Theatre Museum; HB 4904/17)

That statement Michael Chekhov made more than half a century ago still rings true today. Out of the five great Russian directors of the first half of the twentieth century, Vakhtangov remains the most relevant. Vakhtangov's work considerably affected twentieth-century theatrical practices. The concepts that today's theatre artists continue to experiment with, explore, and consider were all approached by Vakhtangov in an unorthodox and highly individual way. Moreover, many of the paradoxes and dilemmas of the theatrical art were resolved by Vakhtangov in the final two years of his short creative life.

In his 1922 production of Carlo Gozzi's[1] *Princess Turandot* Vakhtangov brought an actor's **point of view** on his or her **character** into the foreground, foreshadowing the Brechtian principle of "alienation." In *Turandot*, as well as in other productions he directed at his own studio, Vakhtangov interpreted the problem of an actor's improvisational **freedom** versus formal **discipline**, and paved the way for Jerzy Grotowski (1933–1999).[2] In his productions, Vakhtangov also anticipated Grotowski in his approach to such theatrical aspects as 'act' and 'ritual'.

---

1   Count Carlo Gozzi (1720–1806), an Italian playwright, a proponent of the *commedia dell'arte*.
2   This parallel between Vakhtangov and Grotowski was noted by the Russian scholar Vladislav Ivanov (Ivanov 1999: 95).

The Dybbuk, directed by Vakhtangov at the Habima Studio, made the critics speak of the Theatre of Cruelty before the time of Antonin Artaud (1896–1948). For example, Russian critic and scholar Nikolai Volkov[3] wrote, in 1922, "In *The Dybbuk* Vakhtangov demonstrated how cruel his talent was, how dear the beauty of ugliness was to his **soul**" (Volkov 1922: 20). Contemporary Russian scholar, Vladislav Ivanov, wrote on *The Dybbuk*, "Vakhtangov's cosmic ecstasies did not just anticipate Antonin Artaud's 'cosmic trance.' They also had an indisputable advantage before the fantasies and incantations of the French theatre's poet, as they came fully armed with theatrical means, realized in the art's matter" (1999: 96).

Michael Chekhov, according to his own admission, took notes of Vakhtangov's talks and rehearsals; he was influenced by Vakhtangov's concept of rhythm and **gesture**. The influence in this case was mutual, as Vakhtangov arrived at some of his own conclusions studying the work of Chekhov, the actor.

Edward Gordon Craig (1872–1966) and Max Reinhardt (1873–1943) praised Vakhtangov's productions in the press.[4] Bertolt Brecht (1898–1956) and Jerzy Grotowski carefully studied Vakhtangov's heritage. Grotowski, who trained in Moscow under Vakhtangov's disciple Yuri Zavadsky (1894–1977), frequently mentioned Vakhtangov in his lectures. Peter Brook saw the revival of *Princess Turandot* in Moscow.[5] Among those who feature Vakhtangov in their writings are Lee Strasberg (1901–1982), Eugenio Barba, and David Mamet. One way or another, through agreement or disagreement, direct or indirect influence, Vakhtangov's heritage is present in the works of these masters. As for Vakhtangov's elder colleagues and mentors, such as Konstantin Stanislavsky, Vladimir

---

3 Leonid Volkov (Zimnyukov) (1893–1976), Russian actor, director, and teacher, a member at the Vakhtangov Studio from the time of its founding until 1919. After his departure from the Vakhtangov Studio, Volkov worked at the MAT, its First and Second Studios, at the Moscow Theatre of the Revolution, and at the Moscow Maly Theatre and School.

4 According to Vladislav Ivanov (1999), in 1931 and 1937 Craig wrote articles on the Habima Theatre's London tours. While original sources cannot be identified, reprints of these articles can be found in two journals. The reprint of the 1931 article appears in *Bericht des Gewerkschaftsbundes der Angestellten: Bericht über das Arbeitsjahr 1930*, Berlin: Verlag des GDA, 1931, p. 12. Craig's 1937 article has been reprinted in Habima, English Publication of "Bama," *Theatre Art Journal of Habima Circle in Palestine*, August 1939, pp. 33–34. Max Reinhardt's 1926 interview on the Habima Vienna tour, also from an unidentified source, was reprinted in Itzhak Norman (ed.) (1966) *Be-reshit Habimah* [*The Birth of Habima*], Jerusalem: ha-Sifriyah ha-Tsiyonit, p. 341.

5 In fairness it must be said that Vakhtangov's disciples' interpretation of *Princess Turandot*, issued some forty years after the original premiere, did not impress Peter Brook (1996: 15–16).

Nemirovich-Danchenko, and Vsevolod Meyerhold—all of them acknowledged Vakhtangov's outstanding contributions to the art of theatre, as well as his influence on their own work.[6]

Because of Vakhtangov's lack of interest in theories not supported in practice, his own theoretical conclusion always followed the creation of a practical model. In his final productions, staged within the last two years of his short life, Vakhtangov created the practical model for his method of **fantastic realism**. As for the method itself, Vakhtangov did not have time to write it down, or to explain it fully. The key texts on fantastic realism, featured in the sourcebook, such as *Discussions with Students* (April 1922) and *All Saints' Notes* (March 1921), provide us with a limited understanding of Vakhtangov's concept. This introduction is a partial reconstruction of Vakhtangov's method of fantastic realism, based on his own writings, memoirs by the colleagues, audience recollections, critical reviews and scholarly works on Vakhtangov, and my experience of training at the Vakhtangov School in Moscow, as well as my own research and practices. Last, but not least, this reconstruction would not be possible if not for my fortune to work directly with two of Vakhtangov's students: Vera L'vova (1898–1985) and, my mentor in theatre, Aleksandra Remizova (1903–1989).

Vakhtangov's Theory of Creative Perception

Vakhtangov and the Stanislavsky System

Anyone writing on the Stanislavsky System is bound to encounter one significant difficulty: the theory, as outlined in Stanislavsky's writings, was seldom followed in teaching practices. This is true of the two original and most trusted disciples of Stanislavsky's: his close friend and associate, Leopold Sulerzhitsky (1872–1916), and Sulerzhitsky's student Yevgeny Vakhtangov. Out of all directors and teachers associated with the Moscow Art Theatre (MAT),[7] Stanislavsky only consid-

---

6   Vakhtangov considered Stanislavsky and Nemirovich-Danchenko his mentors and teachers, and yet both men outlived their "student" by more than a decade. So did Vakhtangov's older peer Meyerhold. In their subsequent works these masters reflected Vakhtangov's discoveries and thus carried Vakhtangov's heritage into the future.

7   The Moscow Art Theatre was founded in 1897 by Konstantin Stanislavsky and Vladimir Nemirovich-Danchenko. Vakhtangov worked at the MAT and its three studios as an actor, director, and acting teacher from 1911 to 1922. From 1916 to 1922, Vakhtangov served on the Board and as the informal leader of the First Studio of the MAT, of which he was also a co-founder.

ered these two leaders capable of surpassing Nemirovich-Danchenko and himself at the MAT's helm.[8] Both Sulerzhitsky and Vakhtangov taught Stanislavsky's technique at the First Studio of the MAT. Vakhtangov, who became extremely popular as both a director and teacher outside of the MAT, gave himself generously to numerous Moscow theatre collectives. By doing so, Vakhtangov often incurred the wrath of both Stanislavsky and Sulerzhitsky.

Leopold Sulerzhitsky died in 1916, and Vakhtangov outlived him by only six years—he died on May 29, 1922, at the age of thirty-nine. Later that year Stanislavsky established the MAT School. With both Sulerzhitsky and Vakhtangov gone, Stanislavsky turned to the third and only remaining teacher of his technique who he trusted: Nikolai Demidov.[9] Stanislavsky's letter to Demidov, written on the occasion, featured bitter words on Vakhtangov:

> I am doomed!
>
> I worked with Vakhtangov; he gave me a lot of trouble. They did not recognize him, tried to sack him from the theatre; at the end—he was lured to teach in one place, promised to direct at another; he worked nights at the Habima Studio; as for me—in his entire life he only found 2 evenings to work together on Salieri.[10]
>
> Whatever I do, whatever I prepare—they tear it from my fingers, and I am left with nothing.
>
> (Stanislavsky 1999: 54)

8 See Stanislavsky's letter to the MAT Managing Director Mikhail Geits (Stanislavsky 1999: 379).
9 The name of Nikolai Demidov (1884–1953) is still little known in Russia and is almost unknown in the West. This happened for strictly political reasons connected with the Stanislavsky method monopoly, established in the Soviet Union by Stalin. In Stalinist Russia, Demidov, who disagreed with Stanislavsky on several points, was kept in exile for a large part of his career. The monopoly on teaching the Stanislavsky method, established by some of the influential Stanislavsky disciples, prevented Demidov's name from surfacing for another half a century following Stalin's death. This is why a four-volume edition of Demidov's works did not appear in Russia until this first decade of the twenty-first century. It took Russia this long to discover this important teacher and theoretician and the participant in many important events of the twentieth-century Russian theatre. Without his witness, and without the awareness of his methods, one cannot fully comprehend the development of Stanislavsky's views on the actor training. Only in Demidov's heritage can one find an explanation of the legend, popular in the West, about the sudden turn in Stanislavsky's views that occurred in the last years of his life.
10 Vakhtangov worked with Stanislavsky on the role of Salieri in Aleksandr Pushkin's one-act verse play *Mozart and Salieri*. See p. 31 of the Introduction.

This passionate cry was meant as a reproach to Demidov whose initial reception of Stanislavsky's offer to head the MAT School was restrained. Demidov responded to Stanislavsky's plea and accepted the position. The results he achieved with the students made Stanislavsky proclaim, two years later, "Our school, prepared by Demidov, must carry God in it" (Stanislavsky 1999: 167). As for Demidov himself, in his book *Actor Types*, he made the following peculiar confession:

> If Konstantin Sergeyevich [Stanislavsky] did practice pedagogy, he only did so in the course of rehearsals, in passing: it was done to help the actor bring to life a particular moment of the role. He never taught School—there was no time. His students taught it, starting with Sulerzhitsky and Vakhtangov. For Stanislavsky it was simply impossible to perform consistent and regular control over results achieved by the methods he proposed, as well as the outcomes of the program as a whole.
>
> As for the teachers' work, sometimes it brought good results, sometimes bad ... Why?
>
> Perhaps, because one teacher applied their talent to the "system," another—did not.
>
> Somehow, it came as a matter of fact that, in the case of a teacher's failure, no one ever asked the question: perhaps, *the imperfection of the method* is to blame?
>
> And in the case of success, no one ever asked: perhaps, the teacher, *except for using the established methods, also used some other methods of their own,* sometimes without noticing it?
>
> (Demidov 2004a: 392–393)

Alexander Adashev (1871–1934), a MAT character actor, organized a private acting school in Moscow, where Vakhtangov studied from August 1909 to March 1911. The MAT's leading actors, such as Vasily Kachalov (1875–1948) and Vasily Luzhsky (1869–1931), taught at the Adashev School. Even at the most progressive Russian acting schools or conservatories of the period, students spent most of their time studying parts. The teacher, instead of providing training for specific skills and qualities essential to an actor, would see his or her duty as imposing their own way of acting particular roles on the students. Vsevolod Meyerhold, who trained at the Philharmonic Society's Drama School under Nemirovich-Danchenko, wrote down the following quotation from the French actress Rachel in his 1897 student notebook: "For those with no talent, Conservatory will polish their facilities and make them decent actors; it will kill every talent, however, as it forces them to act its own way" (Maikov 1896: 3, cited in Meyerhold 1998: 135).

Among the Adashev School teachers, Sulerzhitsky stood out because of his involvement with the newly developed Stanislavsky System. The starting point of Stanislavsky's methodological journey was based in the organic creative nature. The organic principles of the creative process conducive to revealing an actor's **creative individuality**—such was the platform Stanislavsky shared with Sulerzhitsky. Vakhtangov, a natural-born director and actor possessing the inborn feeling of truth, accepted Sulerzhitsky's principles as unshakable; they were in perfect harmony with Vakhtangov's own genetic makeup as an artist.

The Creative Individuality

In March 1911, Vakhtangov, who served as prototype for the student Nazvanov, the narrator of Stanislavsky's *An Actor's Work* (also known as *An Actor Prepares*), made his near stenographic record of Stanislavsky's first talk to the MAT youth. Two other talks followed; in Vakhtangov's notes we find the Stanislavsky System's goal, as defined by Stanislavsky himself: "to cultivate in students, abilities and qualities which help them to free their creative individuality—an individuality imprisoned by prejudices and clichés" (Zakhava 1930: 23).

So, what is this mysterious creative individuality, not featured in Stanislavsky's major writings, and, most importantly, what are the means of getting in touch with it? Leopold Sulerzhitsky had this to say on the subject:

> All the intense work of the contemporary director ... concentrates in helping the actor to discover his own self or, as they put it, help him "express" his personality to its inmost depth, and separate in his work what actually represents his true individuality from everything generic and theatrical, from the so called "tone." Although one actor's tone is unlike the other actors', it has nothing to do with their true individuality. Several beloved "tones" (this actor has two, the other—three or six) are always in every actor's arsenal. At times the actor is empty, the role does not want to submit; yet they have to speak and act it all the same. In this case, some "tone," or a combination of tones, immediately comes to the rescue. This conventional manner, this tone can be quite pleasant in some actors, and, in the majority of cases, the press and the **audience** take it for individuality, as it differs with every actor; at the same time, its inner makeup is always the same.

In actuality, this acted mannerism is the fiercest enemy of the individualized experience.

(Sulerzhitsky 1970: 319)

Sulerzhitsky's speeches and writings contain only hints of the organic means that can be utilized in order to inspire a true *individualized* experience in an actor. And, yet, Sulerzhitsky maintained that without this individualized emotional experience, an actor couldn't transform, or live creatively. Unless an actor engages in this highly personal and organic psychological process, their life onstage will remain mechanical, and their **transformation** false, or acted.

Continuing in Sulerzhitsky's footsteps, Vakhtangov developed principles of the inner technique that are based in the individualized emotional experience. An actor's process begins at the crossing of the creative threshold. If this crossing is to be done in accordance with the **organic technique,** the actor should enter the stage *psychologically unaltered*:

> The first state an actor experiences onstage is the one he just experienced in life. One needs great courage not to betray this experience. One must surrender entirely to the power of one's artistic nature. It will do all the necessary things. Don't impose any solution upon yourself in advance. The quality to develop in an actor is courage.
>
> (see p. 99)

Vakhtangov insisted that no matter what the actor experiences upon crossing the stage threshold it would apply to the imaginary reality of the stage. This axiom is based on the fact that, as the actor enters the stage, their creative nature is mobilized to fulfill the artistic **task.** Therefore, the creative nature offers the actor only those experiences helpful in fulfilling the creative task. Moreover, an actor's creative nature is capable of incorporating any seemingly personal psychological experience into the overall equation of their stage task. The main "job" of an actor is to practice complete freedom—that is, to remain true to their actual experiences and not to alter them. The courage to trust these experiences and not to perform anything on top of them or in their stead is the main secret of the organic technique. Vakhtangov had this to say on the matter:

> In life, feelings have an individual quality. Everyone feels differently. If feelings do not come to an actor—he should not imitate them.

Without feelings—what is there to act? Whatever combination of feelings creates itself—an actor should allow it.

One must remember that:

- Everyone experiences something at any given moment;
- Experiences change constantly; and
- Every single experience is individual;
  One cannot forge a combination of feelings, as it appears in life.

(see p. 99)

Vakhtangov insisted that the complex and highly individual psychological accord that resounds at any moment of a human's existence cannot be forged through the work of intellect and will. It can only "happen" to an actor, if the actor "leaves themselves alone," allows themselves full freedom of following their creative impulses, and yields to their creative intuition, courageously following its urges. According to Nikolai Demidov's version of organic technique, as outlined in his book *The Art of Living Onstage* (Demidov 2004b), the courage to freely go with the impulse, not yet knowing where it might lead you, and the courage to wait for the impulse when it is not there—these are the two conditions that sustain the actor's organic creative process throughout the performance.

Sulerzhitsky's idea of a theatre ensemble was equally grounded in the concept of creative individuality. "I maintain," said Sulerzhitsky, "that a good ensemble is only possible if it includes outstanding individualities, and a director of the same kind" (1970: 320). The concept of the creative collective, or ensemble, as the basis of theatrical art is prominently featured in the creative methods of Sulerzhitsky's students, Vakhtangov and Michael Chekhov. Like their teacher, both of these theatre artists firmly believed that each theatrical collective has its own individuality. At the same time, the collective cannot be referred to as the generic "us"; it consists of individual members, each of whom is unique. The role of the director within the creative collective, according to Sulerzhitsky, is to "create the utmost advantageous conditions *for every individuality* in such a way that this not only does not disturb the ensemble, but also does not contradict the idea of the play and, on the contrary, helps to reveal it with all distinction" (1970: 319).

At the heart of the organic technique lies the concept, outlined by Stanislavsky in his early writings on his method. The **creative spirit** of the actor is inseminated by the creative spirit of the author at the time of the **first reading** of the play. For this reason, the first reading has to be carefully arranged so as to create the right atmosphere for the insemination.[11] This is why Vakhtangov put a special emphasis on the 'first spontaneous impression' an actor receives upon the first reading of the play. From the rehearsal records for Vakhtangov's production of *The Lanin Estate*, the reader will see how the director arranged the first reading, making it conducive to the collective's preanalytical intuitive response. Moreover, in accordance with Sulerzhitsky's principles, Vakhtangov considered the job of the director and teacher to ensure that the first spontaneous impression from the play remained alive and guided the collective throughout the entire period of work on the play and into the performances.

Like his teachers, Vakhtangov believed that each role is conceived at this first acquaintance with the play while the rest of the creative process is dedicated to its gradual growth and development. As Vakhtangov would put it: "each rehearsal is a day in the character's life; a series of days forms personality" (see p. 212). It is for this reason that Vakhtangov insisted that rehearsals should never repeat each other and that "every rehearsal is only productive when in it one seeks or provides material for the next rehearsal" (see p. 111). Only under these conditions can the role develop and grow. On the contrary, if the scenes are repeated in rehearsal in an attempt to fix them, the organic growth of the character stops, and it eventually "dies off." This happens because the actor, in rehearsals, stops supplying the needed material, or food, to his or her creative subconscious. According to Vakhtangov, the creative process itself takes place "in the intervals between rehearsals" when the "subconscious processes the acquired material" (see p. 111).

> The role of the director, therefore, is to foresee the sprouts of the role in the actor and to stimulate their growth. Sulerzhitsky describes this process thus: To catch, to lovingly mark every sincere, truly individual moment in the work of the actor, to notice by what means they managed to bring themselves into the state of creative excitement, what helped them with this, and what interfered, to create conditions that are most fitting for the actor's individuality—this is the director's work in relation to any particular actor.
>
> (Sulerzhitsky 1970: 319)

---

11 "The moment of the first acquaintance with the role is paramount. Virginal impressions ... permeate the depth of the artistic soul, the subsoil of the creative nature; they often leave there lasting imprints that underlie the foundation of the role, become the future character's embryo" (Stanislavsky 1991: 48).

Sulerzhitsky's formula of the director's task might strike the reader as being too ideal and, therefore, impossible. And yet, Vakhtangov practically fulfilled this formula in his directorial work. In addition to using the approach of encouraging the live, individual moments in an actor's work, as described by Sulerzhitsky, he often used a "shortcut" approach. Vakhtangov's disciple Boris Zakhava gives us a precise description of Vakhtangov's ability to inwardly transform himself into each and every one of his actors, to literally become them, both individually and collectively, in order to guess his actors' creative intentions, often unknown to them, and demonstrate them to the collective:

> Vakhtangov could formulate with **clarity** and definition what lived in the collective as yet vaguely and indefinitely. When Vakhtangov demonstrated some quality (gesture or intonation) to an actor, the actor felt that this was the exact quality he was missing in order to fully express himself. Vakhtangov prompted to that actor what the actor's own creative individuality subconsciously demanded. Every play would be staged by Vakhtangov differently with a different company. He demanded different things from different actors, who worked on the same role. As a result, every actor, every member of the collective, felt that Vakhtangov was working for his cause; while fulfilling the cause of the collective, Vakhtangov thus fulfilled the cause of every actor, with whom he worked. Vakhtangov could guess the collective's will; he could organize this will and help each and every member express it in their creative work. Vakhtangov composed his productions in such a way that every member of the collective, even those not participating in this particular production, felt it as *their own*. They could say of each quality in the performance: with this quality Vakhtangov expressed me; he expressed me so truly and so fully, as I could not have done myself.
> (Zakhava 1935; reprinted in Zakhava 2010: 234)

In this brilliant explanation, Zakhava reveals the mechanism of Vakhtangov's directorial phenomenon. The phenomenon itself is well documented in literature on Vakhtangov, including Michael Chekhov's 1928 memoir *The Path of the Actor*. In it, Chekhov maintains that Vakhtangov could speak to each actor "in the language of his soul" (2005: 69). According to Chekhov, Vakhtangov's way of working with the actor resolved the eternal theatrical problem of creative authorship:

> Vakhtangov, as it were, invisibly put himself next to the actor and led him by the hand. The actor never felt any coercion from

Vakhtangov, but neither could he get away from the concept that Vakhtangov created as a director. In implementing Vakhtangov's instructions and concepts, the actor felt as if these ideas were his own.

(Chekhov 2005: 68)

Individual Approach to Creative Individuality

The concept of creative individuality implies that each individual actor is unique and, therefore, deserves a different approach from the director. While every actor is individual in their creative makeup, we do, nevertheless, encounter several predominant actor types. These types rarely exist as pure models; any given actor may combine in themselves qualities from different types, and yet every actor leans toward a particular category. With this category, comes a respective way of working on self and on the role.

Nikolai Demidov, in his book *Actor Types*, distinguished the following general categories of actors: the Imitator, the Emotional (sometimes Demidov uses the term "Emotionally Willful"), the **Affective**,[12] and the Rationalist (sometimes described as Rationally Willful.)[13] Sulerzhitsky and Vakhtangov were clearly aware of the existence of these different types of actors, and they utilized this knowledge in their work. Sulerzhitsky understood that rational and willful means of evoking creative conditions work best for those actors who, according to Demidov's classification, belong to the "rationally willful type." And yet, there are other types of actors, for whom Stanislavsky's stress on activity is deadly; by overwhelming them with physical actions, the director is more likely to kill their creativity than to stimulate it. When it comes to the kind of actor described by Demidov as affective, it is the culture of creative freedom, calm, and passivity that appears to be most beneficial.

The affective actor, who is predisposed to heightened emotions, needs to maintain creative calm, passivity, and meditativeness as a foundation for their creative process. Only such psychological background is conducive to the affective actor's ability to perceive creative impulses deeply into their psyche and to express them from the very depths of their creative soul. The culture of creative calm and passivity

---

12 Demidov's use of the term "affective" meaning "passionate" will be discussed further in the Introduction.
13 See Demidov (2004a: Book 2).

is also advantageous for the bordering type of an emotionally willful actor. When writing about a director's necessity to adjust to different types of actors, Sulerzhitsky described this phenomenon thus:

> One actor, for example, according to the type of their creative passion, cannot develop it correctly if the scene is built on mise-en-scènes rich with elaborate movements. Abundance of physical transitions and movements deprives them of their sincerity and leads them toward a false, muscular **temperament**; they can only live correctly onstage and discover their own individualities in a *calmer* mise-en-scène.
>
> (Sulerzhitsky 1970: 319–320)

According to Vakhtangov's many students, their teacher possessed an almost supernatural, hypnotic power over the actor and an ability to inspire a top-rate performance from a seemingly mediocre individual. In actuality, Vakhtangov's hypnotic gift concentrated in his ability to penetrate the unique individuality of the actor to speak with every actor in the language of his or her individuality and use, with each particular actor, only the methods helpful for their creative type. Besides the shortcut approach of demonstrating to the actor, or the entire ensemble, their true creative intention, Vakhtangov utilized other approaches. For a rational actor, whose excitement was purely intellectual, Vakhtangov clarified the **thought** contained in the text, until it reached crystal-clear clarity and inflamed the actor. (This is as close as an intellectual actor can approach the **essence** of a theatrical phenomenon.) With an intellectually willful actor, Vakhtangov spoke the language of analysis and action. With the emotional and affective actors he utilized the culture of intuition and creative calm, etc.

As a creative individuality, both as a director and an actor, Vakhtangov himself belonged to the affective type—the type whose creative process is based in synthesis, an instant intuitive grasp of the character, play or performance as a whole, the power of globalization, the feeling of complicity with the world, and deep passions fraught with potential tragic outbursts. Therefore, Vakhtangov's own creative individuality was ill served by the rationally willful aspects of the Stanislavsky technique. Moreover, his own development was jeopardized by this particular turn in Stanislavsky's methodological search. It was not until Vakhtangov, in the early 1920s, carried out his "tortuous attempt to break out of Stanislavsky's chains," that his own unique individuality could reach its full potential (see p. 131).

The radical act of breaking from Stanislavsky was carried out by Vakhtangov in his legendary *All Saints' Notes*, written in March 1921. In these notes, authored at suburban Moscow's All Saints' Rehabilitation Resort, Vakhtangov severely criticized Stanislavsky and Nemirovich and enthusiastically praised Meyerhold. This alone warranted elaborate cuts made in the document throughout its publication history.

Three book collections of Vakhtangov's literary heritage were published in the former Soviet Union in the period between the late 1930s and the mid 1980s. By 1939 (the year when the first Vakhtangov book collection came out), Stanislavsky was dead. The Stanislavsky System, however, was pronounced the unbending law of the theatre art by the Soviet dictator Joseph Stalin. The same year, Meyerhold was arrested on Stalin's orders. (He was sentenced and shot in a Moscow prison the following year, on false accusations.) Any evidence of Vakhtangov's praise of Meyerhold, and/or his negative comments on Stanislavsky, could have seriously harmed the two institutions founded by Vakhtangov: the Vakhtangov Theatre and its affiliate Theatre Institute (the Schukin Theatre School). This fact did not escape Vakhtangov's Soviet editors, who were closely affiliated with the two institutions. Meyerhold's name was absent from the first Vakhtangov heritage collection (Vakhtangova et al. 1939); criticism of Stanislavsky was also edited out of *All Saints' Notes*. Mentions of Meyerhold were restored in the two subsequent editions of Vakhtangov's writings (Vendrovskaya 1959 and Vendrovskaya and Kaptereva 1984), both published after Meyerhold's posthumous rehabilitation. Vakhtangov's harsh criticism of Stanislavsky and Nemirovich, however, remained absent from these publications. *All Saints' Notes* was not published in the Soviet Union in its entirety until *Perestroika* arrived in the mid 1980s. The first unabridged publication of this document was undertaken by the noted theatre critic and Meyerhold scholar Konstantin Rudnitsky in 1987, in the twelfth issue of *Teatr* magazine (Vakhtangov 1987: 149–151).

The unabridged variant of *All Saints' Notes* appears in the sourcebook for the first time in English. The artistic self-manifestation, carried out in this document, foreshadowed the revolutionary breakthrough of Vakhtangov's final period. At the same time, *All Saints' Notes* features some extreme, if not unjust, views expressed by Vakhtangov on the key theatrical figures of the time—especially on Craig and Nemirovich-Danchenko. The drastic nature of the act ("breaking out of Stanislavsky's chains"), as well as Vakhtangov's irritation with his own failing health, are responsible for these extremes. It is also important to remember that Vakhtangov's notes were private and never meant for publication.

Creative Passion that Arises from Perceiving the Essence

When, in the early 1920s, Vakhtangov summarized his experiences with the Stanislavsky technique, he concluded:
There are three unresolved elements in the System:

1 *Artistry* is the means to immediately become inspired by the material offered by the author. How to reach an ability to become inspired on command is unknown.
2 *Kernel*—this is the kind of starter that creates the character. The character is created when an actor discovers the kernel. The discovery of the kernel is something we do not know. What is cast into the actor's inner world, no one knows …
3 How to allow oneself onstage to strive to fulfill the tasks, to avoid pushing and wait for this striving to come—that is unknown.

(see p. 100)

In a way, all three unresolved aspects of the Stanislavsky technique point to the same underdeveloped area in the method: the area of creative perception. Where do creative inspiration, impulse, and energy come from? What are their sources? How does an actor perceive them?

Around 1917, Vakhtangov introduced a new term into his rehearsal practices. He began speaking to his actors of the '**creative passion that arose from perceiving the essence**'. One cannot fully grasp the essence of a phenomenon intellectually; one can only perceive, or sense, its essence subconsciously. When it comes to the realm of art, the conscious method of perception will be limited in comparison with the subconscious method. As Vakhtangov himself put it on one occasion, "In art—comprehending is experiencing" (see p. 96).

According to Vakhtangov, everything that surrounds the actor-character onstage—settings, objects, sounds, lights, other characters, imaginary events, etc.—contains the artistic essence, subconsciously invested by the author and the theatrical collective. Both characters and their circumstances, therefore, demand the intuitive, **subconscious perception** from the actor. An actor must perceive their atmosphere and, with it, their unique essence.

The crowning achievement of the Stanislavsky technique, expressed through the motto "the subconscious through the conscious, the involuntary through the voluntary" (Stanislavsky 2008: 18), did not satisfy Vakhtangov. His own way of working was the one of an immediate, intuitive grasp of the entirety of the theatrical phenomenon—be it a play or a character, a particular form of theatre or a principle of theatrical technique.

Most directors and actors have to analyze the object of their study, thus breaking it into elements. They need to be able to study the elements separately, one by one. The rationale behind this process is that once an artist comprehends all the building elements individually they will be able to synthesize these elements, or put them back together, and thus grasp the entirety of the play, scene, character, etc. In practice, however, the process of "gathering" often gets postponed until it is too late and at times it does not happen at all. A play, a scene, or a character, being a dynamic, living, and complex artistic organism, can defy the mechanical exercise of "dissection," if it precedes the creative grasp of the whole.

Once the creative flame is burning strongly, analytical techniques can provide an invaluable service in guiding the creative process. An actor who *begins* their work by analyzing their character's circumstances, however, will not go any further than perceiving an *idea* of how these circumstances affect the character. As Vakhtangov would put it, "I can analyze my role logically and psychologically—ideally, but then I come out onto the stage and it turns out that I absolutely do not need to do what I am doing" (p. 117). Armed by this intellectual notion, an actor is able to perform *an idea of their character's reaction.* The intellectually willful actor is well served by the analytical technique and is easily satisfied with the above-mentioned results.

Even the psychoanalytic parallel between a character's circumstances and the personal experiences of the actor (a technique known as emotion recall) is only capable of producing an emotional outcome once. After this singular emotional experience, an actor is bound to mechanically imitate it in performance. Those actors who continue renewing this experience by digging deeper into their personal life on a regular basis end up as nervous wrecks and can seriously damage themselves psychologically. The imitation of the original experience, however, satisfies most of the directors who use this technique; they are aware of its limitations and accept a good imitation as "truthful."[14]

---

14 Audiences also remain temporarily satisfied with this imitation, as they are used to "overriding" the actor's truth-like performance with their own imagination and experiencing, thus making it truthful in their own eyes. Deep within, however, audiences remain dissatisfied with this unilateral process. They might applaud the actors at the end of the performance, but they will never come back to see it again. Moreover, after such a performance, they will probably stay away from the theatre for as long as their individual perception of "cultural duty" lets them.

In truth, the art of imitation has little to do with the Stanislavskian school of experiencing. The school of the emotional experience, or *experiencing*, requires that an actor live with his or her emotions through the course of *every* performance. According to this school, such emotional experience is also a prerequisite to the actor's transformation. As for imitation, it belongs to the school of presenting the part, or, as Vakhtangov would put it, to "the art of Coquelin." The French actor Benoît-Constant Coquelin (1841–1909) was representative of the presentational school of theatre. In his influential monograph *L'Art du comédien* (1894), Coquelin outlined the precepts of his art, summarized by Vakhtangov thus: "cry over your part at home and then bring the results to the audience" (see p. 171).

What are the alternatives to analytical and imitative approaches to character study? An actor can analyze *their* character, of course, and then try to "forget" the results of the analysis and trust *their* creative nature to express these results onstage. Vakhtangov himself often suggested this process to his actors. On one occasion, however, he offered his students an alternative:

> Would you be able to perform the following, somewhat strange exercise: would you be able to go behind the curtain as a little devil and, as a little devil, examine everything backstage. This is an exercise in intuition. Can you do the following: I see myself sitting in a chair. In a similar way, I can also feel myself as a cat. [Michael] Chekhov, while observing a cat, stopped perceiving who was the cat—him or the cat. Through some power of yours, you guess how the object of your concentration feels at this moment. I can sense your will with my entire being. For a second I somehow transport myself into you. There is a distinction between abnormality and delight here. The latter belongs to the realm of art. I can internally somehow penetrate the essence of the given subject; in other words, I can guess its "kernel." This is the principal thing for an actor.
>
> (see p. 106)

As noted, Vakhtangov's own method of study was the one of an immediate intuitive grasp of the very essence of the character, or a play. This method allowed him to embrace the object in its entirety *prior* to the period of analytical dissection. In other words, Vakhtangov's was the method of immediate synthesis. Since every element of the harmonious artistic whole contains in it the **spirit**, the essence of the whole, Vakhtangov relied on his creative intuition to significantly shorten the process of study. By the end of his career, a single hint, one aspect of the whole, would allow Vakhtangov to grasp the entirety of a character, play, period style, etc. In March 1921, Vakhtangov wrote, comparing his directorial intuition with Meyerhold's:

> I feel that my intuition is better than Meyerhold's. He needs to study an historic epoch, in order to grasp its spirit. I, however, from a couple of empty hints, for some reason, clearly and vividly feel this spirit. I always, almost unmistakably, can tell in detail the life of the century, society, class, habits, laws, clothes and so on.
>
> (see p. 131)

The method of synthesis is also characteristic of Vakhtangov's approach to acting technique. Stanislavsky always began the exposition of his training by introducing the actor to separate "elements" of the creative process. Once the actor was familiar with the elements, Stanislavsky introduced him to the whole, to the main goal behind the training. This goal was to awaken and to stir the creative subconscious of the actor. Inevitably, a problem would present itself: an actor was so conscious of the separate elements of their process they were no longer able to create "subconsciously."

Vakhtangov used every means known to him to bring the actor into the creative realm from the very start of the rehearsal process. He never started a rehearsal without previously bringing himself and the company to the **creative state**.[15] The same is true of Vakhtangov's training. In his initial exercises, he would lead the students toward "forgetting themselves" and living subconsciously onstage, for however short a period.[16] Only then did Vakhtangov speak of the elements. Moreover, in his training of the elements Vakhtangov concentrated on one single thing: allowing the student to experience how every single element contained in it the rest of the creative elements and, therefore, a path to the subconscious creative state. In his training, Vakhtangov also started with the essential, with the whole.

Vakhtangov demanded that the actors perceive the soul of their technique. When speaking of movement, speech, and other disciplines commonly classified as "external technique," he would say, "These

---

15 This could be done through inspirational talk, collective singing and storytelling, or any other appropriate means.
16 An example of such an exercise is featured in Nikolai Mikhailovich Gorchakov 1957: 14–21. The English-language version of this book is Nikolai Mikhailovich Gorchakov (1959 [probable year]: 11–19).

subjects are truly needed in theatre school; but one should study them *in order to absorb their essence*. One may not be able to fulfill an exercise in **plasticity** of movement, but one should perceive *the soul* of movement, fencing, etc." (see p. 88). On a different occasion, he told his students: "You must fall in love with the soul of the spoken word" (see p. 123). Vakhtangov was not speaking figuratively, but literally. He wanted his students to subconsciously, or intuitively, perceive the organic nature of every subject—the essence of the phenomenon it trains, as it is present in nature and the eternal works of art.[17] By doing so, Vakhtangov erased the border between internal and external technique. The very process of actor training became the perception of the inner core of the subject.

Creative Individuality as a Basis for the Vakhtangov Principle of Transformation

According to Vakhtangov, the essence of creativity lies in "the richness of an actor's soul and his ability to reveal this richness" before the audience (see p. 88). Vakhtangov's principles of character and **characterization** are based in this concept. In the event the character (or characterization) substitutes for an actor's creative individuality, how can the richness of the actor's soul be revealed? In such a case, an actor is bound to appear spiritually "smaller" than they actually are, especially when the character is interpreted as being spiritually "larger" than the actor. Vakhtangov told the actor, "We don't need characters, characterizations. Everything you have makes up your characterization; you have individuality—this is your character" (see Ivanov vol. II 2011: 149).

Vakhtangov observed that when an actor introduces elements of external characterization they often kill the life of the character. This happens because with these elements there comes a temptation to imitate them. An actor may copy gestures and mannerisms they observed, or discovered intuitively; however, this imitation brings the creative process to a halt. Vakhtangov clearly stated that the creative act ends where imitation begins. When asking his students to exercise in the instantaneous, intuitive grasp of the character's essence, Vakhtangov added, "This is a good way to experience the difference between imitation and transformation. I came to the conclusion that if an actor transforms this way, they don't need external characterization" (see p. 108).

---

17 See Vakhtangov's writings on plasticity, p. 120.

Vakhtangov did away with the Stanislavsky/Nemirovich-Danchenko term of the character's "kernel," as he found it inconsistent with the concept of the creative individuality. In the course of his practice, Vakhtangov understood that what he himself experienced as the subconscious essence of the character differed from the concept of the "kernel" of the role. In Stanislavsky and Nemirovich-Danchenko's view, the kernel is always definable and, therefore, does not constitute the character's essence. The kernel constitutes a certain inoculation to the spirit of the character, allowing an actor to dress the character in a naturalistic physical form. According to Vakhtangov's own description, external characterization (a particular set of gestures, manner of walking, tone of voice, etc.) is activated by "a push of a button"—a triggering of a certain psychological sensation of being somebody else.

Contrary to the "kernel," the character's essence contains in it the character as a whole, and out of it the character organically develops throughout the rehearsal process. The kernel has to be "renewed at every performance" for the very reason that it has nothing to do with the workings of the creative nature and, therefore, has a tendency to constantly die off. Like other intellectually willful elements of the Stanislavsky technique, the "kernel" does not stick to an actor as it does not belong to the realm of the organic creative process.

In 1918, Vakhtangov abandoned the characterization-based process of transformation where the kernel of the character swallows an actor's creative individuality. During his work on Ibsen's *Rosmersholm*, staged as a **mystery**, Vakhtangov's emphasis fell on the spiritual radiation of the character's essence. Therefore, Vakhtangov abandoned physical characterization that did not express this essence. He insisted that, in *Rosmersholm*, an actor's own appearance, plasticity, and voice are more appropriate than the manufactured characterization. He demanded that the "actor should transform by the power of their inner impulse," while preserving their "God-given face" and "God-given voice" (see p. 211).

Physical characterization, as one of the expressive **textures**, however, was preserved by Vakhtangov. Once the creative artist is free to remain himself or herself on the stage, they are also free to use any expressive texture, be it the one of characterization or the one of **grotesque**. For example, Vakhtangov demanded that in the Theatre of Fantastic Realism every "character actor" must discover an archetypal element that stands behind the characterization and express themselves through the grotesque technique. Such was one of the textures of acting in Vakhtangov's final productions, such as *Erik XIV*, *The Miracle of Saint Anthony*, *The Dybbuk*, and *Princess Turandot*.

Michael Chekhov in his own technique has further developed the idea of the archetypal **image** or gesture standing behind the character. Vakhtangov's concept of the character's essence was developed further by Nikolai Demidov in his school of acting, where Demidov calls it the character's "embryo". Unlike the "kernel," the embryo of the role, formed at the first reading, is dissimilar to the fully developed creation of the role, and yet it already contains in it the role as a whole. A gradual, organic rehearsal process, as understood and described by Vakhtangov, is needed in order for the embryo to develop into a full-blown role.

In its essence, Vakhtangov's principle of transformation is much closer to the kind of transformation practiced by the tragedians of the Maly Theatre—starting with the nineteenth-century tragic genius Pavel Mochalov (1800–1848) and concluding with Vakhtangov's contemporary Maria Yermolova (1853–1928). One of Russia's oldest companies, Moscow's Maly Theatre is known as the House of Ostrovsky. Aleksandr Ostrovsky (1823–1886), an influential Russian playwright and theatrical figure, played a crucial role in the history of the Maly. Vakhtangov wanted to find a contemporary non-naturalistic form for Ostrovsky's plays; their flow reminded him of the mighty Volga river (Vershilov 1959: 395). In his 1921 diary notes taken at the All Saints' Rehabilitation Resort, Vakhtangov criticized the Maly Theatre for its tendency to remain fixed, without adjusting to the spirit of the times. At the same time, he was fond of the Maly Theatre actors, who disregarded the Stanislavskian fourth wall and dared to "demonstrate that they are acting" (see p. 156). Somehow Vakhtangov's teacher Sulerzhitsky sensed the connection between Vakhtangov's individuality and the Maly Theatre tradition early on—during Vakhtangov's first year at the MAT, Sulerzhitsky made a prediction: "One day you will be at the Maly Theatre" (Vendrovskaya and Kaptereva 1984: 89)

On the Actor's Creative Passion

In his October 31, 1914, lecture on the nature of the actor's **communication** with the partner, Vakhtangov made the following statement:

One should be attentive to one's partner on the stage. A lack of attention in life translates into attention on the stage. In order to play a lack of concentration, I must be concentrated. This concentration should be my life experience—something alive in me concentrates on something alive in my partner. As for the lack of concentration I must play—it should be affective. Similarly, in order to play a weak character, I must be strong. Otherwise I won't have enough power to play a weak person. In order to play a villain, I must be kind: kind, as far as real feelings are concerned, and evil, as far as affective feelings are concerned.

(see p. 103)

In Vakhtangov's vocabulary, the notions of the *affect* and *affective* are synonymous with an actor's essential skill to "publicly" re-experience emotions and sensations once felt in private life. He insisted that an actor should be able to evoke these "unreal," repeat emotions and sensations "without any external **motivation**," and called them *affective*. In this particular passage, Vakhtangov insists that an actor onstage cannot directly experience the lack of concentration belonging to the character. It has to appear as an "unreal" repeat, or *affective* sensation. At the same time, the immediate "real" stage experience of an actor should be the one of concentrating.

We should note, however, that Vakhtangov's idea of concentration differs from the Stanislavskian willful effort. Vakhtangov's description of concentration implies an involuntary process of the actor "allowing in" the live essence of his or her partner. The actor is not the one concentrating—"something alive in me" concentrates on "something alive in my partner" (see p. 188). According to Vakhtangov, "Creativity is the highest level of concentration. When your entire being is dedicated to a single purpose—then there will be enough energy for true creativity" (see p. 98). Obviously, the "highest level of concentration" Vakhtangov speaks about cannot be evoked by the will alone. Only an actor's "entire being" (will, feeling, and thought) is capable of achieving such a level of concentration involuntarily, through special readiness for the creative act.

In a lecture dedicated to the phenomenon of the affective memory, delivered on October 27, 1914, Vakhtangov said:

In life ... our feelings are always evoked by some real pretext; these pretexts do not really exist onstage; they are always unreal there, so the best we can do is believe in them. There comes a question: can these unreal pretexts evoke real feelings in us? No, not under any circumstances. These unreal pretexts are not just unable to evoke real feelings, they should not do this, or the stage will cease being an art. A source of our special stage feelings that are quite unlike real ones is not in unreal pretexts, but in our ability to relive our emotional experiences ... This repeat emotion is not adequate with the emotions we experience in life.

(see pp. 183–4)

In the preceding passage from a lecture, delivered to the beginners, Vakhtangov does something unthinkable for the teacher of the Stanislavsky technique: he acknowledges the falseness of the stage reality. Moreover, Vakhtangov insisted that, in order to make an actor's art possible, theatre artists and teachers must first agree that this falseness is not an actor's enemy but their friend—a prerequisite to their creativity. Where Stanislavsky taught the actor how to erase the contradiction between life and theatrical reality, Vakhtangov told the actor that their creative **joy** arises from "creating a new truth out of this contradiction" (Leonid Volkov, interviewed in Khersonsky 1940: 72). In 1914, as Vakhtangov delivered his eight lectures to the students, he managed to thread this thought through every element of the system—delicately but firmly.

In Vakhtangov's view, the actor's emotion itself does not arise from their literal conviction that they *are* the character and, therefore, must emotionally respond to the play's circumstances as the character would. If that were so, what would be the point of the actor's skill?[18] If that were so, the actor would not be able to experience the creative joy in the event that their character's circumstances and emotions are, let us say, tragic. Vakhtangov's term "affective emotion" indicates an emotion that is not directly triggered by the fictitious circumstances of the play. In order to perceive the imaginary circumstances as real, and to respond to them with artistic emotions, an actor must be in a specific creative, or festive state. When speaking of the "affective emotion," Vakhtangov refers to creative passions caused by one single fact—a subconscious realization that "I am an artist." He called this ability "artistry."

It is significant that Vakhtangov never asked an actor to believe that their stage environment was adequate to the imaginary environment of the play, but "to have **faith**." By doing so, he established a firm border between the actor's faith and hallucination. A deeply religious person does not believe in things that can be seen but in things unseen. If a true believer could see or touch what they believe in, would their faith have any value? According to Vakhtangov, an actor's faith is the faith *in the invisible* rather than a naive trust that visible things are not what they actually are:

It is quite easy mixing **justification** with hallucination, and therefore

---

18 Indeed, in this case the nature of an actor's skill would be hallucinatory and equal the condition of a mental patient.

we must sense a clear border between them. Applying my faith to my task causes me to become *naive*. This notion should be set apart from its usual interpretation. My faith does not come as a result of my **naivety**; rather, I become naive as a result of my faith. *Faith, achieved through justification, causes naivety.*

(see p. 178)

"Faith," in Vakhtangov's meaning of this word, is an actor's ability to live creatively onstage and to experience creative passions without *literally* perceiving the events of the play and the stage environment as real. This statement of Vakhtangov's may have been interpreted by some of his followers as a step toward **Presentational Theatre**, away from the theatre of the emotional experience. What Vakhtangov's statement truly means, however, is that the process of life onstage does not equal **everyday life** process—onstage an actor engages in a creative process where everything that surrounds them does not equal itself. Therefore, in order to become "real," an actor's surroundings need to be creatively transformed through the prism of an actor's artistic fantasy.

Vakhtangov suggests that an actor's faith is an ability to perceive the *essence* of every event and every object onstage. As any essence, it is intangible and invisible. A theatrical essence, according to Vakhtangov, is festivity, or joy. At the heart of this experience is the heightened sense of living, described by Vakhtangov as the sensation of wanting "to live more than ever" and feeling yourself "belonging to everything living" (see p. 108). This sensation, and not the reality of the character and their environment, is what serves as justification for the actor's experience and causes him or her to live out their creative passions.

The very term "affect," or "affective," is associated, in Russian psychology, with the realm of *heightened* emotions. Even the popular *Ozhegov Semantic Dictionary of the Russian Language* transcribes "affect" as "the state of a strong emotional excitement and loss of self-control." In the Russian understanding of the term, to exist in the state of affect is to be in the heat of passion. This is why one of the three original teachers of the Stanislavsky technique, Nikolai Demidov, used the term "affective" for his unprecedented technique of the passionate actor. Demidov's affective technique is a unique reconstruction of the lost art of the great nineteenth-century tragedians. Vakhtangov's method and technique, as well as his ideal of the emotional life onstage, are closer to Demidov's school than they are to Stanislavsky's system.

Vakhtangov's formula of an actor's creativity differs from the Stanislavskian formula of "living *truthfully* in the *given* circumstances of the role." Vakhtangov's actor lives *passionately* in the new artistic reality *they* create. An actor's ability to shift their point of view on the reality of the stage is their ability to perceive its festive essence. The reality of the stage does not actually change—the shift of point of view is the shift of an actor's mentality—from the everyday mentality to creative mentality.[19] It is achieved through the act of artistic *perception*—by perceiving the festive essence of the stage objects, partners, circumstances, and events, the actor arouses their creative passion. By doing so, the Vakhtangov actor creates a new artistic reality.

The heightened experience of life, put by Vakhtangov at the heart of the creative state, implies the acute sense of its counterpart: death. Therefore, in a state of creative mentality, an actor can walk on the threshold of existence and experience life and death for no particular reason—in everything, and in nothing. Needless to say, in such a state, one does not need any "external motivations" to act, to spontaneously feel any passions or to create any imaginary reality. While in the creative state one does not need to believe in the imaginary circumstances or events as one does not need to take props, costumes, sets, and partners for something "real." In such a state, an actor just believes, just experiences, and just creates.

The technique of creative passion, or the affective technique, represents the highest level of creativity when an actor *creates a new artistic reality on top of the actual reality of the stage.* The actual reality of the stage is included in it, but it is so insignificant in comparison with the new artistic reality that it literally dissolves in it. In other words, the artistic reality, created through the means of the affective technique, has a tendency to swallow the less infectious reality of the stage. As Vakhtangov himself put it on a later occasion: "The moment of passion within the theatrical creative state, when an actor almost forgets that he is onstage is the moment of faith, the moment of truth" (see p. 92).

The reason Vakhtangov notes that the actor "almost forgets that he is onstage" while in the heat of creative passion is that true emotional experience and transformation are impossible without the doubling of the actor's consciousness. The newly doubled mentality instigated by the creative process causes the actor to continually register their own performance onstage. The watching side of this mentality can decrease in moments and become practically imperceptible, or subconscious, but it never disappears altogether.

---

19 As for the audience, according to Vakhtangov, it "believes everything an actor believes" (see p. 89.)

2 The Theatre of Mystery

Vakhtangov in Context

The "pre-revolutionary" period of Vakhtangov's creativity is marked by the director's search for what he called the "Theatre of Mystery." The art of psychological naturalism no longer satisfied Vakhtangov; in fact, his fascination with naturalism ended before he joined the MAT. Similarly, many of the members of the MAT, including Stanislavsky and Sulerzhitsky, refused to be content with what was achieved by the MAT in the productions of Chekhov.

During the period between 1898 and 1904, when the MAT originally approached Chekhov the playwright, Stanislavsky remained under the influence of the Meiningen Ensemble that toured Russia in 1885 and 1890.[1] Under the direction of Ludwig Chronegk (1837–1891), the Meiningen Ensemble achieved impressive results in recreating the illusion of the historic reality onstage. Stanislavsky himself claimed that, in the realm of acting, he followed the line of the intuition and feeling in his interpretation of Chekhov. Vakhtangov insisted that Chekhov's characters, as portrayed by the MAT, were created through the "Meiningen principle projected onto the inner essence of the role." In other words, according to Vakhtangov, the MAT Chekhovian characters were *copied* from life, rather than intuitively *created*.

Vakhtangov was not alone in his judgment. Chekhov himself was dissatisfied with the MAT's naturalistic approach to his plays. The reality of an Anton Chekhov play is a unique *artistic* reality—a creative universe of its own, not just a result of the author's **observation**

---

1 The Meiningen Ensemble was the court theatre of the German State of Saxe-Meiningen, organized by Georg II, Duke of Saxe-Meiningen. The Ensemble productions featured archaeologically authentic reproductions of locations and realistic, fully individuated crowd scenes. The Ensemble toured extensively. Besides Stanislavsky, it also influenced theatrical figures such as Ibsen and Antoine.

of life. Vsevolod Meyerhold, who originated the role of Konstantin Treplev in the MAT's version of *The Seagull*, was convinced that the success of this production with the audience was determined by the sensitivity of the MAT ensemble, an ensemble capable of perceiving the music of the Chekhovian language.

Meyerhold, whose acting was praised by the otherwise critical Chekhov, was deeply dissatisfied with the MAT's naturalistic practices. In 1905, through the support of none other than Stanislavsky himself, Meyerhold was able to experiment with the symbolist **theatrical forms** at the Povarskaya Street Studio in Moscow. The Studio was closed shortly thereafter by Stanislavsky; Meyerhold's productions of Maeterlinck's *The Death of Tintagiles* and Hauptmann's *Schluck and Jau* were seen only by a handful of specialists. Meyerhold continued his search for the forms of theatrical symbolism at the tragic actress Komissarzhevskaya's Theatre in St. Petersburg.

Vera Komissarzhevskaya (1864–1910) was a unique figure in the Russian theatre at the change of the centuries. The original Nina of the failed Imperial Aleksandrinsky Theatre's 1897 premiere of Anton Chekhov's *The Seagull*, she was the only one of the cast to gain insight into the Chekhovian universe. Highly valued by Chekhov himself, Komissarzhevskaya made her fame in the productions of the contemporary realistic, as well as classical heroic repertoires. Despite her enormous success with Russian audiences, especially with progressively oriented students, Komissarzhevskaya embarked on the quest for the theatre of the future. Influenced by the Russian symbolists' movement at the turn of the twentieth century, she opened her newly created independent theatre company to Meyerhold, and she boldly participated in his formal experiments as both actress and producer.

Meyerhold, who conducted his formal experiments with complete disregard of his contemporary actors' creative process, only survived at the Komissarzhevskaya's Theatre for the 1906–1907 season. The failure of her collaboration with Meyerhold did not disillusion Komissarzhevskaya in her search. She continued to be influenced by the Russian symbolists, such as Aleksandr Blok, Andrei Bely, Leonid Andreyev, Valery Bryusov, and Aleksey Remizov. Moreover, Komissarzhevskaya continued to experiment with various forms of **theatricality** at her company, employing avant-garde directors of the time, such as Alexandre Benois (1870–1960) and Nikolai Evreinov (1879–1953), as well as her own brother Fyodor (Theodore) Komissarzhevsky (1882–1954). At the time of her farewell tour of the Russian provinces in 1909–1910, Vera Komissarzhevskaya made a confession to the author Andrei Bely—in a way, a summary of her search for the Theatre of the Future. Bely left the following record of their conversation:

> She is tired of the stage; the stage broke her; she went through the theatre—new and old; both of them broke her, having left a heavy sense of bewilderment; theatre in the contemporary cultural conditions is an end to a man; it is not theatre that is needed, but the new life; the new act will appear in life; it will come from new people; these people are yet to appear; this is why theatrical innovators' strivings break off in a perplexed question; we don't have the actor; he needs to be created; he cannot be created without creating a new man in him; a new man must be cultivated from infancy; ... she decided to dedicate her entire experience and the whole force of her strivings to the creation of a new man-actor; an image of a large institution appears in her imagination, almost a kindergarten that would transform into a school, and even a theatrical university; pedagogue-teachers of this hitherto unseen enterprise must be chosen people, who yearn for a man.
>
> (Bely 1934 cited in Rybakova 1994: 458)

Following the closing of the Povarskaya Street Studio, Stanislavsky continued his exploration of symbolism in collaboration with Sulerzhitsky. The two co-directors introduced the style of symbolism to the MAT stage in productions such as Hamsun's *The Drama of Life* and Andreyev's *The Life of a Man* (1907), as well as Maeterlinck's *The Blue Bird* (1908). In 1909, they invited Edward Gordon Craig to direct and design a production of *Hamlet* at the MAT.[2] Both Stanislavsky and Sulerzhitsky collaborated on this performance with Craig. This historic production opened in 1911; it signified yet another MAT attempt to speak to its audiences of the sacred and essential in human life and nature. In his memoir, *My Life in Art*, Stanislavsky referred to this part of his theatre's repertoire as the line of the fantastic, symbolism and impressionism.

Stanislavsky's interest in theatrical stylization led to the invitation of the director/designer Alexandre Benois to participate in MAT productions, such as Molière's *The Imaginary Invalid* and *The Forced Marriage* (1913), and Goldoni's *The Mistress of the Inn* (1913).

---

2   This was done at the advice of the influential American modern dancer Isadora Duncan, whose own experiments in the realm of movement and dance fascinated both Sulerzhitsky and Stanislavsky.

Benois's last collaboration with the MAT took place in his 1915 *Pushkin Production* which was based on three of the author's four *Little Tragedies* (*Mozart and Salieri*, *The Stone Guest*, and *Feast During the Plague*). In this production, Stanislavsky the actor suffered a major flop as Salieri; the naturalistic style of his acting clashed with Benois's stylized staging and design. Benois, who played an important part in the MAT's government, had to leave the theatre. Stanislavsky took his own failure to heart, and his fascination with this role continued to linger. Shortly before Vakhtangov's death in 1922, Stanislavsky decided to clarify for himself his former student's views on the art of theatre; the role of Salieri was chosen as material for joint practical sessions.

The story of Stanislavsky's fiasco in the role of Salieri illustrates the fact that the MAT's experimentation with theatricality, historic stylization, symbolism, and the fantastic did not go beyond the external realm. It was conducted in the sphere of set design, music, lighting, stage effects, etc. No equivalent of these styles and techniques were discovered in the realm of acting. In fact, no one searched for it at the MAT. The fine old concept of "external characterization" was adapted to new purposes. The external characterization in the "fantastical" productions might have been condensed and "defamiliarized," but the traditional MAT method of an actor's existence onstage was not altered. No new word was spoken in the sphere of the psychology of acting; an MAT actor's approach to character, and their own creative process, in a fantastical production, remained essentially naturalistic.

The fact that the MAT's experiment was conducted outside of the realm of the internal acting technique was enough for Vakhtangov to almost entirely overlook it at the time. The same can be said of Vakhtangov's point of view on Meyerhold's symbolist search. He did not witness Meyerhold's Povarskaya Studio experiments, but he saw his St. Petersburg Studio's productions based on Blok's *The Puppet Booth* and *The Strange Woman*. Moreover, Vakhtangov was an acting apprentice with the Komissarzhevskaya Theatre during its Moscow tour of 1909. Besides Meyerhold's production of *The Doll's House* Komissarzhevskaya kept in her repertoire, Vakhtangov also witnessed the new symbolist experiments she undertook under Fyodor Komissarzhevsky's direction in productions such as Friedrich Hebbel's *Judith* and Franz Grillparzer's *The Foremother*,[3] as well as their exper-

---

3 *The Foremother* was directed by Fyodor Komissarzhevsky in collaboration with Alexandre Benois.

iments with historic stylization, conducted in Goldoni's *The Mistress of the Inn*. In 1910, Vakhtangov saw the *commedia dell'arte* production of Schnitzler's *Columbine's Scarf*, directed by Meyerhold at the St. Petersburg House of Interludes.

Out of the European theatrical innovations, Vakhtangov was acquainted with the formal search, carried out by the German director Max Reinhardt; he also knew of the work of German theatrical reformer Georg Fuchs (1868–1949). Vakhtangov was aware of the experiments in the realm of theatrical lighting and design conducted by the influential Swiss architect Adolphe Appia (1862–1928). Vakhtangov studied the theories of rhythm, speech, and movement of the French masters Émile Jaques-Dalcroze and François Delsarte, as outlined and developed by their Russian disciple Sergei (Serge) Volkonsky (1860–1937). Of Volkonsky's works, Vakhtangov especially valued his book *The Man on the Stage* (1912).

Vakhtangov read the theoretical writings of the Russian symbolists, such as Alexandre Benois, Fyodor Sologub, Valery Bryusov, and Andrei Bely, among others. He read Meyerhold's book collection *On Theatre* (1913), as well as Fyodor Komissarzhevsky's book *An Actor's Creativity and Stanislavsky's Theory* (1916). Vakhtangov was influenced by Richard Wagner and Romain Rolland's concepts of the **Popular Theatre**.[4] Finally, Vakhtangov studied the artistic and cultural theories of the Russian Marxists, such as Anatoly Lunacharsky and Platon Kerzhentsev.

At the MAT, Vakhtangov participated, as an actor and acting coach, in Edward Gordon Craig's production of *Hamlet*. He also acted in Benois's *The Imaginary Invalid*, as well as in the Stanislavsky–Sulerzhitsky productions of *The Blue Bird*. Truth be said, Vakhtangov did not understand the importance of the Stanislavsky–Sulerzhitsky formal search until after the Russian Revolution of 1917. For Vakhtangov, it was the revolution that demanded new forms from a theatre artist. Before the revolution, Vakhtangov felt that the search for new forms in theatre, conducted by both Russian and European theatre artists, was untimely. Vakhtangov changed his attitude toward the search for new forms in the early 1920s; however, it was not just a change in Vakhtangov but also a change in the world. When the revolution arrived, Vakhtangov recognized that the search he overlooked

---

4   A Russian translation of Rolland's 1902 book *Le Théâtre du peuple*, prefaced by Viacheslav Ivanov, was issued in 1919. Vakhtangov left notes on this book; the content of the notes is similar to other Vakhtangov writings on the Popular Theatre featured in the *Sourcebook*.

was the search for the theatre of the future. At the same time, he realized that many of the discoveries of the symbolists became outdated with the arrival of the revolution. Out of the entire heritage accumulated by the Russian theatrical innovators prior to the revolution, Vakhtangov subscribed only to a few achievements. He admired Meyerhold's gift of discovering unique theatrical means to convey not just the world of a particular play but also the entire creative world of its author. He may or may not have known of Vera Komissarzhevskaya's final resolve; however, he certainly would have agreed with its main idea: "the new act will appear in life; it will come from new people; ... I decided to dedicate my entire experience and the whole force of my strivings to the creation of a new man-actor" (Bely 1934, cited in Rybakova 1994: 458).

Vakhtangov's contemporary theatrical innovators hit a dead end with the creation of a new type of actor/human being. The work of "engineering" this kind of actor was the starting point of Vakhtangov's search. The new actor Vakhtangov was striving to develop, an actor totally free in his or her creative process, could afford to be free in his or her choice of creative means. In his final productions, Vakhtangov boldly mixed many of the external textures utilized by his colleagues. One can observe elements of symbolism, expressionism, futurism, constructivism, and grotesque in Vakhtangov's productions.

Vakhtangov's synthesis of these textures, however, was always unique and original, and, most importantly, it was meaningful and live. Motivated by the main idea of the production, Vakhtangov's mixture of external devices was harmonious with the unique artistic world he created in every performance. Moreover, his actors could bring these formal devices to life; in the hands of his contemporary directors the same devices, however beautiful and expressive, appeared external and dead, and unjustified by the actors. Vakhtangov's pre-revolutionary achievements in the inner realm of acting provided a solid platform for his formal experiments in the early 1920s. The inner foundation Vakhtangov created prior to the revolution, his model of the psychology of acting, has proven to be appropriate for any formal device the new era demanded of a theatre artist.

Vakhtangov called the actor a "master, who creates texture" (see p. 127). He demanded that the form in theatre, including the form of the character, should not be copied from life or art but "created, it should be fantasized" (see p. 158). Vakhtangov considered fantasy, the artistic "how," a foundation of the creative process. One has to draw a clear line between imagination and fantasy—the latter was the term consistently used by Vakhtangov. Nikolai Demidov provides the following explanation of this distinction:

> Fantasy is not imagination. Fantasy is imagination in action. An actor who can easily fantasize in their imagination, outside of themselves, is often deprived of their chief ability—to be able to fantasize in action, with their body. This is the only kind of fantasy *intrinsic to the actor.* Actors who possess this quality, as they start their work on the role, may not be able to give a clear answer as to how they imagine their character—they do not see it outside of themselves. As soon as they start rehearsing, however, and try out their character in action, they find out that their body, face and voice already know it all, and can draw a live and complete **image of the character.**
>
> (Demidov 2009: 354–355)

Therefore, Vakhtangov's concept of **fantasizing** has little to do with presentational acting—the type of a process where an actor imagines the ideal image of their character and then faithfully copies it night after night. (The same type of a process is characteristic of the presentational theatre's approach to emotion. It is experienced, or perceived, once. This is enough to memorize the emotion's outer manifestations in order to be able to express it in performance.) Vakhtangov's fantasizing is a hands-on creative improvisation, carried out spontaneously, on the spot. While this kind of improvisational fantasizing is sincere, it has little to do with everyday life and everything to do with an actor's creative process. The emotional life of Vakhtangov's actors was truthful, and yet they remained creatively free in their choice of expressive means. As Vakhtangov himself put it, "Emotions are alike, both in the theatre and in life, but the means, or methods of conveying these emotions are different" (see p. 152).

Vakhtangov's contemporary theatre of the emotional experience only knew two textures of theatrical expression: the idealized physical and vocal form of the nineteenth-century classical tragedians and the naturalistic characterization of the Stanislavskian kind. Vakhtangov has proven that an actor can live truthfully onstage and transform and experience, while having in their possession the entire spectrum of the creative (or fantastical) expressive means previously attributed exclusively to presentational theatre. He did so by substituting for the formula *living truthfully and sincerely as the character* with *living truth-*

fully and sincerely—creatively, as an artist.[5] This important correction made scholars and practitioners credit Vakhtangov with marrying the theatre of the emotional experience with the presentational theatre, or marrying Stanislavsky with Tairov and Meyerhold. In fact, Vakhtangov did no such thing. A synthesis of the presentational theatre with the theatre of the emotional experience was achieved by his close colleague Michael Chekhov in what is known today as the Chekhov technique. As for Vakhtangov, he created a new theatrical method: the method of fantastic realism. An actor's process associated with Vakhtangov's fantastic realism has many similarities with the organic creative process as outlined in Nikolai Demidov's School of Acting. Premature death prevented Vakhtangov from being able to fully develop and explain his method; therefore, the future scholars of fantastic realism will be best served by studying Vakhtangov and Demidov in tandem.

Vakhtangov at the First Studio of the MAT

Vakhtangov's career never really took off at the MAT: he always felt himself something of a stranger at the MAT metropolis. As for the MAT, it did not begin to truly value Vakhtangov until it was too late. One year prior to Vakhtangov's death in 1922, at the celebration of Vakhtangov's tenth anniversary as MAT associate, Stanislavsky expressed his own plans for Vakhtangov in a symbolic gesture. He took the golden MAT founders' pin from his chest and pinned it on Vakhtangov's. It was one of only two such pins, the other owned by Nemirovich-Danchenko. One year later, Stanislavsky clarified his gesture by calling Vakhtangov "the only successor" and "the future leader of the Russian Theatre."[6] Nemirovich-Danchenko had this to say upon Vakhtangov's passing: "Some of the creators ... embellish theatre history, others bring change. But such others are few. In ten, twenty years, we find one person who might produce such change. This is why, for the Moscow Art Theatre, Vakhtangov was the director of such an enormous magnitude" (Sobolev 1922, cited in Vendrovskaya and Kaptereva 1984: 454)

---

5   The mechanism of Stanislavsky's formula is outlined in the third chapter of his book *An Actor's Work* (Stanislavsky 2008: 53). Vakhtangov's formula has been derived by me from the entire body of his creative heritage and practices.
6   Vakhtangov's tenth anniversary as an MAT associate is described in Serafima Birman's memoir (Vendrovskaya 1959: 307). Stanislavsky called Vakhtangov a leader on several occasions; this particular quotation is featured in Vendrovskaya and Kaptereva 1984: 429.

These realizations, however, came in the last two years of Vakhtangov's life. Prior to that, Vakhtangov remained more or less a witness, or an episodic participant, of both the MAT experiments and the MAT tradition. His interests concentrated on the First Studio of the MAT. At the time of Vakhtangov's arrival at the MAT in 1911, the group of MAT associates, as well as the MAT affiliate group (an intermediary group between "associates" and "members of the troupe") was called the "Studio." Shortly after Vakhtangov's arrival, he was invited by Stanislavsky to conduct classes at the Studio. By the time of its official opening in 1913, the Studio received the name of the First Studio of the Moscow Art Theatre.

The First Studio was originally created as a laboratory for the newly developed Stanislavsky technique. This initial purpose of the Studio evolved within the first year of its existence; the success of its productions among the Russian cultural elite, as well as regular audiences, caused the Studio to depart from its laboratory origins. The artistic philosophy of the First Studio was inspired by the creative individuality of the Studio's director, Leopold Sulerzhitsky. In his work at the Studio, Sulerzhitsky managed to extend the MAT's search for the theatre of the "essential" deep into the actor's heart. The First Studio strived to speak of the universally human aspects of life. In its productions it often managed to establish a deep spiritual connection between the stage and the audience. The external and physical aspects of the Studio productions were reduced to the minimum. The Studio space was tiny; its stage was not raised, and the audience of the first row literally sat a few inches from the actors. The sets were modest, and the actors' movements few. The audience's focus went to the slightest nuances of the actor's psychology. The First Studio actors mastered the art of half glances, microscopic gesture, and spiritual radiation.

A man closely associated with Tolstoy, and a follower of his spiritual teachings, Leopold Sulerzhitsky was not just the Director of the First Studio but also its spiritual leader. Indirectly, through Stanislavsky, on whom he had tremendous influence, Sulerzhitsky also became the ideologist of the MAT. His theatrical and human philosophy is well described, or rather "quoted" by Vakhtangov, in his notes *On Leopold Sulerzhitsky*, appearing in Part VI of this volume (see p. 235). Sulerzhitsky's philosophy is grounded in the belief that a man is essentially good and moral. He maintained that cataclysmic events in the history of mankind, and in the private history of a man, always bring out this goodness. A theatre artist must reveal the man's kind essence and, by doing so, create the **festival** of goodness in the theatre. Ultimately, this kind of theatre was supposed to bring the audience and the actor to the state of "communion with God." The very idea that theatre must serve a higher purpose, intrinsic to Sulerzhitsky's artistic views, was further developed by Stanislavsky in his system. Sulerzhitsky's views clearly influenced Stanislavsky's concept of super-super-task, as well as his writings and talks on theatre ethics and the responsibility of a theatre artist. In Vakhtangov's heritage, Sulerzhitsky's views on the theatre's purpose are reflected in the term "**what for**". At the same time, Vakhtangov's views on both the driving force and the final goal behind a theatre artist's creativity differed from the one given by both of his mentors, Sulerzhitsky and Stanislavsky. Vakhtangov's unique creative philosophy is discussed below.[7] The First Studio of the MAT directors, Richard Boleslavsky (1887–1937) and Boris Sushkevich (1887–1946), carried out this vision of theatre in their works. Some of their most well-known productions, such as Herman Heijermans' *The Wreck of Hope* (1913) and Vladimir Volkenshtein's *Wandering Minstrels* (1914), as well as Sushkevich's adaptation of Charles Dickens's *The Cricket on the Hearth* (1914), were prepared under the close supervision of Sulerzhitsky and Stanislavsky. Unlike his colleagues, Vakhtangov was allowed independence in his directorial process. However, Vakhtangov's unorthodox interpretation of the First Studio's credo caused Stanislavsky and Sulerzhitsky to interfere in his early productions prior to their openings.

At the same time, Vakhtangov deeply understood Sulerzhitsky's idea of theatre. He alone gave Sulerzhitsky's theatre an accurate definition by calling it "the Theatre of Mystery." Vakhtangov's own philosophy of the festival, as manifested in the interpretation of plays staged by him at the First Studio of the MAT, was clearly influenced by Sulerzhitsky. All three of Vakhtangov's directorial plans for the First Studio performances featured in Part V of the sourcebook are centered on cataclysms. In Hauptmann's *Festival of Peace* (1913), it is a family cataclysm, a deadly war between family members. Berger's *The Deluge* (1915) features a natural cataclysm. In Ibsen's *Rosmersholm* (1918), the cataclysm is the stagnant and deadly force that destroys anything progressive and lively on the familial Rosmersholm estate. In all three of these productions, Vakhtangov used the cataclysm in order to bring his characters to the state of festival and thus reveal the essential in men. At this point, however, similarities between Vakhtangov's and Sulerzhitsky's philosophies end. The concept

---

7 See also Andrei Malaev-Babel, *Yevgeny Vakhtangov*, London and New York: Routledge (forthcoming in the Routledge Performance Practitioners series) for further discussion of Vakhtangov's philosophy.

of the essential, as well as the vision of the festival as refracted through Vakhtangov's directorial plans, differ from the usual First Studio interpretation. The description of Vakhtangov's philosophy can be found in a diary entry: "There are moments in a man's life when he wants to live more than ever and when he joyfully feels himself belonging to everything living. He becomes vigorous, and both his good and bad seeds express themselves with special vividness" (see p. 108). It is the final line of the quotation that is significant in regard to Vakhtangov's concept of festivity: "both ... good and bad seeds express themselves with special vividness." By introducing the element of the cataclysm into the life of a man, Vakhtangov was striving to strip away the mask people wear in everyday life and to break through to the true, secret human. Unlike the "official" MAT philosophy, inspired by Sulerzhitsky, Vakhtangov's philosophy considered good and evil two parts of one whole and explored the human being as a battleground between these two forces. His idea of festival, or festivity was complex: it encompassed a human being's **desire** "to live more than ever" and to "feel himself belonging to everything living." In his directorial work, Vakhtangov led his actors to a heightened, ecstatic spiritual existence of living at its fullest and experiencing life and its counterpart death with particular acuteness.

The reason Vakhtangov insisted that every performance must become a festival for an actor is that the sense of festivity and "belonging to everything living" was his idea of creativity. Unlike in everyday life, where this experience is rare and mostly suppressed, onstage Vakhtangov continually designed situations that caused his characters, and subsequently the actors, to shed their skin and bare their nerves. At such moments, both characters and actors were forced to lose their masks and live their hidden, "essential" life. An actor, deprived of all defenses and stripped to their human core, according to Vakhtangov, was ready to enter the higher spheres of creativity. By doing so, Vakhtangov aimed to bring his actors, and through them the audience, into the act of communion with a higher force.

In his monograph *Vakhtangov and His Studio*, published twice in Bolshevik Russia, one of Vakhtangov's oldest and most trusted students, Boris Zakhava, had the courage to outline Vakhtangov's philosophy in the following concise paragraph:

> God and Lucifer, Good and Evil, Abel and Cain—those were the problems Vakhtangov struggled to solve ... The *dualistic* outlook was foreign to Vakhtangov; his clear and well-organized intellect had a natural propensity toward the philosophical *monism*. He overcame the duality of Good and Evil through his conception of the Higher Reason that dwelled *above* both of these origins.

God, who opposed Lucifer, was not the highest origin of the world. The Higher Reason exists *above* God and *above* Lucifer, and the two polar origins of Good and Evil submit to it. Human beings, according to Vakhtangov's thought, are the arena of struggle between Good and Evil: God created the man so that his heart would serve as a place where God could carry out his fight with Lucifer, thus fulfilling the will of the Higher Reason—up to his irrevocable and complete victory. Thus, Vakhtangov saw the meaning of the human existence in a constant inner *Struggle*.

(Zakhava 1930: 105–106)

One cannot fully understand any of Vakhtangov's productions outside of this philosophy. It alone can explain the treatment of both Good and Evil in Vakhtangov's productions, where these two forces appear so closely interwoven they become almost indistinguishable. The complexity of Vakhtangov's outlook becomes clear if one takes into account that Vakhtangov does not consider any of these forces as "highest." As cosmic as Vakhtangov's consciousness might have been, he also stood firmly on this earth in his art. His productions never stepped into the realm of the invisible or mysterious. The invisible and the mysterious lived and breathed beyond the threshold of Vakhtangov's productions, but it did not materialize or enter the earthly realm—Vakhtangov's point of view in all of his productions. Vakhtangov's characters who made the full circle of their inner struggle could cross the earthly threshold into the mysterious realm of the final knowing, the realm of the Higher Reason, but at that point they disappeared out of the audience's view. According to Vakhtangov, physically portraying the realm of the mysterious defies its very essence.

Many of Vakhtangov's scholars, after the director's article on his production of *Erik XIV*, elaborated on the concept of the dead and live worlds that existed and collided in each of Vakhtangov's productions. These two worlds were always sought and discovered on the stage, as two different camps of characters, populating Vakhtangov's productions: the courtiers and the commoners in *Erik XIV*, the rich villagers and the beggars in *The Dybbuk*, etc. A close examination of Vakhtangov's theatrical structures, however, reveals that, even though we can usually accept one of these camps as more progressive and, therefore, sympathetic,[8] neither of them is ultimately good and live.

---

8 Needless to say, this assessment will vary, based on the social identity and world view of a particular audience member.

Both Good and Evil in Vakhtangov's productions are *relative*, not *absolute*. Both of the camps, and their individual members, are firmly protected against the inner struggle between Good and Evil by wearing their respective social masks. A social moral that comes with the mask protects them from any doubts and inner struggles. In Vakhtangov's world, only a character who has the courage to shed his or her protective social mask exposes their heart to the ultimate struggle between Good and Evil. By doing so they remain *morally* above the rest of the characters in the play and near the kingdom of ultimate life: the realm of the Higher Reason. Such characters—Erik XIV, Hannan and Leah of *The Dybbuk* (see Figure 3), Frazer of *The Deluge*, Friebe of *The Festival of Peace*, Rebecca and Rosmer of *Rosmersholm*, Virginie of *The Miracle of Saint Anthony*—gain the special knowing at the end of the play or actually step into the other, higher realm.

The Festival of Peace

Gerhart Hauptmann's 1890 play *The Festival of Peace* served as a basis for Vakhtangov's debut on the amateur stage. Vakhtangov directed Hauptmann's play at the Vladikavkaz Student Musical and Drama Circle in 1904. This early production, with the telling title *Sick People,* also featured Vakhtangov in the role of William. Vakhtangov returned to *The Festival of Peace* in 1913 for his First Studio of the MAT production.[9]

In the second act of Hauptmann's play, the terminal illness of the family patriarch brings the scattered, forever-battling Scholzes together by the Christmas tree. In Vakhtangov's directorial plan, the preparations for this forced festival of peace begin in the first act. The director literally invents the force that imposes peace upon the Scholzes. This force for Vakhtangov is the family of the Buchners, whose daughter is engaged to one of the Scholz sons:

> The Buchners reconcile ... Firmly. With confidence. At the end of the first act, and at the beginning of the second, the audience should trust them. At the moment when everyone gathers by the Christmas tree—the audience must feel gratitude toward the Buchners, who have done such a great task so well. [This is necessary] so that the first outburst [of the Scholz family scandal] at the Christmas party would affect me—the audience, and would scare

9   Vakhtangov's *The Festival of Peace* was revived at the First Studio in 1918.

Figure 3
Hannah Rovina as Leah in *The
Dybbuk*, 1922. © The Central Zionist
Archives.

me and inspire apprehension, disappointment, as well as the desire
to rush to the Buchners' aid.[10]

(see p. 199)

One can clearly sense the irony in Vakhtangov's description of
the Buchners, who underestimate the depth and complexity of the
Scholz family relationships. At the same time, Vakhtangov the director
"tricks" the audience by siding with the Buchners so that the Scholz
family scandal that erupts shortly after the temporary "festival of
peace" would ambush his spectators. This is not a mere effect on

---

10 Vakhtangov's quote illustrates his concept of the "directorial bit." Stanislavsky's
meaning of the term "bit" signifies a segment of the play, united by a particular character's task. Vakhtangov expands the concept of the bit, interpreting it as a segment
of the play, united by one particular creative task of the theatrical collective. In his
directorial plan, instead of focusing on the character's psychology as it manifests
itself in the bit, Vakhtangov outlines the effect this particular bit is supposed to
produce upon the audiences and how it should be achieved. Vakhtangov puts the
theatre collective's point of view on the reality of the play ahead of the character's
"objective" reality.

Vakhtangov's part—all of his directorial effects were justified, or grounded, in the main idea of the performance.

Ultimate Good and Evil are beyond the understanding of the Buchners, who are guided by a narrow burgher's morality. This is why the Buchners' striving for the Scholz family peace, in the long run, strengthens the very fear that brought the Scholzes into the state of war. This unconscious fear of the inevitable separation is the fear of death, and it has to be faced, challenged, and overcome. Until then, there will be no peace for any of the Scholzes. This complex philosophic idea concealed in *The Festival of Peace* appealed to Vakhtangov. Step by step, he revealed it in his production.[11]

Two characters in Vakhtangov's *The Festival of Peace* transgressed the boundaries of their class and, therefore, stood on the verge of this ultimate knowing. One is the terminally ill old Scholz, who walked away from his burgher prosperity and spent the last few years of his life as a wanderer. The other one is Scholz's old servant Friebe, who, upon his master's return to the house, becomes more than a servant, but a nurse, or even a mother to his dying master. It was not a coincidence that Scholz and Friebe were performed by Vakhtangov's two favorite actors: Grigory Khmara (1883–1970) and Michael Chekhov. Friebe, as interpreted by Chekhov, was the only character who did not believe in the possibility of the "Festival of Peace" for the Scholzes and yet did everything he could to heal the familial wounds. Somehow, the moral superiority in Vakhtangov's production was reserved for this old man, "all soggy, watery-eyed, an ape, bandy-legged" (see p. 200). Russian Vakhtangov scholar Natalia Smirnova had the following explanation of this phenomenon:

> He [Friebe] was like a crooked mirror of the world that reflected the deformity and emphasized the imperfection of this world. (It was not without reason that Gorky, when he watched the performance, considered Friebe—Michael Chekhov—its main character. In Vakhtangov's interpretation, Friebe was the main character indeed; Gorky rightly guessed the performance concept.)
>
> (Smirnova 1982: 10)

---

11 This idea, of course, is far deeper than Sulerzhitsky's thought that people always unite in the face of death, revealing their good essence.

The Deluge

In 1915, Vakhtangov staged one of the First Studio of the MAT's most famous productions: *The Deluge*. It was based on the 1908 play by the Swedish writer and playwright Henning Berger (1872–1924). At the heart of Vakhtangov's *The Deluge* stood the character of the bankrupt businessman Frazer; the theme of life and death, characteristic for Vakhtangov, was carried out by this character, and the structure of the production was organized around Frazer. Vakhtangov also shared the role of Frazer with Michael Chekhov, who performed it at the opening night. (The two actors took turns performing the part until the time of Vakhtangov's death in 1922.)

The forces of death in Vakhtangov's productions never appeared unmotivated. Their arrival was always carefully prepared or, rather, provoked by a challenge to the unnatural "natural order of things." In *The Festival of Peace*, life as a continuous preparation for death was challenged by the Buchners. In Vakhtangov's *The Deluge* the "order of things" that allows one human being to devour another is challenged by the character of the bankrupt businessman Frazer. By opposing the social order, Vakhtangov's Frazer, who no longer had a social mask of his own, exposed his heart to the ultimate struggle between Good and Evil.

The first act of Berger's play can be considered expository; in it the author more or less introduces characters gathered inside a Mississippi bar on the verge of a natural disaster. Vakhtangov, in his directorial plan, condenses the first act by introducing a strong atmosphere of antagonism that exists between the characters:

> They are all wolves to one another.
> Not a drop of compassion. Not a drop of attention [toward each other]. Everyone looks after their own profit. They snatch [it] out of each other's **hands**. Disconnected. Drowning in business.
> (see p. 203)

The character of Frazer, who, according to Vakhtangov's notes, "wants to live more than anyone else," propels the antagonistic conflict of the first act (see p. 204). In Vakhtangov's interpretation, Frazer revolts against the unbendable law of "natural selection," the law that proclaims that the fittest survives:

Frazer. I don't have a cent to my name, and this scoundrel[12] is now richer than me. I pounce at everything in order to ease my heart and vent my anger—to take it out on somebody ... Frazer has fits [of anger] every time he remembers [the injustice]. He cannot calm down.

(see pp. 203, 205)

In the second act, the signs of the approaching deluge signaled impending death to each and every character trapped inside the bar. At that point, the same Frazer brought the hitherto antagonistic characters into the union of reconciliation. Vakhtangov, who deliberately concentrated the "evil seeds" in the first act, in order to strip his characters down to the essential, achieved the same effect in the second act through opposing means. He wrote on the state of his characters in the second act of *The Deluge*: "Everyone is cleansed. Everyone is truthful. The humanity in them floated up to the surface. Crabs, and sea monsters that got stuck to the human being, got unstuck" (see p. 204).

For Vakhtangov's teacher, Sulerzhitsky, the cataclysmic event and the characters' tendency to form a spiritual union in its face, was the most important point of *The Deluge*. Vakhtangov considered the battle of Evil and Good in a man as most significant. According to Vakhtangov, the Festival of the Hunt begins at the first moment of the play. It precedes the Festival of Peace by a whole act, and it restores itself at the end of the play. In the third act the spiritual union in the face of the deluge is dissolved, as the telegraph brings the news that the deluge was nothing but a false alarm. The characters go back to their evil ways, except for the character of Frazer, as performed by Michael Chekhov and Vakhtangov. In Vakhtangov's production, Frazer left the stage at the end of the third act transformed, lit with an unconscious new knowing (Smirnova 1982: 13).

Michael Chekhov left us a description of Vakhtangov's final performance of the role of Frazer in *The Deluge* on February 13, 1922:

His acting was more than magnificent. All his fellow partners were full of admiration for him. But they were all thinking to themselves that this was Vakhtangov's last performance. And indeed it was— he never acted again. Why did he act so magnificently? Because he

12   In this "inner monologue" of Frazer's, improvised by Vakhtangov, Frazer is referring to his chief rival, Beer, as "this scoundrel."

was asserting his *life* … *Life*, the feeling of *life* … brought the creative state into being. Are we artists all only capable of really feeling life when it is in danger, or when it is fading away? Is it really the case that we will not be able to find our way to a feeling for life, while we are healthy and strong?

(Chekhov 2005: 101)

One might imagine that Michael Chekhov frequently watched Vakhtangov perform the role they shared out of admiration for his talent. Chekhov did admire Vakhtangov;[13] however, the reason behind Chekhov's presence at the theatre that night was more prosaic and grim. Vakhtangov, who was dying of cancer, might faint from the pain and not be able to finish the performance, as had happened on one occasion. Chekhov stood in the wings, ready to step in as Frazer, if necessary (as he had done once before).

Chekhov attributed the source of Vakhtangov's extraordinary inspiration to the fact that the dying actor was asserting his life. And yet Vakhtangov pronounced the formula of creativity as "wanting to live more than ever" and feeling yourself "belonging to everything living" long before he became aware of his mortal illness. Moreover, the "given circumstances" Vakhtangov the director designed for the character of Frazer, as well as his "**super task**," manifested his character's desperate desire to live. The night Vakhtangov gave his final performance of Frazer, his life and art made a full circle and met.

Michael Chekhov witnessed that the excellence Vakhtangov achieved in his final stage appearance was not a singular event. This excellence revealed itself before, as Vakhtangov rehearsed his most famous acting creation: a toy manufacturer, Tackleton. Vakhtangov originated this role in the 1914 First Studio of the MAT production based on Charles Dickens's *The Cricket on the Hearth*. It was directed by Boris Sushkevich under Sulerzhitsky's supervision. Specialists among the audience noted that Vakhtangov's style of acting brought a harsh, if not cruel note to the warm-hearted Christmas tale. With the exception of Vakhtangov and Michael Chekhov, who played the role

13 Chekhov himself considered Vakhtangov "as an older colleague and a teacher in the theatre" (Chekhov 2005: 68). In 1918, Chekhov wrote to Vakhtangov: "Your mission and your business is to move toward your goal, while never getting distracted by ordinary business or, moreover, by defending and justifying yourself. Others will do it better than you. Believe in your mission and think of it alone. You are an extraordinary man, so do your extraordinary work. In my striving for self perfection, I will, perhaps, fulfill the main business, and the main task of living for the ordinary you." (Vendrovskaya and Kaptereva 1984: 186).

of toy-maker Caleb, all other characters in the performance appeared as realistic. Chekhov's portrayal of Caleb was expressionistic in style; Vakhtangov's portrayal of Tackleton was graphic—full of contrast, shadow, and crisp definition:

> Abrupt intonations. Squeaky voice. Croaky laughter. The click of the heel ... One eye is half-closed. A fastidious **grimace** on the lips ... Movements are few. Gesture is reduced to a minimum. You look at Tackleton and wonder: is it a living man, or just a clockwork toy, crafted by Caleb Plummer's skilful hand?
>
> (Volkov 1922: 13)

At the end of the play, Vakhtangov's Tackleton suddenly revealed completely unexpected psychological qualities: his loneliness and melancholy created a nagging sensation in the audience and suddenly made them feel for this cruel Mr. Tackleton (see Figure 4):

> His look is the same. So are the hinged movements ... In the meanwhile, something has happened with Tackleton. His intonations have warmed up. His voice softened. There is anguish and loneliness in his gaze. You can't help but feel that the soulless piece of wood came to life.
>
> (Volkov 1922: 13)

Vakhtangov's soulless toy manufacturer was a human toy, a mechanical puppet that finally revealed a live heartbeat at the end of the play. The image of a human puppet, or a living toy—a reoccurring image in Vakhtangov's works—represents another of Vakhtangov's variations on the theme of life and death. Vakhtangov initially explored this theme in his first Moscow directorial work: a musical miniature *Tin Soldiers*, staged for Nikita Balieff's Chauve-Souris cabaret in 1911.[14] Vakhtangov's *Tin Soldiers* was kept in the cabaret's repertoire for more than a decade. The piece was performed to rave reviews during Chauve-Souris's international tours. When the company took Broadway by storm in 1922, Vakhtangov's *Tin Soldiers* was considered a centerpiece of their repertoire by the New York reviewers, including Alexander Woollcott.

---

14 Nikita Balieff (1877–1936) served as MAT actor from 1906 to 1911. He was the founder of La Chauve-Souris (Flying Bat) cabaret that evolved out of the famous MAT cabbage parties, first into an actor's club and then into a professional theatre enterprise. The Chauve-Souris troupe immigrated from Soviet Russia in 1919.

Figure 4 Vakhtangov as Tackleton in *The Cricket on the Hearth*, 1914.
©Bakhrushin State Central Theatre Museum.

3   Toward the Theatre of Fantastic Realism

Rosmersholm

The theme of revolt and challenge to death, the common theme in Vakhtangov's pre-revolutionary productions, dominates Vakhtangov's *Rosmersholm*. This production, based on Henrik Ibsen's 1886 play, opened at the First Studio of the MAT in 1918, one year after the historic Russian "cataclysm" known as the Bolshevik Revolution. In Vakhtangov's plan for Ibsen's *Rosmersholm*, Rebecca and Rosmer revolt against the dead, stagnant traditions of Rosmer's "noble ancestors." (According to Vakhtangov, this tradition permeates every curtain fold of the familial Rosmersholm estate.) Rebecca and Rosmer's revolt brings on the vision of the white horses—the symbol of death in the play.

In *Rosmersholm*, Vakhtangov strived to break through to "the essential" conflict between life and death, as he did in all of his productions. His directorial plan documents the director's intentions to strip his actors of their everyday life masks, including the Stanislavskian characterization. The method of acting Vakhtangov was seeking in *Rosmersholm* can be described as "confessional." The circumstances he chose and designed for the characters onstage also called for confession: they caused Vakhtangov's characters to appear "spiritually naked," deprived of their regular defenses.

The method of acting Vakhtangov sought in *Rosmersholm* by no means precludes creative transformation. Vakhtangov insisted that his actors preserve their "God-given face, God-given voice" and "transform by the power of their inner impulse" (see p. 211).[1] In March

---

1   The psychology of Vakhtangov's type of transformation has been discussed in the first part of the Introduction.

1921, Vakhtangov proclaimed in the following diary entry his resolve to introduce this new type of transformation to the theatre:

> The theatre of everyday life must die. "Character" actors are no longer needed. All who have capacity for playing character roles must feel the tragedy (even the comedians) in every character part; they must learn to express themselves through the grotesque. Grotesque—tragic and comedic.
>
> (see p. 109)

Vakhtangov assembled an incredible creative ensemble for his *Rosmersholm*, for the first time bringing the MAT together with its First Studio. Rebecca was performed by the MAT leading actress, Anton Chekhov's widow Olga Knipper-Chekhova (1868–1959), the character of Brendel by the MAT tragedian Leonid Leonidov (1873–1941).[2] At the same time, the creative tasks Vakhtangov set before his actors turned out to be too radical for the first generation of MAT actors. In the end, Vakhtangov alone achieved his creative goal as he stepped into the role of Brendel instead of Leonidov (Leonidov took ill before the dress rehearsals).

Vakhtangov's acting in *Rosmersholm* attracted the attention of Nemirovich-Danchenko, who met with Vakhtangov for a detailed conversation following a dress rehearsal. Nemirovich's own production of *Rosmersholm* failed at the MAT ten years earlier. Nemirovich was especially dissatisfied with his production's interpretation of the character of the old philosopher Brendel. Nemirovich insisted that the difficulty of this role lies in the need to "discover the synthesis of satire and drama, necessary in order to perceive this liberal, who went broke before he ever accomplished anything" (Nemirovich interviewed in Khersonsky 1940: 11). According to Nemirovich's own witness, Vakhtangov succeeded at that: "the amazing ease" with which Vakhtangov played Brendel "gave a distinct perception of the tragic forms he was sketching for the new theatre" (Sobolev 1922, cited in Vendrovskaya and Kaptereva 1984: 454) (see Figure 5).

2   Russian tragedians denied invitations to join the MAT troupe as they did not consider the MAT a theatre of their type. Leonidov was the only tragedian on the MAT stage; it happened because he discovered his tragic gift in Nemirovich-Danchenko's 1910 production of Dostoyevsky's *The Brothers Karamazov*. Prior to the role of Dmitry Karamazov that made Leonidov famous he did not distinguish himself in any way among the MAT actors.

Figure 5
Vakhtangov as Brendel
in *Rosmersholm*, 1918.
© Moscow Art Theatre's
Museum.

What was so significant about the character of Brendel, a morally
and physically sunken former teacher of the noble Rosmer, who unex-
pectedly showed up at his old student's doorstep? The photograph of
Vakhtangov in the role shows that, unlike Leonidov, he completely
abandoned the art of physical characterization and turned the role
into a creation of tragic grotesque.[3] In the photograph, Vakhtangov
resembles another classical character who managed to shed his social
mask: King Lear, as he wandered in the heath. A former scholar, and
now a drunkard-beggar and homeless wanderer, Brendel is deprived
of any social status and, therefore, free. "Both Good and Evil seeds"
are battling in Brendel's heart as he makes his way through the world.
This unique interpretation of the character of Brendel by Vakhtangov
explains the note from the director's diary: "Ibsen suffers primarily

3   See Figure 5.

because theatres don't approach him from the standpoint of giant, boulder-like, characters" (see p. 224). Such an approach also explains why Vakhtangov originally required the only MAT tragic talent, the heir to the nineteenth-century tragedians—Leonid Leonidov—for the role of Brendel.

In Vakhtangov's production, Rosmer's old teacher, who once inspired Rosmer to carry happiness and freedom to the common people, now inspired him by the very depth of his own fall. The sight of Brendel caused Rosmer to see himself in the tragic crooked mirror of his teacher's image. Vakhtangov's Brendel sobered Rosmer up and made him abandon his utopian idea of obtaining collective happiness on earth. Once again, Rosmer follows his teacher's example by transcending both of the social masks he previously wore—the one of the aristocrat, and the one of the revolutionary—thus making the final step toward his own inner freedom. Together with his shadowy companion Rebecca, he stands elated on the verge of the special knowing as they leap into the deadly waterfall at the end of the play. As it often happened, Vakhtangov's production appeared to be deeper than his own directorial plan, dedicated exclusively to the relationship between Rebecca and Rosmer.

The *Rosmersholm* psychological and formal discoveries, including the new form of the tragic-comic grotesque, achieved by Vakhtangov in the role of Brendel, paved the way for his final First Studio production: Strindberg's *Erik XIV*. *Rosmersholm* was conceived before the revolution, but it opened after the revolution arrived. The production's lack of success with the audiences lies in the fact that, apart from the character of Brendel, the play did not provide Vakhtangov with material for the form of the grotesque. In the meantime, tragic-comic grotesque, as an expressive means, was a prerequisite to Vakhtangov's future method of fantastic realism. Both a creative method and a model of theatre, fantastic realism belongs to the epoch of "cataclysm." Vakhtangov celebrated cataclysm before the revolution's arrival. All of his productions for the First Studio of the MAT spoke of cataclysm and featured characters caught in between the two worlds: new and old, dead and alive, good and evil.

The revolution arrived and "divided the world into the 'old' and the 'new'" (see p. 165). Time changed for Vakhtangov and his contemporaries; cataclysm, and the fierce struggle between the two worlds, now took place not just in the human heart but in the reality of everyday life. Vakhtangov, the artist of the cataclysm, whose philosophy of artistic festival was grounded in heightened existence on the threshold of life and death, must have sensed that the spirit of the times was meeting him halfway. He began his formal experiments and discovered the expressive means, harmonious with his time—first as an actor in *Rosmersholm* and then as a director in productions such as *The Miracle of Saint Anthony*, *Erik XIV*, and *The Dybbuk*. Vakhtangov wrote about the First Studio work on *Erik XIV*: "It is our times that direct us toward this experiment—the times of the Revolution" (see p. 142). Nemirovich-Danchenko, who dedicated his career at the MAT to recreating the unique psychology of the author in his productions, granted Vakhtangov's *Erik* the greatest compliment he could give: *"Erik XIV* became a performance where, for the first time, the form of the play was discovered, outside of the Moscow Art Theatre walls" (Sobolev 1922, cited in Vendrovskaya and Kaptereva 1984: 454).

The production of *Rosmersholm* was also meant as a preparation for the ultimate mystery Vakhtangov planned to stage at the First Studio of the MAT in 1918: Byron's *Cain*. In the end, Stanislavsky decided to direct this production himself at the MAT. Stanislavsky's production of *Cain* failed miserably and literally closed before it opened. Vakhtangov's "daring" plan for *Cain* never came to fruition (see p. 241).

The Miracle of Saint Anthony

Vakhtangov's own studio (the future State Academic Vakhtangov Theatre in Moscow) was organized in November 1913. A group of university students in Moscow invited Vakhtangov to head their studio. The Studio's name changed several times throughout its existence. For the sake of consistency, in the sourcebook I refer to it as the Vakhtangov Studio. By the time of Vakhtangov's death in 1922, however, the Studio carried the name of the Third Studio of the MAT.

Vakhtangov began his work at the Studio with a play by a contemporary Russian author, Boris Zaitsev, entitled *The Lanin Estate*. This work, conducted exclusively for training purposes, was performed only once, in March 1914. It was followed by formal training, conducted initially by Vakhtangov himself and later by his most experienced students. The Vakhtangov Studio produced no plays between 1914 and 1918, except for three *Performance Evenings*, presented in lieu of classroom work sharings. These three evenings, presented in 1915, 1916, and 1917 were based on dramatizations of short stories by Chekhov and de Maupassant as well as some one-act plays by less important authors. In 1920, Vakhtangov staged at his Studio Chekhov's one-act play *The Wedding*; he revised this production in 1921. In 1920, Vakhtangov rehearsed Pushkin's verse play *Feast During the Plague* at his Studio. Records for these rehearsals are featured in Part VII of the sourcebook. They give us a precious glimpse into Vakhtangov's formal creative laboratory. The work on the Pushkin play was never completed, and Vakhtangov's plan to perform *The Feast During the Plague* in one evening with Chekhov's *The Wedding* was not realized. Two of the most significant Vakhtangov Studio productions are thoroughly represented in the sourcebook. These are Maurice Maeterlinck's *The Miracle of Saint Anthony* and Carlo Gozzi's *Princess Turandot*.[4] Of the two plays, *Turandot* is considered Vakhtangov's testament. It survived over 1,000 performances in its original staging, and enjoyed two consecutive revivals. *Turandot's* longevity is second only to the MAT's production of Maeterlinck's *The Blue Bird*, directed by Vakhtangov's two teachers, Konstantin Stanislavsky and Leopold Sulerzhitsky in 1908. As admirable as it may be, this longevity is also ironic, as Vakhtangov himself insisted that the form of his *Turandot* must evolve constantly throughout the production's life.

A lesser known of Vakhtangov masterpieces, *The Miracle of Saint Anthony* is, nevertheless, significant as a step on the way to the theatre of fantastic realism. This 1904 play by Belgian author and playwright Maurice Maeterlinck (1862–1949) opened at the Vakhtangov Studio in September 1918. In Maeterlinck's play, the relatives of the wealthy old woman, Mademoiselle Hortenze, are gathered in her house for her funeral. They are confronted by an intruder, who introduces himself as St. Anthony of Padua. St. Anthony arrived to answer the prayers of Mademoiselle Hortenze's old maid Virginie, who is seeking the revival of the deceased. Virginie confirms her wishes to bring her mistress back to life despite the Saint's warning that such a turn of events would deprive Virginie of the generous inheritance her mistress left her. The rich relatives, now even richer with the death of Mademoiselle Hortenze, do not believe that they are in the presence of a saint. In the meantime, St. Anthony makes his way into the room where the deceased woman lies in state, and fulfills his promise. Mademoiselle Hortenze's heirs are temporarily moved, but not for long. They quickly pronounce the miracle a coincidence, label the old man as a madman and call the police. As St. Anthony is led away to the police department in the pouring rain, Virginie, the only trusting soul in the house,

---

4   The rehearsal records of Vakhtangov's unfinished work on Aleksandr Pushkin's one-act play *The Feast During the Plague* are also included in the selection. They give us a precious glimpse into Vakhtangov's formal creative laboratory.

follows him, carrying an umbrella above his head. At the departure of the saint and Virginie, the revived woman immediately dies again.

Vakhtangov rehearsed the first variant of Maeterlinck's *The Miracle of Saint Anthony* at his Studio from 1916 to 1918. Similarly to his First Studio works, he continued to search for the **Theatre of Mystery** within this comedy. As the spectators witnessed the characters' mistrust of the miracle, they were intended to "feel moved and embarrassed" by their own lack of faith, thus rising to an elevated moral state. When evoking within the audience this experience, Vakhtangov, according to his own admission, merely followed the author's point of view and intentions.

In his second variant of the production, directed in 1921, Vakhtangov substituted the all-too-human psychology of the Maeterlinck characters for the social psychology of the class of bourgeois, thus anticipating the theatre of Bertolt Brecht. Even with this correction, the two leading characters of the play, St. Anthony and the maid Virginie, still belonged to the realm of psychological theatre. In accordance with Vakhtangov's intentions, the audience was expected to identify with the simple soul Virginie and see Anthony through her trusting eyes— not as a mighty and mysterious saint but as a kindly old man. By doing so, Vakhtangov synthesized the aspect of the mystery with the element of Popular Theatre.

Virginie remained the moral center of Vakhtangov's production as she transcended her social mask in several ways: first by wishing her mistress alive, then by turning down a sizable inheritance, and, finally, in her last image on the stage, by accompanying St. Anthony in his wandering. The audience saw him as a kindly old man—through the prism of popular consciousness, represented in the play by Virginie. The ensemble of relatives at the rich aunt's funeral was executed in the form of the grotesque, also as seen through the eyes of Virginie. In her consciousness, St. Anthony was more real than her rich masters.[5] They appeared to her (and the audience) as grotesque mannequins or puppets, designed to react to any event with a preprogrammed set of gestures. Such reactions were sustained by Vakhtangov with the use of what he called "a period"—the group of relatives would freeze, creating an expressive bas-relief, for a determined duration of time. The group would mold itself into yet another bas-relief as something

---

5   The discovery of Vakhtangov's tendency to present the reality of the play as seen through the eyes of its main character was made by the Russian Vakhtangov scholar Natalia Smirnova (Smirnova 1982).

new occurred, or as the line passed to a different character. These physical reactions, while being individual with each character, always merged into a harmonious sculptural composition; the inner content of every reaction was determined by the psychology of the class. At the same time, Vakhtangov insisted that, while the characters' external movement was continually interrupted, the actors should continue living internally throughout these moments of stillness. He maintained that such "freezes" do occur in life and called his actors to master the psychology of the bas-relief freeze, preserving and varying the individualized experience behind each moment of stillness from one performance to the next (see Figure 6).

In his last discussion with students, Vakhtangov suggested that the combination of symbolic sets and eclectic methods of acting made his second variant of *The Miracle of Saint Anthony* a "transitional form" on the way to fantastic realism. The varying texture of acting in the play, ranging from realism to grotesque, represented pure fantasy of the theatrical collective, thus expressing the contemporary interpretation of the Mystery and Popular Theatres. This aspect of the Vakhtangov production made it the work of fantastic realism. At the same time, the production set belonged to the style of symbolism. While this style of the set was appropriate for Maeterlinck's play, Vakhtangov considered it outdated from the standpoint of the 1921 theatrical aesthetic. For this reason, Vakhtangov could not count even his second version of *The Miracle of Saint Anthony* as a pure work of fantastic realism.

Erik XIV

Vakhtangov's final production at the First Studio of the MAT, *Erik XIV*, opened in 1921. Strindberg's story of the mad Swedish King Erik interested Vakhtangov primarily due to Erik's defiance of a social mask. Deprived of its defense, Vakhtangov's Erik literally became "the battleground between good and evil": "God and hell, fire and water. Master and slave—he, who is made out of antagonisms and squeezed between the polarities of life and death, must inevitably destroy himself" (see p. 141).

From Vakhtangov's notes on the performance, it is obvious that the director was fascinated by the parallel between the events of the play and the Parable of the Wedding Feast from the New Testament (Matthew 22). Like the king from the parable, King Erik in Strindberg's play invites his courtiers to his wedding feast. But King Erik is marrying the daughter of a simple soldier, and "the nobility refuses to attend" (see p. 139). Erik then "orders to assemble the beggars from the gutter

Figure 6 Scene from Act 1 of *The Miracle of Saint Anthony*, 1921. © Moscow Art Theatre's Museum.

and the street harlots from the tavern" (see p. 139). A parable, as a traditional product of popular consciousness, became the core of Vakhtangov's performance.

Strindberg's Erik is torn between the worlds of the courtiers and the commoners. At the end of the play, he falls victim to a coup, staged by a group of aristocrats. In a complete deviation from Strindberg, Vakhtangov's Erik died by his own hand. Erik's death was portrayed symbolically in the production's finale. Michael Chekhov, who played Erik, stepped out of the huge cocoon of his royal cloak. (The cloak itself, as well as the royal crown, was decorated with the arrows of forked lightning; these appeared to be splitting the king.) (See Plate 1.) As Erik drank his cup of poison, he remained in the tight-fitting tunic of a monk. Erik's naked soul, deprived of any earthly baggage and equal to anyone else's, stood in front of the audience. The entire production was staged by Vakhtangov, as if seen through the prism of Erik's tormented, split soul; in the finale Vakhtangov revealed this soul, Erik's "essence," to the audience. Vakhtangov's Erik was meeting his maker "naked," as "it is easier for a camel to pass through the eye of a needle, than for a rich man to enter into the kingdom of God" (Matthew 19:23–24, Mark 10:24–25, and Luke 18:24–25). The sufferings Erik exposed himself to during the play made him, as a character from another Strindberg play would put it, "one of the last."

In Vakhtangov's production, Erik entered the kingdom of God elated, and with ease. (Or did he enter some other great kingdom, the one of Higher Reason, where suicide is not considered a mortal sin?) According to Vakhtangov, Erik did so because he was able to transgress all social masks—be it the one of a tyrant or the one of a popular king. At the end of Vakhtangov's production Erik literally shed the skin of a half-monarch, half-commoner and became "a man."

Even before *Erik XIV* opened with Michael Chekhov, Vakhtangov expressed his wish to his First Studio colleagues to perform the title role of Erik in turn with Chekhov. This wish was granted to Vakhtangov, and a special dress rehearsal was called exclusively for the Vakhtangov-Erik. The First Studio actress Lidiya Deykun (1889–1980), who played the role of Erik's wife Karin, recalled in her memoir this dramatic episode. Vakhtangov, already in Erik's costume, suddenly stopped the dress rehearsal. Addressing Michael Chekhov, he said, "Misha, you took everything from me. I have nothing left for the role" (Deykun 1984: 355).

The Dybbuk

The Jewish Habima Studio (currently the Habima, National Theatre of Israel in Tel-Aviv) was founded in Moscow in 1917 by three teachers of Hebrew language: Nahum Zemach, Menahem Gnessin, and Hannah Rovina. The goal of this organization was unprecedented: it aimed at creating a hitherto nonexistent model of the Hebrew theatre, the theatre of the Bible and of the tragedy, destined, at its maturity, to leave Russia and settle in Palestine. Vakhtangov, who did not speak Hebrew, was responsible for the Habima troupe's original training; the evening of short plays, directed by him, opened the Habima Studio in October 1918.[6] Some of the Habima Studio members did not speak Hebrew either: they had to take regular language classes as part of their Studio "curriculum." Truth be told, even the elder "teachers" did not really know how to speak the language since it was no longer used in everyday life (outside of Palestine). Vakhtangov, who had to coach his inexperienced students "down to every gesture, down to intonations and timbre of voice," used his famed intuition to fantasize the melodies and rhythms of the spoken Hebrew (see p. 327). Vakhtangov's production of *The Dybbuk* opened in winter 1922 and transformed the Jewish Habima Studio into a major artistic force. *The Dybbuk* was performed in its original form for over forty years and kept in the Habima's repertoire until 1965 (Tartakovskaya 2007: 39–43). Throughout this period, *The Dybbuk* remained a required feature of the company's numerous world tours; Vakhtangov's production was one of the chief reasons behind the Habima's international fame, as well as the admiration of such twentieth-century figures as Albert Einstein, Maxim Gorky, George Bernard Shaw, Edward Gordon Craig, Rabindranath Tagore, and Marc Chagall (Ivanov 1999: 156). It would not be an exaggeration to say that Vakhtangov gave birth to what is now the National Theatre of Israel in Tel-Aviv: the Habima.

The story of *The Dybbuk* is based on an ancient Jewish myth.[7] According to the myth, a restless soul of a dead person can live on

---

6　*The Genesis Performance*, directed by Vakhtangov for the Habima opening, consisted of four one-act plays: *The Elder Sister* by Shalom Ash, *The Fire* by Isaac Leib Peretz, *The Sun! The Sun!* by Itzhak Katzenelson, and *The Pest* by Isaac D. Berkowitz.

7　According to the *Encyclopedia of Jewish Myth, Magic and Mysticism*, while "demonic possession has a long history in Judaism, the first reports of *dybbuks* only start to appear in the sixteenth century" (Dennis 2007: 72). Up until the beginning of the twentieth century, the ritual of exorcising a *dybbuk* was frequently performed among the Hasidim.

as a *dybbuk* and enter the body of a living human. The very choice of a myth by Vakhtangov is significant, but so was the choice of the author and the composer for the production. *The Dybbuk* was written by a man dedicated to preserving the Jewish myth, ritual, legend, and folklore. His name was Shloyme Zanvl Rappoport; he was a philosopher, revolutionary, and an author, who wrote using the pen name of An-sky.[8] The composer on *The Dybbuk* was Joel Engel; he accompanied An-sky during his 1911–1914 ethnographic expedition through the *shtetls* of Volhynia and Podolia, collecting the musical folklore of the Jews.

The entirety of An-sky's play revolves around three rituals: prayer at the synagogue, a wedding, and the act of exorcism. Vakhtangov's interest in the play, however, went far beyond its ritualistic and ethnographic aspects. Vakhtangov reinterpreted the play radically, making it serve his leading artistic theme. His version of *The Dybbuk* concentrated on the eternal conflict between the forces of life and death. At its heart was the theme of revolt against death.

The poor young religious-school student Hannan instantly dies at the news that his intended Leah is promised as a wife to a rich fiancé. By doing so, Leah's greedy father, the merchant Sender, broke the prior promise he made to Hannan's late father. (Hannan and Leah were betrothed in their childhood, and, as they grew up, they fell in love.) The group of Jewish beggars at the wedding of the rich merchant's daughter became one of the main driving forces of the Vakhtangov production. (See Figure 7.) In the director's interpretation, the beggars teamed up with the spirit of the poor scholar Hannan, helping Hannan the *dybbuk* to reclaim his intended bride. In the central scene of the second act, the beggars swirled Leah in an ecstatic, violent dance, weakening her body and spirit, thus making her susceptible to Hannan the *dybbuk*.[9] When the Messenger announced that the *dybbuk* entered Leah, the beggars rejoiced at the news.

Vakhtangov directed the dance of the beggars as "the protest-dance, the scream-dance" (Karev 1959: 417). His beggars revolted against the heartless world of the rich who brought them to their current state. They also supported Hannan and Leah in their revolt against the dead, stagnant world they were born into—the world that had no place for

---

8   The hyphenated spelling of the playwright's last name, An-sky, introduced by the author himself, was customary in Russia. In English-language theatre studies, however, the name is usually used without the hyphen.

9   The theme of the beggars' alliance with the *dybbuk* has been discussed by Yosef Yzraely (1970).

Figure 7 Scene from Act 2 of *The Dybbuk*, 1922 (beggars' dance). © Vakhtangov Theatre's Museum.

two loving hearts. Once again, Vakhtangov played out the parable motif of the beggars invited to the "royal" wedding. The Parable of the Wedding Feast had its second incarnation in Vakhtangov's *The Dybbuk*. In this production, however, Vakhtangov's interpretation of the parable was unorthodox, paradoxical. His imagery of the second act that featured the famous beggars' dance was multileveled, complex, and rich with symbolic meaning:

> The crowd of the beggars, invited to the wedding feast, is elaborated by Vakhtangov in the manner of exaggeration. These monstrous faces, deformed bodies and contorted movements, look as if they are taken from the caricatures by Leonardo. If one is to remember the bas-relief of the beggars from *Erik XIV*, the enormity of the distance traveled by Vakhtangov between these two productions becomes obvious. Vakhtangov in *The Dybbuk* demonstrated how cruel his talent was, how dear the beauty of ugliness was to his soul. With greedy curiosity he peers into the crawling tangle of human debris he called into being. He keeps accelerating the tempo of this gray ragged whirlwind more and more. And then suddenly he slices it with the white beam of Leah. Leah the Lily— the bright Ariel amongst the Caliban crowd. Her dancing amongst the chimerical round dance of the people-monsters is exceptional in its strength. Vakhtangov does not spare the whiteness: he stains it with the toad paws, with the touches of apes.[10] He mixes the breath of the rose-maiden with the plague's breath.[11] Vakhtangov, who himself experiences bliss "on the edge of the abyss,"[12] makes the theatre experience it with him.
>
> (Volkov 1922: 20; see Figure 8)

What is significant in this description is the fact that in Vakhtangov's production both Hannan and Leah existed between the world of the rich and the poor, thus also defying social masks and exposing themselves to the forces of Good and Evil. Vakhtangov's beggars did not

---

10 Vakhtangov invested each of his beggar characters with an animal archetype. One beggar woman resembled a toad, another an ape, etc. In doing so, Vakhtangov followed the concept of the grotesque outlined by Meyerhold in his 1918–1919 lectures (Meyerhold 2001).

11 A reference to the following verse from Pushkin's play *Feast During the Plague*: "We froth our goblets, one and all, / And drink the breath of a rose-maiden, / Although it may be ... full of Plague!"

12 A reference to the following verse from Pushkin's play *Feast During the Plague*: "In every battle there is a bliss, / As on the edge of a dark abyss."

Figure 8 Scene from Act 2 of *The Dybbuk*, 1922 (beggars' dance). © St. Petersburg State Museum of Theatre and Music.

help Hannan to claim Leah's body in order to restore the ultimate justice. They had a class agenda of their own; they needed to get back at their oppressors: Leah's rich father and the family of her rich fiancé. Hannan and Leah of Vakhtangov's production became the battleground for the struggle between the rich and the poor. Therefore, the forces of the dead and the living, the good and the evil, appeared as relative categories in the director's interpretation. As was mentioned before, in Vakhtangov's productions these two seemingly opposing forces were so closely interwoven that they often become indistinguishable.

In his article on *Erik XIV*, Vakhtangov spoke of the dead world of the courtiers and the living world of the people. Contrary to his own statement, in the production Vakhtangov portrayed both courtiers and commoners as essentially stagnant and dead. The expressive means used to portray these two camps of characters were different (**statuary immobility** for the courtiers, ethnographic primitivism and one-dimensional bas-relief for the commoners), but the effect achieved through these means was essentially the same. Erik—Michael Chekhov—was the only living character in the production, as he was the only one deprived of a social mask. The rest of the characters in the production were portrayed by Vakhtangov as they were reflected in Erik's soul. Vakhtangov's Erik hated his courtiers and misunderstood his people; that alone justified, in the world of Vakhtangov's production, why the courtiers appeared as lifeless statues, while the commoners looked as if they just stepped out of an ethnographic postcard. Ultimately, living force in Vakhtangov's *Erik XIV* existed outside of the threshold of the production, within the mysterious realm where Erik went in the finale.

Similarly, in *The Dybbuk*, both the rich and the beggars were portrayed through the means of grotesque (schematic, puppet-like plasticity of movement of the rich and the distorted, angular, and broken physicality of the beggars' dance). Neither of these two forces could be perceived by the audience as the ultimate forces of Good or Evil. Both camps were preprogrammed by their social precepts and acted in accordance with them; both equaled their social function and, therefore, were not truly alive and human.

Only the characters of Hannan and Leah remained outside, or rather above, both camps, thus becoming completely exposed—a battleground for the fight between the two social groups. Vakhtangov's Hannan and Leah perished as victims of the never-ending fight between the rich and the poor, but by their death they broke through to each other—into the higher realms, unseen and unavailable to all of us on earth. If there was one social group that could fully identify with Vakhtangov's Erik, Hannan and Leah, or Rebecca and Rosmer, it was the core of the

MAT's audience—the now extinct class of the Russian intelligentsia.[13] This group of people, who prepared the Russian Revolution, was the first to fall victim to it. Those members of the Russian intelligentsia who were still alive and not in exile by 1921 saw themselves in Michael Chekhov's Erik and in the Habima Studio's Leah and Hannan.[14]

The otherworldly realm lived and breathed on the periphery of the Vakhtangov production of *The Dybbuk*. It was present through Engel's mystical music, through the leitmotif of Hannan's spiritual strivings—the Song of Songs, through Leah's striving for the dead Hannah, etc. At the same time, it never physically entered the world of the performance. The Russian theatre critic of the time, Mikhail Zagorsky, remained dissatisfied by the harsh end of Vakhtangov's *The Dybbuk*. Instead of portraying the metaphysical union of the two souls, the Romeo and Juliet of the *shtetl*, united in death, Vakhtangov closed his production with a cruel and utterly unromantic gesture. When the local *tsadik* exorcised the *dybbuk* from Leah, she falls flat on the stage floor. The sprawled body of the dead woman is covered by the Messenger with a dark piece of sackcloth (Zagorsky 1922).[15] What Zagorsky did not understand was that Vakhtangov's *The Dybbuk* could not end any other way. Vakhtangov's concept of the union of the two souls was an otherworldly event. Unlike his MAT mentors, the wise artist never portrayed the otherworldly in a physical form—doing this would defy its very essence, and Vakhtangov's art aimed at the essential (see Figure 9).

13 In 1922, Stanislavsky inscribed his photograph to Vakhtangov as to "one of those deserving of glory, who did not desert his post and stayed to save his art and the Russian theatre" (Vendrovskaya and Kaptereva 1984: 429). Those of the original Russian intelligentsia who did not emigrate or perish in the bloody civil war that followed the revolution were executed in Stalin's purges. The new class of the so-called Soviet intelligentsia, as well as the contemporary Russian intelligentsia, can be seen as heirs to the original class, but even they would admit that the relation is rather distant.

14 According to the Russian director Aleksei Dikiy, Vakhtangov's *Erik* "was perceived as the confession of the theatre that was far from discovering its place within the drastic social change of the time" (Vendrovskaya and Kaptereva 1984: 352).

15 In the original Russian version of the play, the name of this character is identified as the Passerby rather than the Messenger.

Figure 9 Scene from Act 3 of *The Dybbuk*, 1922 (finale). Courtesy of Andrei Malaev-Babel

4   Toward the Theatre of the Future

Theoretical Model of the Theatre of Fantastic Realism: Vakhtangov's Directorial Plan for Tolstoy's *The Fruits of Enlightenment*

In 1919 Vakhtangov began to develop his model of Popular Theatre. Due to Vakhtangov's gift of synthesis, this new model absorbed his Theatre of Mystery, creating an original quality of theatre Vakhtangov later called fantastic realism. An observant reader may have noticed the presence of the theme of social mask, characteristic of Popular Theatre, in Vakhtangov's pre-revolutionary productions. Similarly, we find the elements of mystery in each of Vakhtangov's final productions of 1921–1922. The last time Vakhtangov consciously returned to this concept in his 1921 directorial plan of Tolstoy's play *The Fruits of Enlightenment*, he did so through the prism of fantastic realism.[1]

The form suggested by this directorial plan was devised for the MAT. This form was fantasized by Vakhtangov in harmony with the creative individuality of the MAT's collective. The style of naturalism, characteristic of the MAT, was preserved in the production as one of the possible creative means utilized by the Theatre of Fantastic Realism. Moreover, Vakhtangov insisted that a naturalistic set, furniture, and costumes, outlined in his plan, appear to be "justified." One might ask, what justification does naturalism need since it always appears to be true to life? According to Stanislavsky, the term "justification" is used to indicate a necessity for every theatrical situation, quality or device to be believable from the standpoint of everyday reality. In his directorial plan, Vakhtangov disagrees; he insists that in a work of theatre naturalism should appear *theatrically* justified. It is highly doubtful

---

1   Therefore, Vakhtangov's directorial plan for *The Fruits of the Enlightenment* is featured in Part II of the *Sourcebook*.

that Vakhtangov ever fulfilled his intention of proposing his plan to Stanislavsky.

Vakhtangov's plan outlined a prologue to Tolstoy's play. The setting of the prologue faithfully recreated one of the MAT rehearsal halls; the entire troupe was present onstage for the prologue, and the play was openly introduced to the audience as a performance rather than "a slice of life." This implied a new method of acting and communication between the audience and the stage that broke the Stanislavskian fourth wall. Ironically, according to Vakhtangov's plan of the prologue, the MAT's head, Stanislavsky himself, was to address the audience directly with the following words on the Tolstoy production:

> Let us suppose that this performance takes place at one of the rooms or verandas of the Yasnaya Polyana estate. We will provide a copy, a naturalistic copy, to be exact, of this room or veranda. Let us suppose that we have rehearsed the play here, at the Art Theatre rehearsal hall, and suppose we wanted to show it to Tolstoy. Suppose he is alive, but cannot come [to the theatre], because he is unwell.
>
> We go to the Yasnaya Polyana estate. We take with us no makeup, no costumes, and no furniture. At our disposal we have the Yasnaya Polyana furniture and objects. Those are bed sheets, carpets, shawls, stools, and flowerpots—the modest means, typical for a domestic production. (Replicas of Tolstoy's things, or better yet his real things, should be taken for props, furniture and street wear, such as fur coats, hats, etc.).
>
> (see p. 136)

Vakhtangov's concept of synthesis between the Theatre of Mystery and Popular Theatre is present, in a nutshell, in this quotation. On one hand, the performance appears to be improvised on the spot at a non-theatrical location (Tolstoy's Yasnaya Polyana estate) using the means available at hand. It is openly billed as a performance, and the fourth wall is broken from its very start. All the above principles belong to the Popular Theatre. On the other hand, both the actors and the audience are to imagine that throughout the performance they are acting in the presence of a great man. In Russian thought of the time, Tolstoy represented a phenomenon of the national conscience—a morally superior human being, in whose presence one could not lie. At the MAT and its First Studio, whose ideology was developed by Tolstoy's disciple Sulerzhitsky, such a notion was especially alive. The supposition that Tolstoy is watching immediately demanded an ultra-sincere, confessional quality of acting from the troupe—the very kind of acting

Vakhtangov strived to achieve in his previous mysteries. Moreover, the idea of the presence of a higher being, *to be evoked by both actors and spectators*, was established in the opening speech of the prologue, delivered by Stanislavsky: "[Throughout our work] We never stopped worshiping the memory of the great man [Tolstoy]. And you, who have come to the theatre today, will also remember him actively" (see p. 138).

As we see, Vakhtangov's new method of fantastic realism contains elements of the Theatre of Mystery.[2] At the same time, the nature of communication with the audience in a performance of fantastic realism is close to the one in the Popular Theatre. This type of communication is not only communal but also collaborative. The actor and the audience do more than "co-experience": they co-create the performance. At the same time, the actor and the audience member, in such a performance, do share in a sacred act of communion with a higher force, or a higher being. According to Vakhtangov's plan for Tolstoy's play, this act of memory of the great author and human being would evoke "an atmosphere of grandeur … within the performance, both in the audience and on the stage" (see p. 139). Vakhtangov specifies that the sacred atmosphere is not to be carried from the stage into the audience, as it happens according to the Stanislavskian formula: "Theatre is a temple, the actor is the priest" (Stanislavsky 1993: 413). According to Vakhtangov, the sacred atmosphere is evoked on both sides of the footlights simultaneously, as the audience at the start of the performance is asked to co-create, to become "active." For Vakhtangov, this atmosphere of awe represented the new content of the performance— Tolstoy's "comedy was transformed into a mystery play" (see p. 139).

Practical Model of the Theatre of Fantastic Realism: Vakhtangov's *Princess Turandot*

Already in *Erik XIV*, staged in 1921, one year prior to *Turandot*, Vakhtangov contemplated a prologue, where actors would appear before the audience at the start of the production as their own creative selves. The director, however, abandoned this idea, considering it too radical at the time. The theoretical model of the new type of communion, or creative act, intrinsic to the Theatre of Fantastic Realism, was first outlined by Vakhtangov in his directorial plan for

---

2   The sacred act implies that both communicating parties also exist in a communion with a higher being.

Tolstoy's play. The mystical communion with a higher force was synthe-sized in Vakhtangov's approach with the direct and active co-creative communion between the actors and the audience, characteristic of the Popular Theatre. Instead of communing with the higher being, both the actors and the audience in the Tolstoy play were meant to *bring the higher being to life through the pre-established creative act of memory.* This concept of the creative act was practically realized by Vakhtangov in his final masterpiece, a working model for the Theatre of Fantastic Realism: Carlo Gozzi's *Princess Turandot.*

Unlike Stanislavsky's truth-like, or truthful **action**, Vakhtangov's theatrical act was no longer merely *sincere.* Vakhtangov's creative act produces results that are tangible and real. In that, it is similar to a ritualistic act that allows no division between actors and the audi-ence and is perceived as non-fictional by its participants. In a peculiar way, Vakhtangov's model brought theatre back to its origins. Russian symbolist author, Sergei Rafalovich (1875–1943), whose ideas were not alien to Vakhtangov, described the primeval theatre thus:

> The first criterion of the primary dramatic, or rather tragic, act would be its religiousness.
>
> The second criterion is its popular aspect, or rather, its nation-wide nature; as Popular Theatre indicates the kind of theatre that sees people as something different from better educated circles, and nationwide theatre unites all without distinction.
>
> Third—the synthesis of the arts.
>
> Fourth—improvisation.
>
> At this stage there is no separation as of yet between spectators and performers—everybody is a performer and a spectator at the same time.
>
> There is no separation between fiction and reality, as everything is a reality. There is no mention of verisimilitude, as everything is truth.
>
> (Rafalovich 1908: 185)

All the criteria of the primal theatre, identified by Rafalovich, fit the image of Vakhtangov's Theatre of Fantastic Realism. Vakhtangov's theatre is a merger between the Theatre of Mystery and the Popular Theatre, just as it is also the Theatre of Synthesis of the Arts and improvisational theatre.

Vakhtangov believed that by carrying out the creative act in the performance of fantastic realism, both the audience and the ensemble tangibly evoked the highest force obtainable by a human being on earth—the one of the creative spirit. By doing so, they genetically alter human nature, thus developing a more perfect human and bringing closer a happier future of mankind, as envisioned by Vakhtangov. It was not moral goodness, or the spirit of social progress, that Vakhtangov aimed at evoking through his art, but rather creativity.

Many of Vakhtangov's colleagues and scholars were perplexed by his fascination with the role of Master Pierre from Nadezhda Bromley's 1921 verse play *The Archangel Michael*. Bromley (1889–1966), the First Studio of the MAT actress, poet, and author, wrote a highly original play that divided the Moscow theatre community. The majority considered the play "delirious," while the minority, including Vakhtangov and the Commissar of the Enlightenment, Lunacharsky, considered it a new word in the art of theatre. In 1921 and 1922 Vakhtangov, already mortally ill, continued rehearsing the role of Master Pierre for as long as he humanly could; even on his deathbed he wrote a letter to Bromley, begging her not to pass the role on to Michael Chekhov (see p. 325). The reason for Vakhtangov's stubbornness was that with the role of Master Pierre he could, as an actor, express his theme in art: the idea of the supremacy of the creative spirit. In his notes on the role Vakhtangov proclaimed: "A man's creative spirit is greater than [his] religious and social senses" (see p. 135).

Bromley's tragic farce deals with Master Pierre, a great sculptor, who created a miracle-working copper figure. According to the author herself, "It is the story of the fall and disgrace of a man, who forgot himself and wasted his [creative] gift, of this man's late meeting with himself, [and] with the copper statue." What follows is "despair and death of the statue," Master Pierre's "attempts to create it anew; in the end, the fallen man creates a monster" (Bromley 1959: 326). In Master Pierre, Vakhtangov wanted to perform the tragedy of an artist, who wasted his creative spirit. He himself knew nothing higher, and he lived for its sake. He told his students:

> No matter what universities you graduate from, what you do, how rich you become, you will always be poor, for as long as you don't have art. Ladies and gentlemen, you do not value art; you do not know what you are doing. You breathe art, as you breathe air, and you do not know what that means for you. What will become of you, if you are deprived of air?
>
> (see Ivanov vol. II: 154)

The theme Vakhtangov the actor was not destined to express, Vakhtangov the director conveyed in his *Turandot*. It was the one and only of the director's creations where the threshold of the higher realm came so close to the periphery of the world of the production it practically entered its realm. This sensation of crossing the other-worldly threshold was viscerally felt by the audience; it is documented in the accounts of Vakhtangov's *Turandot*. The critic Nikolai Volkov, responsible, among other works, for the pioneering two-volume study of Meyerhold's theatre, wrote in the posthumous Vakhtangov mono-graph, "Vakhtangov's name is forever connected with the honorable title of the juggler of Our Lady. The gates of heaven are open for Our Lady's juggler. Vakhtangov will enter them" (Volkov 1922: 11).

Nadezhda Bromley, the author of *The Archangel Michael*, wrote one year after Vakhtangov's death:

> Vakhtangov stands between us and the future; this future is the golden age that will arrive by means of transcending tragedy.[3] The first step on this path is Vakhtangov's *Turandot*. Did he himself not personify the transgression of tragedy? Death lived in him for years and breathed through his breath, and yet the vivifying life entered with his step everywhere, across every threshold he crossed. What permeates the emptiness beyond the thresholds he abandoned last? I hear the dance of this emptiness whistle and play—who will fill it?—it is so densely filled with him.
>
> *Turandot* resounds in the emptiness beyond *the last* threshold he crossed in his life,—this is his last victory on earth; he played this victory to the end in his dialogues with his last partner—death.
>
> (Bromley 1923: 35)

Vakhtangov's final productions make it clear that the higher realm, unobtainable on earth, is not the end goal of this art. Making the nation more creative, inspiring their spontaneous, imaginative, improvisa-tional, and free self-expression was Vakhtangov's means of developing a new type of actor-human—member of the society where everyone possesses the free spirit of an actor. Through his art, and through his daily work at multiple schools and studios, Vakhtangov was bringing closer his vision of the theatre of the future:

> The time will come when theatre will be an ordinary event of our life. Theatre will simply be in a square. Everyone, who feels himself capable, will act. Theatre will be free of charge—there will

---

3   Tragedy in Bromley's meaning equals death.

be no admittance fee, or a performance honorarium. It will be a free art for free people. Narrow professionalism will disappear; all naturally talented actors will play.

(Leonid Volkov, interviewed in Khersonsky 1940: 67)

At his Studio, where *Turandot* was staged, as well as at numerous other theatrical institutions, Vakhtangov cultivated the actors of the future. The development of the organic technique that was based in complete creative freedom was one part of Vakhtangov's work. The other part of the work was developing the greater and more spiritually significant being in every actor. Strict discipline of training, rehearsal and performance processes, and ethical lessons were conducted by Vakhtangov at every step of the way. The cultivation of the independent creative spirit in his students, inspiring love for their studio and, ultimately, their art—such were the means utilized by Vakhtangov. Most importantly, Vakhtangov avoided cheap preaching and inspired his students not by his example but by his very existence; he never told his students to be like him, but the talent he exhibited in everything he did, in art and in life alike, caused his students to expand and grow. Through this scrupulous daily work, Vakhtangov practically solved the dilemma, expressed by Vera Komissarzhevskaya: "we don't have the actor; he needs to be created; he cannot be created without creating a new man in him" (Bely 1934; cited in Rybakova 1994: 458).

In his revelations to colleagues and students, Vakhtangov insisted that the qualities that currently belong strictly to theatre artists in time would belong to other members of the future society. Vakhtangov envisioned this society as the union of the free and equal, where everyone will possess the qualities he cultivated in his actors through spiritual training and rigorous work on inner and outer technique: freedom and spontaneity, courage and boldness, and theatrical ethics that implies a strong feeling of the ensemble. This is why Vakhtangov could insist that, in the theatre of the future, "everyone, who feels himself capable, will act."

In Vakhtangov's Theatre of the Future, people coming together for a performance will not be divided into actors and spectators. Shortly before his death, Vakhtangov shared the following parable with his friend and former student, actor Leonid Volkov:

You and I, we both sit in the first row and watch the performance; at the same time, I am also an actor in this production. So, when I am free, I share my impressions with you, as with a friend, and then I say:—It is my cue, now I will play for you. I leave the first row, climb onto the stage and begin to play everything—grief and joy, and this friend of mine believes me ... When I finish, I rejoin him and say—Well, how was it? Good?

(Leonid Volkov, interviewed in Khersonsky 1940: 71)

The fact that Vakhtangov's imaginary spectator, Volkov, was also an *actor, and a friend*, is significant. The kind of relationship between the spectator and the actor, outlined by Vakhtangov, implies that in the future theatre any spectator, at any point in the performance, could enter the stage as an actor. In this model of theatre the Stanislavskian fourth wall is not just dented, it is dismantled for good.

This specific kind of acting was realized by Vakhtangov in *Princess Turandot*. In comparison with Vakhtangov's vision of the theatre of the future, there still exists some division between the actor and the spectator in his *Turandot*. At the same time, this division was brought to a minimum, as Vakhtangov insisted that *Turandot* actors consider themselves proud and dignified servants to their spectators, who, in their turn, will serve the actors tomorrow in their unique field. Every audience member, a master in their own right, associated themselves with the exquisite **mastery** of the actor, demonstrated by every member of the *Princess Turandot* ensemble. Vakhtangov told his actors:

> You are virtually a part of this audience. Today you are performing onstage as artists, tomorrow you "sit in the audience," and those who today watched your acting (as professional art), tomorrow will demonstrate to you their art of the textile or spinning mill workers, the art of a worker at the largest industrial plants ... perhaps, an art of an office worker at a large state institution. Today we are artists in our field, tomorrow—they are artists in their field.
>
> (Nikolai Mikhailovich Gorchakov 1957: 112–113)

One of the reasons Vakhtangov came so close to realizing his vision of the Theatre of Fantastic Realism in *Princess Turandot* is that he staged it as a production performed by actors-improvisers, about another troupe of improvising actors. An actor's free creativity became the higher force that permeated the atmosphere of this production, thus evoking the creative act. The crossing of the actor's creative threshold took place before the audience's eyes and signaled the crossing into the realm of creativity.

The Vakhtangov ensemble members would pick up pieces of fabric lying on the **stage platform** and in their skillful hands, bring these fabrics to life. In the period of one minute, the actors would reveal each fabric's plastic quality, making their pieces dance in the air and form intricate rhythmic patterns. Before the audience could consciously register an esthetically beautiful and choreographically skillful movement, the piece of fabric would become an element of the character's costume—a cape, or a turban, or an improvised beard of a Chinese wise man. The actors were putting on their characters' costumes, that was all. This episode in *Turandot* was synonymous with the moment of climbing up to the stage from the audience in Vakhtangov's parable. It can also be compared with the crossing from the wings onto the stage in the naturalistic theatre. At the same time, Vakhtangov's master-actor had an advantage in that he or she did not need to resort to naturalistic illusion to inspire the trust of his or her friends in the audience (see Figure 10).

In order to fully understand the groundbreaking nature of the Vakhtangov production, let us take a closer look at the structure of the artistic reality, as well as the character structure, created by Vakhtangov in his *Princess Turandot*. At the top of the play, the actors of the Vakhtangov Studio appeared in front of the audience in an opening parade. Instead of wearing their characters' costumes, they wore what Vakhtangov referred to as the "actor's working uniform." This was not Meyerholdian *prozodezhda* (a sack-like jumpsuit used for both men and women alike and designed in constructivist style). Rather, Vakhtangov's male actors wore elegant tails, and his actresses wore evening gowns designed by the leading Moscow fashion designer of the time, Nadezhda Lamanova.The year was 1922, the fifth year of the proletarian revolution, and the period was the one of "military communism." Dressing his actors in tails and evening gowns was a bold move on Vakhtangov's part, and yet it was entirely accepted by the audience. Vakhtangov refused to "reflect his times" literally. The pulse of the contemporary times, however, did beat in Vakhtangov's *Turandot*. It reflected the *essence* of the period: the festive, forward-looking, and hopeful spirit of the time. Vakhtangov actors' uniform appeared to be in harmony with this spirit.

During the parade, each actor was introduced to the audience by their real name, as their creative selves. This introduction was done by the four traditional *commedia* masks: Tartaglia, Pantalone, Brigella, and Trufaldino. Unlike the rest of the cast, they wore traditional *commedia dell'arte* costumes and did not pose as Vakhtangov Studio actors. The acting technique utilized by the masks contained a slight element of characterization. This characterization, however, was treated by Vakhtangov as an artistic texture. It was executed with

Figure 10 Actors putting on costumes at the start of *Princess Turandot*, 1922. © Bakhrushin State Central Theatre Museum.

such skill, lightness and ease that it never overwhelmed the artistic individuality of the performer. Most importantly, the characterization was clearly "fantasized" by the actor. For example, Tartaglia acquired the "characterization" of a three-year-old girl (see Figure 11), while Pantalone, in the good old *commedia dell'arte* tradition, spoke in a dialect. In this instance, however, instead of the traditional Venetian dialect, it was a very recognizable peasant dialect of the Ryazan region of Russia (see Figure 12).

In the eyes of the Russian audiences, the romantic Venice and the utterly prosaic Ryazan existed as two obvious polarities. This and other devices utilized by Vakhtangov made his version of the *commedia* unlike any of the stylistic experiments with the *commedia dell'arte* revival carried out by his contemporary artists both in Europe and in Russia. On one hand, Vakhtangov kept the spirit of the *commedia*

Figure 11
Boris Schukin as Tartaglia in *Princess Turandot*, 1922. © Vakhtangov Theatre's Museum.

Figure 12
Ivan Kudryavtsev as Pantalone in *Princess Turandot*, 1922. © Vakhtangov Theatre's Museum.

alive and ignored its letter. On the other hand, Vakhtangov did not try to plant the *commedia* onto Russian soil and bridge reality and art, as other artists, including Blok and Meyerhold in *The Puppet Booth*, had done. Max Reinhardt, who staged his version of Gozzi's *Turandot* approximately a decade prior to Vakhtangov's production,[4] achieved a breathtaking stylization of China—the actual locale where the Turandot fairy tale takes place. Vakhtangov's Pantalone, who served as a councillor to the Emperor of China and spoke in a Russian peasant dialect made it clear: this *Turandot* takes place in the world of theatre, and nowhere else, and its characters are actors.

The Vakhtangov actors "juggled" their masks with great virtuosity: characterization could increase, at which point it condensed and bordered on the grotesque. It could also decrease, and finally might disappear. In the course of the performance an actor playing a mask could "come out of character" and ask their fellow actor to pick up a set of keys they just dropped on the stage, addressing the partner by their real name. This style of acting made many of the critics and theatre practitioners proclaim that Vakhtangov's actors, instead of playing characters, played their own ironic point of view on their characters.

A more thorough exploration of Vakhtangov's character structure in *Turandot* proves that no actor in this production ever "came out of character." To begin with, the Vakhtangov actors played actors. They were introduced as such, and, most importantly, when the performance began, they remained actors. Vakhtangov asked each of his performers to develop a "character" of the member of the traveling *commedia* troupe. The Vakhtangov Studio actors developed their Italian actor-characters according to the "science" of the Stanislavsky System: they had biographies, elaborate relationships with each other, etc.

The character structure of Vakhtangov's *Turandot*, therefore, consisted of the three following layers: the Vakhtangov Studio actor, the Italian *commedia dell'arte* troupe member, and the Gozzi character and/or *commedia dell'arte* mask (depending on which one of the two the actor performed).[5] In the creative world of the Vakhtangov Studio actor, the Italian actor they performed executed their respective *Turandot* character or mask. The "presence" of the Italian *commedia dell'arte* troupe member was never openly revealed to the audi-

---

4   Reinhardt staged *Turandot* in Berlin in 1911 and in London in 1913.
5   Each of the four *commedia dell'arte* masks, according to Gozzi, also fulfilled some kind of function in the plot of the fairy tale. Pantalone served as a councillor to the Chinese Emperor; Brigella was the eunuch in charge of the Emperor's harem, etc.

ence. It remained the Vakhtangov actor's professional secret, and yet Vakhtangov's hidden device produced a tangible effect upon both the actors' method of creative existence in the performance and its perception by the audience. Vakhtangov's lead actor, Yuri Zavadsky, who performed the part of Prince Calaf in *Turandot*, gave the following description of the phenomenon of the actor's creative existence in this production:

> Vakhtangov strived to achieve from me a "double," or even a "triple" life onstage. I, Yuri Zavadsky, felt myself an Italian actor, who enthusiastically uses his mastery to create the character of Calaf. As an Italian actor, I perfectly comprehend all the naivety and comicalness of my character's situation; as Yuri Zavadsky I, at the same time, convey the stilted style of the Italian **actor's performance**, and sense its symbolic nature.
>
> (Zavadsky 1975: 200; see Figure 13)

Figure 13
Yuri Zavadsky as Calaf in *Princess Turandot*, 1922. © Vakhtangov Theatre's Museum.

This way of living in the performance fit within its theatrical logic and by no means constituted "playing a point of view." The ironic quality, strongly present in the performance, might have been *received* by the audience as the actor's point of view on his or her character. In the meantime, Vakhtangov's actor, who remained at the core of the *Turandot* character structure, lived creatively onstage and expressed their creative individuality, while alternating between several different textures, or techniques of acting.

The Italian fifteenth- and sixteenth-century *commedia* actors, not familiar with the Stanislavskian "truth-like" style, treated their masks and characters accordingly. They used their roles as pretexts to express their festive emotional capacity and improvisational mastery. On the other hand, the Vakhtangov Studio actors, playing the Italian performers, also used the fairy tale as a pretext to master the improvisational skills and learn to "carry their tears to the footlights and lay themselves open to the audience's applause" (see p. 289). Not unlike the *commedia dell'arte* actor, Vakhtangov's master actor was required to live creatively; this means that they could instantly flare up emotionally "without any external motivation" (see p. 114), and they were capable of spontaneous improvisational acting of varying styles.

Actors playing the masks improvised in the *commedia dell'arte* style; at times this included improvising original lines. As in the actual *commedia*, many of these improvisations were "carefully prepared," but some remained spontaneous. Vakhtangov's actors, performing the masks, spent hours of training dedicated to developing the freedom and courage of an improviser. Actors playing fairy-tale characters preserved "the spirit of an improvising actor" (Chekhov 2002: 41). This meant that the quality of their acting was so spontaneous and light that they produced a complete impression upon the audience that their performances were improvised.

The three layers of the character structure were present in every aspect of Vakhtangov's *Turandot*. The artistic reality of the production consisted of the elements that belonged to three completely different realities. (All three of these harmoniously merged in *Turandot*.) The first reality was the one of 1922 Moscow and the Vakhtangov Studio at Arbat Street. The second was of Italy in the times of *commedia dell'arte*. The third reality was of fairy-tale China, the setting of *Princess Turandot*. Elements of all three realities were present in the set, costumes, music, audience experience, etc.

What made Vakhtangov's *Turandot* a revolutionary production signifying a new method in theatre was that *the actors' method of creative existence onstage actually included all three of these layers:*

Moscow, Italy, and China. In the realm of acting, Vakhtangov designed an organic structure that allowed his performers to live truthfully in a fantastic reality. Only this can explain Stanislavsky's address to Vakhtangov after the dress rehearsal of *Princess Turandot*: "In the twenty-year history of the MAT such victories were few. You found what many theatres sought long and in vain" (Gorchakov 1957: 183–184).

Stanislavsky equally accepted Vakhtangov's production of *Erik XIV* at the First Studio of the MAT. He pronounced it "futuristic" and added: "This kind of futurism I understand" (Deykun 1984: 355–356). And yet, the artistic world of Vakhtangov's *Erik* was also created out of an eclectic mix. As noted, in Vakhtangov's production of *Princess Turandot* the director, instead of inviting his audience into the palace of the Chinese emperor, invited them "into the midst of actors, doing their theatre work" (see p. 149). In the production of *Erik XIV*, instead of inviting the audiences into the palace of the historic King Erik, ruler of Sweden in the late sixteenth century, Vakhtangov invited them into the Dostoyevskian "camera obscura" of mad Erik's soul. Like a Dostoyevsky novel, where the author portrayed the reality as seen through the eyes of one of his characters, Vakhtangov's *Erik XIV* projected the image of the world, as it imprinted in Erik's soul, onto the screen of the production.

In his *The Dybbuk*, instead of inviting audiences into the world of the Jewish *shtetl*, Vakhtangov invited them into a deep existential realm:

> You felt that you are being immersed in some strange dream; although incomprehensible, it was thrilling and rousing, and it was making your heart turn! You felt as though you touched upon the mysteries of the earthly existence, flew up into the spheres of hitherto unknown experiences, and came face to face with the fearful demonic evil powers that invisibly populate the woeful life of a man.
>
> (Zavadsky 1959: 296)

A new and distinctly different artistic reality was created in each and every one of Vakhtangov's three final productions. Its inner and outer elements may or may not have been new to his contemporary art of theatre. The combination of these elements, however, was so harmonious in each performance that the artistic world of every production appeared inimitable and unique.

Vakhtangov's death came at the end of the 1921–1922 Moscow theatre season. It was an unusually rich season, even by Moscow standards; it saw such defining productions of the twentieth-century Russian theatre as Vsevolod Meyerhold's *The Magnificent Cuckold* and Tairov's *Phaedra*. And yet, at the end of the season, everyone, including such different theatrical figures as Meyerhold and Stanislavsky, agreed that the season of 1921–1922 was, nevertheless, Vakhtangov's season. *Princess Turandot* managed to absorb the roughness of Meyerhold's constructivist spectacle, completely deprived of the realistic illusion. In its own unique way, *Turandot* also unmasked theatre and revealed its mechanism. The mechanism of Vakhtangov's production, however, was the one of the acting ensemble's creative process and not Meyerholdian bio-mechanics. Where Meyerhold celebrated purposeful physicality, Vakhtangov celebrated creativity. This is why *Turandot* was also able to reflect Tairov's aesthetic of beauty. The gorgeous tinsels of Tairov Kamerny Theatre's productions were absent in *Turandot*, but the feeling of beauty was very much alive in it. Vakhtangov's final creation did manage to merge the incompatible: Stanislavsky's emotional sincerity, Nemirovich-Danchenko's sense of the author's psychology, Meyerhold's sense of the author's style, expressed through rough theatrical form, and Tairov's beauty. Vakhtangov's *Turandot* combined it all and remained an original Vakhtangov Studio creation.

5   Theatre of the Eternal Mask

Vakhtangov's two final discussions with students were meant to summarize the lessons of *Princess Turandot*. In these discussions, the dying Vakhtangov made the following statement: "The next stage of our work will be dedicated to the search for the eternal form ... In time, the means we have chosen will cease being theatrical. We must find the true theatrical means. We must find the **eternal mask**" (see p. 153).

The next stage of Vakhtangov's work at his Studio was supposed to be the production of *Hamlet*. We will never know how Vakhtangov's *Hamlet* would have looked as we will never be able to fully recreate his vision of the Theatre of Eternal Mask. Presumably, his eternal mask would have absorbed the major principles of Vakhtangov's method of fantastic realism as well as his vision of the Theatre of the Future. I am convinced that, with or without knowledge of Vakhtangov, the artists of today's theatre continue to search for the eternal mask and experiment with it, each in their unique way.

I spent the summer of 2008 teaching in London. As any theatre professional, I tried not to miss a single performance that promised a rich theatrical experience. One of the most profound revelations of my London summer came from a new theatre company called the Factory. The company gathered a troupe of actors—extremely free and utterly equal—to perform an improvised version of *Hamlet*. The performance was held at a different location every weekend. The location, wherever it was (the production I saw was performed at a former church that housed a Steiner school and kindergarten), served as the *Hamlet* set. None of the actors gathered that evening knew what particular part they were about to play—the audience was asked to determine the casting at the top of every performance. Moreover, the space was reconfigured after each act. A new special configuration was set, and new conditions thrown into the mix by the ensemble director. These conditions insured that the actors seldom knew where they were going to make their next entrance. As a result, those actors who were waiting for their cues, often lurked in the "house," merging with the audience. Halfway through the production, the audience began to perceive them as friends. It seemed that at any moment an actor might ask an audience member, "Well, how was it? Good?" Another suggestion made by Vakhtangov in 1918 also came to my mind, as I watched this *Hamlet*:

> Ideally, an actor should, together with his partners, analyze and digest the text and proceed onto the stage to create the character. This is [how it should be] in the ideal case, once an actor has trained in all the necessary techniques, or acquired skills. An actor must be an improviser. This is what we call talent.
>
> (see p. 119)

At the time, I thought the Factory's *Hamlet* reached the improvisational limit. That limit was challenged by another company of young actors I encountered performing a version of *The Three Sisters* at the London Gate Theatre. This improvised production preserved Chekhov's division of the play into four acts; however, within each of the acts, performers were free to improvise the order of lines. Moreover, they could also switch parts in the middle of a scene. Suppose you were an actor playing Colonel Vershinin, and another actor suddenly said one of your lines; this meant that you were no longer Vershinin and now had to find yourself another character. At that point, you, the actor of today, found yourself in the position of the actor from Vakhtangov's 1922 parable: "This instant I am not an actor, and the next instant I am an actor; I cross this threshold before my friend's eyes, apparently altering nothing in me; and yet, there, on the other side of the footlights, I am a different person, and you (my friend) trust me" (Leonid Volkov, interviewed in Khersonsky 1940: 71).

To me, these improvised productions of *Hamlet* and *The Three Sisters* realized Vakhtangov's formula of theatre where the new truth is created out of the eternal contradiction between the reality and the stage. This contradiction, a stumbling block for the actor of psychological theatre, became an inexhaustible source of inspiration for an actor of the Vakhtangov kind: the actor of the Theatre of Fantastic Realism.

Part II
Vakhtangov on Theatre, Actor Training, and an Actor's Creative Process

6 On Theatre

FEBRUARY 23, 1918

Three Elements of Theatre: Collective, Audience, and Actor Cultivation

In order to answer the question: "What is theatre?," we need to name its elements. The collective is the first of them. One genius actor is not theatre; it is a monster, a miracle. To prefer one good actor over a good ensemble is to deny the very essence of theatre; the concept of theatre includes the notion of the collective.

The second component is the audience. To be an actor for yourself, in [the privacy of] your own home (Fyodor Komissarzhevsky's expression) is to be in communion with God, to experience ecstasy. This, however, is not theatre, as the art of theatre consists of an ability to awaken a feeling and infect the audience with it; it is an ability to sense and lead the audience.

The third element is **actor cultivation** that allows an actor to merge with the collective; its absence creates a division between the actor and the troupe. This division resembles the one that exists between a member of high society and an upstart who wormed his way in. The unifying element in the troupe is its constancy. Theatre with a constantly changing ensemble is not a theatre. It is an enterprise. Under such conditions the theatre ensemble will not acquire a creative individuality. The actor [in an enterprise] gives it everything he can for a period of six months, while the actor, who is a part of a constant troupe, does so throughout his entire life.

On Contemporary Theatre Schools[1]

The defect of the contemporary drama school is that it teaches a subject for the sake of a subject. Subjects such as diction, plasticity of movement, gesture, etc., are truly needed in theatre school; however, one should study them *in order to absorb the essence of the subject*. One may not be able to fulfill an exercise in plasticity of movement, but one should perceive *the soul* of movement, fencing, etc. When fulfilling an exercise, one must know the "what for" behind it. I cannot give an answer to this question, as everyone, in time, should discover his own answer.

An outdated school graduates separate specialists: "leading men," "comedians," "leading women," etc. A contemporary school should graduate groups of actors who share a common cultivation. These actors, upon graduation, should then be capable of creating a theatre of their own. Otherwise, a single actor will go under, as he finds himself in a foreign environment that does not meet his [cultivated] needs.

School, Studio, Theatre

A school develops an actor. Unlike the school, the studio works on a play and searches for a form through which to express it. A studio has its own author, who inspires the actors through the director. The finished play is performed at the theatre.

The Essence of an Actor's Creativity: Creating New Artistic Reality

The justification of the drama schools is in perceiving the essence of the subjects studied. This is necessary in order to learn to create.

What is the essence of an actor's creativity? It is the richness of an actor's soul and his ability to reveal this richness.

Untruth onstage appears when faith is absent. A theatrical school must develop an actor's ability to believe that "this could happen to me."

In school one must learn to create conditions conducive to creativity. What does it mean, "to create"? Art exists only in moments when the creative process takes place. An actor's art does not materialize. Why do we call saying somebody else's lines creativity? And why should

---

1 On Russian theatre schools of the period, criticized by Vakhtangov, see Introduction, pp. 8–9.

an actor be in a creative state in order to say somebody else's lines? Because onstage everything is untruth, and an actor must develop his ability to trust it, as if it was truth.

The process of transforming a theatrical lie into artistic truth is the creative process.

New Points of View

Creative play in theatre is a play of the new points of view. One cannot believe literally. One must have an ability to take lies for truth, using the power of one's creative imagination; one must know how to instigate a new point of view on what happens onstage.

Believing literally would not be creativity, but a sickness, an hallucination.

Inappropriate laughter that does not come from the essence of what happens onstage is caused by an actor's inability to take the given situation seriously. The theatrical lie should not interfere with **seriousness**; it should not distract.

An object [itself] is the cause of the point of view in life; as for the stage—there I myself awaken the required point of view [on the object]. Adults lose the naivety of a child. When a child is tired of play, it means that he is tired of creating new points of view. A child is naive, which is why he creates new points of view so seriously.

To be serious means to know that I am doing an important work. An actor, creating new points of view seriously, becomes naive. Onstage, it is unpleasant to speak a naturalistic truth; it ruins artistic fiction, as naturalistic truth is deprived of the creative element. The audience believes everything an actor believes.

On Types of Artistic Reality in Theatre

The Moscow Art Theatre was the first to violate the worn-out traditions. They sat actors down with their backs to the audience; created a setting that accurately characterized the place of action; and discovered a new tone for the roles—lyrical or dramatic, etc. The Moscow Art Theatre developed new principles of set design; they introduced whisper, rhythm.

But now the Moscow Art Theatre has developed its own **cliché**— the Chekhovian cliché. Some plays, such as *Rosmersholm* and *Cain*,[2] cannot be played in a Chekhovian style; they don't need details, they are symbolic. The stage should leave more space for the actors' and audience's fantasy. An actor must internalize [the world of] the author.

In Chekhov's works an audience must believe that the actor *is* the malefactor.[3] *Rosmersholm*, however, does not require characterization; it does not need a kernel.[4]

An actor must make the author's circumstances and words his own.

I can make an author's circumstances my own *when they are truth to me*.

A good actor accepts the director's plan right away. Without showing off, he begins to search for the truth, not in word, but in deed. He does not say to the director: "I don't like it"; it is his obligation to accept the form, given to him by the director, and seek a means to express it.

Thus an actor develops an ability to justify the form.

Every theatre seeks its own form.

Everything is truth in a play written by a good author. An author always writes the play *for some reason*. Chekhov's plays bred in his soul. Ibsen revealed his characters' psychology with an extraordinary depth.

An actor must know how to reveal the subtext of a role and how to feel its **through line** of actions.

An author gives structure to the play and the role.

A group of actors take this structure, reveal the tasks, or, to put it differently, they "undress" the play, determine its main action, draw the red line of the **through action**, reach the super task, or the "what for" behind the play.

Besides, one must determine what is accidental in a play.

2 For further details on Vakhtangov's concept of the Theatre of Mystery, his production of Ibsen's *Rosmersholm*, and his plans to stage Byron's *Cain*, see p. 90 and p. 241.

3 Vakhtangov refers to the title character of Anton Chekhov's 1885 short story *The Malefactor*. An adaptation of this story was staged by Vakhtangov at his Studio for the March 1917 performance evening.

4 The concept of the kernel of the role is explained by Vakhtangov in sections such as "Three Unresolved Elements in the System" (p. 100) and "Character Study: Gradual Perception of the Character's Kernel" (pp. 104–5), as well as in the Introduction (p. 22).

A play is a series of justifications, suggested by the author. For the actor to "act truthfully" does not mean to act in a life-like manner but rather to act in accordance with the [creative] *laws* of life.[5]

From talks given at the Vakhtangov Studio from 1918 to 1919
and recorded by Vera L'vova

---

5   In this thought, Vakhtangov expresses the formula of Fantastic Realism—the art that is supposed to create a new artistic reality on stage, using life and nature's organic creative laws, rather than copying them superficially. It is essential to stress that Vakhtangov refers to life's creative laws; not all aspects of everyday life are creative and, therefore, applicable to the stage.

7 On the Actor's Creative Process

On the Technique of the Affect: Truth of Passions and Feelings that Seem True[1]

Everything that happens onstage must be convincing.

"Feelings that seem true" beget trust.

"The truth of passions" begets faith.

The moment of passion within the theatrical creative state, when an actor almost forgets that he is onstage, is the moment of faith, the moment of truth.

There is great truth and small truth.

"I sit there pecking on the table top" is a small truth, but it is needed as a transition to the greater truth.[2]

Psychological, inner truth—is the great truth.

Such inner truth strongly guides the life of the body.

Truth is what I believe at this particular moment.

When the falseness of theatrical events becomes truth for an actor—this is stage truth.

On Cliché Acting

One of the greatest enemies of stage truth is cliché, or artificial acting.

Falseness has become legitimate at many theatres.

---

1 Vakhtangov refers to a famous dramatic formula, developed by the Russian poet Aleksandr Pushkin: "The truth of passions, feelings that seem true, that is what our intellect requires of a dramatist." Pushkin's thoughts on the art of theatre influenced Konstantin Stanislavsky's system of acting.

2 Here Vakhtangov presages principles of the Demidov organic school, such as yielding to small automatic movements, as well as psychological oneness and non-alteration (Demidov 2004b).

There is theatrical falseness that has already become "truth"—this is the dangerous kind.

For example: an actor runs out onto the stage boards; the audience applauds, and an actor takes a bow.

This seemingly has become truth, but it is a lie.[3]

Never give yourself impossible tasks—they are the ones that lead to a lie.

On the Feeling of Truth

There are two ways toward truth.

Firstly, you can hit truth by chance, and then become aware of it, that is, feel it.

Secondly, you can take some action and logically justify it. You must mechanically develop a habit (when given [a task?]) onstage, to go through the following sequence: tensing up muscles—releasing all tension—justifying [the task].

Exercise: arranging each other into [arbitrary] poses [and justifying them].

In this case the feeling of truth must be the controller preventing you from lies and not allowing you to violate the truth.

However, the technique alone does not give you means to act truthfully—you must develop the feeling of truth, a sensation of the threshold between truth and lies.

This threshold should be pushed to a maximum. Sometimes actors are so afraid of falseness that they convey nothing to the audience.

They don't reach truth for the fear of lies.

In justification exercises, for example, one tends to sit down, and continue sitting, while the proper thing to do is to discover activity. Inactivity onstage is never received [by the audience]. When one lives passively, one cannot convey one's feelings.

Every action must be done for some purpose, and it should be done to the appropriate degree. The feeling of truth must die.

---

3   In his final production of *Princess Turandot*, Vakhtangov managed to justify symbolic theatrical truth. In this production, Vakhtangov's actors bowed to the audience as they entered the stage, without ever coming out of character or interrupting the flow of life onstage. This was justified as Vakhtangov staged *Princess Turandot* as a theatrical performance where master-actors became characters. In so doing, Vakhtangov proved that pure theatricality could become truthful. Moreover, he proved that all aspects of such a performance demand purely *theatrical* justification (see p. 291).

In this case when one does not reach truth for the fear of lying, one must overact; this is the only way to understand and become aware of the threshold of truth.

This is when you need the regulator that will show you the needed threshold of truth. This threshold will be new every time.

To sum up, you should not *underact*, as the truth is discovered with bold brushstrokes. If an actor believed in something today, this does not mean that he must also believe the same thing tomorrow.

The preparatory moment for the feeling of truth is an actor's naivety, similar to the naivety of a child.[4]

During tomorrow's rehearsal or performance, the feeling of truth must control the action anew.

Physical truth is simpler, it is easier to fixate, but it must be tied to the inner truth.

An actor must begin with physical tasks.

They must be fulfilled with precision; otherwise there will be no truth.

Some [logical] justification is needed in order to coax the actor's creative nature into believing [the reality of the action]; what comes to an actor instinctively, comes from his subconscious.

> [This translation is supplemented with previously unpublished materials, featured in Ivanov 2011.]

On Actor Cultivation

To be an actor, one should, first, be in control of one's will.

Will is impaired by the lack of discipline, lack of **feeling of the stage**.[5] You must feel the collective.

Everything you convey and do must be fully executed.

Each exercise must be carried to completion; only then can you move on to the next exercise.

The most important thing is to develop one's composure, calmness.

These [qualities] must be acquired through building endurance in ensemble scenes.

In the case that one must arrive at a feeling through an action, one must begin by investigating the physiology [of this action].

---

4   On naivety, see Vakhtangov's lecture, "Faith, Naivety, and Justification," p. 177.
5   When speaking of "feeling of the stage," Vakhtangov refers to artistry.

An actor must be able to analyze and act the basic patterns[6] of roles such as Hamlet, Othello, etc.

Homework: find a phrase, pronounce it beautifully, find music, "yes, no, but," come up with a mob scene, as well as with *prana*[7] [...].

Everything in art must be elaborated, prepared.

One must develop creative initiative. For example, boldly and with clarity, one must divide the role into large bits, and only then begin to divide it further, proceeding from the first division. Otherwise, actors start with the first scene, and soon get stuck there.

An ideal actor should have an ideal order. When finishing one bit, the actor should already see the entire next bit, and instantaneously transform with that bit. In live communion, however, one must allow oneself to finish [the bit] completely, and only then organically move on to the next bit ([with the next] breath).

[This translation is supplemented with previously unpublished materials, featured in Ivanov 2011.]

On Activity and Physical Actions

One must not attack the feeling; on the contrary, one must approach it (what would I do, in order to ... etc.)

One may go along the line of feeling, or along the line of action.

Only things active are worthy of the stage. The most difficult thing is to portray inactivity onstage. It is difficult to select an action that would convey inactivity; in the meantime, inactivity onstage can be achieved only through action.

---

6 When referring to the sources of inspiration behind his Psychological Gesture Technique, Michael Chekhov mentioned Vakhtangov's rehearsal demonstrations: "Vakhtangov had a quality indispensable for a director: he was able to demonstrate to the actor the basic pattern of the role. He did not portray the character in its entirety, he did not play the role instead of the actor himself; rather he demonstrated, indeed played, a sketch, an outline, a pattern of the role. [...] He showed me the pattern of the part of Erik over the course of the whole act—and he did this in no more than a couple of minutes. After his demonstration, the whole act in all its details became clear to me, although Vakhtangov had not gone into these at all. He had simply given me the basic structure, the structure of the character's will, within which I could then position all the details and particulars of the role. (Chekhov 2005: 69–70.)

7 Breath/life in Sanskrit, a key term in the teachings of yoga.

Without action nothing onstage is received [by the audience]. When a human being lives passively, he cannot convey his feelings.[8]

An actor must be able to give an outcome to his every feeling, that is he must *act*, rather than live inwardly.

One must start with the physical action. He ought to determine what kind of physical object he has before him, where he must put it, and why; how is today special, etc.

All this will tie up together, if it is executed in a certain rhythm.

There are two types of [creative] dreaming—active and passive. When I see myself strolling [through the world of the play]—this is passive dreaming. When I see all objects [around me], but don't see myself—this is active dreaming.

How can I make myself act?

By treating myself like a puppy and suggesting to myself those things that entice my will.

[This translation is supplemented with previously unpublished materials, featured in Ivanov 2011.]

On Creative Emotions and Spontaneous Impressions: Working on a Play

In art, comprehending is experiencing.

The scheme of the role is a circle of logical sensations. Elements of feelings are various points [of this circle]. The first point flows out of the second, third, etc.

How does one arrive at the first point, that is, how should one work upon a role?

1   One must take special care to preserve the first virginal impression. The following things get in the way:
     Conversations prior to the reading of the play—preconception.
     "Acted," bad reading.
     Authoritative interpretation of the play.
     Conveying scholarly information.

---

8   Vakhtangov's concept of "activity" and "concentration" should not be taken literally, as a conscious willful effort. Vakhtangov did not tolerate labored and intellectual acting. When, in the following paragraphs Vakhtangov refers to "physical action," he outlines the process where the actor *perceives* the environment. Triggered by subconscious perception, activity and concentration arise *involuntarily*. Grounded in the perception of *physical sensations* from the environment, Vakhtangov's principles seem to anticipate Stanislavsky's Method of Physical Actions.

Demonstrations by the director, done in the early stages.

The play has been read.

One must understand the play's circumstances. It is essential to properly surround yourself [with these circumstances], and "the sincerity of passion" will come.

Circumstances can be divided into external and internal.

2 External.

a) Investigate the plot, according to facts. It is impossible to immediately include the inner meaning [of the facts].

To analyze a play is to take the circle with all its curves and begin to investigate it.

b) [When staging Griboyedov's (1795–1829) *Woe from Wit,*] [a]nalyze the circumstances of the everyday life (French influences [upon Russia], fashion, Moscow after 12 noon, etc.), religious and social circumstances.

3 Internal circumstances.

a) Relationships between people (Princess Marya Aleksevna[9]).

[This translation is supplemented with previously unpublished materials, featured in Ivanov 2011.]

On Preparing for the Performance: The Threshold of Creativity

Your acting should always be preceded by an overture (while putting on makeup).

Before the performance you must "make up your soul"; that is, you must prepare it.

Putting on makeup and changing into costume must be a sacrament. (Salvini[10] used to come to the theatre at 5 P.M. He had an extensive process of preparing for the performance.) You must strive for it and train yourselves in this direction.[11]

Affective [remembered] emotions belong to all five senses [sight, smell, taste, touch, and hearing], as well as to the group of the sensation of pain.

---

9 A powerful "offstage" character in *Woe from Wit*.

10 Italian tragedian Tommaso Salvini (1829–1915).

11 None of these questions can be answered literally in a performance. Whatever an actor discovers in his or her pre-performance meditations must be sufficiently forgotten before stepping onstage. In other words, an actor should allow his or her subconscious to provide the answers in performance.

([For example,] Your heart begins to beat faster, as you recall your first performance, attending a performance by Shalyapin,[12] or, perhaps, an instance when the director took a role away from you. When electricity is absent, the entire action is atrophied, and the level of energy is low.)

[The truth?] of passions—a jealous man—jealousy, ecstatic religious moment. In general, heightened passions cannot be approached directly. One must approach heightened passions in stages. Only such a gradual approach will lead to heightened passions.

Exercises in affective emotions.

Living with an affective emotion requires: (1) to release tension in one's muscles. This requires just as much [muscular] energy as necessary, no less. Following that, one must master narrowing and widening the circle. A mere table lamp might lead you to all kinds of passions.

"An artist who is deprived of the feeling of the stage, will never become an artist, but a mere actor"—Schepkin.[13]

Having narrowed the circle, we delve deep within ourselves.

From what point of view do the through line, tasks, plan, score of my role interest me today? The answer to this question is very important, but it is impossible to answer it without first determining how I feel today.

If, as an example, today I cannot act, for one reason or another, I must analyze myself, look within, talk to my "artist," make an agreement with him—if this is so, just convey the thought, but convey correctly what is needed. By doing so, you can move your artistic feeling toward the required state. This process must be trained and turned into a habit; it must be exercised before every performance.

Otherwise, a man turns into a boor, a woman—into a vulgar broad.

One must learn to use any object onstage, as any object can convey some affective emotions.

Take up a watch and be still—the duration of the exercises can be extended daily.

Creativity is the highest level of concentration.

When your entire being is dedicated to a single purpose—then there will be enough energy for true creativity.

[This translation is supplemented with previously unpublished materials, featured in Ivanov 2011.]

---

12 Fyodor Shalyapin (1873–1938), Russian opera singer.
13 Mikhail Schepkin (1788–1863), Russian realist actor.

8   On the Stanislavsky System

The Main Goal of the System: Absolute Freedom

The system is a method of educating actors. The system is a series of inviolable creative laws (**muscular freedom, object of attention,** task, etc.).

Trust it, and later you will become convinced that it is so.

First and foremost, an actor should be shown the method that would convince him that it is so. The entire teaching is a device, the means to achieve something. This "something" is an absolute freedom!

On Crossing the Creative Threshold: The Organic Technique

The first state an actor experiences onstage is the one he just experienced in life. One needs great courage not to betray this experience. One must surrender entirely to the power of one's artistic nature. It will do all the necessary things. Don't impose any solution upon yourself in advance. The quality to develop in an actor is courage.

No matter what you take from life, everything will apply. In life, feelings have an individual quality. Everyone feels differently.

If feelings do not come to an actor, he should not imitate them. Without feelings, what is there to act? Whatever combination of feelings creates itself, an actor should allow it.

One must remember that:

1   Everyone experiences something at any given moment;
2   Experiences change constantly; and
3   Every single experience is individual.

One cannot forge a combination of feelings, as it appears in life.

The third part of the system: approach to the role. That is, an actor must be taught, etc.—it is a path toward developing an [individual] approach to the role.

At every rehearsal, instead of experiencing, an actor must supply the material for his subconscious.

The Essence of the Stanislavsky System

The essence of the Stanislavsky System (what distinguishes it from other systems) is in the development of individuality, passion, teaching an actor how to approach a role, etc. The system teaches to experience the desire that motivates stage tasks.[1] It teaches [students] how to feel the truth, to dispose of falseness, to justify given circumstances, to communicate, to be in a circle. The system also teaches *artistry*, fulfilling actions onstage; it teaches freedom, etc.

Three Unresolved Elements in the System

There are three unresolved elements in the system:

1 *Artistry* is the means to immediately become inspired by the material offered by the author. How to reach an ability to become inspired on command is unknown.
2 *Kernel*: this is the kind of starter that creates the character. The character is created when an actor discovers the kernel. The discovery of the kernel is something we do not know. What is cast into the actor's inner world, no one knows.

When I approach the role individually, I am seeking the kernel. When the kernel is found, I must take it from the same realm at every performance, but I must take it every time.

At every performance the kernel must be refreshed somewhat.

Sometimes the kernel comes from the external form of the role. Every actor has a different approach toward discovering the kernel. One must believe that, having walked onto the stage in costume and makeup, I cannot remain "myself"; one must achieve a new combination of inner and outer characteristics.
3 How to allow oneself onstage to strive to fulfill the tasks, to avoid pushing and wait for this striving to come—that is unknown.

---

1   In his lecture on the creative task, Vakhtangov says, "An action and the desire to implement it, i.e. *artistry*—such is the essence of the stage task" (see p. 182).

Perhaps, the path to it lies through developing courage. The system is a series of methods that lead to the result, that is to acquiring the mastery of acting, developing creative imagination, freedom and a sense of ethics, an esthetics, etc.

On Super Task and Through Action

Every work [of art] contains the zest that compelled the poet to write it. With Chekhov, it is yearning for beautiful life, with Tolstoy, self-perfection. This zest is the super task.

It pays to assume the kind of task that is closer to the through action.

How does one determine where to cut a bit? This must be decided based on the character who leads the bit, according to the through action.

An actor must understand the author's super task.

The execution of the super task is the through action. Once the super task of the play has been discovered, an actor must be guided by it in his role.

There may be a small task. And what if I deepen it? Then my "I am" will resound in a more complex, significant way.

The deeper you dig into the task, the closer you come to its center, which *is* the super task.

An actor must reach the deepest spiritual super center that includes everything in it. True acting results from the fulfillment of this deepest task.

[This translation is supplemented with previously unpublished materials, featured in Ivanov 2011.]

On Theatrical Ethics

The important result of the system is acquiring the knowledge of self. The positive side of the system is that it draws from true art. An actor, having entered the realm of art, must be a good human being. This is not just a case of refraining from inappropriate laughter on the stage or not getting distracted with trifles before the performance: one must be inwardly pure.

We can only enter art as good people. One must believe that. This means: I enter the theatre, and I will proceed with an open soul with the things I do.

Actors are people of the art, which means special people.

From talks given at the Vakhtangov Studio 1918–1921
and recorded by Vera L'vova.[2]

---

2   Vera L'vova's records were not dated. Mentions of Ibsen's *Rosmersholm* and Byron's *Cain*, both approached by Vakhtangov in 1918, indicate that these records could not have been made any earlier. The schedule of Vakhtangov's work at his Studio suggests that Vakhtangov could not have delivered these talks later than 1921.

9 On Character and Characterization

An Actor's Creative Individuality as a Basis for Organic Transformation[1]

An actor must live with his own passion. We must hear your own voice, your blood, your nerves.

You must be very serious onstage, be able to appraise a fact. I won't accept a single moment that comes from "theatre."

No characterization, you are playing yourselves or rather, as we say, you "proceed from yourselves." Proceed from yourself, and be very serious ...

We must fall in love with the character. Even if I play a villain, even if I play a tragic role of Hamlet. One must be above the character he plays. All this relates to the joy of creation, all this creates a festival.

Every character has something in him we can love him for, some sympathetic qualities.

From September 25, 1916, talk given at the Vakhtangov Studio.

As far as an actor can preserve his own individuality, he must preserve it. In makeup you must subtract, instead of add. You should not put on makeup in such a way that no one would recognize you, but, on the contrary, in such a way that you could be recognized. You should take away some part of your own [features], in order to give what is required.

One cannot search for a character on the side, and then pull it onto himself; a character must consist of the material that you possess.

From January 23, 1917,
talk given at the Vakhtangov Studio.

---

1 On creative individuality, as a basis for organic transformation, see also p. 10.

On Improvisation[2]

Each rehearsal must be a new rehearsal. You must seek the new at every rehearsal, instead of repeating a previous rehearsal, from beginning to end ...

One partner should never tell another what he will do onstage. Everything onstage should be unexpected, and one should react spontaneously. You must develop within yourselves an enormous trust toward the subconscious realm.

From October 30, 1916, talk given at the Vakhtangov Studio.

A day will come when authors won't write plays. You know many plays, but very few works of art. A work of art must be created by an actor.

An actor must be able to play his character in all circumstances, not just within the excerpt from the character's life presented in the play. This excerpt is just a detail, while an actor should perform not a detail but an entirety. An actor should not know what will happen to him as he goes on the stage. He must go on the stage as we in life go about having a conversation, or attending a meeting. When we work independently, we should not rehearse the given play but, in general, learn to shift our points of view on facts. Actors must be trained so that, prior to their entrance, they can be told what they must play: their past, their points of view on those who surround them, their tasks. This enables them to act: their feelings, words, etc., pour out.

This would be true *commedia dell'arte*. This is the ideal. *Commedia dell'arte*, however, is always archetypal. Up till now, no actor dared to perform a non-archetypal[3] role without an author, without memorized lines (to play a character part as an improvisation). Do understand: to prepare a role does not mean to rehearse the given play; to prepare a role means to seek in yourself points of view needed for the role.

From November 29, 1916, talk given at the Vakhtangov Studio.

Character Study: Gradual Perception of the Character's "Kernel"

If the character study is to be pictured as a triangle, then this process can be imagined as a gradual movement from one of the sides of the triangle toward its opposite apex; that is, this process narrows

---

2   On improvisation, see also p. 289.
3   Vakhtangov refers to a "non-stock character" type of role.

gradually. One needs less and less stimulating factors to sense the character, leading to a sensation that is narrowed to a single dot—to the apex of the triangle (the character's kernel).

The following is the process of study.

The reading of the play takes place first. It is followed by its analysis from the literary and artistic standpoint, clarification of the general character of the play and its atmosphere. Then we move to separate personas, to separate characters, we study them gradually, examine their feelings and nature: gradual immersion into this study is what working upon creating a character means. An actor seeks within himself the feelings he needs to experience in order to bring to life the character. He discovers in his soul the buttons he can push to evoke these feelings. Each actor's buttons are individual; they are not like another actor's buttons. Everyone knows for himself what combination of factors he must proceed from in order to experience certain feelings at a given moment, and what button, known to him alone, he needs to push for that. As an actor digs deeper into his role, the number of these buttons gradually diminishes, until the artist can finally control his feelings through one combined button. In one push, he can evoke the entire range of his character's feelings and begin to live his character's life.

In an actor's work, there comes a certain moment of tiredness, an apathy, when he becomes incapable of evoking feelings and starts resorting to clichés in his acting. This is the moment when the wounded soul requires rest for healing and calming; this requires a break from work. An actor of a given level of talent will never go below a certain number of buttons. Soon after the period of rest, this minimum is determined, and with it an actor achieves a certain level of excellence.

Instantaneous Grasp of the Character's Whole

A genius actor is different in the way that he comprehends the character in a reverse order. He immediately, at once, embraces the character in its entirety, thus finding himself instantly at its apex. It is from this place that he perceives the details.[4]

From January 3, 1914,
talk given at the Vakhtangov Studio.

---

4   On instantaneous intuitive grasp of the character's essence, see Vakhtangov's following talk with his students on February 15, 1915 (p. 106).

On Yoga

While reading *The Yogi Philosophy*,[5] one can find lots of exercises. I was amazed by the [number of] terms borrowed from the philosophy. Probably, Stanislavsky [also] borrowed from them. There you find muscular freedom, concentration, faith, naivety, and justification. There you can find an exercise that develops a "sharp eye." The goal of yoga is, of course, human self-perfection.

[One day] I would like to give you an exercise that requires a strong circle, density-wise, and calls for enormous faith. But let's wait with that; in the meantime, exercises in observation.[6]

Exercises in an Instantaneous Grasp of the Character as a Whole

Everyone must describe, but also act it out. Would you be able to perform the following, somewhat strange exercise: would you be able to go behind the curtain as a little devil[7] and, as a little devil, examine everything backstage. This is an exercise in intuition. Can you do the following: I see myself sitting in a chair. In a similar way, I can also feel myself as a cat. As [Michael] Chekhov observed a cat, he could no longer distinguish between himself and the cat. Through some power of your own, you guess how the object of your concentration feels at this moment. I can sense your will with my entire being. For a second I somehow transport myself into you. There is a distinction between abnormality and delight here. The latter belongs to the realm of art. I can internally somehow penetrate the essence of a given person; in other words, I can guess his "kernel." This is the principal thing for an actor. The secret lies in transporting your "self" there. Yogis say "take a pencil, direct your attention onto it"—this is the same thing as

---

5   Vakhtangov most probably was referring to a Russian translation of Yogi Ramacharaka's book (Ramacharaka 1904).
6   On Vakhtangov's concept of observation, see the Glossary and Malaev-Babel (forthcoming).
7   The character of "a little devil," suggested by Vakhtangov, is based on the mythical and mysterial imagery of the popular carnival consciousness. So are all other characters featured in the notable February 15, 1915 session. When Vakhtangov suggested that his students learn to "observe" and enact essentially archetypal characters—a starving person selling an icon, a beggar stretching his hand out, servants—he led his students into the realm of the popular grotesque. According to Mikhail Bakhtin, "the mystery devil [...] is an ambivalent image, like the fool and the clown, representing the destroying and renewing force of the material bodily lower stratum. The devil usually appeared in the mystery as a carnivalesque character" (1984: 266–277).

in Stanislavsky's teaching. This is what I do until I exhaust all of the fantasy I have for the role.

On Grasping the Character's Essence: Toward the Theatre of the Grotesque

If you merely portray what you observed externally, this will be an imitation—the art of Coquelin. But there is also another way. It is not given to everyone, perhaps, but everyone can approach it, at least. What is the external characterization?—the characteristic features that distinguish this person from everyone else on an external level. Everything that constitutes the external characterization of a person is an indispensable consequence of his inner state. It is his inner state that made him such.

I am able to transform, I can feel and think like a given character. This is characterization, in a nutshell. What is the essence of Caleb—it is that he does not much live on this earth.

I am asking myself, what is the character's essence? Everyone creates a character according to their individuality. (According to this individuality, the actor chooses the characteristic gesture, for example, the trembling head [of an older gentleman]). I felt the kernel of the role, the essence of the character,[8] but as soon as the gesture appears, it all [the sensation of the inner essence] vanishes. These [exercises in feeling the person's essence] are the kind of exercises you need to do when you observe.

By March 1st, without fail, everyone must bring the results of their observations.

How would you feel differently while riding a streetcar, etc.

For example: a hungry, ragged lad selling icons in Sukharevsky Square.

A beggar, stretching his hand out.

Portray your servants.

But you should not [merely] portray but portray plus *live*.

---

8   In this 1915 talk Vakhtangov does not clearly distinguish between the origins of two different types of transformation: the kernel of the character (a source for characterization) and the character's essence (a source for organic transformation). At the end of this talk, Vakhtangov states, "I came to the conclusion that if an actor transforms this way [by sensing the character's essence], they don't need external characterization" (p. 108). In a 1918 talk, however, Vakhtangov stated that a non-naturalistic play "does not require characterization, it does not need a kernel" (p. 90). In that talk, Vakhtangov makes a clearer distinction between the "kernel" of the character and the character's essence. On this subject, also see Introduction, p. 22.

This is a good way to experience the difference between imitation and transformation. I came to the conclusion that if an actor transforms this way, he does not need external characterization.

From February 15, 1915, talk given at the Vakhtangov Studio.[9]

Gradual Formation of the Character's "Kernel"

A man's individuality is formed through a series of days his life arranges for him. It applies features to his face and determines his physiognomy. Similarly, his entire spiritual makeup and world view develop day by day.

This is why a particular person naturally reacts to a particular event exactly the way he should react. A man could not care less about expressing himself logically, according to the inner logic of his internal physiognomy with all its features. Nature itself takes care of that, and the reaction takes place instinctively, beyond a man's conscience. He [already] has the kernel of his own personality within him.

The Grasp of the Character's Whole: The State of Festivity, or Creative State

There are moments in a man's life when he wants to live more than ever and when he joyfully feels himself belonging to everything living. He becomes vigorous; his seeds, good or bad, are revealed with special vividness.

In such moments a man becomes inspired, his eyes light up festively, and he fills up with vigorous desires and a thirst for activity. This is a festive moment.

It is the same for an actor.

Day after day, from one rehearsal to another, the image of the role is shaped.

Grain by grain, beyond an actor's conscience, everything he finds for his character imprints on his soul.

A series of performances go by. Here too the work of the formation of the character's kernel continues.

But now comes a moment when this kernel has ripened and an actor no longer needs to worry about expressing himself in accordance with the logic of his character's inner and outer physiognomy. The artistic nature itself will take care of that.

---

9 The typewritten record of this class is kept at the Vakhtangov Theatre Museum, fund No. 231-A.

Only the festivity is needed.

Experiencing the stage as a joyful place.

An actor must fill himself with "an energetic desire" to express, or rather, to create.

At such a moment one does not need to "act."

An actor just needs to fulfill his character's tasks. He needs to be active in his fulfillment of these tasks.[10]

How would one go about developing confidence that this is true?

How would one go about developing an ability to evoke the "creative state"?

These are the theatrical questions the Studio of this year should dedicate itself to.

These are the questions we must go to Stanislavsky with.

No festival—no performance.

Our work is senseless without it. Without it, we have nothing to captivate the audience.

> From September 21, 1916, entry in the
> First Studio of the MAT *Book of Impressions*.[11]

On the Art of Grotesque

The theatre of everyday life must die. "Character" actors are no longer needed. All who have capacity for playing character roles must feel the tragedy (even the comedians) in every character part; they must learn to express themselves through the grotesque.

Grotesque—tragic and comedic.

From March 1921 diary entry made at All Saints' Rehabilitation Resort.[12]

---

10 Depending on the type of actor (rational, imitator, emotionally willful, affective), as well as the type of actor's creative existence in a given performance, Vakhtangov's definition of an actor's activity would change. In a different kind of production, or to a different kind of actor, Vakhtangov advised that an actor should "just convey the thought, but convey correctly what is needed" (see p. 98). Finally, in a performance where the elaborate theatrical form of an actor's performance is fixed, Vakhtangov would suggest that an actor should just fulfill the form, etc.

11 An English translation of this entry was first published in Vendrovskaya and Kaptereva 1982. *The Book of Impressions* of the First Studio of the MAT was originated by Konstantin Stanislavsky and Leopold Sulerzhitsky, who wanted to encourage Studio members and associates to share their thoughts on the art of theatre, Studio performances, training, as well as on the daily life at the Studio. This particular entry preceded Vakhtangov's notes to actors on his production of *The Deluge*. (The following notes can be found on p. 206.) On the First Studio of the MAT's *Book of Impressions*, also see p. 109n11, as well as Malaev-Babel (forthcoming).

12 An English translation of this entry was first published in Vendrovskaya and Kaptereva 1982.

10 On Consciousness and the Subconscious in an Actor's Creative Process

Engaging the Subconscious in Actor's Homework

In everyday life, a person is ready to receive or bring any kind of news—at any moment. The same should be true of the stage. As time goes by, we will learn, without preparation, to meet the challenges of the most passionate moments of the role. You must become intimate with the role. Dreaming about the role should become a habit.

I come to rehearsals prepared. You must not forget that I can only experience and demonstrate a particular place in your role once. You must be ready to perceive it. If you are not capable of perceiving what I give you today, it is forever lost to you. If you are not greedy, not prepared for perception, it is impossible to become inseminated with the role.

Now, how should you work upon your role at home?

Let us suppose that I don't know how I must perform a particular place in a role. I pose a question to my subconscious; I give material to my subconscious, so that it can answer my question. The subconscious contrives an answer out of this material. You want to make do only with the material that I give you. But this is not enough. If things continue this way, everyone who comes to see our performance will say, "someone else created the form of this role." The actors' individualities are missing.

Ladies and gentlemen, do become convinced in the necessity of conscious homework and gain faith in the work of the subconscious in rehearsal. Have you ever been reading a book in class, hiding it under your desk? This unrelated reading is our work on the role—in the street, at work, at home, anywhere in life. When something distracts you from this "unrelated reading," you use any opportunity, any free minute, to go back.

From October 19, 1916, talk given at the Vakhtangov Studio.

Engaging the Subconscious in Rehearsal and Performance

An actor should be prepared for that which will excite him emotionally: I will go onto the stage and I will become emotionally excited with my love for her. This should carry me away. I must become enticed by the thought "I will soon be with her." I come onto the stage with this, and I don't know what will become of me; I don't know if God will send me inspiration or not. If God sends me inspiration, I will feel my complicity with the world, I will feel happy to be alive.

From November 29, 1916, talk given at the Vakhtangov Studio.

Subconscious Perception and Expression

Consciousness does not create anything—ever ... Only the subconscious does. It has an independent ability to choose material for the creative process, bypassing the conscious mind. Apart from that, one can consciously send material for the creative process into the realm of his subconscious. From this standpoint, any rehearsal is only productive when in it one seeks or provides material for the next rehearsal; it is in the intervals between rehearsals that the subconscious processes the acquired material. One cannot create anything out of nothing, which is why one cannot play a role without work—"out of inspiration."

Inspiration is the moment when our subconscious has combined material from the preceding work. At the mere call of our conscious mind, but without its involvement, the subconscious will give everything one single form.

Fire that accompanies this moment is a natural condition, just as several chemical elements being combined into one form naturally produce heat.

Mental elements combined into a particular form amenable for a given individual cause an inflow of energy at the moment of their expression. This energy warms up, lights up, and breathes life into the form. Everything that is invented consciously does not carry the signs of fire. Everything that is created within the subconscious realm and formed subconsciously is accompanied by the extraction of this energy; it is chiefly this very energy that carries an infectious power.

This infectiousness can be described as a subconscious captivation of the perceiving party's subconscious. It is the sign of talent. He who consciously feeds his subconscious and expresses the results of its work in a subconscious way is a talent.

He who subconsciously feeds his subconscious and engages in a **subconscious expression** is a genius.

He who expresses consciously is a master.

He who is deprived of the ability to perceive subconsciously or consciously, and yet dares to express is a mediocrity. For he does not have an individuality. For he, who deposited zero into his subconscious (the creative realm), will express zero.

From November 3, 1917, notebook entry.[1]

Take a bundle of thoughts, throw it into the sack of your subconscious, and go for a walk.

Ready? Not yet? Take another bundle of thoughts, etc., etc.

Everything must be thrown into the subconscious realm.

If a role gets clogged up at a certain point, you must leave that point alone, change the preceding circumstances, and the entire result will be different.

The initial approach—what would I do in such and such circumstances. Take all these circumstances and stand straight at the center of them, in the thick of them. Allow everything in, let it permeate you—and the truth of passion will come.

The art of an actor is in his ability to move himself toward what he will need to give, the ability to reveal what's required of him.

From September 29, 1919, talk given at the Vakhtangov Studio and recorded by Vera L'vova. [Originally published in Ivanov 2011.]

On *Prana* and Creative Perception

There is a vital force in life, and in nature—it is called *prana*.

Prana is a vital force that is spilled all over nature, and is radiated by human beings. *Prana* must be taken from everywhere, from nature. First and foremost, one must breathe correctly, so that *prana* does not vanish immediately upon its entrance.

All food contains *prana*; therefore, you must not swallow up food, but chew it until you reach the state of delight.

Prana affects blood, through food and through air. *Prana* is yet to become our everyday self. "I am [character]," however, constitutes *prana*.

---

1   An English translation of this entry was first published in Vendrovskaya and Kaptereva 1982.

Prana is stored in the head realm—thought—and in the solar plexus—feeling.

Voluntary actions come from the 1st source.

Involuntary—from the 2nd source.

One can sense *prana*, and one can control it.

It is essential to be able to gather, to concentrate *prana*, so that it could be used when necessary.

Firstly, one must be free from any muscular tension.

All sensations require no effort whatsoever.

(The truth of passions is the very *prana* that grows from the solar plexus.)

One should not pretend, but rather be suspenseful. (This would be the development of one's ability to fantasize and concentrate.)

[...]

> From October 8, 1919, talk given at the Vakhtangov Studio and recorded by Vera L'vova. [Originally published in Ivanov 2011.]

On Subconscious Expression

We want to figure out what we want to act in this play. It would be possible, of course, not to do that and act, without further ado, what is written: to work subconsciously. Is there a way to reconcile conscious determination of tasks with the requirement that creativity must be subconscious? Everything we now say about the play we will forget, but it won't disappear without a trace; it will all be stowed in our subconscious realm so that later on it could appear on the stage subconsciously.

When in life we act consciously, we are never ourselves. I am only myself when I act unconsciously. The same is true of the stage. In life, however, I act unconsciously in a particular way—it depends on my subconscious realm's content, as I received it during my life rehearsals. If we come to some agreement, and the actor comprehends with his soul, this goes into the subconscious treasure house, to appear later in the performance.

Going to the stage, I must be convinced that someone else will act for me, that everything will happen on its own.

We cannot demand from actors that they be in a state of creative ecstasy during each rehearsal; they must only be enthusiastic about the work. To be able to act in performance, an actor must gather a lot into his treasure house and "act" nothing in performance. When I can do everything in performance, it is called inspiration. Something one could not possibly "perform," must perform itself, on its own accord.

Let's take *The Cricket on the Hearth*, for example. As the performance progresses, a certain warmth is radiated from the stage, and by the end it fills the audience.

In a similar way, in our play, a smile should accumulate and radiate.[2] Every actor must carry this smile with him, and it should become his "what for".

Author's smile, an actor's creative state (a festive moment) and qualities subconsciously thrown: those are the three essential elements.

With some people, this subconscious realm is closed, this treasure box is locked, and the key is thrown away. This is called mediocrity.

From September 17, 1916, talk given at the Vakhtangov Studio.

Creative Passion that Arises from Perceiving the Essence[3]

A role is prepared when an actor has made the lines of the role *his own*.

An actor must awaken his passion without any external motivation for creative passion; to achieve this, an actor must work in rehearsals chiefly to make everything that surrounds him, according to the play, his own atmosphere and to make his role's tasks his own; this will cause his passion to speak "from the essence." This kind of passion arising "from the essence" is the most valuable, because it alone is compelling and truthful.

This is the very kind of passion I strived to achieve from Khmara, since the very first rehearsal of *Rosmersholm*. I did achieve it with his wondrous help and his faith in the value and attractiveness of such a passion. A single thought: "I must make all my countrymen happy"—this thought, as such, inflamed him and made him Rosmer.

Sometimes an actor who has an excess of noble and moral qualities fails to accumulate enough **adaptations** for the role that calls for villainous qualities. He does not succeed with this character, although all may be well as far as the quality of his acting is concerned—that is, he experienced his role truthfully.

---

2   When Vakhtangov speaks of the author's smile, he refers to the playwright Maurice Maeterlinck's point of view on characters and the reality he portrayed in the play. Here, as well as in the next paragraph, the world "smile" is synonymous with "author's point of view." See Vakhtangov's notes on Maeterlinck's smile (pp. 208–9) as well as his talks with his actors (pp. 257–9).

3   On this subject, see also the Introduction (p. 17) and *The Miracle of Saint Anthony*, January 23, 1917, rehearsal record (p. 266).

Unless an actor makes the essence of the play *his own* and, most importantly, believes that the secret of the true creative process lies in his trust of his own subconscious (that reacts on its own, from the essence), he will be compelled to act using old clichés, developed by bad rehearsals. His acting will be boring and predictable. The audience will know ahead of time what [such] an actor will play.

The most interesting thing in every new role an actor performs is unpredictability ([Michael] Chekhov, Moskvin,[4] Gribunin,[5] Stanislavsky).

Nothing is more important for the director than the ability to approach an actor's soul, that is, to be able to tell him *how* to discover what is required. It is not enough to show a quality to the actor, to analyze the text: the director must also inconspicuously show to the actor a practical way of achieving the task.

"You have such and such task" … Yet an actor does not know how to fulfill it. Through elementary means a director must show *how* to accomplish this task. In the majority of cases, the issue is clear: either an actor does not sense the object of his attention, or he does not organically comprehend his task, or he does not have a firm grip on the essence, or he merely follows the lines, or he deviates from the through line, or he is tense, etc.

From October 1918 notebook entry.[6]

The Essence of Theatrical Reality

I know, from my own experience, that an actor must proceed from the essence. Only in such a case will acting be an art. In an opposite case, acting will be either "theatre" or "life." In actuality, acting must not be one or the other, but the art of the stage. It comes when an actor takes for the truth what he created by the power of his fantasy.[7]

From March 6, 1917, talk given at the Vakhtangov Studio.

4   Ivan Moskvin (1874–1946), one of the leading MAT actors and the company's founding member.
5   Vladimir Gribunin (1873–1933), one of the leading MAT actors.
6   An English translation of this entry was first published in Vendrovskaya and Kaptereva 1982.
7   See chapter *The Essence of an Actor's Creativity*, p. 88.

On Fantasizing[8]

It is necessary ... to know why you need to do what you do. Only then will the festival come. Then you will be coming to stage not to act, but to believe. A path toward this is fantasizing.

Everything that concerns your life in the play, you must know as well as your own mother. When you say, "I have a wonderful mother," it sounds different from saying: "Pushkin's Tatyana[9] is charming."

When a student, well prepared for a Russian history examination, with the knowledge of the sequence of events, historic dates, etc., tells about the reign of Peter the Great, we all sense that he does not truly know what he is talking about. As for the famed historian professor Klyuchevsky,[10] he knew what he was talking about in his lectures. He could speak badly from the standpoint of oratory eloquence, but everyone listened to him in ecstasy. All this because he knew what he was talking about.

The same is true of an actor. An actor will only then be truly satisfied, when he feels that he knows what he is talking about.

Ideal acting, ideal transformation happens when an actor reacts to everything spontaneously.[11]

The art of an actor is in making the foreign, given to him by the author, his own.

From October 18, 1917, talk given at the Vakhtangov Studio.

"What For"

I must need what I do onstage; it should be organically needed by me and no one else. A director, or a teacher, can help you discover a through action, (main) thought behind a bit, etc., but no one can tell you—this is your "what for" behind this stage task. You can only discover it on your own. As you analyze tasks, you often forget about this necessity to search for an answer to the question: What am I doing it for? There exists an intimate side of the role: Why do I, and not someone else, need this?

A child is told: tomorrow is Christmas, and he will remain under this impression all evening and all day tomorrow, all the way up till

---

8   See also Vakhtangov's concept of "saturating yourself for the role," outlined during the September 25, 1916, rehearsal for *The Miracle of Saint Anthony*, p. 260.

9   Tatyana is the main female character of Aleksandr Pushkin's poem *Yevgeny Onegin*.

10 Vasily Klyuchevsky (1841–1911), one of the leading Russian historians of the time.

11 Vakhtangov expands upon this concept in his October 22, 1916, talk at the rehearsal of *The Miracle of Saint Anthony*. See pp. 263–4.

Christmas. There exists some special ability to sense: I need. "I" and "need" are equally important here. It must be necessary for my blood, for my nerves, for my thoughts. If you do not have this "I need," you are a craftsman.

I can analyze my role logically and psychologically—ideally, but then I come out onto the stage and it turns out that I absolutely do not need to do what I am doing. An actor must "gain faith." The very fascinating thing about the stage is that everything there is a lie, and this lie becomes truth for me.

It seems to me that the main reason why true passion is absent onstage for you is that you do not need the Studio. The Studio is not needed, therefore a performance is not needed; a performance is not needed, therefore all these small tasks the author gives are not needed as well.

In order to be passionate, you must know:

- What does the art exist for?
- What does the theatre exist for?
- What does the Studio exist for?
- What does the Studio stage this particular play for?
- What do I play my role for?
- What did I fulfill this particular stage task for?
   From October 11, 1917, talk given at the Vakhtangov Studio.

The Thought[12]

You know that you cannot be in the creative state unless you prepared in advance ... One must be able to entice oneself. Except for those creative conditions you [already] know,[13] there is one more necessary condition. This is the condition I had in mind when I told you, "convey the thought." I assumed that if you convey the thought in every bit you would move along the through action. In the end, of course, an

---

12 On this subject, also see the record of Vakhtangov's rehearsals of Pushkin's *Feast During the Plague* on p. 284.

13 Prior to explaining his concept of "thought," Vakhtangov reminded the actors present in rehearsal about other basic elements of the inner technique: "What I am trying to get out of you—'being serious,' 'gaining faith,' 'appraising a fact'—is entirely missing. This is why you are not passionate, and don't catch fire. Besides, you completely lost control of your muscles. If I were to run a test on concentration, I am convinced that you would not be able to pass it. You are not in control of your inner technique. You must elevate your inner technique. Every day before classes you must exercise. Someone should lead these exercises" (Ivanov vol. II 2011: 171).

opposite thing is needed: as you move toward one definite goal, you will inevitably convey the thought of every bit correctly.

... When one knows what he is talking about, he always persistently moves toward something singular and definite ... With all the lines of the text you must speak the main thought of the bit—not the nearest thought, but the main thought—the one that the nearest thought is spoken for. This is what is called: I know what I am doing.

From October 11, 1917, talk given at the Vakhtangov Studio.

Point of View[14]

Actors should have their points of view ready before the rehearsal, as everything that follows must develop on the basis of the points of view required by the play. Actors should fulfill their tasks, having already acquired points of view toward what surrounds them.

From October 18, 1917, talk given at the Vakhtangov Studio.

On the Theatrical Analysis of Plays and Roles[15]

Suppose you know some person well—you know several significant moments of his life, his character, habits and tastes (what he likes and what he dislikes). This knowledge will make it easier for you to tell how he would act in this event or another. You can invent several situations for such a person and, almost unmistakably, guess how he would find his way out of them. The better you know him, the more details you remember, the better you might sense his character, and the more correctly and the sooner your sense might prompt you how a certain event might affect your friend. When an author writes a play he certainly has a good knowledge of all the people acting in it. The closer he knows them, the truer is the flow of events (in the earlier acts) in the play. And, consequently, the truer is its very ending (the last act).

From March 1919 notebook entry.[16]

On Actor Cultivation

Actor cultivation must consist of enriching the actor's subconscious

14 On Vakhtangov's concept of the point of view of the author and point of view of the creative collective, see pp. 257.
15 This is one of the few notebook entries titled by Vakhtangov.
16 An English translation of the following notebook entries was first published in Vendrovskaya and Kaptereva 1982.

with varied abilities: freedom, concentration, seriousness, **stage intelligence**, artistry, activity, expressiveness, gift of observation, quickness to adapt, etc.[17] There are an infinite number of these abilities.

The subconscious, equipped with such a supply of means, will forge a near perfect creation from the material it receives.

Ideally, an actor should, together with his partners, analyze and digest the text and proceed onto the stage to create the character.

This is [how it should be] in the ideal, once an actor cultivated all necessary means, or abilities. An actor must be an improviser. This is what we call talent.

God only knows what goes on in theatre schools. The main mistake the schools make is that they take it upon themselves *to teach how to act*, while they should be *cultivating actors*.[18]

From October 22, 1918, notebook entry.

On Conscious and Subconscious Elements in Training

The important thing is not to play an *étude* well but to resort to all aspects of our system of training as frequently and as consciously (as strange as it may sound) as possible. This is necessary so that you develop a subconscious habit of using all the abilities we "cultivate."

This can be compared to learning a foreign language.

From November 10, 1918, entry in the
Gunst Studio's *Diary of Independent Works*.[19]

17 See the Glossary for the definitions of terms such as "freedom," "concentration," "seriousness," "stage intelligence," "artistry," "activity," "stage expressiveness," and "adaptation." On "observation," see the Glossary and Malaev-Babel (forthcoming).

18 On the concept of actor cultivation, see the Glossary and Malaev-Babel (forthcoming). On Russian theatre schools of the period, criticized by Vakhtangov, see Introduction, pp. 8–9.

19 The Gunst Studio was opened in Moscow in 1917 by Anatoly Gunst, an artist and actor. Vakhtangov was invited by Gunst to head the Studio in 1918. Upon Gunst's death in 1919, his Studio was "absorbed" by Vakhtangov's Studio. Gunst Studio's *Diary of Independent Works* was kept by the students, who were required to provide regular accounts of their independent work on exercises, *études*, and scenes. Vakhtangov, who taught at the Gunst Studio from 1918, systematically read students' accounts and wrote comments on their work. An English translation of this entry was first published in Vendrovskaya and Kaptereva 1982.

11 On the Organic Outer Technique

On Plasticity of Movement

Actors should train in *plastique* not so that they can dance or acquire a beautiful gesture or posture but in order to imbue their body with the feeling of plasticity (cultivate it). Moreover, plasticity is present not just in movement but in a piece of fabric tossed by a nonchalant hand, in the surface of a frozen lake, in a cozily sleeping cat, in suspended garlands, and in a still marble statue.

Nature does not know things not plastic: a breaking wave, a swaying branch, a galloping horse (a wretched nag even), the succession of day and night, a sudden whirlwind, flying birds, a tranquil mountainous expanse, a waterfall, madly leaping, the heavy step of an elephant, a hippopotamus's ugly form—all of it is plastic: there is no clumsiness here, no embarrassment, no awkward tension, deliberateness or staleness. There is nothing stiff or dead about a cat fast asleep, but, oh my God!, how stiff is an eager young man darting to get a glass of water for his sweetheart.

Actors should engage in long and diligent work to consciously *cultivate* the habit of plasticity so that later they can unconsciously *express* themselves in a plastic way. This applies to their ability to wear a costume, adjust the volume of their voice, achieve physical transfiguration (through a visible external form) into the form of the character they portray, allocate their muscular energy efficiently, and model themselves into anything in gesture, voice, or musical speech. Actors should also be able to achieve plasticity in the logic of their feelings.

From October 30, 1918 notebook entry.[1]

---

1 An English translation of this entry was first published in Vendrovskaya and Kaptereva 1982.

Plastique **Class**

I am in bed; I cannot come to you; I won't see you for a long time, and yet I need to tell you how vital it is to train in *plastique*, and how vital it is to *know how* to train in it, so as to understand the essence of "plasticity" as one of the most essential actor's qualities. You must learn how to sense *modeling*, and the *sculpture* of the role, scene, play; without the quality of plasticity one is unable to do this. It is almost impossible to acquire the quality of plasticity unless you train in *plastique* skillfully.

This is in short.

You will find a detailed and fascinating account of it in a wonderful book by S. Volkonsky, *The Man on the Stage*, published by the Apollon publishing house. Read it, and you will be attending the *plastique* class as eagerly as you now attend your speech class and acting exercises.

Next time I will tell you about *solfeggio*.

Ye. Vakhtangov

From November 8, 1918, letter to the Gunst Studio.[2]

On the Spoken Word

A phrase must first be cleared grammatically. All words must be finished, but some words must be said *lovingly*.

Feelings must be threaded through your *favorite* word.

Do not color the nearest words, but rather go along the line of action.

Speech and tone must be placed in the vowels.

In a poem, if you try to achieve a singsong quality, or color words and phrases, the inner meaning will be lost.

In text analysis, one should be first guided by the thought, searching for the *most important words*.

One must give the right meaning to the word—then the feeling will come.

To start with, one says the words of the scene in a grammatically sound manner—the feeling will follow.

Dull speech results from a mere recitation of facts, without the emotional experience.

When the quality [of speech] turns out to be dull, one must consult the compass—the through action.

---

2   An English translation of this entry was first published in Vendrovskaya and
    Kaptereva 1982.

- *Forte* does not mean loud; it means *not piano. Piano, pianissimo* must be based in the sound of the voice, not in whispering.
- *Pianissimo*: lazily telling about what took place.
- *Piano*: stressing the things I enjoyed.
- *Forte*: asserting, assuring that it happened exactly as I say.
- *Fortissimo*: I contest.
- *Forte-fortissimo*: I disallow.

An intention to say the line "simply" will result in it being not simple, but bland.

There are two kinds of simplicity: simplicity of the poor and of the rich imagination. Only the latter is good, for it conveys not just a bare form but also the inner content.

You must fall in love with single words and use them to convey thoughts. Then your speech will be colorful, interesting.

You must develop a habit to identify important words immediately [spontaneously, intuitively], rather than doing it in a mechanical way.

When the thought is concentrated just in one or two words, the rest of them will remain only relatively stressed.

What is to be done when a certain moment in the role isn't going well? You must simply understand what you are saying, to fantasize yourself a story.

Exercise. Fantasize circumstances for a random phrase.

It is impossible to express the thought without steeping it in feeling.

It is not enough to convey the richness of sound in every word; you must convey its thought, i.e. its feeling.

You must develop a rich register of sounds in your voice.

You must learn to find beauty in everything—in word and in sound.

An actor must use words the way Chekhov used pen and ink. A singsong quality of speech must be substituted by your love of words, or love of sounds.

[When reciting poetry to musical accompaniment?] A speech phrase must always correlate with musical phrase.

Home exercises: choose a phrase, speak it beautifully, discover different subtexts for "you," "no," "but."

You must master your vowels. We don't have cheerful "AH," rich "AH," playful "BAH," ferocious "BAH," poetic "BAH," "GAH," "DAH," etc. It is necessary to train them all.

You can make your speech very significant *through pauses*: "I ... curse ... thee."

Rhythm depends on the inner logic. Without rhythm, you can understand nothing: the logic is missing. Vivacity can and must be conveyed through slow rhythm; every word, however, must have liveliness.

In a big theatre one needs many times as much passion, firmness, [expressive] speech patterns, etc., than at a studio.

To make sure that one sound does not drown out another, one should take one's time; to do that, an actor must discover the necessary inner state.

Intervals in speech must be justified.

You must fall in love with the soul of the spoken word.

As we begin to love our vowels, we develop the need for slowness. Slowness and distinction must be motivated and justified by our intuitive, inner feeling.

You must conform to vibration so that one sound does not override the other. This calls for developing the timbres, the sonority of your voice.

To avoid shouting, you must develop sonorous and flying vowels.

You must discover the right feeling, the right intonation by making bold mistakes; otherwise the fear of overacting will make you tense.

What must one do when one is afraid to speak? He should immediately redirect himself toward the required thought and put all his effort into conveying it.

From talks given at the Vakhtangov Studio, in September, October of 1919, and recorded by Vera L'vova. [This translation is supplemented with previously unpublished materials, featured in Ivanov 2011.]

Part III

Fantastic Realism

12 Axioms of Fantastic Realism

Lectures to Deliver at the First Studio (of the MAT)

1 On the stage rhythm.
2 On the theatrical plasticity (sculpture).
3 On gesture and on hands in particular.
4 On the feeling of the stage, rhythm, plasticity, clarity, **theatrical communication**.[1]
5 On the **directorial architecture** (composition of the play).
6 On the theatrical form and theatrical content.
7 Actor: a master who creates texture.
8 Theatre is theatre. Play is a performance.
9 Presentational art: the mastery of acting.
10 The through line of the theatrical performance.
11 Thought, word, phrase, bit of the role. The essential components of theatre: play, a pretext for a performance; actor-master, equipped with both inner and outer technique; director, a sculptor of the theatrical performance; stage platform, a place of action;[2] designer, musician—director's collaborators.
12 Every kind of performance calls for its own form of stage platform: Shakespeare, Molière, Gozzi, Ostrovsky, etc.

From 1921 notebook entry.[3]

---

1 By "theatrical communication" Vakhtangov implies partner and ensemble communion in rhythm and in movement, direct and indirect communion with the audience (including the backstage staff), as well as the direct and indirect communication between the actors outside of the "character mask," or by the means of the "character mask."
2 On Vakhtangov's concept of the stage platform, see the Glossary and Malaev-Babel (forthcoming).
3 No month or day shown. An English translation of this entry was first published in Vendrovskaya and Kaptereva 1982.

13 Fantastic Realism and the Russian Theatre (*All Saints'* *Notes*)

On Meyerhold and Stanislavsky

I am thinking of Meyerhold. What a genius director, the grandest of all who lived before us, and of all who exist today. His every production is a new theatre. His every production could produce an entire movement. Stanislavsky as a director is, of course, lesser than Meyerhold. Stanislavsky does not have an individuality. All of Stanislavsky's productions are banal. The first period of Stanislavsky's productions: imitating the Meiningen Company. The second: Chekhovian theatre. (During this period, the Meiningen principle was projected onto the inner essence of the role—the emotional experience.) It amounted to naturalism of the same kind. All naturalists equal each other, and a production staged by one of them can be easily taken for the production of the other. Meyerhold is original.

In some of his works, he senses true theatricality, does not rely on the authority of the books, and seeks historical aspects and forms of theatre intuitively instead of reconstructing them. In such works, he is almost a genius and cannot be compared with Stanislavsky. I even think that he is a genius. Why, oh, why did life put one above the other?

I know that history will place Meyerhold above Stanislavsky, because Stanislavsky only provided theatre for one segment of Russian society, bourgeoisie and intelligentsia, for two decades. Meyerhold gave roots to the theatres of the future. The future will give him his due. Meyerhold is higher than Reinhardt, higher than Fuchs, higher than Craig and Appia.

On Stanislavsky and Nemirovich-Danchenko

Stanislavsky's theatre is already dead and it will never be reborn. I rejoice at that. It is strange to say, but I now remember even *Three Sisters* [1901] and *The Cherry Orchard* [1904] with unpleasant feeling. I am disgusted at *Julius Cesar* [1903], even though it amazed me at the time. Perhaps this is because I also can stage like that, and so can anyone who received some training in the school of naturalism. Anyone—even a nondirector—any layman who is enthusiastic enough to spend time with illustrations and Hottenroth.[1]

As for Nemirovich-Danchenko, he has never been a director. He is not a master of form, nor [artistic] qualities. He does not have the feeling of rhythm and plasticity. He lived off Stanislavsky's fantasy. He is a misunderstanding as a director. His significance in the Russian theatre: supplier of literature. He suggested Ibsen, Chekhov.

Both Nemirovich and Stanislavsky, due to their immense practice, know the actor. Meyerhold does not know [the actor] at all. Meyerhold does not know how to evoke the required emotion in an actor, the required rhythm, or the required theatricality. Nemirovich and Stanislavsky know how to do that—or rather Nemirovich only knows how to analyze a role and a play psychologically and evoke a particular emotion in an actor. And Stanislavsky, who does not know much about psychology, builds it intuitively (often much loftier and finer than Nemirovich). He knows the actor ideally—from head to toe. He knows him down to his intestines, can see through his skin, foresees his thoughts and his spirit, but he [Stanislavsky] does not have any command of theatrical form in the noble meaning of this word. He is a master of characterization and of unexpected character adaptations. However, he is not at all a master of a theatrical performance. This is why he brought theatre to the philistine level, having taken away flashy curtain, the actors' entrances, the orchestra—in short, having taken away all theatricality. Instead of taking it away, he should have ennobled it, transformed the pathetic theatricality of his [Stanislavsky's] days into the true and lofty theatricality of the golden days of theatre—[theatre of] antiquity, for example.

On Fashion and the Eternal in Art

Art nouveau is a vulgar style. The time will come when the interior

---

1 Friedrich Hottenroth (1840–1917), German lithographer, painter, and author. Vakhtangov is referring to Hottenroth (1884–1891) *Trachten, Haus-, Feld- und Kriegsgeräthschaften der Völker alter und neuer Zeit* [*National Costumes, Domestic Utensils, Agricultural Instruments and Military Weapons from Antiquity to Modern Times*], 2 vols., Stuttgart: G. Weise.

decorations of the Moscow Art Theatre will seem vulgar. Will the halls of Versailles, or antique terrace of the Greek palaces and Roman theatres ever be perceived as vulgarity? Will the auditorium of the Bolshoi Opera Theatre—rich and theatrical, all adorned with velvet and gold—ever look vulgar in the eyes of the people of the future? Never! As for Morozov's mansion[2] in Vozdvizhenka Street, or Ryabushinsky's mansion,[3] these and other palaces were built by merchants without an ennobled sense. These are vulgar, because they are pretentious. The same kind of pretentiousness is in the decor of the Moscow Art Theatre—it is the deliberate modesty of the merchants. They are trying to say: we are not garish. Look how modest everything is at our place. We've got art-nouveau style. Their modesty is immodestly loud. The "immodesty" of the Bolshoi Theatre is modestly quiet.

On Stanislavsky and Sulerzhitsky

Stanislavsky's personality, his selfless dedication and purity command boundless respect. I don't know a single person who would not respect him. Then why is he alone? Why is it that, apart from the very very young, no one is interested and excited at the opportunity of working with him? (By the way, *The Drama of Life* [1907], *The Life of a Man* [1907], *The Blue Bird* [1908]—these are Stanislavsky's works in collaboration with Sulerzhitsky; there is more from Sulerzhitsky in these works. They do not represent Stanislavsky's individuality.)

On Alexander Tairov and his Kamerny Theatre

Tairov is, undoubtedly, a talented man. He has absolutely no knowledge of an actor. He is in need of the Moscow Art Theatre students. He will never create a theatre of eternity. He is as much of a bourgeois as Stanislavsky. But he has got a feeling of form, truth, however banal and loud. A human spirit is beyond his reach: he cannot spring up to the deeply tragic and the deeply comic. His theatre is also a triviality (every fashion is trivial until it passes). The Moscow Art Theatre

---

2   This Moscow mansion stylized in neo-Moorish style was built between 1895 and 1899 by the architect Victor Mazyrin for the Russian millionaire merchant Alseny Morozov. Despite its Moorish motives, the mansion is eclectic in style; it is considered one of the early examples of the Russian art-nouveau style.
3   This Moscow mansion in the Russian art-nouveau style was commissioned to the architect Fyodor Schechtel by the manufacturer Mikhail Ryabushinsky and built between 1900 and 1903.

at least can be put in a glass case and displayed as a museum item. Kamerny Theatre that changes fashion every year will remain a triviality, naturally.

On the Moscow Maly Theatre

Maly Theatre is old-fashioned. It is sweet, like an old granny with her bonnet, modest black beaded dress and prunella shoes at the time when everyone already wears tights, high boots, and a short silk blouse with pockets. Its [Maly Theatre's] naive assurance of the sanctity of its mission—to awaken kind feelings among their contemporaries—has its rightful place in the glass case; it is a sin to take off the dead granny her prunella shoes and to make her wear the high boots to her grave. [As for] Kamerny Theatre[, it] will one day become as an old courtesan—disgusting, painted and dressed up according to the latest fashion.

On Meyerhold and the Theatre of the Future

All theatres of the near future will be formed and founded in the way Meyerhold has long foreseen. Meyerhold is a genius. And it pains me that no one knows it ... This includes his students (by the way, all these Bebutovs[4] and Bassalygos[5] are quite mediocre). I never copied him, and I never will. In my torturous attempts to break out of Stanislavsky's chains, I, on my own, a year ahead of Stanislavsky, started speaking of rhythm and plasticity, arrived at the feeling of rhythm, learned what the expressive plasticity is, what the **attention of the audience** is, the feeling of the stage, **sculptural modeling**, statuary immobility, **dynamics**, gesture, theatricality, stage platform, etc., etc. Today I reread Meyerhold's book *On Theatre*, and ... was stunned. The same thoughts and words, only beautifully and clearly expressed. I can't speak like that, I don't know as much, but I feel that my intuition is better than Meyerhold's. He needs to study an historic epoch, in order to grasp its spirit. I, however, from a couple of empty hints, for some reason, clearly and vividly feel this spirit. I always, almost unmistakably, can describe, down to the smallest detail, the life of the century, society, class, habits, laws, clothes, and so on.

4   Valery Bebutov (1885–1961), Russian theatre director, an associate of Meyerhold.
5   Dmitry Bassalygo (1884–1969), Russian actor and public figure. Bassalygo was in charge of the local trade-union committee at the First RSFSR (Russian Soviet Federative Socialist Republic) Theatre, headed by Meyerhold.

On the Feeling of the Author

Meyerhold has an extraordinary feeling of the play. He is quick to resolve it [the play] one way or another. And his way of resolving it is always such that it could be used to resolve a number of similar plays. Stanislavsky, up till now, only felt one play—*The Seagull*—and in its vein he used to resolve all other Chekhov plays, and Turgenev, and (oh, my God!) Gogol, and (oh, my God again!!) Ostrovsky and Griboyedov.[6] Stanislavsky knows nothing else. Nothing more can be learned from Stanislavsky. Boleslavsky was right when last year he said words that stunned me at the time: "Stanislavsky can give me nothing more, I will go to Craig." By the way, Craig also will not be able to give anything. The screens of *Hamlet*[7] are his quintessence, his extract, the conclusion of his plan. As for the eternal testament that Craig pronounced a long time ago—"create everything intuitively"—one does not have to travel to Craig for that. The trip would be especially useless for Boleslavsky, since one cannot learn intuition, and this part of him is completely atrophied. He is trivial in *The Wreck of Hope* and *Wandering Minstrels* (the best of this production is created by Stanislavsky's intuition); *Balladina*[8] and *The Ragged Cape*[9] represent the exceptional brilliance of his anti-artistic work. (Sushkevich's theatricality in *The Robbers*[10] was old-fashioned and unpretentious, and in that sense—in the sense of theatricality—*The Robbers* stands immeasurably higher than *The Ragged Cape*, even though, at first glance, we all thought differently.)

May naturalism in theatre die!

Oh, how one can stage Ostrovsky, Gogol, Chekhov!

6 Vakhtangov refers to various representatives of realism in Russian theatre, such as Ivan Turgenev (1818–1883), Nikolai Gogol (1809–1852), and Aleksandr Griboyedov (1795–1829).
7 Craig's design for the 1911 MAT production of *Hamlet* was based on twelve tall screens. Vakhtangov was influenced by Craig's design ideas. For further information on Craig's influence, see Malaev-Babel (forthcoming).
8 First Studio of the MAT production, based on the 1834 play *Balladina* (*Balladyna*) by the Polish romantic poet and playwright Juliusz Słowacki (1809–1849). It was directed by Richard Boleslavsky in 1920. Konstantin Stanislavsky oversaw the production and participated in rehearsal work.
9 St. Petersburg Bolshoi Drama Theatre production, based on the play by the Italian playwright Sem Benelli (1877–1949). It was directed by Richard Boleslavsky in 1920.
10 St. Petersburg Bolshoi Drama Theatre production, based on the play by the German poet, author, and playwright Friedrich Schiller (1759–1805). It was directed by Boris Sushkevich in 1919.

I now have an urge to get up and run to share what is germinating inside me.

I want to stage *The Seagull*. Theatrically. The way Chekhov has it.

I want to stage [Pushkin's] *The Feast During the Plague* and Chekhov's *Wedding* [1889] in one evening. *Wedding* has *The Feast During the Plague* in it. These plagued people do not know that the plague has passed, that humanity was emancipated, that one does not need [to invite] generals to their weddings.[11]

In Chekhov's plays we find tragedy rather than lyricism. When a man shoots himself, this is not lyricism. This is either an act of triviality or heroism. Neither triviality nor heroism has ever had anything to do with lyricism. Both triviality and heroism have their tragic masks. Lyricism, however, has had everything to do with triviality.

I am tired.

From March 1921 diary entry made at All Saints' Rehabilitation Resort.[12]

---

11 Vakhtangov crossed out this text in the original.
12 This is the first unabridged English-language publication of this seminal diary entry. The unabridged Russian original was first published in 1987 in the Soviet Union *Teatr* magazine. An abridged version of this diary entry appeared in English in Vendrovskaya and Kaptereva 1982.

14 Expressive Means of Fantastic Realism

Notes on the Role of Master Pierre in the Working Script of Bromley's *Archangel Michael*[1]

Summer 1921, All Saints' Rehabilitation Resort

What Constitutes a Farce

- Elements of yearning and spontaneity, light treatment of facts.
- Naivety.
- This is not eccentricity.
- Lucile (the mob)—she is extraordinarily simple.
- Pierre moves from farce to tragedy.
- Essentially he is a tragic figure.
- Farce is a quality.[2]
- An actor must believe his despair, rapture, laughter.
- No one thinks (except Carrie).
- Not a single moment without *greed*. Blood.

First rehearsal, October 31, 1921 (conversation)

- Timbre of voice.
- **Mouth.**
- Accent.
- Rhythm.
- Body.
- Eye.

---

1 This is the first English-language publication of Vakhtangov's notes. On the First Studio of the MAT's production of *Archangel Michael*, see Introduction, pp. 70.
2 This thought is very similar to Michael Chekhov's concept of style, as outlined in his seminal book *To the Actor* (2002).

- Grimace.
- Tempo.
- Overtone.
- Degree.
- Apostrophe.
- Motive.
- Drunk in the prologue.
- Cynical.
- Fearless as a drunk.
- [Pierre] should not mock, but rather feel himself in the right.
- [Pierre should] Believe in his Joieville fantasy.
- A goner, but oblivious to it (tries to drown it in wine).
- Greed.
- He is haunted by visions.
- His hair is a mess.
- He whistles.
- His joints are heavy.
- [He is] Swollen.
- Pierre is a deeply moral creature; otherwise he could not have fallen so.
- Sodom does not attract him.
- Prologue
- Delirium.
- Revolt.
- Statue.
- Waging a face-to-face fight.

December 7, 1921

[Pierre] should be heavier, older.
To the end, I must not use a single vulgar intonation. [He is] [n]oble to the end.
My goal is to rehabilitate hell. (N[adezhda] B[romley])
The people demand miracles, [Pierre] exploits beauty (N[adezhda] B[romley])
Pierre and Anne are harmonious.
She loves him as he was in his youth. For him it is tragic.
A man's creative spirit is greater than [his] religious and social senses.

(Ivanov 2011)

15 Theatrical Models of Fantastic Realism

The Production Plan for Tolstoy's *The Fruits of Enlightenment*[1]

DECEMBER 10, 1921

I must propose this to K. S[tanislavsk]y

Prologue

The curtain opens.

The stage represents part of the Moscow Art Theatre dress circle foyer. A long table, the kind that is usually set for the rehearsals.

Behind the table and on benches along the walls sit all the actors performing *The Fruits of Enlightenment*, just as they are, that is without makeup and in their usual plain clothes (I think, it would even be better to keep everyday clothes, those usually worn in rehearsals).

Except for actors, there may be people not participating in the production. These can be different people every time—whoever happens to be present at the theatre. Not even actors, perhaps, but stagehands, administration. Sometimes, when possible, Tolstoy's friends—Chertkov,[2] Gorbunov,[3] etc. They may also speak.

Vladimir Ivanovich [Nemirovich-Danchenko], perhaps.

During the first few performances, Vladimir Ivanovich's presence would even be desirable.

During the first performance the entire staff of the Moscow Art Theatre can be present, that is all groups—studios, stagehands, orchestra, etc.

---

1   This is the first English-language publication of Vakhtangov's plan. For further information on Vakhtangov's interpretation of *The Fruits of Enlightenment*, see Introduction, pp. 66.
2   Vladimir Chertkov (1854–1936), Russian author, a close friend of Tolstoy, who shared his religious, moral, and political views.
3   Ivan Gorbunov-Posadov (1864–1940), Russian author, publisher, and Tolstoy's close friend and follower.

At the center of the table sits Stanislavsky (and Vl[adimir] Iv[anovich]).

Stanislavsky gives a general short ring on the bell and begins to address the gathering. He speaks:

On the contemporary art of the theatre.

On what is required of the actor.

On contemporary audiences.

On the Moscow Art Theatre's goals.

All of it quite brief, in plain language, and chiseled

On the reasons why *The Fruits* ... are staged.

On the idea of the play.

On the fact that he only sees one **contemporary form** for *The Fruits* ... which he will propose later, based on the above-mentioned acting requirements: maximum expressiveness, both inner and outer.

Then Nemirovich-Danchenko, or someone else, speaks of the theme that, at the present moment (the moment when the play is performed), concerns the Moscow Art Theatre or theatre in general.

Then Vladimir Mikhailovich Mikhailov [1861–1935, MAT actor] gives a short account of the history of the first performance of *The Fruits* ... He says that Tolstoy wrote this play for his friends and guests, who wished to put on a performance.

During this account, there may be interjections—questions from any of those present.

Then Stanislavsky continues.

"Everything you just heard defined our production plan. Let us suppose that this performance takes place at one of the rooms or verandas of the Yasnaya Polyana estate. We will supply a replica, a naturalistic replica, to be exact, of this room or veranda. Let us suppose that we have rehearsed the play here, at the Art Theatre rehearsal hall, and suppose we wanted to show it to Tolstoy. Suppose he is alive, but cannot come, because he is unwell.

We go to the Yasnaya Polyana estate. We take with us no makeup, no costumes, no furniture. At our disposal we have got the Yasnaya Polyana furniture and objects. Those are bed sheets, carpets, shawls, stools, flowerpots—the modest means we have at our disposal, typical for a domestic production. (Replicas of Tolstoy's things, or better yet his real things, should be taken for props, furniture and street wear, such as fur coats, hats, etc.)"

Then Stanislavsky walks onto the proscenium—they bring on the house lights and close the curtain behind him.

Stanislavsky says to the audience approximately this:

"This kind of a meeting we had at the start of rehearsals for *The Fruits of Enlightenment* on such and such date. We worked days on end. Today we give you the performance (he names the cast).

We never ceased to worship the memory of the great man [Tolstoy].

And you, who have come to the theatre today, will also remember him actively.

Make him alive again. May he be with you now, here, in this audience. May the performance go on, as if in his presence, at the Yasnaya Polyana estate.

While this performance lasts, go in your imagination to the place where Tolstoy lived for some years and from where he fled to die. Laugh, if you feel like laughing, as Tolstoy would have also laughed: after all, he wrote this play laughing, and with a smile.

Stanislavsky exits behind the curtain.

In the meantime, behind the curtain they have revolved the stage: the Yasnaya Polyana room and veranda stand preset for the performance.

They take out house lights.

The curtain opens, and the play begins.

No makeup, no costumes. All actors appear as themselves, dressed as they would dress if today they were going to visit Tolstoy.

Tolstoy's portrait can be hung on one of the walls.

Curtain comes down at the end of the first act.

For the second act, they change furniture and props on the same set; this is repeated for the remaining acts.

(Perhaps, once the scene change is done by the actors in front of the audience.)

In the last act, during the final lines of the play, Stanislavsky enters the stage and heads for the proscenium.

They close the curtain behind him. As Stanislavsky stands in front of the curtain, he says:

"The performance is over. The next performance is on such and such date."

(As they used to tell the audience at the imperial theatres, when the lead actor announced performance schedule from the stage.)

In my opinion, this could achieve the following:

1   The feeling of the contemporary in the staging.
2   Justification of a naturalistic set.
3   Justification of naturalistic furniture and props.

4   The performance gains a solemn quality.
5   Fulfills the desire not to obstruct an actor's mastery with stage makeup, wig and costume.
6   An atmosphere of grandeur is created in the performance, both in the audience and on the stage.
7   All, even small roles, become elevated as terribly significant and critical in the eyes of the actor.
8   The comedy is transformed into a mystery play.

Erik XIV[4]

Erik ... Poor Erik. An ardent poet, a sharp mathematician, a sensitive artist, a riotous dreamer—he is doomed to be a king. His royal vanity calls him to reach across the sea and offer his hand in marriage to Queen Elizabeth of England, whose heart is occupied by the Earl of Leicester. And next to this, his rebellious soul of an artist, seeking an outlet, brings him to the Gray Dove Tavern, where he meets the daughter of a simple soldier, whose heart is occupied by the warrant officer Max. Erik needs a friend; he seeks him among the nobility. He takes into his confidence Gullenstjerna, an aristocrat, for he is "first and foremost a man." And next to this, at the very same Gray Dove Tavern, he befriends the freeloader Persson, "a scoundrel, destined for the gallows," and makes him his adviser, for he is "my friend, brother, and a good man."

Having sent all his noble courtiers invitations to his wedding ceremony, he also personally invites the soldier Mans, and his poor relatives. The nobility refuses to attend, and he orders assembled the beggars from the gutter and the street harlots from the tavern [see Figure 14].

Just like the King from the New Testament [Matthew 22].

But, suddenly, Erik kicks at the people and curses them as swine. As soon as Gullenstjerna wants to stop the people, who have gotten far too loose, Erik, the merciful, forbids him to touch "these babes." Let them enjoy themselves. A married man, he contemplates, "Whom shall I marry?" He asks Persson to become his adviser in the affairs of the state and appoints him an all-powerful procurator. If, however, Erik ever feels Persson's reins, Erik will "throw him off." A humble man,

---

4   An abridged version of this article was printed in the periodical *Kultura Teatra*, No. 4, 1921. An English translation of this article appeared in Vendrovskaya and Kaptereva 1982.

Figure 14
Michael Chekhov as Erik
in *Erik XIV*, 1921. ©
Bakhrushin State Central
Theatre Museum.

he marries the soldier's daughter. As soon as the wedding ceremony
is over, enraged over the actions of the nobles, he yells at her: "Go to
hell!" just as she reaches out her soothing hands to him. "We should
not act to the detriment of the law and civil rights." "I don't feel like
killing; not since my children were born." "War is always inhumane."
"What does the law say on this matter?" These are the words Erik
speaks at every step of his horrid life. And, at once, without hesitation,
he bribes, incites murder, and calls for the executioner. Moreover, he
interrupts the executioner, takes up the sword himself, goes to kill and
kills. He accuses the nobles of treason, summons members of the state
council and brings his case before them. Persson obtains the guilty
verdict for the nobles. In the meantime, Erik has already announced to
the country his pardon for the nobles.

Erik is a man born for misfortune.

Erik creates in order to destroy.

He is torn between the dead world of the pale-faced and blood-less courtiers and the live world of simple people. He passionately desires peace, but there is no peace for this doomed man. Death and life gripped him in a vice of the inescapable.

Inclined to bestow gifts, he turns down the Polish princess and allows his brother Johan to seek her in marriage. And a few minutes later, he gives orders to capture Johan, "catch him dead or alive, cut off his hands and feet, if he resists."

At times he is angry and at times gentle, sometimes insolent and sometimes common, rebellious today and submissive tomorrow, trusting in both God and Satan. He can be recklessly unjust but also recklessly merciful, as smart as a genius but also ridiculously help-less and lost, at first decisive and lightning-quick and then slow and hesitant.

God and Hell, fire and water. Master and slave—he, who is made out of antagonisms and squeezed between the polarities of life and death, must inevitably destroy himself. And so he perishes.

Common people remember the parable of the king from the New Testament, court trumpets play the funeral march, a gentleman-usher carries the regalia Erik left behind: crown, mantle, orb and scepter. He carries it to the next in line, and the next in line ascends onto the throne in rhythm with the funeral music.

An executioner stands behind this throne. Monarchy will perish sooner or later, as its very essence is full of self-contradiction. It, too, is doomed.

Arrows in the crown, arrows on the sword, arrows on the garments, on the faces, on the walls.

When the Studio of the Moscow Art Theatre chose Strindberg's play (interest toward Strindberg in Germany has turned into a "cult," according to *Theatre Culture* magazine), it set itself a task of producing theatrical spectacle where the inner content would justify the form, remote from the historic truth. We transformed all inner and outer aspects of the play based on our feeling of the contemporary. [See Plate 2.]

Similarly, the theme of the play, and the style of acting (the dead world of the courtiers being portrayed in a monumental, sculptural, and laconic style; the living world—Mons, Karin, Max—portrayed with passion and realistic details), as well as the style of the set and costumes, divorced from all existing approaches—all of this has been dictated by our feeling of the contemporary.

This is our Studio's experiment in seeking theatrical forms for theatrical content (the art of experiencing the part). Up till now, the Studio, faithful to the Stanislavsky teaching, insistently strove to master experiencing in acting. Now the Studio enters the phase of seeking theatrical forms. In doing so, it also remains faithful to the teaching of Stanislavsky who seeks expressive forms and shows the means to achieve it (**breath**, sound, word, phrase, thought, gesture, body, plasticity, rhythm—everything in a special, theatrical sense, its inner justification coming from the nature itself). This is the first experiment. Our times directed us toward this experiment—the times of the Revolution.

March 22, 1921.

Audience Address at the Dress Rehearsal for An-Sky's *The Dybbuk* (Draft)[5]

An-sky originally wrote his play in Russian. He then translated it into Yiddish. [Hayim Nahman] Bialik [1873–1934], a major Jewish poet, translated the play into Hebrew at the Habima's suggestion. The play has been written in a naturalistic style; it is a play depicting everyday life. From this point of view it presented difficulty for theatrical treatment. It needed to be resolved either naturalistically, or realistically. Neither of these means were accepted, for the times we live in require forms that ring true today. We felt that neither naturalism nor realism were vital today. We wanted to produce a theatrical performance (saturated with passion), while also preserving the essence of the **mundane** situations.

Then I tried out a form, which I would call theatrical realism. Actors' genuine organic attention to each other and genuine emotional experience, according to the Moscow Art Theatre's school (i.e. what I learned with Stanislavsky) were taken as a principle of the stage acting. As for the means to express these (attention and emotional experience), I was seeking them in contemporary life, in the reality of today. [See Figure 15.]

My collaborators in this work were designer Natan Altman [see Plates 3 and 4],[6] Yuri Engel,[7] who composed the music, as well as

---

5   This is the first English-language publication of Vakhtangov's address.
6   Natan Altman (1889–1970), Russian Jewish artist and theatre designer.
7   Yoel Engel (1868–1927), Russian Jewish composer and researcher of Jewish musical folklore.

Figure 15 Scene from Act 3 of *The Dybbuk*, 1922. © Bakhrushin State Central Theatre Museum.

Lev Laschilin,[8] who helped with the dances, and Yuri Zavadsky and Faleyev, who helped with makeup.

All of the Habima, headed by Nahum Zemach [1887–1939], helped me in my directorial work (gave me special references) with unprecedented scrupulousness.

1921.

Notes in the Director's Script of Gozzi's *Princess Turandot*[9]

Attempt: Writing a prologue for the parade.

1 Address to the audience ... the young actors of the 3rd [Studio of the] Moscow Art Theatre will attempt to act Gozzi's play as they experience both rhythms and the form of the *com[media] dell'arte*. Rhythms and forms prompted by the present times must find a response in the hearts filled with G[od's] blood, as it streams through the rhythms of our days.

2 Introduction of the troupe. (Young, cheerful, healthy. They are not daunted by the hardship of our days. They own the future. They don't fear mistakes. They don't fear failure. They have courage to correct mistakes. They have the bravery to keep going.) May each speak of themselves.[10] Each [speaks] of themselves—briefly—not more than four verses. Must say [original incomplete]

1920.

Requirements of the Participants of the Actors' Parade at the Start of *Princess Turandot*[11]

Utmost composure.

Complete confidence in myself as an actor, creator, artist. This begets self-respect coupled with complete modesty.

---

8 Lev Laschilin (1888–1955), Russian ballet dancer and choreographer, affiliated with the Bolshoi Theatre in Moscow.
9 This is the first English-language publication of Vakhtangov's notes. The Russian original was first published in Amaspiuriants (1996).
10 On the specific creative state of an improvising actor, described by Vakhtangov in this document, see also records of *Princess Turandot* rehearsals, p. 293. Vakhtangov's original plan that actors introduce themselves was changed later. See Introduction, p. 74.
11 Published in Nikolai Mikhailovich Gorchakov 1957.

No show of false modesty whatsoever, and nothing ostentatious. I am your servant, and I am proud, endlessly proud of being a servant of the people.

Clarity and purity in everything: thought, word, diction, voice, movement.

Complete composure onstage. Nothing extraneous, superfluous— shifting from foot to foot, for example, is a crime. Mixing up your place with your neighbor's is an even greater sin; the one who committed it condemns himself to moral suicide (must leave the Studio for a week). Exchanging glances with the partner where it is forbidden—is a blatant violation of our rules and must be regarded as an act of public dissipation. To break the line—is to admit one's lack of talent.

To break the rhythm and symmetry—is to kill your inner artist.

I, Vakhtangov, am in charge of (and inflict penalty for) the parade!
December 1921/January 1922? [see Figure 16][12]

Address to the Audience of the Dress Rehearsal for the Vakhtangov Studio Production of *Princess Turandot*[13]

Our teachers, our senior and junior friends! You must trust us that the form of today's performance is the only form possible for the Third Studio. This form is not only suitable for the *Turandot* fairy tale but also for any tale of Gozzi. We were seeking a contemporary form for Gozzi, which would express the Third Studio at the current stage of its theatrical development.

The form required that we don't stop at conveying the fairy tale's content but also approach certain theatrical techniques. These techniques might go unnoticed by the audience, but they are absolutely essential to the actor training.

Any play is a pretext to organize at the Studio, for half a year, special training required to master a particular form.

We are just beginning. We don't have a right to offer our audiences performances featuring magnificent actors, as such actors are yet to form. Years are required to develop true masters of the stage.

---

12 According to Gorchakov, Vakhtangov wrote his note on the *Turandot* prologue "approximately a month prior to the planned end of rehearsals" (Nikolai Mikhailovich Gorchakov 1957: 151). In a letter to Meyerhold from January 17, 1922, Vakhtangov states that he plans to open *Turandot* on January 30, 1922. (In actuality, *Turandot* did not open until late February.) This indicates that Vakhtangov wrote his note in late December 1921 or early January 1922.

13 An English translation of this address appeared in Vendrovskaya and Kaptereva 1982.

Figure 16 Actors' parade at the start of *Princess Turandot*, 1922. © Vakhtangov Theatre's Museum.

In the meantime, we are selecting people, discovering theatrical laws, absorbing everything Stanislavsky offers. So far, we do not even dream of the kind of a performance a full-fledged theatre could give. Until the time when we could form a troupe from the masters we cultivated based on our laboratory method, we will continue presenting laboratory works.

Presently we are seeking contemporary forms for Ostrovsky, Gogol, and Dostoyevsky. The three plays by these authors are a mere pretext to search for a form and, therefore, to seek the means to express it. In a similar way, *Hamlet*, which we chose for our work, is also a pretext. We know that we couldn't play *Hamlet*, but we also know well that working on *Hamlet* will excite the Studio and reveal to the Studio a lot of things it does not yet know.

And now, allow me to introduce the performers. The role of Princess Turandot is played by [Tsetsiliya] Mansurova [1897–1976], who graduated from the Studio school this year. This is her first public performance. She never acted before. The play's plot requires that her face remain masked for the time being.

Prince Calaf is played by Zavadsky. He already appeared in *The Miracle of Saint Anthony*.

Adelma—Turandot's rival—is played by [Anna] Orochko [1898–1965]. This is also her first role, if you don't count school performances.

Zelima—Turandot's friend—is played by Remizova, a third-year student in our school.[14]

Barak—Calaf's tutor—is played by [Iosif] Tolchanov [1891–1981].

Timur—the father of Calaf—is played by Zakhava.

Altoum—the emperor of China and Turandot's father—is played by [Osip] Basov [1892–1934].

Skirina—Zelima's mother—is played by [Elizaveta] Lyaudanskaya [1896–1940].

Ishmael is played by [Konstantin] Mironov [1898–1941].

The orchestra is formed from the Studio forces. The other kind of orchestra would be rather expensive and unnecessary. You will

14 One of the future leading directors of the Vakhtangov Theatre in Moscow, Aleksandra Remizova was the youngest member of the original 1922 *Princess Turandot* cast and a second-year student at the Vakhtangov Studio school at the time. (She entered the Studio in 1920 at the age of seventeen.) Since Stanislavsky and the MAT elders were watching the dress rehearsal of *Turandot*, Vakhtangov "promoted" Remizova to the third year in his address; according to the MAT rules, a second-year student was not permitted to participate in professional productions.

encounter different kinds of instruments here, even down to the hair combs.

The form of this production does not require serious music, so the music is composed by N[ikolai] I. Sizov [1886–1962] and A[leksandr] D. Kozlovsky [1892–1940] to be in harmony with everything else.

Aside from the accuracy of the orchestration, we can guarantee absolutely nothing.

We commissioned the translation of the text from [Mikhail] Osorgin [1878–1942]. The sets have been sewed by the female student body under the supervision of Ignaty Nivinsky [1881–1933]. Podol'skaya assisted him. Dresses are made by [Nadezhda] Lamanova [1861–1941] out of simple fabrics allotted by the State for the Studio warehouse. Cheap silk for lining, thick flannelette, sackcloth—these are the materials Nadezhda Petrovna Lamanova had to deal with. Tailcoats are made by ... well, we better not mention that. I have finished.

February 27, 1922.

16 Two Final Discussions with Students

First Discussion

On Stanislavsky's Naturalism and Meyerhold's Theatricality

When Meyerhold speaks of theatricality, he implies the kind of a spectacle where the audience does not forget, not for a second, that they are present at the theatre and does not cease, not for a second, experiencing an actor as a master, who plays a role. Stanislavsky, on the contrary, demanded that the audience forget that they are at the theatre and feel themselves in the atmosphere and in the environment inhabited by the characters in the play. He rejoiced when the audience, on coming to see *The Three Sisters* at the Art Theatre, came as if to visit with the Prozorov family—not to the theatrical production. He considered it the highest achievement. Stanislavsky used to say this: "As soon as the audience sits in its place and the curtain is open, we immediately take them in, we make them forget that they are at the theatre. We take them into our world, into our surroundings, into our atmosphere, into our current stage environment."[1]

On Theatricality, True and False

As for us, as for our understanding of theatre, we take the audience into the midst of actors, doing their theatrical work. Stanislavsky wanted to dispose of theatrical vulgarity, wanted to do away with it once and for all. So, he labeled as "theatrical" everything that even

---

1 Vakhtangov is paraphrasing Stanislavsky's first lecture to the MAT Studio, delivered on March 10, 1911. Vakhtangov's stenographic record of this lecture is printed in Stanislavsky (1993: 152–155).

slightly resembled old theatres, and the word "theatrical" became a swear word at the Moscow Art Theatre. It is true that everything he criticized was indeed vulgar; however, in his zeal to ban vulgarity, Stanislavsky also banned the true and necessary theatricality. This true theatricality consists of serving a theatrical production to the audience in a theatrical way. What makes a performance theatrical?

To begin with, it requires such an execution, such a theatrical treatment, acting-wise, which would allow the audience to consistently experience the actor's mastery. When a talented actor demonstrates his mastery, when the theatrical treatment rests in the hands of a true master, it sounds theatrical. But when a mediocre actor imitates a talented master, while contributing nothing of his own, it has the ring of vulgar theatricality.

For example, this is how things stand with pathos. When a talented master, who feels his part and conveys it with theatrical pathos, the audience accepts it and the actor's pathos inflames them. When a mediocre actor imitates him, however (formally, of course), without the inner burning, this does not affect the audience; such an actor does not inflame them. Things can be made even worse if a mediocre actor also happens to admire himself during his performance.

There is no doubt that theatre should have a painted curtain, orchestra, and ushers, who are dressed in the uniform of the theatre. There is no doubt that theatre should have spectacular sets, spectacular actors, who can wear their costumes well, who can demonstrate their voice and their passion. There is no doubt that theatre should have applause—all this is doubtless because these are elements of true theatricality. But when all this is done in a mediocre fashion, when the poorly dressed ushers walk about the theatre, while poor musicians sit in the orchestra, and a mediocre actor tries to demonstrate the passion he does not have and shows off his mediocre costume—it all has the ring of vulgar theatricality. Stanislavsky came down on all this; he started driving all this out and searching for truth. This search for truth led him to the truth of the emotional experience, that is he started demanding real, natural emotional life onstage, forgetting at the same time that an actor's emotion must be conveyed to the audience through theatrical means. Stanislavsky himself also was compelled to use theatrical means. Of course, you know that all Chekhovian productions are never performed without the backstage language: the chirping of the cricket, music band, street noises, street sellers' shouts, or clock chimes onstage. These are all theatrical means, discovered for Chekhovian plays.

On Atmosphere in Theatre and Art

KSENIYA KOTLUBAI:[2] And what about atmosphere? Isn't it also a *theatrical* achievement?
[VAKHTANGOV:] No, no atmospheres should exist in the theatre. Only joy should exist in the theatre, and no atmospheres. There is no such thing as a theatrical atmosphere. When you look at a naturalistic painting, do you really perceive an "atmosphere"? It strikes you with its content, but, as you view it, you forget about the artistry. I remember the effect [Ilya] Repin's [1844–1930] painting *Ivan the Terrible Murdering his Son* had on me. I used to stand before it for hours; I was afraid to approach this painting, but I perceived it only from the standpoint of content. The blood, Ivan's eyes, especially the eyes of the murdered son. But now when I look at this painting, it fills me with disgust. But I want to continue.

On Naturalism as a Theatrical Form

Stanislavsky once told us how they worked on one of Chekhov's plays: "We are sitting by the theatre cafeteria in semidarkness, upset; all of us quite depressed. Nothing is working. Suddenly we hear a clawing sound. It was a mouse. We began listening in silence, and we felt that the required atmosphere had come."
And here I suddenly got it. I understood that the secret of the Chekhovian plays' success at the Moscow Art Theatre is in the correctly discovered theatrical means.

On Truth and Theatricality

Of all Russian directors, Meyerhold is the only one who felt the theatricality. In his time he was a prophet and, because of that, he was not accepted. He projected at least ten years ahead of his time. Meyerhold did the same thing as Stanislavsky. He was also disposing of vulgar theatricality, but he did it through theatrical means.

2 Kseniya Kotlubai (1890–1931), Vakhtangov Studio's co-founder, teacher, and actress, one of Vakhtangov's closest students. Kotlubai served as Directing Assistant on *Princess Turandot*. After her teacher's death in 1922, Kotlubai left the Vakhtangov Studio and became the director at the MAT and Nemirovich-Danchenko's Musical Theatre.

Symbolist theatre was necessary in order to break and destroy vulgar theatricality. By disposing of it through symbolist means, Meyerhold arrived at the true theatre.

Stanislavsky got carried away by genuine truth and brought the naturalistic truth onto the stage instead. He was seeking theatrical truth in the truth of life. Meyerhold arrived at the true theatre through the symbolist theatre, which he now rejects. At the same time, Meyerhold got carried away by the theatrical truth and took away the truth of emotions. Truth, however, must be present both in the theatre of Meyerhold and in Stanislavsky's theatre.

Stanislavsky got carried away by truth in general and brought the truth of life onto the stage, and Meyerhold, while taking the truth of life away from the stage, also took away the theatrical truth of emotions. Emotions are alike, both in the theatre and in life, but the means, or methods of conveying these emotions are different. Quail is quail both at home and at the restaurant. But at the restaurant it is served and cooked so that it rings as theatrical; at home, however, it is homemade, not theatrical. Stanislavsky served truth as truth; he served water as water, quail as quail. In the meantime, Meyerhold disposed of truth altogether, that is he kept the dish, kept the recipe, but instead of cooking quail, he cooked paper. The result was a cardboard feeling. As Meyerhold was a master, he served it artistically, restaurant-style, but it was uneatable. At the same time, destroying vulgar theatricality through the means of symbolist theatre brought Meyerhold to true theatricality with its formula: an audience should not, even for a second, forget that they are at the theatre. Stanislavsky, through his destruction, arrived at the formula: the audience should forget that they are at the theatre.

On the Contemporary and the Eternal Forms in Theatre

A perfect work of art is eternal. Only a work in which the harmony between the form, content, and material has been discovered can be called a work of art. Stanislavsky only found harmony with the sentiments of the Russian society of the time, but not all that is contemporary is eternal. All that is eternal, however, is contemporary without fail. Meyerhold never sensed "today"; he only sensed "tomorrow." Stanislavsky never sensed "tomorrow"; he only sensed "today." Ideally, one should sense "today" in the day to come and "tomorrow" in the present day.

When the revolution came, we all felt that things in art cannot remain the same. We did not yet know the form—the real, appropriate form, so in *The Miracle of Saint Anthony* we achieved a transitional form. The next stage of our work will be dedicated to the search for the eternal form. In Chekhov's plays, the forms of life and theatre coincided. Today the theatrical means we employ in *The Miracle of Saint Anthony*—"exposing the bourgeois"—coincided with life's demands, with the demands of today. This time, however, will pass. No one will expose any longer, because socialism is not a proletarian society: it is the society of equal, content, well-fed people. When poverty, and the very notion of poverty, disappears, there will be no need to expose bourgeois. Therefore, in time, the means we have chosen will cease being theatrical. We must find the true theatrical means. We must find the eternal mask.

The Summary of the First Discussion

Today we clarified how Stanislavsky, while banning vulgar theatricality from the theatre, brought in the truth of life, and how Meyerhold, at the start of his work, by taking truth out of the symbolist theatre, took away the theatre's blood. This happened because Meyerhold buried the mundane truth before it actually died. Meyerhold could only have done it when the old had become obsolete, or dead. But it was not yet dead; it just hit a dead end. In the meantime, Meyerhold already began burying it; he dug it in and started making a new living man, using dead means. That was futurism. As for Stanislavsky, he arrived at the moment true theatricality died. He began building a living man using living, genuine means; he created a living man who had a real heartbeat and real blood. This man began to live real life and left theatre, as theatre became life. Now the time has come to bring theatre back to the theatre.

Why is the Maly Theatre at a deadlock? The Maly Theatre is at a deadlock because it absolutely cannot rightly interpret the contemporary and instead goes on using theatrical means of the olden times— the very means Stanislavsky was banning. At the time when one man was burying them, and the other was resuscitating, breathing new life into them, the Maly Theatre kept living as if nothing had happened, not sensing what went on in the theatrical atmosphere.

April 10, 1922.

Second Discussion

Naturalism, Realism, and Fantastic Realism

[VAKHTANGOV:]   Please ask questions.

BORIS ZAKHAVA: I think that today we should speak of theatricality, of true theatricality.

[VAKHTANGOV:]   All right. In theatre I seek contemporary means of treating the performance in the form that would ring as theatrical. Let us take the mundane in life, for example. I shall try to treat it differently from the Art Theatre, which treats it as the truth of life, projected onto the stage. I want to find a **condensed form**, a form that would be theatrical and, therefore, would be a work of art. The method of treating everyday life, provided by the Art Theatre, does not beget a work of art, because it is deprived of creativity. All it has is a fine, skillful, condensed result of life observations. I want to call what I do "fantastic realism." You, Kseniya Ivanovna, do not like this—why not?

KSENIYA KOTLUBAI: I don't like it, because, in my view, Vakhtangov should bring back to the stage the words in their true and only meaning. What you want to call fantastic realism is simply realism to me. I don't want you to apply any terminology to your pursuit.

[VAKHTANGOV:]   I don't feel like speaking now. Why don't you try to identify the difference between naturalism and realism.

BORIS ZAKHAVA: In my view, naturalism accurately depicts what a naturalist artist observes in reality. Naturalism is a snapshot. As for the realist-artists, they extract from reality only what strikes them as the most important, most essential. They toss away the insignificant details and select the typical, the important. However, in their creative process they constantly deal with the same material as everyday life does. Such art exists, and it should neither be confused with naturalism, nor with what Yevgeny Bogrationovich seeks. You can't call what Yevgeny Bogrationovich seeks simply "realism," unless you get rid of what stands between naturalism and what Yevgeny Bogrationovich seeks.

[VAKHTANGOV:]   I could, perhaps, instead of calling what I seek fantastic realism, call it theatrical realism, but this is an inferior term: everything in theatre should be theatrical. It goes without saying.

KSENIYA KOTLUBAI: I am convinced that some well-formulated definition of realism does exist. You say, Boris Yevgenyevich, that a realist-artist sorts the important from the unimportant. This is completely wrong to me. In my mind, realism in art, and in theatre in particular, equals an artist's ability to recreate, to create anew what he receives from the material that inspired him. Material gives the master-realist certain impressions, certain ideas. They afterwards create this idea in their specific art, using the means known to them alone.

[VAKHTANGOV:] So, you are implying that Boris Yevgenyevich gave the wrong definition of realism. To your mind, realism is a new creative act performed through a means completely unlike the impressions that fed the artist. Give me an example. What is Andreyev's play *The Life of a Man*, as staged by the Art Theatre?

KSENIYA KOTLUBAI: From my point of view, this is not true realism, and here is why: it is an attempt to project onto the stage the symbolist content of the play using symbolist means, just as they are provided by the author. This is not a recreation of a symbolist play on the stage. Everything Andreyev wrote is projected onto the stage untouched.

[VAKHTANGOV:]   This is not true. All characters, acting in the performance are created by the director, not by Andreyev. Andreyev does not write that such and such a character is fat and has a speech mannerism. Andreyev wrote the text. In the meantime, the actor-artist creates a character (a human being), dresses it, according to his own sense, invests it with particular (in this case—schematic) movements, discovers how it walks, speaks and sits down, etc. *The Life of a Man* and *The Drama of Life* are fantastic realism.

BORIS ZAKHAVA: Are you of the opinion that [Maxim Gorky's] *The Lower Depth* [1902] is naturalism?

[VAKHTANGOV:]   Definitely, this is pure naturalism. The theatre misinterpreted Gorky. To my mind, he is a romanticist, while the theatre treated him naturalistically, rather than romantically.

Kseniya Ivanovna, you say that we are searching for realism. Here is an example: the second act of *The Dybbuk* (the wedding) asked for an inserted scene that would justify the duration of time that passed onstage. We needed the audience to believe that the band had time to reach the bridegroom; otherwise it appeared that the band returned almost immediately upon leaving. For this purpose, I inserted a scene with two girls watching the band. The girls carried out the Chekhovian business of jumping up on benches, watching, applauding. I created a fine scene. Everyone loved this scene. Like me, they also felt that the scene had something Chekhovian in it. Nevertheless, this scene had to go, because it differed from the rest of the play in its method of theatrical

treatment. There now even exists a term: "The *Dybbuk* method."
What is *Turandot?*

KSENIYA KOTLUBAI: It is true realism.

[VAKHTANGOV:]   It is fantastic realism. Show me another performance like *Turandot.* Blok's *The Puppet Booth*, perhaps, in Meyerhold's staging. However, in Meyerhold's production actors did not play actors, and that is just the point. *The Puppet Booth* only featured an external depiction of theatre, that is, the stage wings represented stage wings, and there was the prompt-box, etc. By the way, this was done according to the author's directions. In the meantime, [in *The Puppet Booth*] the actors played characters depicted by the author.

An actors' performance can be found in antiquity—in Shakespeare's and Molière's theatre. Today only a few big actors— [Eleonora] Duse [1858–1924], [Fyodor] Shalyapin [1873–1938], Salvini—as they act, demonstrate that they are acting.

Realism does not take everything from life but, rather, what it needs to recreate the given scene; in other words, it only places onto the stage things that act. At the same time, realism takes the truth of life, and it gives the audience real feeling. Sometimes it also gives insignificant details, and then it turns into naturalism, because insignificant details belong to a snapshot. *The Pushkin Production* at the Art Theatre is realism. Have you seen insignificant details in it, or perhaps in [Aleksey Tolstoy's] *Tsar Fyodor* [1898]?

Meanwhile, in *Tsar Fyodor*, a *boyar* could give some insignificant details, and then it would turn into everyday life, or naturalism. Sometimes the author of the play does not provide insignificant details, but the naturalist-director introduces them. Since you came into the room from the street, where it is snowing, the naturalist-director will be sure to make you stop in the foyer, talking and shaking off snow, etc.

A play can be directed naturalistically, or using the method of fantastic realism. And the latter will be the strongest, because a sculpture is intelligible to every nation.

They try to treat opera naturalistically or, in the best-case scenario, realistically. I would treat it the way talented singers instinctively do. You can never fool the audience. A singer should emphasize: I am singing; that is why I come onto the proscenium. Stanislavsky stages opera naturalistically. He would not permit an actor to come onto the proscenium.

Presently, in *The Miracle of Saint Anthony*, we are mixing

external symbolism, in the set, with realism and fantastic realism. There is not a trace of naturalism in *The Miracle of Saint Anthony*'s acting. Form and the means of treatment are of paramount importance in fantastic realism. The means should be theatrical. It is very difficult to discover a form harmonious with the content that is also presented through the right [theatrical] means. If you take marble and begin forming it with wooden hammers, nothing will come out of it. An appropriate instrument is required to break marble.

When Luzhsky picks a play, he starts contemplating, "What means should I use in staging it? Why don't I treat it as 'Sèvres porcelain'."[3] This can be done, of course. But the harmony between content, expressive means, and form is missing here. *Angot's Daughter*[4] is misinterpreted, because the very genre—operetta—requires operatic means. [The style of] "Etching" has nothing to do with it. Consequently, the form has not been discovered; neither was the etching carried throughout the play—it begins after the act has ended. An etching is something immobile and very solemn, even if its subject is light. The chief thing is that an operetta is treated using dramatic, unoperetta-like means.

Author, Time, Theatrical Collective

Why is [*Princess*] *Turandot* being received? Because in it we discovered harmony. The Third Studio performs the Italian fairy tale by Gozzi on January 22, 1922. The expressive means are both contemporary and theatrical. The content is in harmony with the form, like a single chord. This is fantastic realism; this is a new direction in theatre.

The Drama of Life and *The Life of a Man* at the Art Theatre were treated in the method of fantastic realism. Today, however, *The Life of a Man* would be unpleasant to watch because it was treated with theatrical means of that period, i.e. the age of decadence.

Why is *The Life of a Man* not being received? Its form was discovered in the bourgeois taste. *The Life of a Man* is synonymous with the

3   Vakhtangov is referring to the production of Molière's 1668 play *George Dandin; ou Le Mari confondu* (*George Dandin; or, The Abashed Husband*), staged by Luzhsky at the Vakhtangov Studio in 1920. Luzhsky stylized his production after Sèvres porcelain, and Vakhtangov, who could not tolerate stylization, closed it after the first dress rehearsal.
4   *Mrs. Angot's Daughter* (*La Fille de Madame Angot*), an 1872 operetta by the French composer Charles Lecocq, directed by Nemirovich-Danchenko and Luzhsky at the MAT Musical Studio in 1920.

Ryabushinsky Mansion in Moscow. As soon as the order and peace have been established, exposing bourgeoisie would become old-fashioned, and *The Miracle of Saint Anthony* will require a new angle of view, in terms of its theatrical treatment

The Form Should Be Created, It Should Be Fantasized

KSENIYA KOTLUBAI: The works of art that survived the centuries are realistic. Realism existed in every art. In theatre it did not exist because the theatrical means that could convey the works of theatre as realism have not been discovered. This is why what used to be called realism, to me is a trade-off form, expressing nothing essentially.

[VAKHTANGOV:]   Precisely. This tradeoff form *is* called realism in theatre. In the meantime, I will continue calling what I seek a fantastic realism. One can master naturalism in theatre, for naturalism is faceless. One can also master realism. The world of Gogol, however, is the world of fantastic realism. In the meantime, in the Art Theatre's production of [Gogol's] *The Inspector General* [1921], [Leonid] Volkov, who plays Osip, creates a naturalistic character. Lilina[5] and the rest—create realistic characters. [Michael] Chekhov's Khlestakov, however, is the character treated in the method of fantastic realism. Volkov is no theatre, while Chekhov is theatre.

   Naturalism in theatre should not exist, and neither should realism. Only fantastic realism should exist. Rightly discovered theatrical means give an author a true life onstage. One can master the means; as for the form—it should be created, it should be fantasized. This is why I call this fantastic realism. Fantastic realism exists; it must now be present in every art.

April 11, 1922.

---

5   Mariya Lilina (1866–1943), a leading character actress of the MAT since its founding and the wife of Stanislavsky.

Part IV
Popular Theatre

17 Theory and Practice of the Popular Theatre

On Popular Theatre

The art should not lose touch with the people. It should either be *with* the people, or *against* the people, but never outside of the people.

Theatre is not *for* the people. It is *with* the people.

An artist should, instead of teaching the people, discern the people's soul. An artist should rise up to the people, having understood their height, rather than lifting them up to him; in his arrogance, investing himself with special powers. Apollo—the sky. Christ—the earth. These are the two elements of art. Pagan beauty and Christian love. The eyes, peering up into the illusive heights, and the hand, held out to the real suffering brother.

Theatre-creating people are yet to encounter their theatre-creating artist.

The art should meet the people's soul. The people's soul, having met the soul of the artist who beheld the words of the people's soul, should produce a true universal creation (a myth, perhaps).

An artistic striving must seize the word enchained in a people's breast. Without the help of an artist, this word will crawl upon the earth, and will never find its form. It will be trampled by the heavy foot of Time.

To achieve his victory, an artist must have his Antaeus' earth.[1] The People are this earth.

---

1 Antaeus: in Greek mythology, the son of the sea god Poseidon and the earth goddess Gaea. Antaeus compelled all strangers passing through his country to wrestle with him. Whenever Antaeus touched the earth (his mother), his strength was renewed. Heracles discovered the source of his strength and, lifting him up from earth, crushed him to death.

Only the people create; only they carry both the creative force and the kernel of the future creation. An artist, who does not draw upon this force and does not seek this kernel, commits a sin before his own life.

An artist must draw from the myth—from this eternal deposit of creative crystals formed in the people's soul; from this quintessential clot of treasures we call "human emotions," accumulated by the people and deposited over centuries; from this ocean, saturated by eternal wisdom. Everyone who saw the sun left his immortal part in this ocean—the part he carried within him, and which alone justifies why he was born to see the sun. From the myth must an artist draw the living fire to fuel his strivings toward heaven.

The Higher Reason must crystallize the Immortality, having heated it in the furnace of the living soul. To do so, it had chosen the only possible form—that of a man.

By the miracle of the universe, the Higher Reason tempted a man to stay in the earthly existence. This miracle is here to lure a man. If not for it, mankind would stop multiplying and conveying its form from generation to generation—the form of a man, who, according to the Higher Reason's will, unconsciously inherits Immortality.

The world will correct its existence as soon as Immortality has ripened.

Everything that accumulated within the people is immortal without fail. An artist should fix the eyes of his soul on it.

The people *experience* reality. They reflect real values in their souls and reveal these truly experienced values in the images kept in people's memory—in the popular art.

An artist crystallizes and completes images previously kept in the popular art.

The people preserve [values] in symbolic images.

Theatre must never be the theatre in charge of "national temperance."

Theatre should not be turned into an opium den.

There is a longing, a yearning for the art that lives in the people. Artist, overhear it!

An artist must not arrive at the ready forms of the popular art; neither should his worship of people give impulse to his strivings but rather his religious duty.

On his way to the Eternal, he will meet the eternal people, forever yearning for God; he will become fertile by the kernel of Immortality and gather life-giving juices for the creation and completing of the artistic images.

Only the one who has a talent for an individual intuitive grasp is an artist.

March 31, 1919, notebook entry (Ivanov 2011).[2]

The Directors' Section[3]

It is imperative that the Popular Theatre's productions feature mob scenes, be grandiose, and of the heroic repertoire.

A new building must be erected for the Popular Theatre, otherwise the Bolshoi Theatre must accommodate the Popular Theatre.

The directorial board must consist of the representatives from all theatrical trends—Stanislavsky (Art Theatre), Tairov (The Chamber [Theatre]), Komissarzhevsky (Komissarzhevskaya [Theatre]), Maly Theatre (Maly Theatre).

These representatives cannot be employed on a full-time basis. We must obtain their consent to grant their service at such a time when TEO approaches them.

All Moscow directors must be registered.

Submit the idea of the House of Theatres as the first type of Popular Theatre.

House of Theatres should be given at the disposal of:

On Day One	Art Theatre: Chekhov's plays.
On Day Two	Maly Theatre: Ostrovsky plays.
On Day Three	Chamber Theatre: *Columbine's Scarf.*
On Day Four	Vera Komissarzhevskaya Theatre.
On Day Five	Moscow Art Theatre Studios: *The Cricket on the Hearth? The Deluge? Twelfth Night?*
On Day Six	circus, variety show, the best and most interesting productions by the touring theatres.

In terms of creative implementation of the large idea, and in terms of initiative coming directly from the Directorial Board, there is only

---

2   This is the first English-language publication of Vakhtangov's diary entry.
3   The Theatre Office (TEO) of the People's Commissariat for Education, headed by Anatoly Lunacharsky, was established in 1918. Vakhtangov was invited to head the Theatre Office's Directors' Section. He made two notebook entries in preparation for this work: "The Directors' Section" and "Why Would I Want to Work at the Theatre Office?". Vakhtangov's illness precluded him from being able to execute his duties. The Popular Theatre by the Kamennyi Bridge in Moscow, organized by the TEO, opened in December 1918 and only survived for one season—almost exclusively on the Vakhtangov Studio's repertoire.

one [task] the Directorial Board has—the creation of a true Popular Theatre.

A talented director is a national heritage.

The real and truly Popular Theatre that would reflect and foster the revolutionary spirit of the people can only be created according to the concept of the House of Theatres I propose; i.e. each school (trend) must implement their production at the House of Theatres in the spirit of their trend, and yet in the vein, and on the scale of the Popular Theatre.

Popular Theatre that offers productions featuring theatrical treatment by a particular theatre group is no longer popular. This would either be Popular Art Theatre, or Popular Maly [Theatre], or Popular Chamber [Theatre]. The theatre that is needed, however, is Popular Theatre per se, the kind where revolutionary people will find *everything* they possess.

Let us say that all five theatres take a great interest in staging *The Dawn*, and each theatre stages it in its own way. In such a case, the Popular Theatre won't stop being popular, as long as all five productions are featured at this theatre.

In this instance, the Popular Theatre's repertoire would be simple:

Popular Theatre
The Dawn
by Verhaeren

Tuesday	performed by the Art Theatre
Wednesday	performed by Maly Theatre
Thursday	performed by Chamber Theatre
Friday	performed by Vera Komissarzhevskaya Theatre
Saturday	performed by the Proletkult Studio
Sunday	performed by the touring Reinhardt troupe, or by the Petrograd Proletkult workshop.

March 1919.

18 Philosophy of the Popular Theatre

An Artist Shall Have to Answer[1]

"An artist shall have to answer,
when the guest arrives,
why he has not filled
his lamps with oil."

V. Ivanov, *By the Stars*[2]

The red line of the Revolution divided the world into the "old" and the "new." There is no corner of human life through which this line has not passed, and there is no person who has not felt it in one way or another. The sharp line of the Revolution dramatically shaped the following three categories: people who want to remain in the past and defend this past (as far as taking up arms); people who accept the new and also defend this new (as far as taking up arms); and those who "passively adapt," waiting for the results of the struggle between the first two groups. The corporeal, spiritual, emotional, and intellectual sides of human life have all been stirred by the hurricane the likes of which has never been seen in the history of the Earth. Its whirlwind is spreading the flames of destruction further and further, wider and wider. Mankind's dilapidated structures are burned to the ground. The area enveloped in the flames of renewal is growing. Yet there are still naive people hoping some fire brigade would arrive to put out the flames that have smoldered for centuries in the people's core. They still fancy they

---

1 This article was published posthumously on May 29, 1924 in the *Izvestiya VTSIK* newspaper.
2 Vyacheslav Ivanov (1866–1949), Russian poet, playwright, historian, and theatre theoretician. His book *By the Stars* came out in 1909.

see instigators, and they are still waiting for these rebels to be caught, and the former prosperity to return (with the French rolls). If they only took the trouble to look at the pages of books that, instead of telling the history of the tsars, talk about the life of the many-faced being whose name is the People. They are the ones who, with their own hands, raise an individual to the summit of life, or bring death to those who break from them. It is they who unseal the crater of their boundless soul expelling lava that has accumulated over centuries of menacing silence. You mistook this silence for thoughtlessness! Your loud prosperity alongside their silent poverty seemed to you as it should be. Now they have screamed. Now they have broken the thick silence. They let out a cry into the world. Their cry is lava; their cry is fire. Revolution is their cry.

When the Revolution turns toward us its hurricane steps, its red-hot footprints burning the line that divides the world into "before" and "after," how can She leave the heart of the artist untouched? How can the artist's ear, having heard the cry into the world, fail to recognize whose cry it is? How can the artist's soul help feeling that the "new" he has just created has become "old" no sooner than She [Revolution] made her first step? If something created in the old world is beautiful, it must be brought to the people, for the people broke their silence precisely because things beautiful were always kept from them, for they are now demanding the return of what was taken from them. Mankind does not have a single truly great work of art that is not the incarnate finish of the people's creative powers, for the artist always overhears the truly great in the people's soul.

When the Revolution comes, and it comes when all that is truly beautiful in all spheres of life becomes the domain of the few—this means that the People demand the return of their own. The artist has no need to fear for his creations: if they are truly beautiful, the people themselves will preserve and take care of them. The People possess this extraordinary sensitivity. It is the artist's duty to do this.

But that is not all.

If the artist wants to create the "new," to create after the Revolution arrives, he must create "together" with the People. Not *for* them, not *for the sake of them*, not *outside* of them, but together with them. In order to create the new and be victorious, the artist must have his Antaeus' Earth. The People are this earth.

Only the People create; only they carry both the creative power and the kernel of future creation. The artist who does not draw on this power and seek this kernel commits a sin before his own life. The soul of the artist must meet the soul of the people, and if the artist beholds in the People the word of their soul, then their meeting will produce a truly popular creation; that is the truly beautiful.

In the people's voice there rings the centuries-old deposit of crystals that formed in the people's soul. The wealth of human emotions actively experienced by the people and deposited over centuries is heard in this precious sound. The people's voice is like the ocean, saturated with ancient wisdom. The immortal part of everyone who has ever seen the sun—the part he carried within him that justified why he was born to see the sun—was deposited into the ocean of the people's voice. Here, in this voice, the artist must hear the living fire of his own strivings toward heaven.

May the artist who is chosen to carry the spark of immortality fix the eyes of his soul on the people, for that which has taken shape within the people is immortal. And the People now create new forms of life. They create them through Revolution, for they never had, and still don't have other means to cry out to the world about injustice.

"Only on the shoulders of a great social movement can real art rise out of its state of civilized barbarity to the heights it deserves."

"Only Revolution can call back to life from its depths what it wrested from the conservative spirit of the previous cultural period. What it swallowed will reemerge more beautiful, noble and all-embracing."

"Only Revolution, and not Restoration, can give us again the greatest works of art."

This is what Richard Wagner says.

Only Revolution ...

Which "people" do we speak of?

After all, we are all the People.

We speak of the People who create the Revolution.

April 1919.

"Beyond the Limits of Human Comprehension"

Over there, beyond the limits of human comprehension, upon the unreachable heights of the immaterial worlds, above the stars, in the chasm of the outer spaces, freely breathes the beautiful world—the world of ideas. For millennia mankind has peered with inquisitiveness upward. With determined persistence, it refines its thought—daringly, fearing not the immeasurable height. Tirelessly, century after century, the mighty creative spirit of mankind strives to permeate this bright kingdom, and it steals from it one idea after another. And here, on the dirty and coarse Earth, equally tirelessly, lasting from generation to generation, it builds the manifestation of the idea.

From the notebook of 1919–1921. [Originally published in Ivanov 2011.]

Part V

Transfiguring the Stanislavsky System

19 Lectures on the Stanislavsky System[1]

Lecture 1

The Classification of Contemporary Theatre

You have gathered here, ladies and gentlemen, to study theatre, and, by doing so, to expose yourselves to art at large. This is why, first and foremost, we need to agree on what we understand by "theatre." We know of many different theatres that can be categorized as entertainment institutions. Each of them carries something unique, something that sets them apart from each other, sometimes even drastically: Korsh Theatre, Nezlobin Theatre, Maly Theatre, Drama Theatre, Art Theatre, Saburov Theatre, etc. This is why we need to divide all these theatres into separate groups, classify them, and then clarify the difference between the type of theatre we plan to draw upon for our exposure to art and all the other institutions that call themselves by the same name.

The easiest way to classify theatres is to take, as a basis, an actor's approach to his part, as practiced at different theatres.

Firstly, an actor can approach a role with an aim of exploiting it for his own egotistical interests. We will call a theatre of this type an *exploitation of art*. Secondly, an actor might approach a role in order to experience its emotions, discover the equivalent form of the emotions in his homework, and later present before the audience the results of this work. (Coquelin—"cry over your part at home and then bring the results to the audience.") Such is the Maly Theatre school, the school of presenting the part.

In the old days, there was yet another approach to a part when an actor, having memorized his lines more or less decently, in all other

1 This course of lectures was delivered at the Vakhtangov Studio; lecture records compiled by studio members.

aspects relied on his inspiration, or as they also call it, "his gut feeling." As a result, one out of a hundred performances he would play well by living in unison with the emotions of the role. In our time, however, theatres practicing such an approach to a part do not exist, and typically actors consider it their duty to prepare their role one way or another.

The fourth type of theatre is the **theatre of experiencing** the part. In it an actor strives to live in unison with the emotions of his role and lure the audience with these emotions.

To sum it all up, the major theatre types are presentational theatre and theatre of experiencing. In a presentational theatre an actor's main task is to use his external expressive means (intonations and mimicry) in order to portray different emotions. As a result, an actor develops a special stereotypical approach, also known as cliché, for every emotion. An actor uses it to portray a feeling. As soon as he has marked different moments of his role as "joy," "laughter," "anger," "contempt," etc., he already knows what to do. He knows (they even print special instructional manuals for it) that clenching one's eyebrows and fists portrays anger, while extracting certain sounds from one's throat and contracting certain facial muscles conveys laughter, etc. What they do not know is this: absolutely no one needs this, and a human being should be ashamed of occupying himself with such a craft. This is all false, and a dog's smile won't evoke joy in anyone. We, however, decided to study the true art of experiencing the role, the art of expressing ourselves, our very souls, before the audience.

On a Theatre School

Now I must clarify the difference that exists between a school and a theatre. This is necessary because in my practice I often see students forgetting that they are in school and thinking that their goal is creative work. Creative work is only possible in a theatre. It is in a theatre that an actor creates, while in a school he prepares for future creative work.[2] This is why a school's goals are, firstly, determining a student's

---

2   This thought of Vakhtangov's can be easily misunderstood. For Vakhtangov, true creativity equals spontaneous expression of an actor's subconscious. Since in school students need to put conscious attention on the technique, true creativity is not possible at the school, according to Vakhtangov. (See Vakhtangov's entry in the Gunst Studio *Diary of Independent Works* from November 10, 1918, p. 119). This does not mean, however, that Vakhtangov did not lead his students immediately towards the subconscious in his classes and rehearsals. He did so constantly by creating conditions that allowed his students to cross the first creative threshold (the threshold of the subconscious), and he appealed directly to his students' subconscious in his character and role demonstrations.

individuality (for example, his natural inclination toward comedy or lyricism); secondly, developing his natural abilities; and, thirdly, providing him with methods to approach his future theatre work.

No such thing as performance exists in school, while at the theatre a performance is the time for actor's creativity. In school we must:

1   acquire outer technique—a skill of being in control of our voice and body;
2   acquire inner technique—our soul's ability to repeat emotions;
3   develop fantasy.

The stage is different from life—it is more beautiful than life, and fantasy is an actor's second nature. To sum up, our body and voice (outer technique), our feelings (inner technique) and our fantasy—these are the school's subjects. As you see, teaching how to act is not one of the tasks; this is not the task for a school to undertake. The task of a school is to prepare the ground for the future creative work. The essence of the creative work that takes place at the theatre is transformation.

The Outline of the Course in Inner Technique

Now let's take a closer look at our work to come. It will consist of practical work, working on a play and of my lectures on theatre theory. In addition to that, we will engage in a series of exercises aimed at developing skills outlined in my lectures. What is the aim of these exercises? These exercises will:

*   make you accustomed to the internal discipline (you will learn how not to treat each other as competitors);
*   make you observant (being observant in life and being observant as an artist are two different things);
*   develop your ability to be in control of your soul, that is at any moment to be able to discover within yourself a necessary emotion;
*   they will develop your fantasy;
*   an actor should never say "I don't feel like acting"; he should always want to act, to create. This urge for creative work—let's call it *artistry*—should also be developed through these exercises;
*   these exercises will develop your taste;
*   they will develop your emotional range, will remove its excess or supplement its shortage;
*   they will train you to be in control of your concentration;

- will train you to analyze a play and a role;
- will give each of you your specific, individual approach to the part;
- will help you to know yourself;
- finally, they will develop in you an ability to sense clichés in your acting, and to immediately ban them. All these put together must develop in you ...
- a skill of revealing yourself [creatively] in front of an audience.

You see how many tasks stand before you, none of them being the task of learning how to act. That is, the school only teaches self-control. Stanislavsky said that an actor must exercise daily, so that his passion does not fall asleep, his warmth does not cool off, and his taste does not degrade.

One might try to contradict that this is impossible. The answer is: in such a case, don't dare count yourself among the ranks of those approaching art.

Exercises do not take much time: having begun doing them, you don't notice how you incorporate them into your everyday life. Only through exercises can one develop an organic need for work.

In school, I must basically transform; my entire nature must transform, amalgamate. I would even go as far as to say: "we must change as human beings, become better, kinder people."

All together we must transform each of you, and thus prepare the ground for future creative work.

A person must transform—but what ways lead to this?

The plan of the course:

Part I: Preparatory work
1   Muscular freedom.
2   Concentration.
3   Faith, naivety, justification.
4   **Circle of attention.**
5   Stage task.
6   Memory of action, memory and feeling.
7   Tempo: increased and decreased energy.

Part II: Working method
1   Communication.
2   **Public solitude.**

Part III: Analysis of a play and a role

Plate 1
Ignaty Nivinsky's
design of King
Erik's costume for
Erik XIV, 1920.
© Moscow Art
Theatre's Museum.

Plate 2 Ignaty Nivinsky's set design for Act 1 of *Erik XIV*, 1920. © Bakhrushin State Central Theatre Museum.

Plate 3 Natan Altman's set design for Act 1 of *The Dybbuk*, 1921. Set model (reconstructed later). © The Israel Goor Theatre Archives and Museum (non-profit organization).

Plate 4 Natan Altman's design of the beggar costume for *The Dybbuk*, 1921. © The Israel Goor Theatre Archives and Museum (non-profit organization).

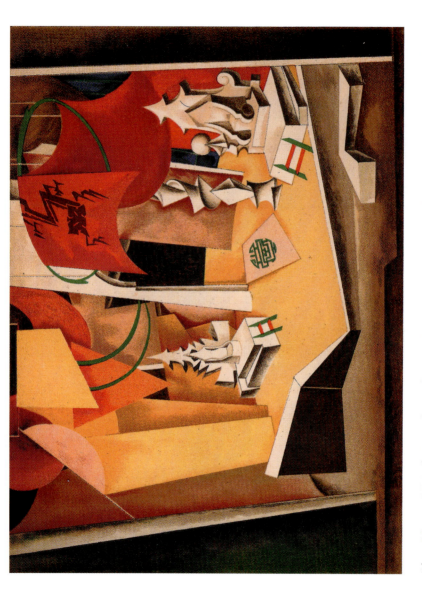

Plate 5 Ignaty Nivinsky's set design for Acts 2 (Scene 2) and 4 (Scene 7) for *Princess Turandot*, 1921. © Bakhrushin State Central Theatre Museum.

Plate 6 Ignaty Nivinsky's design of Pantalone's costume for *Princess Turandot*, 1921. © Bakhrushin State Central Theatre Museum.

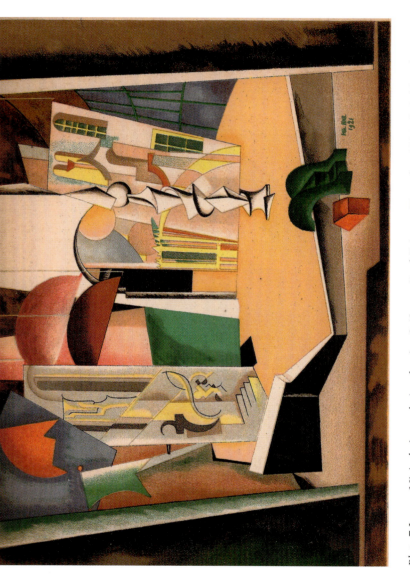

Plate 7 Ignaty Nivinsky's set design for Act 2 (Scene 4) of *Princess Turandot*, 1921. © Bakhrushin State Central Theatre Museum.

Plate 8 Ignaty Nivinsky's design of Tartaglia's costume for *Princess Turandot*, 1921. © Bakhrushin State Central Theatre Museum.

Plate 9 Ignaty Nivinsky's set design for Act 3 (Scene 6) of *Princess Turandot*, 1921. © Bakhrushin State Central Theatre Museum.

Plate 10
Ignaty Nivinsky's design
of Calaf's costume for
Princess Turandot, 1921. ©
Bakhrushin State Central
Theatre Museum.

Part IV: Outer characterization.

Muscular Freedom

Now that we are done with the required introduction, and the plan of the course is outlined, let's proceed with its first part: studying materials connected with preparatory work.

Stanislavsky observed significant actors, talked to them, compared them with the run-of-the-mill and insignificant actors. By doing so, he discovered what outstanding actors had in common and what related them to each other. These common things include muscular freedom, which all significant actors possess during their creative work. (Not-so-significant actors possess it when they are lifted to the heights of true creativity.) An actor can only create when he is completely free. Creative work is unthinkable in a stage of tension. As soon as an actor loses his muscular freedom, he substitutes his emotions with cliché. This lack of muscular freedom is caused by an overload (muscular tension) or a lack of energy. Muscular tension causes actors to perform a whole lot of unnecessary movements, such as adjusting their cuffs or hair, studying their nails, closing their cigarette case and using a lot of completely unnecessary energy. Sometimes, in the opposite, muscular tension prevents actors from doing things they could and should do: lighting a lamp on the stage or pouring a few glasses of tea becomes an impossible task—matches break, a glass shakes in their hands, and they get exhausted waiting for water to fill the samovar.

Muscular Controller

To sum up, an actor's muscles should be free at every moment of his presence on the stage. Such is one of the necessary prerequisites for the creative work on the stage.

What should one do in order to acquire muscular freedom and get rid of muscular tension? In order to do it one needs to develop an inner muscular controller, which would make the actor sense when he lacks freedom and eliminate muscular tension. However, would this controller itself prove to be an obstacle? Not if it is developed to the extent when you stop sensing it, so that it works in a completely spontaneous, automatic way. In order to develop such a controller one must constantly exercise using every incident when one experiences muscular tension. It is beneficial to start your day with such exercises. As a result, you will begin sensing every muscle of your body, and that will help you, when necessary, to acquire muscular freedom in seconds. You must know, though, that even then there will remain a certain element of muscular tension. In the future we will discuss how to get rid of it.

October 10, 1914. [This translation is supplemented with previously unpublished materials, featured in Ivanov 2011.]

Lecture 2

Concentration

The second prerequisite of the creative state is concentrated attention: in brief, concentration. By sending our attention in some direction we are going to create a center of attention. It is clear that one cannot have two centers of attention at once; no one can simultaneously read a book and listen to a conversation in the next room. At any given moment, you can only concentrate your interest upon one object. Such an object we call *an object of attention*. A sound, a physical object, a thought, an action, your own emotion or your partner's emotion can all become an object of your attention.

How can we attract our interest to one particular object? We can concentrate our five senses either on some object, or on a sound (hearing). Similarly, we can concentrate our thought power on some thought and our inner feelings on a feeling, be it our own feeling or our partner's. *An actor must have an object of attention at every second of his existence on the stage.* Otherwise, an actor won't be able to experience the required feelings at his own will.

Having an object of attention onstage—be it some physical object, a feeling or a thought—and living your own independent life before the audience is bliss. It is for this bliss that people go onto the stage. Many spying eyes are directed at you, while you are recalling some tune and not feeling these eyes directed at you. Moreover, you listen to your own soul; your own feelings constitute the object of your attention. It is this kind of concentration that destroys the remainder of muscular tension your controller could not remove. Muscular freedom and concentration closely depend on each other. When you are concentrated, you are necessarily free; however, a lack of muscular freedom won't allow you to concentrate your attention. This is why, first of all, one must destroy tension, as far as possible, and then discover an object for your attention. The remaining trace of tension will then disappear in its own.

To sum up, you must learn how to lure your concentration. In order to be concentrated, you must develop a skill of (1) instantaneously discovering an object of attention and (2) luring yourself with this object.

October 13, 1914.

Lecture 3

Faith, Naivety, and Justification

An audience will only trust the actor and find him sincere when the actor trusts in the importance of his own actions and words. No sooner than the actor begins to doubt this importance, be it only for a second, he will feel awkward and ashamed of his deceit. Therefore, everything he does onstage will become superfluous and false. One can only create when one has faith in the importance of one's creative work. What should one do in order to gain this faith? In order to do it, one should discover a justification: the cause of every given action, situation, sensation, etc. For example, let's swiftly assume some physical position, however odd: lift up a hand, a leg, or sit in some peculiar way and then try to find a justification for the assumed position. Let us suppose that you are sitting in a chair, having lifted your right leg and left hand. This is an extremely awkward position, and yet if you justify it by imagining that someone is pulling a tight-fitting boot off your right foot, while you hold onto a post with your left hand, so they don't pull you off your chair, you will immediately feel freer in this awkward position; it will become sensible. Only then will you believe in the necessity of this position when you find a justification for it. Once I feel that a particular justification is quite credible, I won't feel ashamed putting myself in this position. Justification is a path toward faith.

Not a single object, action or accident should remain unjustified onstage. Imagine that you are playing the role of an aristocrat, while the stage manager left a cigarette butt on your table: you must justify this; if your partner is laughing at you from backstage, that too must be justified. Your partner being late for his entrance does not mean that your colleague-actor is gaping, rather it means, perhaps, that the person you expected did not arrive on time, for some reason. This will cause you to take some actions; it will awaken some new sensations rather than throwing you off and causing you to come out of character. Justification is a cause that precludes any doubts. In order to train finding quick justifications, one must develop his fantasy. After all, as frequently as we receive justifications from an author, we have to discover them ourselves. This is why we need to develop our fantasy through exercises that consist of justifying:

1   a physical pose;
2   a place;
3   an action;
4   a sensation;
5   several unconnected situations, etc.

At this point, though, it is necessary to issue a certain warning. It is quite easy mixing justification with hallucination, and therefore we must sense a clear border between them. Applying my faith to the task before me causes me to become *naive*. This notion should be set apart from its usual interpretation. My faith does not result from my naivety; rather, I become naive as a result of my faith. *Faith, achieved through justification, causes naivety.*

It is this kind of a naivety actors must develop in themselves. I become naive when I can, in all sincerity, relate to my theatre colleague as if to my father, uncle, foe, etc., depending on our relationships in the play. The necessary feeling will come if I achieve physical freedom, find an object of attention, discover (through justification) faith in the importance of what happens onstage (or acquire naivety) and, finally, carry out a series of actions.

To sum it all up, today's lecture leads us to the following conclusion:

An actor, at every given minute, must believe in the importance of what happens onstage.

October 13, 1914.

Every seemingly absurd action, onstage and in life, will stop being absurd, if one justifies it. For example, I can spend hours trying to stand a pencil up on its sharp end. This occupation will become important to me, once I discover its cause. (I want to discover the pencil's center of gravity, I made a wish, etc.) These causes for actions that inspire my trust, we will call justifications. When it comes down to it, our every role is nothing but a justification for a series of situations.

Thus, in order to gain faith, one must discover a justification.

Example: lift up your hand—justify why you lifted it. Take up the Roman warrior's pose—justify why you took it. Try to believe that you carry a basket with fruits, although your hands are empty, justify … Justify that you wash your hands, although there is no sink, no water, no soap—find our trust in this . . .

Find your trust in the action of threading a needle, although there is no real needle and thread, etc.

The path to justification lies through fantasy.

Exercises develop a habit of justification, and they also develop fantasy.

Onstage, fantasy arrives on its own, when you need it most.

What is the right way of justifying? It is the way of the subconscious striving to justify. How shall you exercise? In the early stages, I even suggest assuming absurd tasks; make sure that it is difficult to believe in these tasks.

Choose the most nonsensical exercises, the kind of exercises that make you uncomfortable. (For example, if you come upon a postcard with some pose, be it the most mannered pose, go ahead and assume this pose, and justify it for yourself ...)

Exercises in justification may include:

- [physical] pose;
- place;
- movement;
- physical state;
- series of unconnected positions.

For example, I dictate a series of actions: (1) listen, walk, watch, move away, or else (2) open the drawer, put a chair up on a desk, take a handkerchief out of your pocket, then some other absurd actions . . . I can give you complicated tasks. Justify:

- for the role of Hamlet—take up a sword, break it, throw, run, listen ...
- for Othello—to forgive Desdemona;
- for Harlequin—to shake Pierrot's hand;
- for Polichinelle—to throw money around.

(Justify with your feelings, rather than with your brain.)

Let us say that you need to justify a state such as "listening." If, while listening you hear a nonexisting sound, this is no longer fantasy but hallucination. There exists a certain border. Due to a number of circumstances, a certain feeling (a very particular feeling too) always arrives, as I justify a concrete situation. The cases when the feeling arrives on its own, not as a result of a justification (for example, I just took up a physical position, and the feeling arrived)—this is an exception.

October 16, 1914. [Originally published in Ivanov 2011.]

Lecture 4

The Circle of Attention

Everything we have examined up till this point—muscular freedom, concentration, faith and naivety—we will now unite under one notion: *the circle of attention*. The circle of attention is a concentrated state, distinguished by free muscles and faith in the importance of what happens onstage. This circle can be expanded or contracted. An ability to swiftly shift the boundaries of the circle is one of an actor's very important qualities.

Exercises in the Circle of Attention and Memory of Physical Actions

Try to produce the following actions while keeping your hands absolutely empty (using no physical objects whatsoever, but rather sensing them by the power of your fantasy):

1 embroidering;
2 hand-washing laundry;
3 shining riding boots;
4 sculpting with clay;
5 making preserves;
6 styling hair;
7 untying a string on a box of candies;
8 making a fishing rod and fishing;
9 starting a stove;
10 getting dressed;
11 cutting out a pattern;
12 cleaning a gun;
13 gluing together a box;
14 playing with dolls, etc.

It goes without saying that you should choose exercises close to your individuality.

October 20, 1914.

Lecture 5

A Stage Task

Imagine some kind of a mob scene. A street fair, perhaps: you see a picturesque sight, lots of people selling, buying, bargaining. You will agree that a scene like that won't occupy you for more than ten minutes. Something else is needed in order to make it enticing; it needs events and actions. A stage does not tolerate immobile, statuary moments. Inactivity does not have a place onstage, and, therefore, an actor comes onto the stage to carry out actions. This means that, prior to entering the stage, an actor should have some task. Firstly, he needs to know *what* he is supposed to do onstage and, secondly, *why*: the *motive* of his action. The nature of this goal will determine how he feels himself onstage. Let us suppose that my task is to ask my grandfather for money; the motives behind my asking may be quite varied. I might be soliciting a contribution for some charitable cause, I might need money to buy a new tailcoat, or to pay my tuition, etc., etc. It is obvious that my emotional experience onstage would change depending on my action's motive. Therefore, onstage one must have an action resulting from several tasks. The creative work onstage then can be defined as a clear, logical, and beautiful fulfillment of a number of tasks. This fulfillment must be beautiful without fail. Things not beautiful in life onstage can become beautiful if this beauty is transformed through the prism of creativity. Real, authentic life should not exist onstage, for such life ceases to be art (base naturalism).

Three Elements of the Stage Task[3]

Let's now move onto the analysis of the stage task, without which we cannot imagine a single stage situation. A task is comprised of three elements:

1 motive (why I have entered the stage);
2 desire (what I am fulfilling a given motive for);
3 *how I am fulfilling it,* something we will call *adaptation*.

It is this final element—adaptation—that determines an actor's level of talent.

---

3 On three elements of the stage task, see also Vakhtangov's talk with the actors at the rehearsal of *The Lanin Estate* on January 18, 1914, p. 252.

Motive and desire are typically conscious elements (even though in certain cases they can arise subconsciously). I consciously determine why I have come onstage (my motive) and why I am fulfilling it (my desire). As for adaptations, or how I fulfill my motive, they arise subconsciously and depend on those accidents arising onstage while I fulfill my task. Let's say that my task is to calm down an upset person; I am calming him down, fulfilling my motive; I feel compassion, tears come to my eyes; these tears are my adaptation. What is the essence of a stage task? A stage task should always be grounded in action; it can be nothing but action. As for an inactive moment—feelings—it comes as a result of action, a result of resolving a given task. One cannot play feelings, they should come to us on their own, beyond our will. We have already agreed that we are not here to *present* our feelings— such is the task of the presentational theatre; our task is to *experience* them. Such is the main goal of our beautiful theatre—theatre of experiencing. A task then is what I must do onstage, my action. A stage task only has a right to be called that when action has begun. Up till that moment it does not exist; a stage task cannot exist on paper. An action and the desire to implement it, i.e. artistry—such is the essence of the stage task. An element of will characterizes action. One cannot play feeling, one must play tasks. I calm someone down—this is action, and compassion is a feeling (this action's result); I ask for money (this is action), and I get angry because they won't give it to me (this is feeling); I escape from prison (action), and I despair because I can't escape (feeling); I hold my laughter (action), I laugh (not an action); I hold my tears (action), I cry (not an action), etc.

As I ask for money, escape from prison, or hold laughter or tears—in all of these cases I manifest my will. Therefore, in all these cases we are dealing with actions. In those cases when we deal with actions' result, with feeling—i.e. when I get angry, despair, laugh, this takes place beyond our will, and sometimes even against our will (I don't want to cry, but I do). A feeling is not my will's doing; it is a doing of nature.

October 23, 1914.

Instead of "motive," we will sometimes say "task." Desire also often coincides with task. As for emotion, it remains above it, so to speak. One must first arrive at a firm intellectual understanding that one must not play emotion.

When performing one must transform to the point when even during intermissions one maintains the required emotion. The task must be divined—intuitively. When we remain in a creative state, nature does our job for us.

An actor produces a character while fulfilling a number of tasks. When sensing the character intuitively, an actor can arrive at producing the correct character right away, having never performed it before—just by solving the tasks.

The first emotion an actor brings onto the stage is his actual psychological experience.

Everything that happened with an actor throughout the day, everything that formed his experience—we shall call it a complex of accidents. An actor arrives at his creative act with this complex of accidents. (This is the first stage [of creativity].)

An actor's second emotion is evoked by the task: having created his circle of attention (the second stage of creativity), he fulfills the task, or rather a series of tasks, according to his role—these tasks inspire emotion.

The combination of these emotions creates the character's gamut.

[Vakhtangov's students perform *études* in the circle of attention; to those who performed one *étude*, Vakhtangov gives the other *étude*—in the physical state—"I am at home" (one of the calm domestic moments, without any extraordinary events).]

October 24, 1914. [Originally published in Ivanov 2011.]

Lecture 6

Affective Memory[4]

In our last lecture we clarified the following thesis: one cannot play feelings: they come on their own as I resolve my task, or as I adapt. Then how do these feelings arise and what is the essence of the emotional experience onstage?

Just as with the help of our five senses we memorize taste, smell, the form of an object, its color, etc., we can also memorize our inner feelings. Once we have experienced a certain event, our soul memorizes the feeling through which we react to this event. In cases when we get to experience a particular event often, the feeling through which we react to this event becomes familiar—we grow accustomed to it. As the same circumstances repeat, we can also repeat our feelings, memorized by our soul. In life, however, our feelings are always evoked by some

---

4 See the discussion of the term "affective" in the Introduction, pp. 25–7. On the subject of affective memory, see also Vakhtangov's talk with students at the rehearsal for *The Lanin Estate* on December 23, 1913, p. 246.

real pretext; these pretexts do not really exist onstage; they are always unreal there, so the best we can do is believe in them. There comes a question: can these unreal pretexts evoke real feelings? No, not under any circumstances. These unreal pretexts are not just unable to evoke real feelings, they should not do this, or the stage will cease being an art. The source of our specific stage feelings, that are quite unlike real ones, is not in unreal pretexts, but in our previously mentioned ability to relive our emotional experiences. This repeat emotion is not adequate with the emotions we experience in life.[5] This is why, in opposition to life feelings, we call our stage feelings *affective*. They are guided by completely different laws than those guiding our emotions in life. In addition to our affective (repeat) feelings, the stage also has a place for the feelings we experience in everyday life. These everyday feelings, however, can only be of two kinds: either I am pleased with the fact that I experience repeat feelings well, or I am displeased when I experience them badly, insincerely. As I leave the stage, having finished my role, all of my affective feelings immediately leave me, and only one of the two life feelings remain.

We see now what a big difference there is between the affective and real experiences. In life, once we experienced grief, for example, could we rid ourselves of it in a minute? Moreover, could we, in five minutes, move from grief to an equally sincere joy? Onstage, however, this happens left and right; an actor who experienced the most profound grief in one act has to start the next act in carefree gaiety, and vice versa. Usually actors think that they ought to spend tons of energy onstage, but that is not so. Those actors who leave the stage exhausted and fall in a chair, their forehead perspiring, usually do one of two things: either they show off, or they act with enormous physical tension. In the later case, their exhaustion is of a physical nature, and, as we know, physical tension is alien to a creative state. Suppose we experienced required emotions onstage the same way we experience them in life. In this case, after a performance we might have been committed to an asylum, or sent to a hospital, or, even worse, given our last rites.

To sum up, onstage we are dealing with the affective or repeat feelings.

---

5   This statement seemingly contradicts a later statement made by Vakhtangov in his final talk with his students: "Emotions are alike, both in the theatre and in life, but the means, or methods of conveying these emotions are different" (see p. 152). On the nature of this "contradiction," see p. 34.

I already mentioned that in the event that we dealt with our real emotions onstage, theatre would cease to be art. Just imagine that an actor, whose role asks him to hit his partner, actually does that. A partner would be in pain, and he would feel offended. How do you think an audience would feel in such a case? Without a doubt, they would pity the beat-up actor; they would not feel sorry for the character this actor performs, but the actor himself. It is not the character that would get beat up, but an actor, and, therefore, not a trace of art will remain here. It would be quite a different story if the other actor would use his affective memory to evoke the affective feeling of pain and offence, while the first actor, without actually striking his partner, would experience an affective feeling of guilt—only in this case would we be dealing with art. Feeling pain when someone actually beats you, feeling grief when your father dies, or rejoicing as you receive an inheritance, etc., is no big art.

Even in the event that you were to actually experience all this onstage, it would still fail to evoke a festive feeling in your soul—a paramount stimulus urging people to engage in art. Neither would it evoke your creative joy, since the creativity itself would be missing.

Affective life resulting from a stage task being solved—such is the life in the theatre of experiencing. Thus, the circle of attention comes first, then comes the task, and then, as a result of its resolution (or, to be more precise, in the process of its resolution) come our affective feelings.

It is also important to note that these feelings represent an actor's personal feelings; out of these personal feelings an actor creates his character. An actor experiences his own emotions, and that results in the audience receiving an artistic image of the character they create: Hamlet, Joan of Arc, Khlestakov, Chatsky [*Woe from Wit*], etc. Every actor [who performs a particular role] would have the same tasks as his colleague performing the same role, and yet their characters would come out different. This happens because each of them creates his role out of his own emotions. Each of these actors has got his own individual adaptations. Every feeling contains, without fail, a tiny bead of another feeling. I can experience fear differently, due to the complex of accidents. Fear will, nevertheless, always remain fear. There is no such thing as special fear, for every case of life. On stage, it is not the situation, but the emotion that matters.

Someone might contradict us by saying, "If an actor creates a character out of his own emotions, then what should he do if he never experienced a particular emotion?—let us say, he was never on the brink of death, never stood facing the mouth of a revolver, never committed forgery, etc." In reality, no feeling exists that a grown-up person has not experienced. He might not have experienced a situation he meets onstage; as for the feelings—he has felt them all. Moreover, onstage he is capable of experiencing up to 50 percent of a feeling he only experienced at 5 percent in real life. Such is the power of our affective memory. As for why this happens, I have no idea.

Thus, in life, an actor may not meet the same causes he comes across onstage. As for the feelings evoked by these causes, he has undoubtedly experienced them. In the event that he has not experienced the kind of fear one feels while facing the mouth of a revolver, he certainly has feared a mean dog, etc. No person exists who never felt fear. There is no such thing as a special fear, a different fear for every occasion.

Pretexts play no role onstage, since they are unreal. It is not these situations that matter, but the feeling. In order to experience joy onstage, one must experience it in life. In life it was certainly caused by a fulfillment of a particular life task, however subconscious. One can fulfill this task onstage, in which case it will become conscious. As for its result—repeat feelings—they will arise subconsciously. My joy might apply to any pretext—it is irrelevant. I don't care why I might experience joy—be it an inheritance or escaping from prison; as long as I get to express my feelings publicly—that is the source of my creative joy.

Just as we memorize our feelings, we can also memorize our actions. Thus come repeat actions. Our soul keeps a memory of our feelings, while our muscles remember our actions. It is not our mind that remembers them, just as it is not the mind keeping memories of tastes, smells, colors, etc.

October 27, 1914. [This translation is supplemented with previously unpublished materials, featured in Ivanov 2011.]

Lecture 7

Tempo, an Increased and Decreased Energy

There are a number of actions that we fulfill without altering our habitual state, or, as we will call it, our habitual tempo. Each of us has a habitual tempo of our own, typical for our fulfillment of life tasks—be it having dinner, studying, talking on the phone, etc. Suppose something occurs (an event) while we fulfill our task. This event might disturb our habitual tempo. Such an event introduces a new justification for our task and causes our tempo to alter. For example, if I am accustomed to having my dinner in a particular tempo and someone tells me that I must be somewhere else in ten minutes without fail, my tempo will change. It will change because I acquire a new justification for my task. Let's take another example: I am about to depart on my trip, and I am now at the train station. The tempo of my actions following the first bell will differ from the preceding tempo, and it will change even more following the second bell. When I solve my task in my normal tempo, I experience my normal feelings. When my tempo switches to moderate, my feelings begin to deviate from the norm. An increased tempo will make me feel extremely excited. The same is true on the stage. Based on these discoveries, we will now distinguish between increased and decreased energy. Decreased energy is common for a state of melancholy, boredom, depression, while increased energy accompanies vigor, joy, laughter, etc.

Any stage task, without exception, can be transposed into a different tempo. Let us suppose, my task is to cook fried eggs. If I justify this task by the fact that I am doing this against my will—they are making me cook fried eggs—the tempo in which I solve this task might become slow, and my energy decreased.

If I justify the same task by the fact that I must feed someone at once, I will start fulfilling the task in a faster tempo and my energy will increase. In my third lecture I showed you some exercises in fulfilling different tasks while being in a circle. Find different justifications for these exercises, and they will help you practice an increased and decreased tempo.

October 30, 1914.

Lecture 8

Communication

When actors are interested in their actions onstage, so is the audience. A stage dialogue will never be interesting unless the actors are interested in talking to each other. When two or more actors enact something onstage, an interaction, a mutual interest, arises between them. We act upon our partner with the strength of our entire self—not just with our words and appearance but with our whole being. This influence of my self on the self of my partner we will call "communication." During such communication with my partner, his spiritual experiences become an object of my attention. We shall also call it a partner's living spirit. I should never imagine a partner reacting to my words and actions. I should not console him and tell him [literally] not to cry when he is not even mildly upset, much less crying. I should only react to what my partner actually gives me. When my partner plays a king, I should respond to him, to my colleague, as to a king. At the same time, I influence him as my colleague, instead of imagining a king in his place. Otherwise I would have turned my adaptations into clichés. I must always adapt to something living, to something that [forever] evolves.

Thus, the essence of communication is an exchange of feelings: something alive in me acts upon something alive in my partner and vice versa: something alive in my partner acts upon me. Only communication can create an audience's interest toward what happens onstage. This is why actors, as they learn their lines, should not memorize gestures and intonations. When studying their roles, they should never search for the character's tone [of voice]. Otherwise their adaptations will become conscious, communication will disappear, and everything happening onstage will turn into something extremely empty and cold. As I communicate with my partner, I have a particular task; my partner's living soul serves as an object of my attention, and I am adapting to it. In the event when only one of the partners lives onstage, there is no communication, and acting becomes impossible. In such an event, the living partner will have nothing to act upon. Presentational acting usually occurs at such moments when a partner does not live, and a rare performance will have no trace of it. This is why you should learn to ban it as soon as it appears. This is the most important thing. In order to do it, you should develop a similar controller to the one serving to remove muscular tension. Thus, one should be attentive to one's partner on the stage. A lack of attention in life translates into attention on the stage. In order to play a lack of concentration, I must be concentrated. This concentration should be my life experience: something alive in me concentrates on something alive in my partner. As for the lack of concentration I must play, it should be affective. Similarly, in order to play a weak character, I must be strong. Otherwise I won't have enough power to play a weak person. In order to play a villain, I must be kind: kind, as far as real feelings are concerned, and evil, as far as affective feelings are concerned.

Try to fulfill the following exercises:

1   Kseniya Ivanovna [Kotlubai] and Natalia Pavlovna [Shilovtseva]. ([Natalia Pavlovna] came to [Kseniya Ivanovna] to sew curtains.) Here is the simplest task; you ought to act nothing. I interrupted you and told you to go up onto the stage. Where would you like to be now?

[Kseniya Ivanovna]:   I want to be in my room.
[Natalia Pavlovna]:   I will go to her to do sewing.

Neither of you can believe that this is indeed [Kseniya Ivanovna]'s room. You can, however, believe that this is [Kseniya Ivanovna]'s lamp. Try to believe this, and exchange some conversation. I repeat: communion only arises in those cases when I say things for my partner. In those cases when I say or do something for the show, for the audience, communion dissipates.

To play a lack of attention on the stage, one must be concentrated. [As a character,] I may not want to be [concentrated], and yet [as an actor,] I do. In order to play tiredness, I must be energetic.

In the case that I am tired, this would be life, not art. One must live with affective emotions. When it comes to being silent, you can either share that silence, or be silent separately …

2   Natan Osipovich [Turayev] and Yushkova, here is a justification for your task: Yushkova sees [Natan Osipovich] for the first time. She has an appointment with him, in his office.

A Public Solitude

While communicating, an actor must do everything for his own sake, rather than for the sake of the audience. I must listen to my partner because I am interested in learning what he is going to say, and I should speak to him because I am truly interested in telling him something.

Furthermore, when I am alone, I am simple, natural. As soon as someone comes into the room, I become different; and when I arrive at a ball, I transform completely. At the same time, an audience's presence should not transform me when I am onstage the way it transforms me in life. When I am alone onstage, I must remain as I am alone with myself in life. This will be public solitude. Public solitude differs from the circle of attention in the way that the circle of attention could be created when we are alone, while public solitude requires an audience. Therefore, public solitude is a circle of attention assumed in front of an audience.

More exercises.

3   Dubinina and Yaitseva: you are alone at the Studio; fantasize; justify why. I need you to experience communion. At the start, you tense up, but later tension goes away. You forget that you are onstage. Forgetting it fully is impossible; however, the true circle

makes you feel pleasant and easy.
4   Protopopova, Malikova, Zimnyukov.
5   Krotkova, Zakhava, Kastorskaya (at Krotkova's, talking about her apartment, and about a play).
6   Igumnova and Westerman (preparing for their roles).
7   Igumnova and Ostreiko (met at some courses).
8   Shpital'sky, Lapshin, Lanina [Kotlubai] (riding a streetcar, on their way to the Studio). Your relationship toward each other and those around you should justify that you sit in a streetcar. Lanina does not know them.

October 31, 1914. [This translation is supplemented with previously unpublished materials, featured in Ivanov 2011.]

20 Materials on the Stanislavsky System

Plan of the [Stanislavsky] System (As I See It)

A. General Part

I. Contemporary Theatre

GENERAL CONCEPTION OF THEATRE

1 Three types of theatres:

    a Presentational Theatre.
    b Theatre of Experiencing.   } Based on approach to the role.
    c Theatre of the Craft.

2 On actors' clichés.

II. Basis of the Stanislavsky Teaching

1 Attributes of the subconscious (creative attributes).
2 Conscious path toward enriching the subconscious.
3 Actor cultivation (the actor's outer and inner technique).

III. On the Abilities an Actor Must Possess (Developed by the System)

IV. Stanislavsky Teaching as a System of Actor Cultivation

B. Methodological Part

1   Cognition of the methods (the thought).
2   Organic concentration (sensory organs).
3   Artistry (the will).
4   Affectivity (the soul).
5   The creative element (the spirit).
6   The means of working on self and on the role (the method).

C. Practical Part

Work on Self

1   Exercises in attention. Attributes of attention:

    a   Muscles.
    b   Concentration (the object).
    c   Faith and naivety.
    d   The circle of attention.
    e   Physical action.

2   Exercises in communicative ability. Attributes of the soul:

    a   The living spirit of the partner (the object).
    b   The inner action.
    c   The task (three of its elements: action, desire, adaptation).
    d   Increased and decreased energy (degree of passion in task fulfillment).
    e   Justification: **appraisal of the fact.**
    f   Creating the past of the role.
    g   Creating the today of the role.
    h   The *I am.*
    i   Exercising artistry.

D. Affective [Repeat] Emotion

1   The emotion doctrine.
2   Complex and primary emotions.
3   The roots of emotions.
4   Nature of the affective [repeat] emotions.
5   An actor's soul as material for the character.

E. *Creative Part*

Work on the role

TRANSFORMATION (CREATION OF THE CHARACTER)

1   Spiritual transformation.

   a   The gamut of feelings.
   b   The inner character.

2   Physical transformation. The concept of outer characterization.
3   The kernel of the character. The method of working on plays and roles.
4   Play analysis

   a   The first reading, literary analysis, historic analysis, artistic analysis, theatrical analysis.
   b   Division into bits.
   c   Through action.
   d   Unsealing of the text.

5   Role analysis

   a   Clarity.
   b   Division into bits.
   c   Discovering the kernel.
   d   Discovering the tasks.
   e   Discovering the through action.
   f   Creating the past of the role.

6   *Études.*
7   Rehearsals (complex of accidents).
8   Performances

   a   Preparing for the performance.
   b   Using the inner technique.
   c   "Freely manipulating (juggling) the role."
   d   Perfecting the role.
   e   The play's growth.

9   "The completion of the play."

March 1919.

To Those Writing on the Stanislavsky "System"

There is no book so far by Stanislavsky himself. He never breathed a word in the press of the laws he discovered for the art—the art of theatre in particular. Nevertheless, how many judgments on the so-called "Stanislavsky System" have already appeared, and continue to appear, in newspapers, magazines, and book collections. Even an entire book has been published devoted to the criticism of Stanislavsky's teaching.[1] The author of the book, however, is determined to criticize Stanislavsky's teachings, expounding them as he sees fit.

When such articles, or such a book, fall into the hands of those working directly with Stanislavsky, they can't help but puzzle, wonder, and patiently wait for the moment when Stanislavsky's works are published.

What will these bold and hasty critics say when they see for themselves that their brilliant and passionate lines, dictated by the indignation of a noble heart, were instigated by their own insinuations. What, for example, will Komissarzhevsky (a man who assumes that Stanislavsky "rejected creative fantasy") say when he finds out that Stanislavsky considers fantasy "the actor's second nature," and that his entire "system" of actor training is built exclusively for the triumph of the creative fantasy? What will Komissarzhevsky say if he reads that Stanislavsky does not reduce the play to "three, four, or two particular feelings," as Komissarzhevsky maintains, but to one thing only, although not a *feeling*, but an *action*? This action inspired the author to write the play, and the task of fulfilling it united the actors on all phases of their creative work, down to the very performance. What will Komissarzhevsky say if he reads that, in Stanislavsky's terminology, "the play's through-action" is not the "predominate feeling," or "predominate tone" (as Komissarzhevsky assumes), but rather that the through action is exactly what these simple words indicate? It is the action that runs through the entire play.

Is it fair to subject to criticism a huge part of Stanislavsky's teaching on emotions when only the single term "emotional memory" reached one's ears? How can one begin by guessing at the essence of this term ("If we presume that Stanislavsky uses the term 'emotional memory' in the sense," etc., says Komissarzhevsky) and then proceed to prove this essence absurd? What is the purpose of this, and what is to be gained

---

1   Vakhtangov refers to Komissarzhevsky's book *An Actor's Creativity and Stanislavsky's Theory* (1916).

by it? Would it not be simpler to wait until Stanislavsky himself says what he wants and how he wants it?

A book criticizing a teaching and appearing before the teaching itself is pointless if only because its references to the teaching, to quotations and terms, may prove ridiculously unjustified. What if it suddenly turns out that the criticized book contains no such statements, definitions or terms, or (worse still) that these terms mean something else rather than what the critic implied?

A critical review published before the appearance of the criticized material may and must be dismissed lightheartedly, with good humor and cheer. It makes me somewhat sad, however, when I encounter, in a magazine article, an attempt to give a summarized account of the practical part of the teaching, penned by someone who was introduced to the teaching directly by the teacher. It is sad because the dry formulas of a summary will never give the full voice to that which is dear and precious, was obtained through extraordinary creative intuition and brought much enlightenment and joy. A summary without a book never gives much, since it excludes the opportunity to reference the book. It leaves a chaotic impression, unless it is compiled according to the plan and system of the book itself. The practical part of the book is bound to suffer the most in a summary. This is especially true when things described in the practical part, due to their delicate structure, require a detailed, clear, and exhaustive presentation.

Volume 2–3 of the *Gorn* magazine, published by Proletkul't,[2] features an article entitled "On the Stanislavsky System." I know the talented author of this article well. I know his keen sense and understanding of Stanislavsky's teaching. I believe in his good intentions in writing this article, and yet I cannot help but reproach him.

Not for the form, not for the absence of a logical plan, not for the lack of system—those cannot be achieved anyway in a short article. I cannot help but reproach him for conveying the particulars isolated from general principles and for pointing out details of the practical part without stipulating overall goals, fundamentals, or an overall plan.

If one can give an account of the teaching before the author himself does so, such an account can only be written in a form of a general overview. An account of a purely practical part, based on a strict

---

2   Proletkul't (Proletarian Culture) was a literary and cultural educational organization that functioned between 1917 and 1920. Its goal was to create the proletarian culture in Russia and to instigate the creative activities of the masses.

systematic assimilation, might be harmful to those who take it as a manual for practical work onstage. One cannot learn from a book how to write poetry, fly an airplane, and develop in oneself the abilities an actor must have; even less so can one instruct in a book how to teach stage art.

Michael Chekhov, the author of the article in question, promises in his introduction to say two things: "what is the system, how it was created and why actors need it—this is first; and second, how those who call themselves enemies and adversaries of Stanislavsky's theory view his system."

A brilliant and quite thorough plan. It would be so if ... Michael Chekhov would not break it from his opening line. He did not tell what the system is, and he mentioned nothing of how it was created. Yet many exciting things can be written about this with love and care. Instead, Chekhov, above and beyond his promise, relates at great length how to work with a student and what the student should do.

If this is a practical guide, it does not reach its goal, for the practical part of Stanislavsky's teaching cannot be explained in three to four magazine pages. This would take several volumes (I am not exaggerating). If this is an introduction to the system for those uninitiated, these persons receive a false and inaccurate impression of it, due to the sketchiness of the information.

Even if this is a summary, it is simply incorrect as it is not systematized and far removed from the historically formed plan life itself has developed. The system is called a system when everything in it is systematically consistent. If it is an exposition of Stanislavsky's teaching, then what does it have to do with the practical advice to students and their instructor that takes up three-quarters of the article?

Finally, I was quite disappointed by Michael Chekhov's statement that he intends to give a "complete and detailed exposition" of Stanislavsky's system.

I imagine that only the person who created this system can give a "complete and detailed exposition." I imagine that any exposition of the system by a third party is bound to suffer from a lack of such "completeness." I imagine that the author of the article "On the Stanislavsky System" won't be upset with me if I permit myself to doubt the wisdom and timeliness of any exposition of Stanislavsky's teaching before Stanislavsky himself publishes his work.

March 1919. A slightly edited version of this article appeared in *Vestnik Teatra*, 1919, No. 14. The original version is featured in the *Sourcebook*. First English translation of Vakhtangov's article appeared in Vendrovskaya and Kaptereva 1982.

Part VI

From Director's Diaries

Toward the Theatre of Mystery

21 On the Production of Hauptmann's *The Festival of Peace*

Notes in the Director's Script

The Buchners reconcile ... Firmly. With confidence. At the end of the first act, and at the beginning of the second, the audience should trust them. At the moment when everyone gathers by the Christmas tree, the audience must feel gratitude toward the Buchners, who have done such a great deed so well. [This is necessary] so that the first outburst [of the Scholz family scandal] at the Christmas party would affect me—the audience—scare me and inspire my apprehension and disappointment, as well as my desire to rush to the Buchners' aid.

Everyone who desires to be pleasant always puts you off by his very desire to be pleasant.

An actor who possesses natural-born pleasantness must use it (seek himself in the role), instead of seeking outside of himself.

From the Director's Diary

JANUARY 31, 1913

4th [rehearsal]

The following things are important to me:

- The Buchners are guests.
- Augusta is lonely.
- Ida and her mother do not yet notice the squabbling and consider this an insignificant mundane occurrence, the kind that can happen in our family too.
- Frau Scholz is conceited, but inclined to work.
- Friebe is an artist; he revels in his work.
- The general atmosphere of the scene: they are waiting, very anxious, hurriedly make arrangements for the [William's] arrival.
- Festival.

FEBRUARY 6 [1913]

7th rehearsal

We did the scene three times, ending with Fritz's arrival. Searched for [Michael] Chekhov's [role of Friebe] characterization.

FEBRUARY 7 [1913]

8th rehearsal

We discovered gentleness for Mrs. Buchner.

For Friebe we discovered some of the characterization (he is all soggy, watery-eyed, an ape, bandy-legged) [see Figure 17].

FEBRUARY 14 [1913]

11th rehearsal

By all means we must find an external characterization for Frau Scholz. She should proceed from the grumbler.

For Friebe—his meeting [with his master, Fritz Scholz] ...

Lidiya Ivanovna [Deykun] [role of Frau Scholz] should totally rid herself of her own manner. It consists of some kind of stillness and

Figure 17
Michael Chekhov as Friebe and Grigory Khmara as Fritz Scholz in *The Festival of Peace*, 1913. © Bakhrushin State Central Theatre Museum.

theatrical vigilance; overall, it is something completely vague and unnecessary.

FEBRUARY 20 [1913]

16th rehearsal

Scholz needs gentleness. Take out all theatrical tension ...
  In 2–3 rehearsals we must start blocking.
  The whole of the first act has been analyzed.

ACT I

Christmas Eve. They are waiting.
Family scene. [Frau] Buchner reconciles.
He [William] might arrive any minute.
Like a bolt from the blue.
Impression of the arrival.
A mess. ("This one [Robert] is starting at it too")
[Frau] Buchner acts.
Robert alone, takes off the mask.
(Vivacity.)

FEBRUARY 25 [1913]

21st rehearsal

Robert and Augusta go back and forth between quarreling and making peace ...
  Rehearsal went very well. Everyone was concentrated and free. We did quite a lot. It is interesting to watch.

FEBRUARY 26 [1913]

22nd rehearsal

We discovered the scene between Friebe and Scholz.
  Since the text is very vague, I find that it can be improvised in a form of a monologue, interrupted by Mrs. Scholz when she feels like it.

MARCH 1 [1913]

24th rehearsal

Boleslavsky [role of William] should stop playing "fingernails." Stop playing child-like hands.

He should not play a village lunatic. I stopped him from playing a baby, playing naivety.

Everything should be deeper and more serious.

He should not play the general state of his character.

His character is weak because he wants to be strong. But he fails.

No need playing a weak person.

Friebe should lead the scene as if he resolved to kill himself.

APRIL 3 [1913]

Rehearsal in costumes and makeup

Present are K[onstantin] S[tanislavsky], Leopold Antonovich [Sulerzhitsky], and those young actors from the theatre troupe who responded to the open rehearsal announcement.

After the rehearsal K. S. made his comments. Overall he approved of what was done so far, and he gave guidance for the future work.

AUTUMN 1913

A few days after the [season] gathering of the troupe, we continued our work on *The Festival of Peace* …

I broadened the actors' tasks. I made transitions between the bits more vivid. I tried to achieve a **full stop** following every bit. I changed interpretations of some moments in the play for almost every performer. I freshened the tasks by introducing new adaptations …

We are yet to manage well the end of the II act; it requires enormous, 100 percent effort and concentration.

Transitions between the scenes are still vague, one scene overlaps with another; we rush too much.

I plan to dedicate several final rehearsals to the end of the II act.

I am striving to achieve a buildup throughout the play, from one bit to the next.

NOVEMBER 13, 1913

The dress rehearsal

Present are K[onstantin] S[tanislavsky], Leopold Antonovich [Sulerzhitsky], and the troupe.

After the rehearsal K. S. made general comments, without mentioning details.

22 On the Production of Berger's *The Deluge*

Director's Notes

JANUARY 18, 1915

On the [role of the] actor.

Lonely. A bit overly familiar. Says his monologue gloomily, without bravado. About thirty-five. Ten years on the stage.

JANUARY 19, 1915

They are all wolves to one another.

Not a drop of compassion. Not a drop of attention. Everyone looks after his own profit. They snatch [it] out of each other's hands. Disconnected. Drowning in business.

Among them, O'Neil has a reputation as a queer fish, but "a smart man." One can sense wisdom in his words.

Frazer lost his fortune.

Beer is about to marry a rich woman for her money. [He is] Consumed by the desire to profit.

Nothing human is left in them. And this is not just today; this is how it is every day, their entire life.

For O'Neil, only bread is sacred (deep meaning—labor, invested in the bread).

[On the role of] Frazer. I don't have a cent to my name, and this scoundrel[1] is now richer than me. I pounce at everything to ease my heart and vent my anger—to take it out on somebody.

Act II is all repentance.

---

1 In this "inner monologue" of Frazer's, "improvised" by Vakhtangov, Frazer is referring to his chief rival, Beer, as "this scoundrel."

Joy and tender emotion. Everyone is cleansed. Everyone is truthful. The humanity in them floated up onto the surface. Crabs, and sea monsters stuck to the human being, got unstuck. The human cleansed through his love for another human. Let's die together. As we hold each other's hands. They opened their souls to each other.

[Michael] Chekhov should take out the vaudeville.

Richard [Boleslavsky][2] must be constantly reminded that he must find the serious Boleslavsky.

In Act II, I should strive to achieve from Geirot the kind of Geirot who cast off everything Geirot-like. Otherwise he will not be simple and sincere.[3]

Baklanova[4] should be as she is.

Geirot should speak in a simple voice.

[The character of] O'Neil—scoffs at himself and everyone else.

[Act] II

Richard [Boleslavsky] should say the monologue about himself without a jest. [He should] withdraw into his shell. He felt his guilt. I am drowning. His hands dropped. Oh, if only I could cry … If only I could ease my heart. Alone, I am alone … Wise man, who is tired of suffering, surrounded by such miserable, shallow people.

Committing his speech to memory is a must.

[Act] II

Chekhov should listen to his feelings.

[They are all] disheveled, uncombed, neckties came out from their vests. They straighten all this in Act III.

[The character of] Frazer. Wants to live more than anyone else. [See Figure 18.]

[I must] speak to Leopold Antonovich [Sulerzhitsky] about set models.

Going over your lines before rehearsal.

2   Richard Boleslavsky was replaced by Grigory Khmara in the role of O'Neil later in the rehearsal process.
3   Aleksandr Geirot (1882–1947), member of the First Studio of the MAT from 1913, performed the part of Beer in Vakhtangov's production.
4   Olga Baklanova (1893–1974), member of the First Studio, performed the character of Lizzi in Vakhtangov's production.

Figure 18
Vakhtangov as Frazer in *The Deluge*, 1915. © Bakhrushin State Central Theatre Museum.

MARCH 11, 1915

Fast tempo should not come from rushing.

The black man should not be anxious or embarrassed.

I should wean Smyshlyayev[5] from the false tempo of speech.

An American is prompt, but not in a hurry.

The mundane becomes the spiritual: all people live with only one thing (telegraph).[6] Relationships—losers and winners.

Frazer has fits [of anger] every time he remembers [the injustice]. He cannot calm down.

Charlie [Smyshlyayev] forgot that he is curious. Obliging boy, friendly, talkative. Interested in bar keeping.

They are forced to wait for the rain to stop; an American is not used to sitting without business.

Vaudeville is disappearing from Misha's [Michael Chekhov's] acting ([his character's motto now became:] "I may be bankrupt, but I am an honest bankrupt").

She [Lizzi] is anxious—incorrect inner state—take out the smile.

Remind [the actors] what they act this play for. Talk about the kernel. Act II is the central act: humans. Acts I and III: the animalistic in men.

---

5   Valentin Smyshlyayev (1891–1936), Russian actor and director, served at the MAT First Studio from 1913. Smyshlyayev performed the character of Charlie in *The Deluge*.

6   In Berger's play, as the deluge subsides, the news is being delivered to the characters gathered at the bar via telegraph.

[Actors] should not feel free to approximate their lines.

Rehearsal is a search of [the creative] state in the play—from the actors' **perspective**. In early rehearsals—a structure is outlined—from the director's perspective.

DECEMBER 13, 1915

Tomorrow is the first performance of *The Deluge*. The play I took close to heart, the play I loved, the play that burned in me, the play I felt, and, most importantly, the play I knew how to convey to the audience.

And then came other people: Sulerzhitsky and Stanislavsky; they came, crudely forced themselves onto the play, insensitively trampled upon everything mine, bossed around, without asking me, cut it and axed it.

And I am indifferent to *The Deluge*.

It is alien to me and cold.

Indifferent, strangely calm, I look at the orchard hacked by an axe.

I feel no pain. I feel no regret.

I just want to be silent. Silently silent.

From the First Studio of the MAT *Book of Impressions*

SEPTEMBER 21, 1916

The Deluge[7]

I was out of luck. I watched the performance when you "acted."

Forced me to accept your characters.

Persistently tried to convince me that you are *this* kind of a person, not *that* kind of a person.

You played the shadows of the past.

Feebly and palely.

The first act seemed unnecessary, long, empty, and unpleasant.

The stage pattern of the second act helped me guess what it should have been.

The third act was well acted.

The following actors had clear through lines: Smyshlyayev. He had both tasks and spontaneity. (No need to swagger when drunk, better not to swagger at all in the second act.)

---

7   The section preceding this entry is featured on pp. 108–9.

Zeland[8] is good. (In the third act keep your eyes fixed on the telephone longer. You have a good face in that moment.[9])

Baklanova only [has a through line] in the first act.

In the second act she does not have the right to change the essential part of the blockings: this breaks the entirety of the scene, its sculptural finish, so to speak.

On Sushkevich, I want to agree with Bromley.[10]

Geirot must talk to K[onstantin]. S[tanislavsky]. about the second act.

He is so cold that I don't know how to inspire his passion, or what could inspire it.

Bondarev[11] and Lazarev[12] are doing well.

A lot should be written about Chekhov and Khmara.[13]

I would rather talk to them in person on an occasion.

They disappointed me most of all. They both act well. But they act so very wrong.

Misha, despite himself, turns it all into a farce.

I don't think (not even for a second) that he does this deliberately; I know how seriously he approaches his role.

It upsets me even more. I myself play the same role and, probably, a thousand times worse than him, but may this circumstance not silence me, and may I be permitted to say all this.

I badly want us to find a day we could dedicate entirely to [the rehearsal of] *The Deluge*.

OCTOBER, 1916

Geirot, each performance is a *new* performance.[14]

---

8 Dmitry Zeland (d. 1922), an actor at the First Studio of the MAT from 1914. Zeland performed the role of the Customer in *The Deluge*.

9 Vakhtangov must be referring to the actor being free from the "facial mask"; such freedom results in strong emotional radiation.

10 In the preceding First Studio's *Book of Impressions* entry, Nadezhda Bromley wrote about Sushkevich's performance as Stratton: "Sushkevich is much more moving and truthful than in the dress rehearsal."

11 Aleksey Bondarev (1882–?), an actor at the MAT and its First Studio from 1908 to 1924. Bondarev performed the role of the actor Gugins in *The Deluge*.

12 Ivan Lazarev (1877–1929), an actor at the First Studio of the MAT, performed the role of the inventor Nordling in *The Deluge*.

13 Grigory Khmara performed the character of O'Neil in *The Deluge*.

14 Grigory Khmara commented on Aleksandr Geirot's lack of creative mood, as well as his passive attitude toward his creative work. Aleksandr Geirot defended himself: "Suppose an artist would be forced to paint the same painting day after day, what kind of creative mood would he be in?" Vakhtangov's comment is written in response to Geirot's statement.

23 On the Production of Maeterlinck's *The Miracle of Saint Anthony* (First Variant)[1]

From the Notebook

JANUARY 11, 1917

During *Anthony*, [the audience must always be cheerful.][2] We must make sure that they feel Maeterlinck's smile: kindhearted and pleasant, without a trace of malice. Maeterlinck addresses this smile to his characters, the people he single-handedly put into such a peculiar situation.

Let us suppose that St. Anthony did come to these [rich] heirs. Let us suppose that this miracle did occur. How would these people respond to it—after all, that they are religious and just prayed for the deceased?

Naturally, they would not believe [in the saint] ... They would certainly turn him out, and they would certainly feel humiliated. But the miracle did occur, whether they wanted it or not. Here, they can see it with their own eyes: the deceased old woman is alive. How will they take it now—these petty, ridiculous people? It is so clear: if a dead person has risen, this must be God's doing; for as long as this earth exists, people do not know another force, except for the power of God, a force that could resurrect the dead.

Naturally, these people do not believe that he is a saint. Certainly, she never really died, since she is alive. Certainly, something is fishy.

Nevertheless, they are certainly grateful to this strange man.

But he wants nothing in return. Strange people—these "saints." How do we repay them? Give them money, treat them to a cigar, present

---

1   Rehearsal records for both variants of this production can be found on pp. 257–81.
2   Text in square brackets is missing in Vakhtangova et al. 1939, in Vendrovskaya 1959, and in Vendrovskaya and Kaptereva 1982. It has been restored in Vendrovskaya and Kaptereva 1984.

them with a necktie or a pipe ... All this seems too modern-sounding, spiritually deprived, and awkward. What is this?

At this gentleman's order, Auntie stopped talking and lost her tongue.

Oh, this is blackmail; this is something criminal. We must call the police. And the police arrive—the only powerful tool people have to protect against crooks, drunks, madmen, and blackmailers, when their impudence reaches the limit. Just think: not only do these people pose as saints, they also act as saints, as far as performing miracles. This is too much. In such a case, we must go all the way.

True, calling the police is inviting a scandal ... But in this case we have been left no choice.

24 On the Production of Ibsen's *Rosmersholm*

What I Would Like to Achieve in *Rosmersholm*

1 In acting.
2 In stage furniture, sets and blockings.
3 In the interpretation.
4 In the main line [or through line] of the play, in connection with the play's content.
5 In bits of the play.
6 In the general atmosphere.
7 In the impression upon the audience.
8 In the characters.
9 In the performance.
10 In rehearsals.

Actors

Naturally, I would like to achieve what I consider to be the ideal for every actor. It is impossible to define this top achievement in a few words.

I consider that the most important thing is to create conditions that would allow the actor to preserve, in full measure, "his own individuality."[1] Under these conditions, the actor entering the stage would not know at all how a particular line, or even a segment of his role, might sound today. Not even approximately. I want the actor to remain completely faithful[2] and calm, to remain himself all the way through, in blood and thought, and, whenever possible, to refrain from using makeup. He should only slightly emphasize the important

---

1 Meaning "creative individuality."
2 On Vakhtangov's concept of "stage faith," see Introduction, p. 25.

features on his face and de-emphasize the ones that interfere [with the right image]. Why can't Rosmer, the character, have the face of the actor Khmara? Why can't the character of Kroll look like the actor Lazarev? Why can't Rebecca be exactly like Olga Knipper-Chekhova? Rebecca is younger than Knipper-Chekhova—that's all. This is the only way in which Knipper-Chekhova's face should be altered, and not by making her look younger, but by masking [subtracting] anything that could age Rebecca. Let's worry less about the wigs. They should be avoided completely. The actor [Leonid] Leonidov does not need one either, even though the author says that his character has long hair.

God-given face, God-given voice. Actors should transform by the power of their inner impulse.

The basic condition will be the actor's *faith* that he, the actor, is put into circumstances and relationships indicated by the author—*he personally* needs what his character needs in the play. Suppose the actor understands his character well. Suppose he *understands* that the steps specified by the author are the only logical steps. Then, suppose the actor finds the very idea of living in these circumstances *tempting* and comes to *love* (without sympathizing) something about the play and his character. Finally, suppose the actor becomes *convinced* of things his character is *convinced* of and *feels the necessity* to spend a couple of hours in the atmosphere of Rosmersholm and *prepare for the festivity* that the creative process offers. By doing all that, the actor will be transformed, and, at the same time, he won't lose his own creative individuality in anything.

I do not want the actor to ever perform a particular place of his role the same way, with the same degree of intensity. I want those feelings, and their intensity, to be truthful to today's performance; I want them [feelings] to arise in the actor naturally, on their own accord.

Suppose a particular moment turns out paler than in yesterday's performance. The truthfulness of the moment, of its subconscious logic, will compensate for that paleness. Such a moment would never feel sunken in the generally truthful flow [of the play].

The most awful thing is when an actor tries to repeat yesterday's success, or when he prepares for the climax. [In life,] These climactic moments usually result from [spontaneous] self-expression; in other words, they result from my reaction to the causes that lie outside of myself. The form of this reaction depends on my individuality. In fact, both the form and strength of my emotional response are determined by the fact that I *cannot* possibly react differently to this external cause. How can one possibly prepare for this [reaction], and how can one recall and wish to repeat yesterday's form, however successful it may have been?

I wish that the actors would improvise the entire performance.

After all, they do know who they are, as well as their relationships with other characters; they share [their characters'] thoughts, aspirations and wants. What could be possibly preventing them from living, i.e. engaging in their characters' actions?

Actors must not develop clichés.

Each rehearsal is a new rehearsal.

Each performance is a new performance.

Actors should:

1   know what they are doing on the stage at this particular moment, and why they are doing it;
2   should "have past";
3   in rehearsals, should develop the correct relationships toward other characters in the play;
4   should desire and act in a way specified by the author (it is understood that these desires and actions have to be accepted by the actors as the only ones possible and logical for their given character);
5   should know their lines.

That's all. I maintain this, and I undertake to prove it, if necessary. For the time being, I assume that we, Art Theatre-cultivated artists, take this for granted and *require no proof.*

All rehearsals should be used for:

1   subtle, scrupulous and creative *text analysis* (main idea, subtext);
2   *defining bits and tasks* (what and why);
3   forming relationships (because each rehearsal is a day in the character's life; a series of days forms personality);
4   *organically cultivating within yourself,* for the duration of the rehearsal, the same attitude toward the world, and world outlook, as that of the given character.

To sum up, I see a group of people *prepared*, throughout a series of rehearsals:

• to relate to each other as required;
• to have the pre-curtain "baggage";
• to strive to fulfill their desires;
• to know the inner and outer aspects of the play.

Today this group takes up, for their theatrical festivity, the author's situation and *carries out* their strivings. Each member of the group meets obstacles on their path and tries to overcome them. Some people win, and others lose. Let the winner rejoice because he has won and not because he is supposed to "play" joy.

Let the loser mourn because his desires were not fulfilled, not because he is supposed to "play" grief. Let joy and grief come on their own, at the strength and to the degree that the performer is capable of *today*.

I want actors to be *serious* in these aspirations, instead of pretending to be aspiring. I would like them to organically need what their characters need. *They. Organically. Need.* All three of these words are important and equal.

With calm and conviction, the actors strive toward what's most important for them or, rather, they strive to fulfill their life purpose. By doing this, they transform subconsciously, while the audiences, observing them from the side, define on their own what kind of people these characters are. Actors should not indicate with your behavior onstage: this is who I am, according to my own plan.

I want the actor Khmara to become inspired with the dream of making "all people happy," by awakening in people the desire for happiness.

I want Knipper-Chekhova to support Khmara's dream and help him carry it out and show him the ways to fulfill it (to abandon the Rosmersholm estate, to live, to act, to work).

I want Leonidov, the actor, to feel that now is the time to lay his sacrifice on the altar of emancipation. I want him, while passing by Rosmersholm, to call on his student Khmara and to incite him to the same great step. At Rosmersholm I want him to meet some unfamiliar faces. Or, better yet, he should not anticipate meeting anyone.

I want the actor Lazarev, with all his love and sincerity, to start rescuing his friend Khmara from the claws of this terrible woman who can bewitch anyone—from Knipper-Chekhova.

I would like the actor Cheban[3] to mock Khmara. He should take this opportunity, since Khmara, who ruined Cheban's life, is now also vulnerable to exposure.

---

3   Aleksandr Cheban (1886–1954), First Studio of the MAT actor and director from 1913 until 1936, and then an actor at the MAT. Cheban originally rehearsed the role of Mortensgard. Vakhtangov replaced him with Boris Sushkevich during the rehearsal period.

I want the actress Sheremetyeva[4] to observe all this and actually draw her profound conclusions and make decisions based on what she sees—all this without any predetermination whatsoever.

I don't want the performers to do anything theatrical on the day of the *Rosmersholm* performance; neither do I want them to be called to rehearse other plays on these days.

I want *Rosmersholm* to be performed no more than once a week.

I want actors to love this performance and feel festive when its day comes.

I want actors to await it eagerly, as people await Easter after the Good Friday.

Set, Stage Furniture and Props, Blockings

I cannot imagine painted backdrops, no matter how hard I try.

Neither can I imagine set constructions.

Out of all Moscow Art Theatre designers ([Alexandre] Benois, [Mstislav] Dobuzhinsky [1875–1958]), [Victor] Simov [1858–1935]), Gordon Craig comes the closest [to the ideal].

I imagine heavy, somber, dreadful drapes.

These are not the drapes of the theatre school stage.

Neither are these the abstract drapes.

This is not a "directorial concept."

These drapes are a fact.

They actually exist.

They are the drapes of the Rosmersholm estate.

These drapes are steeped in the centuries; they have their own life and history.

They carry silence and order, austerity and stableness, brutality and unbending will.

These drapes saw Rosmer's great-grandfathers, his grandfathers, and his father. They remember the touch of Beata's tender, helpless hand.

Austere, faded tapestries and portraits have been looking down from these drapes-walls on several generations.

A single will and a single spirit has always reigned here. The only reason these heavy sofas, tables, and armchairs—massive, ancestral, and silent—keep their stillness and don't die of shame for the only

---

4   Anna Sheremetyeva, an actress at the MAT. Sheremetyeva performed the role of Frau Helthes in the production of *Rosmersholm*.

black sheep in the Rosmer family, is that their body is wooden, and they cannot move.

You do feel, though, how gloomily they lowered the eyelids of their soul, and how hopelessly these witnesses to the past grandeur keep their silence.

The drapes, and the antiquity of furniture, gloomily tolerate this frivolous novelty—these vibrant, presumptuous flowers that appeared after the death of their true masters. These flowers never dared to even peek into this darkness and peace before.

Oh, if only the old folk *saw* this …

Large, massive room. Nothing new except flowers. All as it used to be, only now, for some reason, there is joy outside the windows, and the windows are open, and there is a new aroma of gardens and fields mixed with the usual smell of ancient wood and drapes.

When the lamp is lit, it becomes even darker and gloomier in this room. Then the portraits' austere, unmoving eyes sharpen, as they pierce the darkness below the ceiling. They gaze persistently at the bright spot—the circle around the lamp, where only the faces of the new people, excited at something new, can be seen brightly and softly.

Then the sofas and armchairs squeak in their own language. They understand each other.

Then the folds of the ancient drapes rustle and whisper.

When the lamp is lit, the outline of the furniture and the drapes is barely visible. In the narrow field of light—people's faces appear, especially their eyes, and the faint outlines of their clothing; perhaps, the clothing is not even visible. Above them are the piercing eyes of the portraits.

The faces of Rosmer and Rebecca, thin and pale, reflect the subtlest curve of their spirit and thought. Their eyes are horrific and alive with overwhelming desires. They are horrific, because it is terrifying to see such a transformation in an actor. These eyes are joyfully excited, as they are not the eyes of those who lie, but of those who believe.

When this room is filled with light, the drapes and furniture noisily shudder, and the portraits freeze from the bright light, hiding their faces, turning their backs and burying themselves in the walls, corners, and folds. They do it so as not to bare their shame under this insolent upstart light. They do it to block from their senses the new flowers' cursed fragrance.

Never mind, these people will not escape these walls.

Let Rebecca go on knitting: she will knit her own shroud.

Let her water these tasteless red and yellow flowers: she will grow her own funeral wreath.

Let Rosmer neglect his research and his family genealogy: he will either return to them, or die.

Let him spend his days with this sorceress, this alien woman with her shadowy past: he will suffer when he remembers Beata.

Let them believe in their clear conscience—the day will come when these apostates find out what it means to betray us in their forgetfulness.

Let them, pathetic creatures, dream of leaving this house for the so-called active life—they don't know they will meet the white horses.

We already sense the tremulous shadow of their wings.

We already feel their chill and hear them approaching.

This is what Rosmersholm—dead, archaic, stagnant, and vengeful—thinks.

And so Rebecca did make her shroud.

And her flowers did become a funeral bunch.

And Rosmer too walks to his death, as his conscience is no longer unclouded.

The white horses darted past. There is no getting away now …

Now the dead Rosmersholm is triumphant.

The sofas, tables, and armchairs squeak—they can breathe freely now.

The drape folds rustle viciously.

The portraits' eyes gleam.

Praise be to the gods of the past—we have been rid of the evil spirits.

The white horses will take them right now.

They have been crushed, those pathetic, tiny creatures that dared trespass against what is ours …

But what's this?

Why do these people, condemned to death, look so bright and radiant?

Why is this woman so festively clad in her shroud, and why are the flowers in her hands so joyful?

Why does a triumphant Rosmer embrace her, and walk toward the dreadful footbridge so freely, resolutely, and radiantly?

The drapes, the sofas, tables, armchairs, tapestries, and the eyes on the portraits hesitate, confused and frightened, on the very threshold of their intended triumph.

The golden and airy sun shines on their foolish, deceived, frozen faces brighter and bolder than before.

The red and yellow flowers turn their heads joyfully to the window …

Remove the drapes, carry out the furniture, take down the portraits—for *they* have died, *they* are corpses now.

They could not withstand the daring flight.
The white horse had come for *them.*

Interpretation

Brief and simple.
"This is a work of poetry that deals with people and their fate."
Ibsen himself said so.

Rosmersholm stands noble, but hopelessly frozen in its own nobility; instead of creating new life, it relives its days—century after century.

The last, childless leaf of the once powerful family branch—Johannes Rosmer—lives out his days in this house. Rosmer lives with his pale and gentle, morbidly passionate wife, Beata.

Rosmer's mind, that was just beginning to awaken under Ulrich Brendel's influence, was silenced. Now Rosmer sits, humble and quiet, over his books of family trees and genealogy.

Apparently he is a bad husband, since this strange Beata always leaves him disappointed.

Yes, he cannot return her sensuality.

Yes, she suffers because of it. But so does he.

Otherwise, things are quiet and peaceful, as always.

And then enters Rebecca.

She is attracted to this aristocrat-pastor.

Wild woman that she is, she must get what she wants. But the minister does not see her passionate eyes and does not understand her few daring, provocative, yet seemingly casual words.

He trustingly initiates her into the world of his thoughts. He trustingly accepts her novel books; he is trustingly inflamed with alien feelings. What Ulrich Brendel planted in him long ago is reawakened. He is ablaze with ideas that had never occurred to him before. He shares this new blossoming of his heart with Rebecca nobly and gently.

Rebecca is conquered. Her personal desires vanish on their own. Rosmer's lofty spirit ennobled her.

She is now dreaming with him.

She awakens Rosmer's confidence that he can and must carry out his dreams.

Rosmer must leave Rosmersholm and seize his life by the horns.

What should be done about Beata?

She is a weight around his neck.

Rebecca disposes of her in her own way, which she does not regard as sinful.

Now Rosmer is free; he can go.

She will help him.

The first thing he must do is explain to his old friends, represented by Kroll, that he is no longer one of them.

This is not an easy thing for Rosmer.

Accidental and fatal visit—a call from his former teacher Brendel, a passive dreamer like Rosmer. Brendel breaks with his solitude (spiritual Rosmersholm); he is on his way to "seize life by the horns."

No, now is not the time to waver.

He should immediately follow Rebecca's persuasion.

He tells these frightening words to Kroll.

Kroll is stunned; he left upset and agitated.

This was to be expected. But Rosmer will convince them all, and they will understand him.

Rebecca knows, though, what this breakup means and what will follow it.

She secures a backup support from Mortensgard. True, he is a dishonest man, but does it matter that the means are impure when they bring about the triumph of truth?

Kroll, before he left, recalled Beata and the white horses.

Mortensgard, before he left, reminded Rosmer of Beata.

Rosmer began to waver. Rebecca must hurry. She must rescue the situation, quick, quick.

Otherwise, the spiritual child born of their spiritual union will perish.

But Rosmer cannot be saved: he is poisoned with remorse (as he puts it), for he summoned the white horse that came for Beata.

Weakened by her shadowy past, Rebecca despairs of breaking the Rosmersholm-bred notion of conscience.

She has nothing left to do but relieve Rosmer's soul of its burden and tell him who summoned the white horses.

"Rosmer, it was I who killed Beata. Now your conscience is clear. Go alone into the new world."

So Rebecca has been deceiving him. She wormed her way in here for her personal gain, killed Beata, enticed him, and now calls him away.

He can no longer trust her with anything.

Back to his friends, old and trusted.

Back to the old days.

And he did go back. And he repented.

Where will this awful woman go now?

"Some place, it doesn't matter to her."

"And what about him?"

"He will kill himself for he does not want to live like that—being unable to ennoble men."

Why did she do all this?

"I loved you, Rosmer."

"I don't believe you."

"I desired you, passionately."

"What are you saying?"

"You ennobled me, and my desires vanished."

"That can't be true, I can't ennoble anyone."

"You ennobled me."

"Prove it."

"How do you want me to prove it?"

"Follow Beata."

"Joyfully."

If this is so, then he can believe her.

"Yes, that is so."[5]

"Then we shall die together!"

"We won't be able to live—you with your past and me with mine. If we went on living, we would be defeated. We would go on living, condemned by the living and the dead."

"But I have a new outlook: we are our own judges, and I will let no one, living or dead, triumph over me."

"Joy ennobles the soul, Rebecca."

"We shall die joyfully."

---

5   From this point on, it is impossible to discern which one of the characters speaks a particular line of the improvised final dialogue between Rebecca and Rosmer. I call it improvised, because these are not exactly Ibsen's lines; they don't necessarily come in the order Ibsen put them, and some of them are contributed by Vakhtangov. These lines, probably, represent Vakhtangov's idea of the subtext for the final dialogue between Rebecca and Rosmer. There is another possible explanation as to why Vakhtangov did not record which character speaks which line. It is possible that, according to Vakhtangov's idea, by the end of the play Rosmer and Rebecca, who stand on the verge of special knowing, merge into one spirit; in such a case, it is almost impossible to distinguish which one of their voices speaks a particular thought. In Ibsen's play, when Rebecca asks Rosmer, "First tell me this. Are you following me, or am I following you?," he replies, "We will never be able to sort this out entirely." And Rebecca agrees with this view. *Rosmersholm* is not the only performance directed by Vakhtangov where a man and a woman are able to achieve spiritual liberation, or new life, through a complete merger of their entities. This also happens to Ida and William in the final scene of *The Festival of Peace*, with Lizzi and Beer in the second act of *The Deluge*, and, most notably, with Hannan and Lea in the famous *Dybbuk*. As pointed out in the Introduction, Vakhtangov's philosophy was a monistic philosophy, so he probably did view man and woman as a part of one whole that can only achieve its completeness and liberation, or new life, through merger.

"You have the joy now."

"So do I."

"To keep it, we must die."

And so they die.

That is the play's interpretation in a brief and intentionally shallow form.

Some may say this is not an interpretation but a synopsis.

Not true, it is an interpretation. It is true that it revealed nothing new and extraordinary other than what the author intended.

The author, however, intended nothing more than this.

If you read Miss Appolonskaya's interpretation,[6] you won't find the play's content there. She *explains* that Rosmer represents Christianity, while Rebecca is paganism, while the footbridge is the border that joins them, etc. All of it is contrived, and all of it is untrue. Anything at all can be concocted this way.

The author says, this is a work of poetry *that deals with people and their fate.*

No symbols whatsoever.

Striving for it [new life].

This is, roughly, the play's through action.

Not the striving, even, but the very act of carrying out this striving in order to achieve the goal.

Rosmer must want the new life (and know his old life).

And so must Rebecca. The through action of their roles cannot be defined without this desire.

Rosmer's through action is to closely listen to his conscience and keep it pure.Rebecca's through action is to maintain Rosmer's faith in the purity of his conscience (at all costs), even at the cost of self-sacrifice.

The Play's Bits

They depend, of course, on the main line of the play, on its through action.

A bit must be defined as a phase on the journey that brings the goal of the through action nearer to its conclusion.

The through action: fulfilling the striving for new life.

Therefore, *the major* bits, based on the main action, are:

---

6 Inna Apollonskaya (Stravinskaya) (1876–1970), Russian actress, director, and author. Vakhtangov refers to her book *Ibsen's Theatre* (1910).

1   Rosmer announces his "defection," influenced by Rebecca.
2   Rosmer doubts the cause of Beata's death. Rebecca tries to put his suspicions to sleep.
3   Rebecca reveals her sin, so that Rosmer does not doubt [the purity of his conscience].
4   Rosmer and Rebecca cannot carry out their plans.
5   Rosmer and Rebecca triumph by their death.

These are the five *major* moments; they determine the five *major* bits.

The major bits are supported by auxiliary bits.

This clarifies the meaning of bits such as Kroll's arrival, Brendel's arrival, the second arrival of Kroll, Mortensgard's arrival, Kroll's third arrival, and the second appearance of Brendel.

Let the audience arrive at their own general conclusions. This is the life of [two] souls, striving toward beauty and dying with joy, to the amazement of all Rosmersholm.

The Main Line (or Through Line) of the Play

The main line of the play must be sought in Rosmer and Rebecca's relationship. It is not Rosmer who propels the play. It is not his striving that determines the play's through action.

Nor does Rebecca propel the play. Nor does her striving determine the play's through action.

The through line of the play is in the two of them fulfilling their striving for new life.

Fulfilling being the key word.

This fulfillment is necessary in order to achieve the new life.

Under Rebecca's influence, Rosmer conceived a thought that men could be made happy if one was to arouse their desire to "free their minds and purify their wills."

Rebecca enticed Rosmer to take up this role: awakening people's minds.

The question arose before Rosmer: Can he do this? After all, this would require a pure conscience that is free of sin. He ended up answering, "Yes, I can, for my conscience is clear. Then Rebecca encourages him to act. He must go and carry this out, and in order to do this, he must first proclaim his new beliefs and leave his conservative circle.

Rosmer carries this out.

Then Rebecca persuades Rosmer that he must make connections with Mortensgard, for Kroll will take revenge, and Rosmer must be able to defend himself.

Kroll's statement convinces Rosmer that Rebecca is right, so he starts making connections with Mortensgard.

But Kroll and Mortensgard said something that shook Rosmer's confidence in the purity of his conscience.

The question arises: how did Beata die?

It must be answered: otherwise, this sin is on Rosmer, and without a clear conscience he cannot go to people as a preacher of the [spiritual] cleansing.

And he implements the solution that would answer this "question."

Rebecca sees Rosmer's entire thought process, as it unfolds in his head; she distracts him, acting on him by the power of her conviction. She reminds him of their beautiful dreams about a life together, and urges him to be sensible, showing him the path he should take—in short, she distracts him from his thoughts. For their common sake, she tries to keep Rosmer's conscience undisturbed.

Rosmer did not find his answer.

Rebecca has one more means of influencing Rosmer, provided that he does not stop upon his way: to reveal the truth.

She does it, for their common sake.

He can be on his way now—she will remove herself.

Broken, Rosmer rejects his desires to build a new life, for he no longer believes Rebecca and, consequently, does not believe in their mutual conclusions.

He will believe, if she proves [it] by her death.

Rebecca will do this too, to realize their common goal.

But now Rosmer can no longer go to the people: he has a sinful past.

They must die to redeem their sin.

They must die joyfully, for joy ennobles the soul.

And so they both carry this out.

They did not succeed in achieving their main goal, but they did work to carry it out.

The relationship between Rosmer and Rebecca should be stressed with particular clarity in every main bit.

Every auxiliary bit should concentrate on [their] point of view on Kroll, Mortensgard, and Brendel.

The bits of the roles now depend on the play's main and auxiliary bits.

The main bits of all the roles must lie in the play's main bits, and the auxiliary bits of every role—in the auxiliary bits of the play.

The main idea behind the main bit of a role must not be diluted by the auxiliary ideas behind the other bits. The performer should know well what, in his performance, is of the essential and what is of an incidental nature. As for things incidental, the performer should utilize them to support the main idea.

The essential is what the performance cannot do without.

Everything auxiliary could be cut (one should not do it, of course) without detriment to the essential.

1918.

Notes in the Director's Script

Ibsen is dramaturgically sound.

1   The question of naturalness.
2   Why does the Studio need *Rosmersholm*?

[A question] for the character of Kroll: Where is his passion directed?
    Try to achieve the following:

- appropriating the words;
- no overacting;
- inner characterization;
- accentuating the units.

Without that, the audience is submerged into a dream. This would not be a theatrical impression. Expressive means connected with diction [illegible]. Other means are [one degree] below.

Revealing the facts.

Strong theatrical diction is important.

The play begins with something bothersome for the conservative circles. Kroll dominates. He is extremely agitated.

To [simply] *live* with this emotion is not truthful.

Emotion keeps mum, roars with laughter, yells, kisses.

Ah, this is so funny—this is from the realm of emotion.

I hate you so, I am ready to strangle you—from the realm of emotion.

Hurrah—emotion itself.

[Emotion is only present] [w]here it exists articulately.

When any drama is staged, an actor instinctively searches and strives for the emotion. One must know the realm of emotions perfectly.

Selfless love. What kind of selfless love?

Spontaneous passion, for 2–3 seconds.

To be useful to people (altruism).

Unsatisf[action], that is carried forth.

I must do everything to make Khmara enchanting.

Actors must do less walking.

And more sitting.

Ibsen suffers primarily because theatres don't approach him from the standpoint of giant, boulder-like, characters.

During the next stage of the work, we must discover something that would impart poetic form to the play.

Brendel remembers an idea of Rosmer; he remembers him as one would remember an aroma.

The through action is something of a hurricane that blows away everything in its path, including Rosmer.

Rebecca possesses a revolutionary spirit, and it inflames Rosmer.

1918. (Ivanov 2011)

From the Diaries

APRIL 13, 1918

Today we had the first dress rehearsal of *Rosmersholm*. The Art Theatre was watching. Leonidov got sick, and I suddenly had to step in for him as Brendel. My work of two years is finished.

How much have I lived through ... Onward, onward!

Part VII

Vakhtangov at the MAT and its First Studio

25 On the Inception of the First Studio of the MAT

From Notebooks

MARCH 4, 1911

Conversation with Vladimir Nemirovich-Danchenko

[NEMIROVICH:] Please take a seat. Well, what would you like to receive from us, and what would you like to give us?

[VAKHTANGOV:] I would like to receive everything I can; as for giving—I never even thought about that.

[NEMIROVICH:] What exactly do you want?

[VAKHTANGOV:] I want to learn the work of the director.

[NEMIROVICH:] Just in the directing field then?

[VAKHTANGOV:] No, I will do everything you let me.

[NEMIROVICH:] How long have you been interested in theatre?

[VAKHTANGOV:] Always. Consciously, I started working eight years ago.

[NEMIROVICH:] Eight years? What did you do?

[VAKHTANGOV:] I have a little experience: I acted, directed in amateur groups; I teach at one school; I studied a lot with Leopold Sulerzhitsky, and I have been to Paris with him.

[NEMIROVICH:] Really? What did you do there?

[VAKHTANGOV:] Assisted Leopold Antonovich [Sulerzhitsky] a bit.

[NEMIROVICH:] This is all well, but you ask too much.

[VAKHTANGOV:] ?

[NEMIROVICH:] I pay Boleslavsky 50 rubles. I can offer you 40 rubles.

[VAKHTANGOV:] I am quite satisfied with 40 rubles.

[NEMIROVICH:] Let's do this: from March 15 to August 10 you will be getting 40 rubles, and then time will tell. We will get acquainted in a practical way.

[VAKHTANGOV:] Thank you.

This is all.

MARCH 10, 1911

I received my first summons from the MAT.[1]

MARCH 11, 1911

First conversation with K. S. Stanislavsky. Suler[zhitsky] introduced me to Konstantin Sergeyevich [Stanislavsky].
"Your last name?"
"Vakhtangov."
"Glad to make your acquaintance. I heard a lot about you."

MARCH 12, 1911

I graduated from the [Adashev Theatre] School.

MARCH 14, 1911

A meeting at the theatre on the Cabbage Party.[2] K. S. Stanislavsky to me:
"I heard that Vakhtangov does Vasya [Vasily] Kachalov quite well. Perhaps, you will do an imitation of sorts?"

MARCH 15, 1911

I am officially taken on as an associate at the Moscow Art Theatre. K. S. Stanislavsky's second lecture. K. S. to me, having looked through my notes of his first lecture:
"Good job. When did you manage? You are a stenographer."

MARCH 24, 1911

A party at Adashev's.
Stanislavsky's third talk.

---

1   On March 10, 1911, Vakhtangov made a stenographic record of the first lecture Stanislavsky delivered to the Studio.
2   A cabbage party, or *kapustnik*, is an MAT New Year and Lent tradition. The company would gather, usually following an evening performance, to perform semi-improvised scenes, usually of a burlesque nature. MAT actors, these priests of high art, entirely transformed in *kapustnik* evenings. *Kapustniks* provided necessary psychological release to the MAT troupe. Vakhtangov first came to the attention of the MAT elders as an actor in a *kapustnik* evening. MAT *kapustniks* evolved into a professional cabaret company, Chauve-Souris, where Vakhtangov collaborated as director. See September 6, 1911, diary entry on p. 231 and Introduction, p. 46.

APRIL 12, 1911

I don't want any names in the theatre. I don't want the audience being able to sort out their sensations while still at the theatre. I want them to take their sensations home; I want sensations to linger. This is only achievable if performers (not actors) in the course of a play expose their souls to each other truthfully (with new adaptations for every performance). We must expel theatre from theatre. We must expel an actor from a play. We must expel makeup, costume.

APRIL 15, 1911

I want to form a studio where we would learn. The [main] principle: we must accomplish everything on our own. Everyone is a leader. We must test K[onstantin] S[tanislavsky]'s system on ourselves. Accept it, or reject it. Correct it, complete it, or take out the false. Everyone who enters the studio must love art in general and the art of the stage in particular. We must seek joy in our creative process. We must forget the audience. We must create for our own sake. Draw pleasure from our own work. And we must be our own judges. From day one, I plan to institute lessons in plasticity, voice, and fencing. Lectures in the history of art and costume. Once a week we will listen to music (invite musicians). Here we will carry all the fruits of our thoughts, all our exciting discoveries: humorous sketches, musical pieces, short plays.

AUGUST 3, 1911

K. S. asked me to form a group among the Moscow Art Theatre troupe and start training them in his system.

AUGUST 4, 1911

K. S. suggested that I develop training exercises.

AUGUST 5, 1911

K. S. promised a space for the training, and the required finances. He assigned me to stage a few scenes (miniatures, excerpts) and show him.

AUGUST 7, 1911

At the *Hamlet* rehearsal K. S. assigned me to oversee Tezavrovsky[3] and Bersenev[4] doing exercises.[5]

AUGUST 8, 1911

I have been to Nemirovich to talk about my position at the theatre and about my honorarium.

AUGUST 9, 1911

K. S. told me, "Work. If anyone says a word, I will tell him: goodbye. I need a new theatre. Let's act in secret. Don't mention my name."

AUGUST 14, 1911

Stanislavsky told me, "Every theatre has its intrigues. They should not scare you. On the contrary, it will be a good school for you. Work. Take those who trust you. If the theatre administration asks what it all means, tell them, 'I don't know, I am acting on Stanislavsky's orders.' I will provide the money you need. Don't worry where it comes from. You will have a salary of 60 rubles."

AUGUST 15, 1911

Stanislavsky introduced his sister[6] to me. She suggested that I work with her and her ward. I spoke with Mchedelov[7] about Khalyutina's School.[8] They offer me 6 rubles per two-hour lesson.

AUGUST 20, 1911

Stanislavsky told me, "I made a mistake of explaining my system in

---

3   Vladimir Tezavrovsky (1880–1955), Russian actor and director; worked at the MAT from 1905 to 1918. Tezavrovsky played the role of Osric in *Hamlet*.
4   Ivan Bersenev (1889–1951), Russian actor and director; entered the MAT in 1911. Bersenev played the role of Fortinbras in *Hamlet*.
5   On performance of *Hamlet* at the MAT, see Introduction, p. 30.
6   Zinaida Sokolova (1865–1950), Stanislavsky's younger sister, worked as an actress at the MAT during the season of 1912–1913. Sokolova assisted Stanislavsky in his work on the system and served as a teacher for the Bolshoi Theatre Opera Studio and Stanislavsky Opera Studio.
7   Vakhtang Mchedelov (1884–1924), MAT director and founder of the Second Studio of the MAT.
8   Sofya Khalyutina (1875–1960), an actress at the MAT. From 1909 to 1914, Khalyutina headed a private acting school in Moscow.

one lesson. Many don't get it. I am afraid this will cause conflicts. Beware." I replied, "I have my own method of teaching."

    K. S.:   "Do you want me to come to your first class?"

    Me: "No, that would make me self-conscious."

[AUGUST 25, 1911]

I established the Studio.[9]

SEPTEMBER 3, 1911

First lesson at the Khalyutina School.

SEPTEMBER 6, 1911

Balieff asked me to direct a skit for his Chauve-Souris Cabaret.[10]

SEPTEMBER 7, 1911

Discussed the staging for Chauve-Souris with the artist Sapunov.[11]

MARCH 5, 1912

Suler[zhitsky] suggested going to London to direct Baring's *Double Game*.[12] Honorarium: 60 rubles a day, and I would have to pay for my own travel.

MARCH 6, 1912

Asked Nemirovich to let me go to London.

MARCH 9, 1912

They did not let me go to London.

MARCH 17, 1912

Spoke with K. S. about the Studio.

---

9 This bold statement is accurate, as the word "Studio" in Russian refers both to a theatrical institution that includes a strong component of training, and to the actual classes. As Vakhtangov originated regular training at the First Studio of the MAT, he did actually "establish" the Studio.

10 See Introduction, p. 46.

11 Nikolai Sapunov (1880–1912), Russian artist and theatre designer.

12 Maurice Baring (1874–1945), English author and playwright.

SEPTEMBER 1, 1912

First gathering of the Studio ...

SEPTEMBER 2, 1912

Gathering at Stanislavsky's house. Developing the repertoire.

SEPTEMBER 9, 1912

K. S. Stanislavsky read [Anton] Chekhov's [short] play *On the Highway* at his house.

SEPTEMBER 15, 1912

We read Molière's *Imaginary Invalid* at the Studio.

OCTOBER 6, 1912

The opening of our Studio. Let it be so.

[This translation is supplemented with previously unpublished materials, featured in Ivanov 2011.]

26 On the First Studio of the MAT Artistic Philosophy and Esthetics

On the Feeling of Today: Response to the First Studio Actor Aleksandr Geirot

Sasha Geirot!

Firstly, prodigal son,[1] do not write on the left side of the ledger—leave it to the leisurely and witty commentators—and, secondly, my dove, if you want my opinion on what you wrote, be so kind as to clarify what it means "to reflect the great era—in our theatre and in our creative work."

Does it mean that we need to perform a play that reflects our era?

In this case, either indicate such a play or, be so kind, if time permits, do write one.

Does it mean that the nature of our productions should reflect our era?

As far as I am aware, principles of theatrical productions never depended on war.

Does it mean that our creative work must have some kind of a great goal in such an era as ours?

The Cricket on the Hearth, The Deluge ...

Let us suppose that it is characteristic of some era that the art comes to meet the worn-out soul of a man. In such a case, our era would be reflected in the very fact of the production, and in the choice of plays.

When we all lie in our own cemetery (laid out according to Stanislavsky's plan) (by the way, do not leave for the Kamerny Theatre; they won't even have a decent cemetery), then a historian will write, "The early twentieth century era was reflected in theatrical art, for the most part, in the choice of plays. German and Austrian plays no longer

---

1   The actor Geirot left the MAT for Tairov's Kamerny Theatre and then came back to MAT.

pleased the short-sighted translators, as they failed to bring abundant royalties. The repertoire consisted predominately of the plays written by the representatives of those nations fighting against the Teutons.[2] Preference was given to plays that awakened kind feelings and reconciled with the era's nightmarish life. In that respect, the Studio of the Moscow Art Theatre was especially notable. Cute boys and girls (they were very young back then, eaglets of the Russian stage, so to speak) felt keenly the spiritual demands of their era's Man."

This is what the historians will write, if they don't feel lazy, as I do now. If you do write a play and, we, young eaglets, perform it, then, of course, the historian will be obliged to mention you.

Don't do it, for God's sake! Do not reflect the era! And, for the love of God, do not leave for the Kamerny Theatre! Otherwise, the historian might write that our era was reflected in theatre by the fact that Geirot, tormented by the desire to reflect the era, deflected our trust in him as a faithful studio member.

Your friend, rather well inclined toward you,
Ye. Vakhtangov.

August 15, 1915, entry in the First Studio of the
MAT *Book of Records*.[3]

2   The Teutons or *Teutones* were a Germanic tribe.
3   One of the several books instituted at the First Studio by Sulerzhitsky and Stanislavsky, where Studio members were supposed to enter their thoughts about art. Apart from Sulerzhitsky's moral writings, this entry by Vakhtangov appears to be one of the most "serious." Most of the entries in the book were of an irreverent, humorous nature.

27 On the First Studio of the MAT Traditions and Perspectives

From the Diary[1]

APRIL 14, 1916

In our theatre, at the Studio and among my own students, I can feel a need for the uplifting. I can feel their dissatisfaction with a performance depicting "the mundane," even if it aims for the good.

Perhaps, this is the first step toward "romanticism," toward a turnaround.

I too imagine something ahead.

A kind of festival of feelings, reflected onto the uplifting spiritual realm (what kind of spirituality?), rather than onto the virtuous, so-called, Christian feelings.

We must rise, even if only one foot high, above the earth. For now.

From the Notebook: On Leopold Sulerzhitsky

You left us, our superb and noble Teacher. How many days running have we heard your voice, listened to your wise and simple words, and seen you here in this audience, on these chairs, and here on this stage. The memory of you fills every word of our roles, every subject of our plays, and our every step backstage. You are not among us, but you are inside us, insisting and demanding.

The universe is full of riddles, and of the mysterious. We cannot penetrate their essence, and we never will. If we were to succeed, the riddles and the unsolvable would cease to be, and without them there is no harmony that makes up the universe. To penetrate the mysterious

---

1   This is the first English-language publication of Vakhtangov's diary entry.

and solve the riddle is to destroy the world and its greatest mystery: man.

An hour comes when, by accident or through the natural course of events, a man leaves his friends and all that is beloved and dear to him and departs forever. Where does he go? How can we know, and how can we ever find out?

Perhaps you are among us even now.

Perhaps you hear everything we say about you now.

We do not know this.

[And we never will.]²

We believe that you are among us.

These words we say of you, we say them to you and to no one else.

We would not say them if we did not believe. Nor would there be the sacrament and the mystery of our communion with you. Suppose there is nothing mysterious in the universe. Suppose all is ashes and dust. Suppose in the next world there is no place for a man's spirit, and it also is ashes and dust—even then you are alive and will live for as long as you are in us. "The dead who are remembered go on living as if they never died."³ You made it impossible for us to forget you, and we will not be able to forget you until we ourselves are ashes.

You shall live with us, up till your last disciple's final hour. How can we forget you, so pure of heart?

You are our teacher.

You, who is strong of spirit.

You, who knew beauty and felt it in every speck of life.

We can see your whole self so vividly, as vividly as an hallucination. We can see you as you were, for you revealed your entire self to us.

We are just about to hear your steps on the iron stairs, the slow, unconscious steps of a man concentrated on great yet simple thought.

You stop there at the door, and we know: you opened it, fixed your attention on the knob; you leaned your forehead against the door's sharp edge. You are swaying: we hear the heart-wrenching tune of the *Miserere* waltz.⁴ You are lost in thought, and you endlessly turn the key in the lock.

---

2   Text in square brackets is missing in Vakhtangova et al. 1939, in Vendrovskaya 1959, and in Vendrovskaya and Kaptereva 1982. It has been restored in Vendrovskaya and Kaptereva 1984.
3   A quotation from Maeterlinck's *The Blue Bird*.
4   Music to the MAT's 1910 production of Semyon Yushkevich's play *Miserere* was written by composer Ilya Sats (1875–1912).

You now search with your lips for the humor of the French horn. You found it; your eyes are squinting, your hair is falling down on your forehead. You carry out the waltz of the French horn boldly and loudly, sparkling with the bouncing humor of this instrument, lit up with the deafening angst of your beloved friend's music.

Every actor knows that what happens with him on the stage is unreal, and yet he believes that it happens with him—that is why he can truthfully respond with his feelings to the call of imagination. He believes.

Similarly, we, his students in this Studio, know that he died, and yet believe that he is among us; therefore we can speak as though he is among us.

This is what we say to him.

You see, we remember you.

You, who have been torn from us and cannot come to us from the kingdom of spirits, must shed a smile from there.

We know your smile well; we can feel it without seeing it.

Here you are at *The Cricket on the Hearth* talk.

Your pencil fiddles across a scrap of paper, making spontaneous marks and crossing them out.

Now you put your pencil down, slapping it on the tablecloth.

This means that you had arrived at something. All concentration, you become absorbed in your thoughts, then pick up your pencil again, and, summoning us with its gesture, you tell us, "I don't know, perhaps *The Cricket* requires a special approach. Maybe we shouldn't begin our rehearsals as we used to do it; maybe we better go right now to the Strastnoi Monastery, stand there for a while in silence, then come back here, light the fireplace, and sit around it together, reading the Bible by candlelight."

You used to tell us:

"Get to the heart of Dickens, open it, and then the heart of the audience will be open to you. Only this goal makes it worthwhile, even imperative, to perform *The Cricket*. People's lives are hard; you must bring them a pure joy. When you pick a play to be staged, ask yourselves what you are staging it for."

Could we ever forget this testament of yours, for as long as the Studio exists?

You see, we shall remember you.

Here we are, showing to you, for the first time, our independent work on *The Deluge*. We show you the first two acts. How delicately you approached this far-from-finished work!

What thoughts you had, and what you foresaw in the play!

Here you are, barely holding back your laughter, covering a chuckle. Your joyful eyes penetrate the essence of each performer. At the climactic moment, you suddenly give way to the stored-up laughter. All but tumbling off the chair and hopelessly trying to overcome a new wave of laughter, you say,

"Hold on, hold on. Stop for a minute, you devils!"

Our actors grow still in their places, while holding on to the thread of the scene; they wait for you to calm down, and then go on with the act.

"Oh, what funny people!" you say after the showing. "They are all so warm-hearted and nice; they each have a perfect chance to be good, but they have been corrupted by this rat race, by the dollar, and by the stock market. Discover their kind heart, and let them reach ecstasy as they revel in their newly revealed feelings. You will see then how the audience opens up their hearts. An audience needs this, because they too have their rat race, gold, and stock market ... Only this goal makes it worthwhile to perform *The Deluge.*

You see, we remember you.

Here you are, at one of the rehearsals for *The Festival of Peace.*

"It is not their wickedness that causes them to quarrel, but rather it is their essential goodness that causes them to reconcile. That is the main thing. Give out all the warmth you have in your hearts, seek support in each other's eyes, and gently encourage each other to open up your souls.

"By this and by this alone will you carry the audience along.

"Don't allow hysteria, kick it out, don't get carried away with the effect it produces on the audience's nerves. Strive for their heart instead."

You made a fairy tale out of your short earthly life. In your last days you dreamed of a fairy tale:

"It would be good to stage *The Chimes.*"[5]

You left us one more work to do. We shall approach it remembering you, and our every step in it shall be made with you. The serene song of the chimes will reach you; it will carry to you our love and gratitude, and it will tell you once more that we remember you. If it is true that the dead who are remembered go on living as if they had never died, then you are still living and will live until the end of our days.

The Wreck of Hope.

---

5   The idea of producing a stage adaptation of Charles Dickens's 1844 Christmas book, *The Chimes,* never materialized at the First Studio.

"Natural disasters united people. They huddled together. But they did not gather to tell [each other] about the horrible. You should not play that. They gathered to be closer and seek support and compassion from each other. Be kinder, as you cuddle up to each other, open your aching heart."

Wandering Minstrels.

"Never mind that they are tired and lost, hungry and ragged. Lift up your souls to God; seek peace for the exhausted in Him. They walk toward the truth, and they carry Christ. Notice how in the second act they all beam with the notion of their great mission—to carry the truth. The closer you come to finding this opportunity to commune with God, the more your audience will understand you."

And this is on theatre at large:

"Not just a spectacle, not merely an artistic reproduction, and not the beauty alone; the theatre has and must have yet another goal— God. An actor is not just an artist, but a high priest."

Is our life enough to achieve this goal?

In your modest office upstairs, there is a small shelf with our studio ledgers. You built the shelf, and you started every ledger. There are about fifty of them … and in each we find your commentaries and notes addressed to us. In each we find your quintessential morals derived from many private cases in our [Studio] life. In each of these lines, no matter how short, you appeal to us for mercy, love, sensitivity, and good relations. Your every suggestion and comment was motivated by the heart.

Here are a few of them:

"The purpose of the art is to compel people to be attentive to each other, to soften their hearts and ennoble their morals."

"The human [in you] only begins at the moment when you personally spend even the tiniest bit of attention on the personal life of those around you."

"Don't give in to false shame and try to learn, if only a little bit, about the lives of the people who do your dirty work. If you try to bring even an ounce of enjoyment into their lives, believe me, it will not go in vain."

"If every wall of our Studio, all of it, shall be soaked with the work applied to its improvement, then you will see how the Studio shall grow, how valued and respected it will become, and how anybody's thoughtless or negligent behavior shall become offensive to everyone."

"Be ashamed of your lack of faith, cut it out quick; look around you quick, look each other in the face, feel that you are now the group not to be reckoned with, held together not by a rotten string but by something stronger than that. Often sense each other, and hasten to hammer the rivets into the frame of the new ship called 'The Studio'."

"The more you sacrifice, the more you gain. This is not from an anthology, but from life."

"Just remember that you must hasten to feel your strength in unity—unity with each other and with your creator—the Art Theatre. The sooner the better; I feel it in my heart."

January 25, 1917.

From the Diary

OCTOBER 25, 1918[6]

It would be good to commission the following play:

1   Moses (tongue-tied). His wife. Aaron. Perhaps, he saw an Egyptian beating a Jew. Killed him. That night, in his tent, excited, tells about it … God speaks to him in the night. God orders him to go to the pharaoh, and enables him to perform miracles, so that he would show signs. (The rod.) Moses, who feels his people's pain, inflamed by the idea to liberate his people, prepares to appear before the pharaoh by dawn.
2   Moses before the people. His speech.
3   At the pharaoh's.
4   In the desert.
5   Moses before the people with the table of covenant.
6   Centuries go by.
7   Scattered.
8   Night. Far beyond the limits of the tangible space, there is a light. A song of hope of one thousand approaching breasts is heard in the night. They are coming; the people are coming to build their freedom. Curtain.

THE IGNATYEV CLINIC, NOVEMBER 24, 1918

Why is my heart so heavy today? What an incessant feeling. It is like a premonition of something. It's vague, and that makes me uneasy.

---

6   This is the first English-language publication of Vakhtangov's diary entry.

Yesterday they held a dress rehearsal of *Rosmersholm* ... [7] And they did not even tell me ahead of time that it was called ... Neither did they inform me [about it] after the fact ... Two years I worked with them day after day, and they did not even find it necessary to remember me ... Perhaps, this is natural. Perhaps, this *is* genuine. Perhaps, if they would drop me a line, then *that* would be insincere and formal. One must accept things as they are. I can see clearly now that not only am I not dear to the Studio, but that it does not need me. Well, it is not that it does not entirely need me, but that it can do without me. Yet I cannot submit to this; I must be where I am needed.

After all, it is time to start thinking of daring to take wing. There is no daring at our Studio. Daring next to [Konstantin Stanislavsky] is nonsense; no daring can be realized, unless he recognizes it, while the very fact of his recognition will cancel the daring.

Bolsheviks are noble precisely because they are lonely and misunderstood.

I have no grounds to support my daring, or to be lonely and misunderstood, but I, for example, see well that our Studio is going downhill, and that it does not grow spiritually.

I want to flutter my wings, but there is nothing to flutter with. I must stage *Cain* (I have a daring plan, even if it is ridiculous). I need to stage *The Dawn*,[8] I must adapt the Bible. We must play the rebellious spirit of the people.

A thought just flickered in my head: wouldn't it be good if someone were to write a play without a single individual role in it. Only the mob would perform in all the acts. A Rebellion. They storm a barricade. They overtake it. They rejoice. They bury their fallen. They sing the universal song of freedom. What a curse not being able to manage it myself. And there is no one to commission it from: all our talents are so shallow, and those who would be willing—are mediocre.

[This translation is supplemented with previously unpublished materials, featured in Ivanov 2011.]

---

7 *Rosmersholm* opened at the close of the 1917/1918 theatre season. This entry is written on the occasion of the "brush-up" dress rehearsal at the start of the 1918/1919 season.
8 An 1898 play by the Belgian symbolist playwright Emile Verhaeren (1855–1916). Vakhtangov did not get a chance to realize his plans.

Part VIII
Vakhtangov Rehearses

28 Theatre of the Emotional Experience

Rehearsals of Boris Zaitsev's *The Lanin Estate*[1]

First Reading of the Play: First Spontaneous Impression

DECEMBER 23, 1913

The first meeting featuring Vakhtangov. He arrived late, did not have time to read the play, and therefore started the rehearsal by reading the first act out loud. Soon he got tired and asked members of the group to take turns reading the play. Vakhtangov commented on diction, voice, the style of reading, etc. At the end of each act, he asked everyone to express their opinion on prominent scenes of the act, as well as its general atmosphere.[2]

The First Spontaneous Impression of the Character and Character's Point of View

He also asked the actors to describe some of the characters, as if they stood before us. He asked questions: "What color does she like?," "What kind of heels does she wear?," etc.[3]

---

1   Records compiled by the Vakhtangov Studio members.
2   On Vakhtangov's concepts of the first reading of the play and first spontaneous impression, see the Glossary and Malaev-Babel (forthcoming). When speaking of atmosphere, Vakhtangov, according to the MAT terminology of the time, refers to it as "the general mood of the act." On Vakhtangov's concept of atmosphere, and how it differs from the MAT concept of emotional mood, see the Glossary and Malaev-Babel (forthcoming).
3   On Vakhtangov's concept of fantasizing about the role, see the Glossary and Malaev-Babel (forthcoming).

We read three acts. Vakhtangov noted that everyone was taken by the play, and therefore we can work on it.

On Method

With this in mind, Vakhtangov started clarifying the goals of his method of training. He is pleased to promote the Moscow Art Theatre idea; it is this idea that he will convey to us as we study the art of the stage. This art has two sides to it: the outer technique, and the inner.

When it comes to the first side (diction, voice, gesture, mimicry, makeup, etc.), Vakhtangov is not a specialist in this realm, and so he won't work with us on it.[4] The goal of his training is in perfecting the inner technique. In order to present a character onstage, an actor must understand and reproduce the character's feelings, then express these feelings through words and situations. Inner technique consists of an ability to live the life of the character being created.

On Repeat Emotions (or Memory of Emotions)

The majority of feelings are known to us from our own life experiences, except that these feelings were formed in our soul in a different order and according to a different logic than the one required for the character. Therefore, an actor's task is to retrieve the imprints of the required feelings from different corners of his own soul and lay them in an order, required by the logic of life of the character being created. This alignment of the spiritual fragments is accompanied by pain, just as in every surgical procedure; this pain is characteristic for every kind of creativity, and successful portrayal is only possible when the wounded areas heal and the soul settles down.

---

4   Vakhtangov was a master of the outer form and external technique, as evidenced from his work as both director and actor. In the student production of *The Lanin Estate*, however, Vakhtangov concentrated exclusively on the inner side of the character, and on the internal technique—for strictly pedagogical reasons. In addition to that, by the time of *The Lanin Estate*, Vakhtangov did not subscribe to the MAT approach to the outer form, expressed in the concept of "external characterization." (See Stanislavsky 2008: chapter 23.) Vakhtangov could not share his disagreements with the MAT on the subject of the external form with the young students so he simply stated that he is not a specialist in this realm.

Director as an Inner Technique Coach, Play and Role as Pretext for Training, on the Inner Affinity with the Character

Vakhtangov's role in this will boil down to guiding and easing this spiritual breakdown. "I will be your mirror, I will mirror your mistakes and help you correct them." However, for the success of this work, he needs to know our characters and the essential elements of our souls. Moreover, he needs to know us as we are when we are unobserved. In order to get acquainted with us, he will conduct *études*. The play and the roles will serve as a kind of aid in our study of the inner technique. The play and the roles won't be a goal. The final result, the production, will be seen only as a means for the process of training the technique. In choosing a role, one must be guided by the inner affinity with the character and the adequacy of the major [spiritual] elements—not by the attractiveness of the external aspects of the role. One cannot create a character through external portrayal. While creating a character, an actor can either proceed "from himself" or "from the character," that is, he will either adjust the character to himself, or adjust himself to the character.

Actor and the Audience

Theatre is impossible without the audience. However, an actor's ideal quality is his ability to dismiss the thought of being watched by the audience and to forget that his life onstage is not restricted by the circle of the stage characters.[5]

Final Notes on the First Reading

Vakhtangov gives notes on the unnaturalness of the tone and the theatricality of the readers. He asks us not to recite but to converse with our interlocutor, to feel the partner, to feel the meaning of the language.

---

5 Vakhtangov's statement on the relationship between the actors and the audience is simplified for the specific pedagogical purposes of *The Lanin Estate* production. On Vakhtangov's concept of the audience, see the Glossary and Malaev-Babel (forthcoming).

The *Étude* Technique: Searching for the Atmosphere, Shifting Point of View on the Surroundings

DECEMBER 26, 1913

Vakhtangov conducts an *étude* of the first act.

The *étude* determines that the general atmosphere of the first act is calm, joyful. Therefore, Vakhtangov asks those trying out for the roles of Lanin, Turayev and Elena to evoke a matching feeling.

In order to do it, they must divorce themselves from their surrounding setting and recreate an image of spring: budding trees, sun, grass, an open terrace. This will evoke the feeling of warmth and fragrance.

They must try not to get distracted from this image by the objects that surround them. Therefore, they must substitute for these objects by imagining other objects. Alternatively, they could give the existing objects a different meaning and thereby "justify" them for the spring.

They must make a gradual transition to the required feeling by discovering beauty and pleasantness in their surroundings. They should evoke a calm, pleasant inner state through comfortable physical position, pleasant memory, or any other possible means. The audience must see that this joy is not taken from within but from without, from the image of spring, "from out there." Vakhtangov asks the actors to talk amongst themselves about anything—as their own selves, without experiencing their character's emotions.

An actress trying out for the role of Elena has difficulty sensing spring. Vakhtangov gives her a matchbox and asks her to sense a bird in it, to pet it, to caress it, to stroke it, to seek the bird's beak with her lips. "Now throw it," Vakhtangov says. "I can't," and she presses the box to her chest. This is how Vakhtangov awakens the required feelings. By their manifestations, he detects an actor's spiritual elements and their closeness to the chosen role.

On the Inner Affinity with the Character

JANUARY 2, 1914

We read the first act out loud, taking turns. For the most part, the female roles are being examined. This examination reveals a drastic difference of opinion on the role of Kseniya. Two variants of this character are being sketched, with regard to two different actresses: one is of a person close to nature and the countryside, the other close to the city, "a capricious boarding-school girl."[6] The first variant is generally acknowledged as being truer [to the author's intentions].

JANUARY 3, 1914

We read the second act, actors now reading their respective parts.

Both actors trying for the role of Fortunatov proved to be unsatisfactory: one of them let us feel the scholar but did not express joy, naive eccentricity; he was too monotonous. The other appeared more as a young naively joyful student and did not reveal the scholarly aspect ...

Vakhtangov does an *étude* with an actor playing Lanin. He sits him down by the stove and asks him to feel himself by a fireplace, to carry on freely and evoke a pleasant inner state. As Lanin, he may think pleasant thoughts, hum and whistle, smoke and do anything he feels like doing, in order to awaken the required feeling ...

JANUARY 6, 1914

We read the fourth act.

The following *études* for the character of Fortunatov were conducted with the two actors: at his studies, in conversation with his wife, at the art gallery, at the restaurant, at the tailor's, and others. The assessment remained the same: one of the actors had sincerity, and spontaneity, naivety, but he was more of a poet than a scholar. The other actor was a pedantic scholar: monotonous and artificial.

The opinions split fifty-fifty: the two actors drew lots, and the winner got the role ... The author, Boris Zaitsev is expected at the next meeting.

JANUARY 10, 1914

A general meeting with Boris Zaitsev.

He arrived before Vakhtangov.

Upon Vakhtangov's arrival, Zaitsev began to talk about characters. Vakhtangov announced the cast and asked Zaitsev to describe the characters, as he imagined them. Zaitsev replied that he would rather listen to our opinion first. We went down the list of characters, starting with Lanin. While posing questions and expressing our opinions, we forced Zaitsev to express his view on the characters he created. The notes he gave us were fragmented and brief, yet vivid and clear ...

---

6 "Boarding-school girl": an idiomatic expression, used to indicate either an innocent and naive or an unsophisticated young lady.

In addition to discussing characters, we also discussed their relationships, as well as emotions and moods.

Throughout the discussion, Zaitsev referred to himself in the third person: "Author wanted to say ..."

On Atmospheres and the Through Action of the Play

JANUARY 16, 1914

Together with Boris Zaitsev and Vakhtangov, we determined the general atmosphere of every act, as well as the through action of the play. Everyone expressed their opinions, while Vakhtangov drew conclusions and Zaitsev either agreed or made amendments. It was revealed that the [through] action of the play consists of gradual intoxication with love.

Vakhtangov sees the rainbow of the fourth act as some cosmic force that looks down at the people's sufferings with cold indifference. In his opinion, the fourth act provides a juxtaposition of nature's heartless grandeur with the sores and abscesses of the human life at the "estate." This is why he saw the "estate" as something abnormal and ephemeral—as something one wants to leave for a different, healthy life.

[According to Vakhtangov,] At first one feels good at the "estate." As time goes by, however, one begins to suffocate in the estate atmosphere and want to seek sobriety in a different life. Following Vakhtangov's interpretation, he was reminded of the content, and of the appeasing atmosphere of the fourth act. At that point, Vakhtangov agreed with Boris Zaitsev, who insisted that the rainbow was a symbol of peace.

An analogy between the action of the play and a summer storm was drawn. On a fine day, the clouds suddenly gather, distant thunder is heard; then the storm bursts out with its deafening thunder. And then it goes away as quickly as it arrived, leaving upon itself sparkling teardrops and fresh, purified air.

Prior to this discussion, Vakhtangov already mentioned that he felt separate moments of the play and saw qualities of some scenes. The discussion gave him a clear grasp of the atmosphere and the sequence of action, and it helped him discover the overall structure of the play.

Boris Zaitsev agreed with the opinions expressed and gave the following brief characterization of his play. Life is a canvas for the events that take place in its separate parts. These events grow, pile, collapse and rise again—this goes on forever and ever. An estate is one of such "spots." Life in it also fulfills its cycles: intoxicating spring repeats at the estate, just as it did centuries ago; people swirl in whirlwinds of love, laughter and tears, bliss and suffering—just as people who came before them. Calm and contentment come to surpass passions; people are taking a rest from what they experienced, and the new generations repeat anew their fathers' and grandfathers' path.

Vakhtangov indicated how delicate the action of the play was—like a fine spider web. This requires that the style of acting be especially delicate, so as not to break the main chain of events. Actors should always remember the general direction of the play so as not to overcast it with atmospheres and purely decorative events. In the view of this, it is permissible to cut sections of the play that interfere with, or overcast the main action.

On Play Analysis, Play Bits, Atmosphere, Directorial Bits

JANUARY 18, 1914

Vakhtangov started with theory.

In order to better understand the play and its through action, the play with its acts is divided into smaller "bits." This division can be done either according to action or atmosphere; in the first case we discover thresholds where different events begin and end, causing the play's action to take a different direction. In the second case we divide acts into parts united by the same atmosphere—the beginning of a new atmosphere signifies the beginning of a new "bit." The parts of the play that differ from each other in their atmosphere constitute "directorial," or unconditional bits. The atmosphere of the "directorial" bit must be played by all participants of the given scene, thus creating the general atmosphere, an ensemble. As for the atmosphere of the entire play, or its *leitmotif*, it results from the fulfillment of the through action.

The result of a particular actor's performance—an overall "motif" of the role—comes to light through the individual acting bits.

The "Kernel" of the Role

It is not sufficient for an actor to define the performance's bits and atmospheres. An actor must also discover the "kernel" of the role. Each actor discovers the role's kernel in his own individual way. The kernel of the role is what helps an actor to logically recreate the life of the character or to "live in character." Having discovered the inner kernel of the given role, an actor acquires the feeling of the character and behaves in every situation only the way his character would behave.

The kernel prevents the actor from making a gesture or assuming an intonation, inappropriate for his character. The kernel also compels an actor to seek situations and words logically necessary for the character.

The Feeling of Truth

Everything said and done on the stage must be truthful for me, for the actor, first and foremost. Only then will the audience believe in what we portray; otherwise the impression we create will resemble a situation when a person hands out a piece of paper and asks: "be so kind as to break this 20-ruble note." In such a case, a performance would become an obvious and impudent lie. In addition to that, an actor's point of view on his partner must be justified by this partner. Thus, one can only console someone who is sad; unless the one being consoled expresses sadness, the consolation will appears false.

On Stage Task and Its Three Elements

Every role contains a series of "tasks" an author put in it; an actor's job is to define and fulfill them. An actor's creativity lies in beautiful and clear fulfillment of these tasks.

Each task consists of three elements: action, desire (motivation), and the way it is fulfilled (adaptation).

An actor's every step is justified by a certain desire. While living in character, an actor, at any given moment, wants something; an action is born out of this desire and is followed by the feeling that comes last. Thus, the feeling is determined by two elements of the task: desire (motivation) and action. For example, an actor might need to hide (this is his action), but his motivation can be different. He may be hiding in order to escape someone chasing him or in order to scare someone, etc. This is why different feelings might be born [out of this action]: fear and excitement in one case, vigor and smile in the other, etc. Feelings, evoked by an entire series of tasks, constitute the "gamut" of the character's feelings. Stage acting is the fulfillment of tasks. Born emotion can be expressed externally. This expression is called "adaptation"; adaptations are characterized by the performer's talent; the more talented the actor, the more different forms of adaptation he gives, the more varied the fulfillment of tasks.

A bad actor has a small stock of resolutions to various tasks, and he monotonously uses them as needed. In all his roles he acts on clichés, as they call it.

Back to Analysis, the Flow of the Day

JANUARY 20, 1914

The first-act bits were determined. Bits' borders were outlined, according to [changes in the] action. First bit—up to Elena's arrival, second bit—up to the arrival of the Fortunatovs and Kolya.

The time of action and the life of the characters prior to the rising of the curtain were determined. This was done so that the audience could experience the play not as a life just begun but as a continuation of life. The day was outlined approximately so: Lanin gets up before everyone else, he relishes morning, walks in the garden. Natasha comes out soon after. Around 8 A.M. the Fortunatovs drive in. Lanin sees them from the distance. Lanin and Natasha drink tea; they come here, having settled the guests in the side wing of the house. Gradually Kseniya and Yevgeny arrive, and Nikolai Nikolayevich arrives last. They take their time drinking tea and chatting in a morning fashion. Around 2 P.M. they eat lunch without the Fortunatovs, who are asleep. At lunchtime Turayev arrives. After lunch they disperse in different directions, and around 4 P.M. Lanin, after taking his rest, comes to sit on the terrace. Turayev joins him after a walk, and they are found conversing over wine, as the curtain opens.

Preparatory *Études*

The Flow of the Day

The company did an *étude* to explore the day, ending at teatime. [An actor playing] Lanin did experience the morning time, but did not love those around him; he was dry, reticent. He did not produce the impression of a host, the estate owner, and he remained indifferent to the arrival of the Fortunatovs.

Natasha satisfied the director; overall she was close to her character. She did not, however, express her love for Lanin. Yevgeny entered well, but did not feel the tea. Kolya was shy. General shortcoming: lack of sensation of the morning, air, aroma, and inability to act without the set and props; the sensation of thirst, of food, was lacking at tea. Actors must learn to act using affective memory—that is, being able to recreate, by memory, movements that correspond with various actions and objects. The Fortunatovs rehearsed in the next room.

Fortunatov felt a man who arrived at a new place.

In order to convey a small part of the estate life within the four acts of the play with freedom and ease, the performers must feel the entire process of the characters' life on the estate.

On Repetition

JANUARY 21, 1914

An *étude* of the first two bits was done, and Vakhtangov suggested to those performing that they use atmospheres from the previous *études*, while refraining from reproducing old gestures. In general, all previous external expressions of the atmospheres experienced must be forgotten. The *étude* proceeded satisfactorily, even though it was done for the first time, mostly due to the preparatory *études*. Lanin was goodhearted, while Elena was acting with some sentimentality. They did not succeed at experiencing the Fortunatovs as new, unfamiliar people.

Back to Analysis: Corrections and Clarifications

At the end, logical and psychological analysis of the bits was done, and the cast met many obstacles resulting from the author's inexperience as a playwright. When it came to justifying lines and relationships, many of these justifications were stretched thin.

Preparatory *Études*: Playing the Lines vs. Experiencing

JANUARY 26, 1914

Performers were asked to start by reawakening the feelings of the first bit and then move onto the second bit ... A common defect was observed: actors were moving along the plane of text, instead of going along the plane of feelings. At every moment, an actor should live with the feelings and atmospheres of that moment, rather than playing lines. When this happens, the lines can even contradict the feeling. When playing lines, life is not created, and phrases remain without the inner content.

Miscellaneous Notes

MARCH 5, 1914

The second act was rehearsed (off book up to Elena's entrance, and then on book).

Upon the reading of the entire act, the director remarked:

Actors should have greater attention toward their partners; [the actor playing] Fortunatov ... rushes terribly. (Rushing should be expressed through the inner state, but an actor should not express the feeling faster than it arrives.) ...

[An actor playing the part of Kolya] Has an unnecessary melody in speech ... the director advises actors to use their own words—that will make their speech simpler ...

[The actor playing] Nikolai Nikolayevich should use *his own passion* for the tasks of the role ...No screaming and horror [are needed] in the scene with Kolya, but instead Nikolai Nikolayevich must watch so that everyone feels the intensity of his gaze ...

On Atmosphere

MARCH 7, 1914

Performers spoke of their roles in the third act. The general quality [of the act] is the one of sadness; intoxication with love is at its utmost ... This sadness, however, has tragedy in it; the tragedy is simple here, as it is simple in Chekhov.

On Taste and Manipulation of the Audience's Emotions

The director was offended at the moment [in the third act] where Natasha starts waltzing dreamily. Not everyone agreed with the director on this point. The director objected: "the scene is awfully banal and 'tired'. It is not original, borrowed from Chekhov." It is objectionable to play sad, melancholy waltz in background. To do this is to fool the audience. They are being fooled every time the director evokes a mood in them bypassing the actor—through the setting, or music. The director accepts Natalia [Shilovtseva]'s proposal to substitute the waltz with [Edvard] Grieg's *Solveig's Song*, for example.

On Theatricality

Vakhtangov says of the end of the act: "It is not good; it is lifelike, and not theatrical. It is tiresome, like the rest of the act."

On Emotional Restraint

MARCH 9, 1914[7]

The initial bits of the fourth act were read, discussed and performed ...

The character of Turayev is greatly depressed; a deep feeling should always be expressed simply, without hysteria.

The director said: if you want to express tears on the stage—suppress the weeping, hide the feeling—it will be stronger this way.

Non-Naturalistic Set

MARCH 9, 1914

Rehearsal was held at the Hunters' Club. The first act was blocked. The director had a thought: the set of the play should consist of stage curtains. The play should be performed in costumes and makeup—with no sets.

All that is needed, as an important detail, is the balustrade in the first act, benches and steps, as well as the columns in the fourth act.

On Festivity

MARCH 25, 1914

During the performance, the director would like to maintain a festive atmosphere backstage.

---

7 From this point, rehearsals enter their final period. Vakhtangov begins to put special emphasis onto the analysis of each character's circumstances and psychology. The play is being criticized, certain scenes and sections cut. And finally, the performance *mise-en-scène* is being set.

29 Toward the Theatre of Mystery

REHEARSALS OF MAETERLINCK'S *THE MIRACLE OF SAINT ANTHONY* (FIRST VARIANT)[1]

On the Author's Point of View

SEPTEMBER 17, 1916

The Miracle of Saint Anthony will amount to a full production, despite the small size of the play. If it is played well, the audience will leave satisfied ...

The play requires qualities of sharpness and compactness in acting.

Let us now talk about the play. What attracts us in this play and gives us warm feelings? Why did Maeterlinck write this play? Why does it read so well? It is not the extraordinary nature of the situation that is important but something else. We laugh at ourselves a little, when we laugh at the characters of this play. We understand all of them so well. What is so familiar in this play, and what unites us with its author? We feel pity for Anthony. The meeker he is, the more moving. St. Anthony says: "I came to answer your prayers." This outlines the through action.

Maeterlinck wrote a comedy, and comedy always mocks at something. In this comedy, however, Maeterlinck does not mock the way others do, but in his own unique way. His is not an exposing

---

1 Vakhtangov rehearsed the first variant of his production of *The Miracle of Saint Anthony* from September 1916 to September 1918. Rehearsal records compiled by studio members.

laughter of Shchedrin,[2] nor is it Gogol's tears,[3] etc. This is a mere smile. Maeterlinck smiled at people.

What shall we play here? Guests [at the funeral] are just a mere background; breakfast is also a background. What should we play on this background? It is imperative to play Maeterlinck. We could afford not to play Scheglov,[4] or Sutro,[5] but we were obliged to play Chekhov. The same is true of Maeterlinck. Chekhov's *Huntsman*[6] depicts an everyday life in Russia, and national types. *The Miracle of Saint Anthony* is typically international. National characterization is of little relevance in this play. Policemen of all countries have something in common; they all say the same: "I need to see your identification." Characterization in this play can be as it may. Virginie can be played this way, or the other. As long as you play her heart.

Upon watching this play, the audience should feel moved and embarrassed. The audience should be muttering under their breath: "We are no better … "

This play is a smile of Maeterlinck, as he somewhat divorced himself from *Aglavaine and Selysette*, from the Blind, from Intruder, in short, from everything that exposed the screams of his soul. He distracted himself from this, lit up a cigar, snacked on partridge, and felt himself again. Perhaps, at that time, he dined with his friends, the priest and the doctor:

What if a saint would appear on this earth?

Well, this cannot be—said the doctor—I don't believe this.

Oh, we are such sinners—the priest replied—The Lord won't grace us with his mercy.

In short, neither one allowed for the possibility of such a fact, although under different pretexts.

This is how Maeterlinck wrote this play—lightly, without hysterics, without reproaches on the account of the people. He wrote it while his heart was at rest.

2   Mikhail Saltykov-Shchedrin (1826–1889), Russian satiric author.
3   Vakhtangov is referring to a particular aspect of Gogol's satirical gift. The author was often capable of revealing the tragedy behind the comedic, or, as Gogol himself would put it, "tears invisible to the world."
4   Ivan Scheglov (Leontyev) (1856–1911), Russian humorist and vaudeville author. Scheglov's vaudeville *Female Nonsense* was featured in the Vakhtangov Studio's April 26, 1915, performance evening.
5   Alfred Sutro's one-act play *The Open Door* was featured in the Vakhtangov Studio's December 1916 performance evening.
6   An adaptation of Anton Chekhov's 1885 short story "The Huntsman" was featured in the Vakhtangov Studio's performance evenings.

Why is it that Virginie alone accepted the miracle, and we are at her side?

This play cannot be played so that Achille, Gustave, and the others repulse the audience. They are all nice people. We understand them perfectly.

There is no pretence in this play. Everything in it is pure truth. Including St. Anthony's arrival—this too is pure truth.

If Christ were to come to a dungeon, or to an insane asylum, we would accept it at once. But suppose we were told that Christ came to an ordinary apartment where there is a private doctor, dinner jackets, cigars, partridges, wine—this we cannot accept ...

Where does Maeterlinck's smile come from? This smile resembles the kind of smile Lilliputians evoked in Gulliver. Indeed, let us imagine a man small enough to drown in this ashtray. We don't feel like laughing when someone says, "Let's save a drowning man." However, when someone says it about a Lilliputian drowning in an ashtray, we do feel like laughing. Or else, let us imagine a little cow from the Lilliputian kingdom—a cow that can fit in the palm of a hand. When someone says, "Let's milk it," once again, we would feel like laughing.

SEPTEMBER 25, 1916

The play is being read at the rehearsal table.

[*Vakhtangov*:] Last time we spoke about characters in this play being quite clear, and of their international aspect. Each moment of the play is significant. We also said that there is not a single reproach toward people in the play; we spoke of Maeterlinck's smile ...

Every character has something in him we can love, some sympathetic qualities.

What can Achille be loved for? For being so preoccupied with his partridge, for wanting so sincerely to give something to Anthony. We understand him at such a moment, we sympathize with him. Indeed, what can one possibly give to a saint? A tie pin? Ridiculous. A cigar case? Ridiculous. To treat him to some wine? Equally ridiculous. Achille is in a predicament, and we understand him quite well.

The funniest thing about Gustave is that he takes everything to heart, he is easily excitable. His temperament is completely opposite to Achille's.

The funniest thing about the priest is his "oiliness." His job is talking to God: this occupation formed certain professional methods. When he sees Anthony, he is not quite convinced that this is not a saint standing before him. This is why, just in case, he speaks to him as to a saint.

The funny element in the doctor is his professional self-confidence, despite the fact that he understands nothing.

Joseph is fire: all we see is the flying tails of his coat.

Mademoiselle Hortense: an old lady, a capricious child.

Everything about the police sergeant is brief, quick, articulate. He knows everything in advance. Tremendous confidence in his own righteousness.

What touches us in the character of Anthony? Which of his qualities make us smile? We are moved by his submissiveness, by some kind of heightened attention. He listens very attentively.

To sum up, each of the performers must discover his character's leading quality that would move and evoke a smile. The only reason we don't see the funny sides of life is that we pay no attention to them. One must look from afar, with the eyes of a man who is divorced from life. Every man is dreadfully torn between what he thinks, does, and wants. People want a miracle: all right, let's send them a saint! They are rich heirs: let's resurrect their rich aunt, etc. In all these people you must find something amusing, something that touches you.

If I stand somewhat above and abstract myself, I won't be able to look at a man the way Shchedrin looked. We see that everything human makes us smile and seems small when compared to the higher deeds.

A very touching moment in the play is when Virginie asks for a blessing. This is not something merely human and mundane; this is something spiritual; this is a moment of true communion with God. And it is immediately followed by something human and mundane.

Saturating Yourself for the Role

How should you work? Keep reading the play informally; try to feel it, to dream, to fantasize about it, and some part of you will become captivated. This is called *saturating yourself for the role*. If you saturate yourself for the role, this will appear onstage unconsciously. Today I dreamed some, and tomorrow it will act itself out beyond my will.

It is equally necessary to saturate yourself for the role of Anthony. Only this is more difficult. Everything is too unusual.

On the Essence of the Bit

SEPTEMBER 27, 1916

[*Vakhtangov*] *To Aleyeva*: Do you know this kind of a state? Imagine that you just finished writing your school paper; it is time for bed, and for your nightly prayers. You are in the right mood, you make the sign of the cross, saying your prayer—everything is as it should be. Suddenly the door opens and your little sister comes in. You feel the calamity coming: the girl will spill ink on your paper. So, without leaving your meditative state, you scream in the direction of the door: "Aunty, take little Lizochka." And suddenly this very Lizochka comes to the table, picks up the inkwell and pours ink on your paper. You involuntarily let out, "Lizka, damn it, what are you doing?" All this a mere second after saying the Lord's Prayer, etc. This is how Virginie feels.

You must find how to make a sudden shift, but you should not play it for the laughs. This is not written to arouse laughter.

You should not feel good about yourself when saying: "please, resurrect."

On Regular Acting Exercises

OCTOBER 2, 1916

Last year you had exercises, and now these exercises are gone. I won't open a single performance if there are no exercises. Please, don't put me into an awful position of carrying you all. It is necessary to appoint someone who would lead exercises and take attendance. You should exercise daily, if only for quarter of an hour. It does not matter if an exercise succeeds or not. As long as you are working.

On Character Essence and Point of View

About Joseph. He carries the dish in style. When unable to push Anthony out—utter astonishment. His tailcoat drooped on him, and all his style, all his starchiness, disappeared at once.

On Gustave. When Gustave decides to defeat Anthony through meekness, he truly becomes meek, without pretence.

On Achille. Achille has a certain point of view on the priest: he cannot see him without laughing. At the breakfast table he constantly chuckles at him. The same happens now onstage. When he says: "Saints are your department," it means, "Now it's his turn to try [getting rid of the man]." In general, Achille is a big joker. Very lazy. Eating and sleeping are his main occupations.

Étude Technique

Now we should search [through the following *étude*]. A beggar came to the house where people are busy having breakfast; he makes it difficult for them to continue with breakfast.

On Subtext and Underwater Current

OCTOBER 9, 1916

The play is being read at the rehearsal table.

[*Vakhtangov*] *To Vershilov*:[7] What right do you have to intonate when you have nothing inside? Read it simply so that we could see that you are searching for the structure of the role. Don't intonate at all. Otherwise you start with the second phase, when it is essential to first go through the initial phase. When you read, an expert's eye immediately sees what will happen next; why, even an ordinary audience member senses it vaguely. You are playing the end—at the beginning. Don't act the words of the role. You should act so that the audience senses the undercurrents below the words. Discover that which makes your phrase sound this way or another.

When we say something in life, we always have an undercurrent. I never ask what time it is only to find out the time. I always do it for something else. I must discover such undercurrents that are required by the play. An undercurrent might lead you astray. If you take a wrong direction, I will let you know. Your job is to choose a direction, whether it is right or wrong. You must seek undercurrents. This is the subject for homework. It is essential to lay out the gamut of your role in a particular logical sequence.

What does Gustave live with at the moment of Achille's entrance? "Oh my, a scandal, oh my, it is about to break out."

Here comes Achille, which means, it already broke out.

"What is going on?"

"Don't you see for yourself?"

This "Don't you see, don't you get it?" is heard behind each of Gustave's lines. This is the tonality of this place in his role.

As soon as Achille understood, everything changed: Achille asked: "Is he drunk?" Gustave replied: "Drunk. How did you guess it?"

---

7   Boris Vershilov (1893–1957), Russian director and teacher, one of the founding members of the Vakhtangov Studio. Vershilov left the Studio in 1919 and joined the MAT and its Second Studio. Vershilov played the role of the Police Captain in *The Miracle of Saint Anthony*.

This phrase should also sound like: "Don't you see for yourself? No, not drunk, sober. He [Anthony] is a sober fool."

"Then push him out of the door."

"Oh my, what a brilliant solution he has found: how come we did not think of it ourselves. We can't push him out, that's just it!"

On the Threshold of Creativity (Psychological Non-Alteration)

OCTOBER 19, 1916

This is how we shall work from now on. You will start by telling me what you are doing onstage throughout your entire role. You will proceed to acting at the rehearsal table. Do it without altering the psychological state you just experienced "in life." At the start of your acting give yourself leave to feel exactly what you felt before you began to act. Start acting without as much as changing the position of your body, or adjusting in any other way.

On the Actor's Organic Process

OCTOBER 22, 1916

An actor playing Gustave tells what he does in the course of the role.

[*Vakhtangov*:] You are [merely] stating facts, and you consistently remain on the same plane. On the contrary, your irritation must constantly increase. If you begin at 15 degrees, you should gradually reach 30 degrees. If at the start you don't have 15 degrees, you can start with 1 degree, but then rise up to 15 degrees, as long as there is an increase.

Besides, the very way you tell [what you do in the role] is incorrect. You should do it in the form of a search, instead of answering to me personally. I don't care what adaptation you choose at the first rehearsal. All I care about is that your tasks flow out of your points of view, as determined by the play. You should fulfill these tasks while remaining yourself. In early rehearsal work, you should know what you must do. You should realize that your particular actions, and no other actions, are a necessity. They should become organic, that is, you should agree with the author in everything. You must believe that all this happened to you.

To sum up, firstly I must know why I came to the stage; secondly, [I must know] what I want from my partner; and thirdly: I must have a particular point of view on my partner.

As everything that is "you" accumulates in the play, it will cause you to become different. A complete merger between my entire being and the author's character is needed. This cannot be achieved instantaneously, however, one must move toward it.

If you prefer, I will work with you the way I did last year; I will erase your individualities and impose on you my own form and adaptations. This work will not be joyful. Work will only be joyful when you bring to rehearsals the result of your homework.

Shifting Point of View on Facts

OCTOBER 30, 1916

I kept thinking that you are not shifting your points of view on facts. How do we make the arrival of St. Anthony an event? In the course of seven rehearsals you all fizzled, ladies and gentlemen. All your personal qualities have been used up. As I told you already, I don't want to impose my qualities on you …

You must experience [the atmosphere of] mourning. No noise whatsoever at breakfast, no gaiety, no murmur of voices. Deep inside they all wait for partridges to be served. In the meantime, everyone must maintain the rules of propriety and behave as appropriate on such occasions.

On Tempo and the Essence of a Bit and Character

JANUARY 6, 1917

[*Vakhtangov*] *To Aleyeva:*[8] You are gradually getting the feel of your role. The kernel is discovered. Bits are beginning to take shape here and there. You must dispose of your individual pauses; the audience won't receive them at all. You speaking quietly is indicative of the fact that you are not carrying out your role in Maeterlinck's tempo. When you clean up energetically, then you stop "reporting" your part from the stage, and begin living instead.

---

8   Yevdokiya Aleyeva (1898–1973), Russian actress, a member of the Vakhtangov Studio from its inception in 1913 until 1919. One of Vakhtangov's favorite students, Aleyeva left his Studio in 1919 and joined the MAT. Aleyeva rehearsed and performed the role of the maid Virginie in the first variant of *The Miracle of Saint Anthony.* From the rehearsal records of the second variant of the production, it appears that Aleyeva came back to the Vakhtangov Studio in 1921 to reprise her role of Virginie. This information, however, could not be confirmed by any literature on the production. Kseniya Kotlubai is known to have played the role of Virginie in the second variant of the production.

To Alekseyev:[9] Anthony became somewhat frozen. Anthony is the most ordinary person. We would not want the audience to experience him as some kind of a romantic hero. [At the moment] You are kind in your own right, while you should be kind *to* her, toward Virginie. Anthony is a modest, quiet, harmless old man, but there is a force in him. People who do not break their inner laws carry such a force. Seek, Alekseyev, the point of view on Virginie. You should not be saintly in your own right, but rather in your manifestations. Otherwise you will end up playing a "theatre" saint.

Aleyeva dropped the prescribed, "pharmaceutical" manner of acting. Alekseyev, however, kept it; he only plays what is in the text. What does Anthony live with? He lives with his concern that Virginie would be at ease, would not get scared, that she would understand him, etc. These are all very simple tasks. Similarly in the second act there should be no such thing as a pseudo-classical tone, theatrical pose, etc.

To Everyone: Seek the tempo. Those places you know well according to tasks, you convey well.

To Aleyeva: Clean up faster, but do not let go of the kernel. As you search for fast tempo, keep the kernel.

Point of View

JANUARY 9, 1917

[*Vakhtangov*] *To Alekseyev*: No need to play a saint. Playing a saint is everyone else's job.[10] You must treat people with good-hearted irony and play your point of view on them as if they were children: "I know you feel strange that I am St. Anthony. I understand that, in your mind, 'of Padua' would even sound witty if it came after 'The Madman.' Nevertheless, this is so. I am the St. Anthony of Padua."

You must discover how you "wait" as Virginie goes to get Gustave; Anthony waits actively. He sees everything, notices, studies, and he finds a point of view on everything: "What a strange people."

---

9 Vladimir Alekseyev, a student at the Vakhtangov Studio from 1914 to 1919, rehearsed and performed the role of St. Anthony in the first version of *The Miracle of Saint Anthony*.
10 The saintly quality of St. Anthony will be created by everyone else in the cast responding toward Alekseyev's character as to a saint.

Creative Passion that Arises from Perceiving the Essence

To Zimnyukov:[11] Leonid Andreyevich, you say the lines of your role, while your soul remains at rest. You must achieve the sensation of blood rushing to your head when you show Anthony the door, and he does not obey. In order to achieve this, you must gain organic faith.

JANUARY 23, 1917

[*Vakhtangov*] *To Zimnyukov:* There is one answer to all stage problems: passion that arises from perceiving the essence. I react to the fact that I cannot pull Anthony away from the wall. This is not a generic feeling. Surprise should not be prepared in advance, somewhere on the shelf of your soul. It should appear spontaneously, if you appraise a fact.[12] You must approach Anthony with complete calm. You should just believe in the essence: the house, the foyer, the fact that there is a pilgrim before you, etc.

When you say, "She [Virginie] cannot look at the poor with indifference," you should know what you are talking about, you should fantasize three to four incidents that justify this line.

An actor thinks that he must be agitated. This is not true. An actor is not supposed to be agitated, but he must know what he is talking about.

On Creative Individuality

To Aleyeva: You must speak with your voice, the very voice you speak in life when you are old. Or do you think that in life you are always young?

On the Essence of a Bit and Character

JANUARY 29, 1917

[*Vakhtangov:*] Boris Ilyich [Vershilov] was serious. In the scene when you pull Anthony, you have not found a thing. This is why Boris Ilyich's entire [through] line is incorrect. You must remember: a scandal is

---

11 Zimnyukov was the real last name of the actor Leonid Volkov. (See p. 5n3.) Volkov played the role of Joseph in the first version of *The Miracle of Saint Anthony.*
12 See the Glossary on the definition of the terms "appraising the fact" and "shifting point of view on the fact."

about to break out at any moment. You are helpless, but you don't play a helpless person. On the contrary, you must be very energetic.

Boris Yevgenyevich [Zakhava's] character is taking shape. Antakol'sky's[13] character is not shaping up. You are *playing* your character, you don't have faith, you don't solve your tasks, and you do not communicate. The priest is all about insidiousness, slyness. Feel that you are here for the free lunch. Search for the comedy in the situation: I, a holy father, am being forced to show the door to a man who calls himself a saint.

Aleyeva already has simplicity, has a point of view on the saint. There still remains a lot you don't play to the end. You earned your right to "work" all your scenes up to Joseph's entrance. After that, you should continue searching. What you discovered by now, must be artistically developed.

To Alekseyev: Do not play surprise, when the doctor listens to your chest. In general, you must not play a fool. Anthony sees it all; he can see through all of them perfectly well. He can see that they are trying to fool him.

Now is the time to discover [the form for] the group of relatives. You don't have the right kind of "ensemble." You look a little like the Bolshoi Opera chorus. Discover the "ensemble's" tasks. Strive to fulfill these tasks with greater precision. When you notice the lack of precision, do stop and repeat it again. Take away what is extraneous. Only this kind of work will warm you up for your acting.

On the Essence of the Directorial Bit

FEBRUARY 13, 1917

In the scene of blessing, Anthony now has the following task: in this one moment he should give Virginie more than she has been given in her lifetime. His task is to calm her, to calm a human soul who has suffered so much. "No fear of the great sacraments"—this is what Virginie must play; this is what makes her different from everyone else.

---

13 Pavel Antakol'sky (1896–1978), Russian poet, playwright, director, and actor, a member of the Vakhtangov Studio from 1914. Antakol'sky authored two verse plays rehearsed at the Studio and also was responsible for the lyrics to the *Princess Turandot* songs. Antakol'sky played the role of the Curé in the first variant of *The Miracle of Saint Anthony*.

On the Character Essence

FEBRUARY 14, 1917

On the ensemble [of relatives]: everyone has come here for the inheritance. Every single person. Otherwise, there is point in featuring this group. Everyone in the group must smolder with some inner fire: envy, perhaps. They are all funny in their small human feelings and desires. Each figure is a [symbol of a] human flaw.

Shik,[14] for example: "I wish everyone would respect me and know what I am worth. No matter how much I inherit—even if it is all twenty-two houses—I will still feel wronged." She resembles a bird.

I see everyone with sharp elbows and rough hands.[15]

Point of View and Task

MARCH 5, 1917

Act II of *The Miracle of Saint Anthony* is being read at the table.

[*Vakhtangov*] *To Boris Ilyich* [*Vershilov*]: Everything must arise from one definite point of view. "What is going on, what kind of world do we live in?"

Task: to find a way to thank Anthony.

On Improvisation

MARCH 6, 1917

When I see such rehearsals, I begin to doubt: not what I teach, but if it is worth striving to achieve it.

Perhaps we should compromise: let's make and keep (make a cliché out of) a finely created stage pattern. In this case, everything will be well and good. The only thing is, my work will show in everything; you will not be there, and we will end up with a forced pattern.

Aleyeva did not make a cliché out of anything. For better or for worse, it is all from life, with no overacting.

---

14 Elena Shik-Elagina (1895–1931), Russian actress, director, and teacher. Shik-Elagina was a member at the Vakhtangov's Studio from 1915. She rehearsed and performed the role of the deceased aunt, Mademoiselle Hortense, in *The Miracle of Saint Anthony*.

15 This image was later developed to the degree of "grotesque" by Vakhtangov in the second version of *The Miracle of Saint Anthony*, when Vakhtangov redirected the performance in January 1921. See Introduction, p. 54.

Boris Ilyich [Vershilov], however, acted clichés all through. I can accept poor and colorless acting, but I won't accept a cliché. The ensemble is trying with all its might, but nothing comes out of it. The crescendo is not happening, and they are not the heirs. Boris Yevgenyevich [Zakhava] acts well, but he acts on his own.

On Festivity

If Boris Ilyich possessed some kind of exceptional external appearance, perhaps he would have the right to perform as he does. He would not have this right before art but rather before people. Boris Ilyich does not have this exceptional appearance, and he does not have this right. How can you gladden the hearts of the audience? Only through your feelings. Every person's feelings are interesting. You can gladden the hearts of the audience by your faith.

On the Character Essence

MARCH 7, 1917

Yevgeny Bogrationovich suggests all students speak about the rehearsal.

[*Vakhtangov:*] All notes are given very well. What is good, and what is bad—has been said already. It is only left for me to say why it was good or bad.

It was said that [the character of] Anthony used to be eccentric, and now it has become more ordinary. At the same time, he now appears to be moved by the call of God. This is absolutely true. This happened with Anthony because I tried to guide Alekseyev so that he would not make a cliché of his affective emotion, of his saintly elation. In a different play, perhaps, one can proceed from this elation, but here one should proceed from an ordinary, simple, kind man.

As I told you already: he sees everything, he has a wise eye, he understands people, and he sees their weaknesses through and through. You must convey from the stage what a staunch believer he is. You must speak the way modern cabinet members speak. [At the moment] You don't express such degree of conviction. This conviction has nothing to do with an ecstatic way of expressing yourself, nor with [an actor's] theatrical agitation. A man you play [now] is not capable of resurrecting anyone.

On the Feeling of the Author

The most awful thing is that no one feels the author. Anthony insists that he be let into the deceased woman's room; he could enter it on his own, if he wanted to. [Instead] He insists that he be called for, that they would recognize him [as a saint]. This is why he keeps observing [everyone around him]. He only stops observing when he resurrects [Mademoiselle Hortense].

[At the moment] The Doctor[16] only plays self-confidence. You can add the following [circumstance] to it: I did not get a chance to finish my trout.

On Improvisation

Yevdokiya Andreyevna [Aleyeva], you are moving through the performance well. You are now improvising. Later we will keep the best of what you discovered, and introduce the derived pattern as mandatory.

On Task

MARCH 16, 1917

[*Vakhtangov*] *To Alekseyev:* You are blessing (Virginie) rather badly; you are not caressing her at all. You should caress with your blessing.

Preserving the First Spontaneous Impression from the Play Following a Run-Through

MAY 2, 1917

What should come? What did we strive to achieve? Every second you must sense Maeterlinck's individuality, sense his humor, his smile. This should come from the play.

What is it that should come from an actor? He must remain himself. [He must] appraise a fact and react to it seriously, organically. It is important to satisfy the part of the soul that contains the first impression from the play. If you could see yourselves from the side, you would have said: this is not it. Why "not it"? Because this impression is completely unlike the one you received when you read the play

---

16 Meaning the actor Zakhava who played the part of the Doctor.

for the first time. The director and teacher are important as far as the first impression is important.[17] As a rule, six or seven rehearsals go on in a fresh and productive way. During the following rehearsals the director sustains the fire from the first spontaneous communion with the author. Then come rehearsals when the actor no longer burns [creatively], when he turns everything into clichés and stops sensing the partner; he knows not only what the partner is about to say but how he is about to say it. Before [I left], the form of your performance was in an infant stage, but everything was alive. Now everything is composed better, but it is also dull, monotonous; the author has disappeared completely, and you don't know where to search for truth, for the artistic truth. All memories of the first impression are gone.

On Repetition

Aleyeva turned everything into clichés ... Completely inattentive: you see nothing, your reactions are not organic, but mechanically professional, you have no tasks whatsoever, for the duration of the entire act—not a single task. Your role is ready. You must only discover one single thing: how to be alive. You must stop searching for an old woman. You must be Aleyeva all the way. Your acting today was not mediocre, it was unforgivable. Anyone could play it that way. This means that any depersonalized man can be on the stage. You completely lost Aleyeva. You only repeated a few old intonations, having removed the causes that used to evoke these intonations. In doing so, you lost their soul. Therefore, you completely deadened your intonations and turned them into an embalmed corpse.

How to go forth with your work? You must go to the stage as if for the first time. Remember the first impression, get rid of your speech characterization, and forget completely that this is a comedic part (by the way, it is not at all comedic).

---

17 On the "first spontaneous impression," see the Glossary and Malaev-Babel (forthcoming); on the role of the director in the theatre collective's creative process, see Introduction, p. 9.

Synthesizing Elements of the Technique: "What For," Festivity, Point of View, Passion that Arises from Perceiving the Essence, and Artistic Reality

OCTOBER 18, 1917

Ye. B. Vakhtangov asks Aleyeva:

"What do you do before Gustave's entrance?"

"I clean the room."

"What do you clean the room for? You don't have true feelings, because you do not know what you clean the room for."

"For the solemnity."

"What do you need solemnity for?"

"I want Aleyeva to become Virginie organically through the correct point of view on everything that takes place.

"Virginie needs solemnity so that 'she' [Virginie's deceased mistress] will feel it. And Virginie cries because she knows that 'she' won't feel it."

"I don't see that you love your mistress. Without that you cannot play Virginie.

" … Up till this point, you played without a festive sensation, and you continue playing this way—this is because you do not believe in the truth of the imagination. She who cannot believe is not an actor.

"You, Aleyeva, do not have faith, you do not have any mistress, just like Boris Yevgenyevich [Zakhava] does not have a wife in *The Enemies*.[18] No matter how much he tries to believe, he can't. That means that he is not yet an actor. He is a student, but not an actor. It is not difficult for you, Aleyeva, to create a mistress for yourself, because you believe easily onstage.

"I want all of you, including the ensemble of relatives, to believe in what you are doing."

---

18 Vakhtangov is referring to Maxim Gorky's 1907 play *The Enemies*. Excerpts from this play were used at the Vakhtangov Studio for scene study work.

30 Toward Fantastic Realism

REHEARSALS OF MAETERLINCK'S *THE BLUE BIRD*[1]

Notes on Act 1

OCTOBER 2 [1919].

How shall we approach the dream? Elements of this [psychophysical] state are: wonder, observation, I adapt toward the new [rules?] in the dream.

How shall I apply the state of activity on the stage?

I must take up: what would I do . . .

I must take up [illegible].

I must adapt—examine, be sly (if I am scared), I want to disappear, so that the fairy does not notice me.

A child thinks that if he freezes, a thief won't notice him. You must find strong faith in that.

Take advantage of the new circumstances. (I must hurry to read the book.)

You must strive to remember the dream.

The dream is exciting (you want to lie, oh, so quietly), this strongest desire manifests itself imperceptibly.

To compare [the dream] with reality.

In a dream, the body is gone; only the spirit is there, and this spirit is free—it can do anything.

I want to make sure this is a dream.

You cannot think; otherwise it will vanish.

The dream must be preserved. It will affect everything.

---

1 Vakhtangov rehearsed *The Blue Bird* at his Studio in October of 1919. Rehearsal records by Vera L'vova.

OCTOBER 16, 1919

Notes on Act 4, Scene 3: The Kingdom of the Future [The Azure Palace]

The [psychophysical] state in the Azure Kingdom—complete calm, satisfaction, plenty of sun, it is easy to breathe, like in Heaven. Every role requires the past and the expectation of the future; the combination of these two factors creates the perspective of the role.

The otherworldly sensation, it cannot be played from the head. Nature should come to life in order to activate the superconscious ... Nature can only come to life when the material aspects [of the role] become concrete.

This requires the memory of some past life.

Some justification is needed in order to make the nature trust [the reality of the stage]; it will come instinctively, thus bringing with itself the superconscious.

Only 1/10 of the role can be prepared; 9/10 of the role should remain subconscious; it must not be touched.

An actor can only approach the inner intensity by experiencing the entire gamut of his role's emotions.

Every actor must invent something for themselves.

Time is *fatum*.[2]

When time is disregarded, one may not hurry, revel in work, be an actor.

The hypothetical philosophy of the Azure Kingdom is thus.

People are born more than once.

Somebody lives "out there."

Time takes away.

Those unsatisfied did not get a chance to complete things "over there," so they strive for "something."

They die and find themselves on some planet; in the end, an ideal human is formed; a god, perhaps.

All this is for the sake of the future.

They are searching for what it is that they should create; inquisitiveness, constant thoughtfulness.

In the end, they will arrive at the universal feelings—love, compassion, etc.

If you desire to play heroic repertoire, first and foremost, you must develop your soul, voice, etc.

An active task—creating the future.

2   Destiny, fate (Latin).

We must [absorb] the vital *prana*, so that later we could fly into our lives and carry this vital energy.

I must [approach] this state. I must talk about the loftiest things I can speak of at this moment.

I must philosophize about things that could lead me toward the sun, toward bliss. I must build the steps that should bring me to the blissful state.

Notes on Act 1

OCTOBER 26, 1919

The nature of the awakening.

It takes a long time to distinguish it, you keep adapting to it, and finally realize that this is not a mountain, but a jar.

Fear must be played the following way: I want to be brave, I want to hold myself in check.

In order to speak of the otherworldly, you must be sure to attract your partner's attention—with a pause, with your eyes, etc.

Maeterlinck does not write conversations between one material body and the other but rather between one eye and another, between the two souls.

An actor's invisible rays must penetrate his partner, down to his very center.

Happiness is found in the selfless faith, in the [ability to] "discover happiness within myself."

Tolstoy, Christ.

If Maeterlinck's dialogue about "the other world" is not conducted in the right rhythm, nothing good will come out of this.

Plenty of radiation-permeation is needed . . .

(We rehearsed the first act of *The Blue Bird*, listened to the music, searched for the dream, and for the rhythm.)

Maeterlinck must be performed with eternity in mind, once and for all—Balmont[3] to the Moscow Art Theatre.

OCTOBER 29, 1919

When the music plays, the thought assumes the quality of the music.

When an actor gets accustomed to living with rhythm both in words and in movements—the fairy tale will come.

[Originally published in Ivanov 2011.]

---

3   Konstantin Balmont (1867–1942), Russian symbolist poet.

REHEARSALS OF MAETERLINCK'S *THE MIRACLE OF SAINT ANTHONY* (SECOND VARIANT)[4]

Notes on Act 1

MARCH 31, 1920

Vakhtangov: [...] Yevdokiya Andreyevna [Aleyeva]—Virginie. Forget, if possible, that you have been working on placing your voice and come out of character. You had a lot of good things: you treat the wreaths correctly, you lean well on your mop. I can sense that you do it out of your trust in Anthony. You ask well: "Have you seen the street?" You should receive Anthony's blessing sincerely, simply. You can act better than you did last time. When you got carried away, you could do anything—you became free. You had good characterization, clarity.

In the second act—the moment with the glasses is not good—not enough seriousness, you suddenly became young. You must find the point of view on Anthony, and then you can do whatever you feel like doing.

Anthony's persistence vanishes. I [Anthony] want my tone of speech to show that my resolve is unbending [see Figure 19].

With the arrival of the relatives we must bring to the stage satiety, calm, guts stuffed with partridges, prosperity. Virginie the maid, your passion will spontaneously come upon you. Your job is to restrain it and tap into your kindness when speaking.

I would like everyone to be satiated, content, concentrated. They don't pretend when they stand by the coffin. They do think of death. Tears pour out, but feelings are missing. How much time have I wasted on this—my business can't wait! It is dinnertime now. I paid my respects to the deceased, and now I can go eat. They sit down, they are eating already. Greasy lips. The deceased woman no longer exists. They quietly drink champagne. In half an hour everyone is drunk. Curé[5] says something. Everyone listens respectfully. "He is at his best." "What do you expect, where else have you seen such a funeral?" And suddenly Anthony arrives.

---

4   These rehearsal records, made by Vera L'vova, were originally published in Shikhmatov 1970.
5   The French name for the priest.

Figure 19
Yuri Zavadsky as Anthony in *The Miracle of Saint Anthony*, 1921. ©
Vakhtangov Theatre's Museum.

The first meeting with Anthony is ironic. No suspiciousness is needed. The essence: Virginie is the only one who believes, and no one else.

You must play them as good-natured. They come out, the taste of partridge still in their mouths. Anthony amuses them, maybe they even touch his clothes. When they say, "Turn him out," it is said calmly. All of it with ease; this is what servants are for—they will do it all.

A good-natured mood goes so far that Gustave, while coming out, can hum some tune; after all, he has got a million thoughts in his head, there is more business to be done, more business ...

No need to be surprised at the sight of Anthony. Bourgeois, in general, are never surprised. The fact that these people look after themselves well should be evident in everything. Gustave [O. N. Basov] comes out as if nothing has happened. He stands and looks. Bored eye. You think, "Oh, my God, living is so hard!" We must hang a walking stick [on the coat rack]. Take it in your hand and approach Anthony with it. "You are beginning to annoy me"—the stick is hung back on the coat rack. You should play Gustave's little potbelly and his short hands. A Frenchman is always tipsy, just a little. A German can only permit himself a drink on Sunday; however, he gets drunk.

Footman Joseph [R. N. Simonov[6]]. In his master's [Gustave's] presence he was one kind of a person. After Gustave's exit, he is another. First he fans himself—he is hot. After Joseph failed to push Anthony out, Gustave begins to help him, rolling up his sleeves, getting ready. You should be pushing him out in a businesslike manner. When they fail to push Anthony out, their surprise keeps mounting. The tempo changes. We must push him out quick, quick. It is necessary to remember that your hands are greasy. They push him out seriously, busily, as people who pull a desk full of books. You should not forget to appraise the event of failing to push Anthony out.

During the entrance of relatives and guests all attention [should be] on Anthony. You enter leisurely; you saw what situation Gustave and Achille [N. O. Turayev[7]] find themselves in. You asked politely, calmly, separating your speech with small pauses. Each of the characters can command the audience's attention in a particular segment of the scene, but only when he feels the theatricality of his situation. "Nothing can surprise us! We are buddy-buddy with the police!"—this is on everyone's mind.

We are wealthy—don't forget that. Everyone wealthy is well fed and content.

They see the poor on Sundays.

We need to create a crescendo in this scene. Each of the women should demonstrate herself—here I am!—and exchange glances [with each other].

6   Ruben Simonov (1899–1968), Vakhtangov Studio actor from 1920, served as the artistic director of the Vakhtangov Theatre from 1939 to 1968.
7   Natan Turayev (1892–1959), Russian actor and theatre manager. Together with Boris Zakhava, Kseniya Kotlubai, and others, Turayev organized the Vakhtangov Studio in 1913 and remained a Vakhtangov Theatre actor through 1925. He played the role of Achille in *The Miracle of Saint Anthony*.

V. K. L'vova's[8] point of view: curiosity. Her point of view on E. V. Lyaudanskaya[9] is caution. You must act what life onstage brings you. For example, Gustave disappeared, my Gustave, we have to go look for our husbands. When women arrive, men look at them silently: "As if things were not bad enough already, look, here come the women!" Gustave treats his wife's question with silence. Achille's wife questions her husband. No answer from him whatsoever. Then the women begin to besiege Gustave.

DECEMBER 7, 1920

Gustave: "He wants to revive Mademoiselle Hortense."

The Ensemble of Relatives: "What is that?" (They freeze in indignation.)

This must be sustained with clarity. It is as if they suddenly bumped into something. They soon forgot about it, however, and continued to carry on as busily and gaily as they did on their entrance. The group surrounding the *curé* is cheerful, they roar with laughter. They don't give Anthony much thought. We could easily do away with this one. When they call the *curé*, they already know that a performance is coming. Conversation between Achille and the *curé* draws constant reactions [from the group of relatives]. The *curé* is comical—each of you should find a point of view on him. The *curé*, as he tries to show Anthony the door: "The Great St. Anthony!" Laughter in the crowd of relatives and guests, but it is immediately cut short. When they all bow to Anthony—suppressed laughter.

The *curé*: "The deceased revered you above all other saints."

Ensemble of Relatives: "Yes, yes." (Laughter; everyone is convinced that Anthony will now go away. The *curé* points at the front door.)

Anthony: "No, here." (He points inside the house.)

Ensemble of Relatives: "What is this?" (Everyone straightens up with clarity and grows serious.)

"Yes, yes." (Seriously and very attentively. The eyes of the relatives and guests are pointed at Gustave. They silently ask, "Why don't you chase him out?")

Gustave: "He has a colossal power."

8   Vera L'vova played one of the female relatives of the deceased Mademoiselle Hortense in the production.
9   Elizaveta Lyaudanskaya played one of the female relatives of the deceased Mademoiselle Hortense in the production.

The Ensemble of Relatives: (A turnaround. They don't know what to do. Object—Anthony, they turn to him. Then, with utter earnestness, they call the doctor.)

The Doctor [B. Ye. Zakhava] should approach Anthony right away. It is better to play caution. Squirm less. Shoot with your little eyes at Anthony more.

Notes on Act 2

Maeterlinck introduced a miracle, and here is how people received it.

The doctor does not believe at all: after all, it is embarrassing; we are intelligent people; we can't believe in miracles.

Gustave. I can't even bring myself to pray, let alone tolerate a live saint. To us he is a blackmailer—push him out. When the miracle happened, the resurrection of Mademoiselle Hortense—I am not going to try making sense out of it. I don't what to know what it is. At the same time, we can't let him go like this. We won't give him much. Everything you see here is yours, but we all know that you won't ask for it, it is of no use to you.

When the relatives become certain that Anthony does not want money, they begin to find him quite endearing. They try to come up with a gift for him. They offer it with embarrassment. Oh, he does not accept. Then, "Would you like to have breakfast with us? No?" He starts annoying them. It is better to send him to the kitchen.

They keep talking with him, but the main focus is on the broken parquet plank. This man is still here, but I already forgot about him. "But the floor … we must redo the floor." Everyone becomes occupied with the floor.

"Can we get you a chair?"—a bourgeois joke. Gustave's speech—complacency. He speaks, while his eye keeps surveying the room—did I say it well? Everything sounds sincere. His speech is intended to evoke the following reaction from Anthony: "Please, I don't deserve all this! …"

When Gustave says "everything is yours," he knows that he would give nothing—this is why he says it with such ease. All of the guests should support this very atmosphere.

The appalled bourgeois call for the police to remove Anthony.

It is only as Gustave tells the story to the police captain that the ensemble of relatives begins to understand the meaning of what has happened. "Well, certainly," etc. The end of Gustave's speech is drowned by the chorus of voices. The police captain takes off his cap when he drinks the wine.

No sooner than Anthony has been led away, then Auntie sinks down on her pillows and dies again.

Everything drooped on everyone, it all became unnecessary. Ah? What? They are stunned. Auntie sinks down. Everyone looks, but no one understands anything. During this moment, you must sense your neckties coming undone, swelling colors, etc. You must loosen your muscles and wish to ask something, but your tongue does not obey you.

31 Fantastic Realism

REHEARSALS OF PUSHKIN'S *FEAST DURING THE PLAGUE*[1]

Task, Action, Thought

FEBRUARY 23, 1920

Vakhtangov works *Feast During the Plague* at the table.

[*Vakhtangov*:] Today we will attend to the thought, to the text. Let's try reading the entire text, selecting important words. Only let's agree to be serious. Search in stillness. It is possible to discover *a pose that lasts an hour.*

Ruslanov[2] speaks the monologue of the Young Man:

> Most noble president! May I remind
> About a man familiar to us all,
> Of one, whose jokes and entertaining tales
> Sharp repartees and humorous remarks,
> Most biting in their solemn gravity,
> Enlivened our table conversation
> And drove away the gloom, which nowadays

---

1 According to Vakhtangov's diary entry made in March 1921 at the All Saints' Rehabilitation Resort, the production of Pushkin's *Feast During the Plague* was supposed to be performed in one evening with Chekhov's *The Wedding*. Vakhtangov never finished the production of Pushkin's piece. These rehearsal records, made by Vera L'vova, were originally published in Shikhmatov 1970.

2 Lev Ruslanov (1894–1937), Russian actor and theatre manager; entered the Vakhtangov Studio in 1920. Together with the actor Osvald Glazunov, Ruslanov served as an administrative head of the Vakhtangov Theatre in Moscow until the time of his death. Ruslanov rehearsed the role of the Young Man in *Feast During the Plague*.

Infection—our visitor, inflicts
Upon the most brilliant of our minds …

[*Vakhtangov*] *To Ruslanov*: Let's set aside things such as the characteristics of Pushkin's verse, and the coining of text; let's first simply bring the thought to life. We must find a task. The first part of the young man's monologue is addressed to the President of the Feast, the second to everyone present. Simply say the thought, without any ornamentations, but with communication—otherwise the thought won't convey. Everything will come from the quality of the word "remind." You must stress "enlivened."

> Task: call to cheerfulness. I can no longer be silent.
> Action: I remind everyone, through the President of the Feast, of what took place.
> Thought: I can't bear it any longer.

Use only the most important words to convey this thought. Try it this way: glance everyone over, perceive their numbness, and experience the desire to disengage them from this state. Speak your lines out of this.

Ruslanov attempts to fulfill his notes. Vakhtangov stops him.

You do not perceive their state; they gave themselves over to the charm of death, *and I cannot* disengage them from it. Speak your lines out of this.

Sculptural Modeling

Then Vakhtangov addresses all of the actors:

First prepare your actor's instrument. Model yourself. You must find madness on every face. First prepare the instrument, then the inner life. It is imperative to find the madness of despair, the eyes that look at things and do not see them. ("I no longer need any of this.")

Discover this on your own, through the means of sculptural modeling, in stillness, you being your own sculptor.

Searching for the Atmosphere

Rehearsal moves from the table to the stage.

Let us search through the use of *études*. A theme has been given, but no lines. You can move and walk. Expand, be artists, search for this madness on your own. Then sit down [at the table] and speak. Fantasize: night, street, groans, emptiness, whispers, hoarse voices. Discover how they drink, wait. Stir yourselves up. It is all right for each of you to do this separately first—later you will all come together. Think about the meaning of death. They sit, drink, groan. Speak of something else. ("Ladies and gentlemen, why did I live?—Get away from me, don't yell, you devil!") Start a dance. Search for the fever of 104 degrees. Don't be afraid to speak the simplest words.

Sculptural Modeling

Vakhtangov moves to the next bit of the play.

I would like for the President of the Feast to embrace Mary. Mary has agreed to sing. It is imperative to find the following tableau. Everyone listens. We must find despair in the hands. Support your heads with coarse hands.

Turayev,[3] we will now model [forms] out of you. Your actor's instrument is not yet prepared. Don't let go of what you discovered for the President of the Feast. You must release all of your body—that helps.

Now then, let's start the bit—when everyone prepares to listen [to Mary]. Everyone makes movements toward her.

The Thought

MARCH 8, 1920

Vakhtangov's notes:

Let's start reading and searching for the thought. [I am referring to] the main thought, the one that determines why I speak a rhetorical period.[4] This is not an external search, but an organic one, in a theatrical sense.

Express the thought, for which you speak. In life we intonate depending on the thought that we want to express. Thought and inner state produce feeling. In rehearsals the right inner state is not at all vital. We must rehearse in our actual inner state, as it is. The result might be incorrect, but for the rehearsal it is not important. *What we need at this point is for everyone to speak organically.* During this time on the stage we, firstly, prepared our actor's instrument; secondly,

---

3 Natan Turayev rehearsed the role of the President of the Feast.
4 Rhetoric period is a complex sentence, especially one consisting of several clauses, constructed as part of a formal speech or oration.

searched for 104-degree fever; and thirdly, tried to determine the main thought contained in the text.

Now let us define this thought with *all* of Pushkin's lines.

When we discover the inner state of *The Feast*, when the words start pouring out freely, when the communication is there—only then will we begin to coin the lines.

Having grasped the thought first, we must then begin to speak it, paying no attention to the words. This will help us avoid cliché acting. "Nerve without the thought is drunk. Give the right thought to the nerve—you will get the correct feeling": this is what Vladimir Ivanovich Nemirovich-Danchenko says.

You must know how to allocate stresses. In order to express the thought theatrically we must stress those words that best express this thought.

Ruslanov speaks the monologue. Vakhtangov stops him.

To call someone to be cheerful does not mean yourself being cheerful, or cheering someone up. When all you play is a thought, without any point of view and action, you get a dry account.

At the Kamerny Theatre speech turns into a recital, because they do not carry out actions.

Point of View: Task

MARCH 13, 1920

Feast During the Plague (onstage).

[*Vakhtangov:*] First prepare an actor's instrument, find the necessary inner state, then fantasize.

Ruslanov speaks the monologue of the young man.

Ruslanov, you do not have a point of view on the President of the Feast. Act upon those present with your entire being. "Let it be so"—hopeless solemnity. Ruslanov, instead of waiting for something inwardly, you are merely pausing. You must fasten your eyes on them. You must become horrified at their immobility. As for everyone else, you must all appeal to the President of the Feast.

On Spontaneity

Every occurrence on the stage must be used: if a prop falls down, it must be acted upon.

Point of View: Task, Rhythm

To Turayev: Try inviting the entire company to ask Mary to sing. The President of the Feast must, from the very beginning, withdraw into thoughts of his [deceased] beloved. He does not allow anyone to touch that subject. "I need this song to be drunk. I communicate with the grave. I want no screaming and noise at this time. I want silence." Underneath it: darkness, fire, madness.

Silence must be seen and heard. A cry accentuates silence. We should make the silence merciless and constantly await its resolution.

The President of the Feast: first and foremost—do not tear me away [from my thoughts], allow me to stay in my shell. I need this quiet song in order to preserve the silence; this is why I am calling on everyone else to invite her [to sing]; their movements move Mary to sing.

"So that next we …"—this is addressed to everyone. I urge everyone to listen, and I promise what will follow.[5] After Mary's song, the President of the Feast himself breaks his silence and wants to say a toast. You must feel yourself in the presence of death—all of you. You must find the rhythm so that the words pour out on their own. Everyone must guard themselves from everything—from the plague. One may speak very slowly and yet still hold on to a thought in one's head.

On Set Design

The door should be taken off. The partition can be turned into a street lamp. The bottom of the window will be blocked by people. All of the lower space will be left dark. Black velvet outside the window. Houses in the distance—like skeletons.

Costumes: one common cape [covering the entire group of actors sitting at the table. Huge folds. I would like torches on the stage, flickering flame. *The Feast* should be performed inside Pushkin's frame.

[This translation is supplemented with previously unpublished materials, featured in Ivanov 2011.]

---

5 So that next we return to merriment / With greater madness, like someone who was / By visions separated from this earth.

Rehearsals of Gozzi's *Princess Turandot*[6]

Schiller's Turandot

In spring 1920, at the Vakhtangov Studio's small, two-storey building on Mansurov Lane, one of the female studio members got an idea to take up an excerpt from Schiller's play, *Princess Turandot*, for her independent project. Wanting to receive her teacher's approval, she came to Vakhtangov for advice and instructions, holding the respective Schiller volume in her hand.

Vakhtangov read the play. He became interested in it and, in the autumn, reluctantly decided to stage this fairy tale as one of the Studio's repertory productions. He made this decision as he could find no other play for the Studio. His choice was guided by our usual repertoire shortage, rather than by his great enthusiasm for the play.

The following, in short, is the initial directorial plan for Schiller's *Turandot*, as conceived by Vakhtangov: as the audience walks up the theatre staircase, they already find themselves surrounded by the atmosphere of the fairy-tale performance they are about to see: the theatre lobby, its foyer and auditorium, are decorated in the Chinese style; the performance itself goes on not just on the stage but also at different parts of the auditorium; it emerges in the least expected places, and the audience finds itself surrounded by the fantastical China and its fairy-tale tragedy.

Vakhtangov went to work. He spent several nights with pencil in hand working on Schiller's text. Vakhtangov was getting rid of the overly wordy sections that failed to propel the action. By doing so, he strived to achieve the laconic, clear, and coined quality of text he so valued onstage.

When the text was ready and the time came to start working with the actors, Vakhtangov's grave illness made itself known with an unprecedented strength. Vakhtangov was compelled to go to the health rehabilitation resort for a long period of time, having designated Yuri Zavadsky to carry out the preliminary work with the actors.

After Christmas, as the Studio somewhat settled in one part of its new building on Arbat Street, Vakhtangov came back from the resort. He did not, however, go back to work on *Turandot* right away. He had to first finish his work on the revival of *The Miracle of*

---

6   *Princess Turandot* rehearsal accounts were prepared by Boris Zakhava, in consultation with other Vakhtangov studio members. These accounts were originally published anonymously in *Printsessa Turandot* 1923.

Saint Anthony. Once this job was finished, and the performance was shown to Stanislavsky and Nemirovich, Vakhtangov faced the necessity to, once again, settle back to work on *Turandot.* He was shown the excerpts from *Turandot*—the result of the work conducted in his absence. They were performed by the fairy-tale characters alone; the *commedia* masks were yet to be featured. The result of the showing was completely unexpected: Vakhtangov refused to stage this play.

Vakhtangov felt that playing this fairy tale in earnest is impossible, unfathomable; he categorically rejected his initial plan of the production. As for any other way he could, or should, have staged *Turandot,* he did not know it.

Vakhtangov taught that every play asks for the one and only theatrical form that belongs to this play alone, as realized by a particular theatre collective at the given time. The form of every performance, therefore, must satisfy the following requirements: firstly, it should be organically connected with the essence of this particular play; secondly, it should satisfy the contemporary demands at large; thirdly, it should be a natural and integral manifestation of the given theatre company, a manifestation of the theatre collective's creative individuality at that given moment in its development.

As Vakhtangov did not yet know or foresee the only contemporary form of realizing *Princess Turandot* on his Studio's stage, he decided to decline staging this play …

The Studio Board made an attempt to persuade Vakhtangov not to issue his final verdict and attempt to begin the work; … Vakhtangov held no high hopes for the play. However, yielding to the attack that was waged on him, he said: "Well, all right. I will try to start fantasizing. What if we do it this way …" Then he added, as a side note, "I don't know anything yet. I might say nonsense." Suddenly, Vakhtangov grew enthusiastic. A completely new, harmonious and incredibly exciting plan of the future performance emerged before his listeners.

The New Concept

The actors in this performance should not play the fairy tale about the cruel princess. They should not merely convey the content of this fairy tale to the audience. Who cares if Turandot falls in love with Calaf? On the contrary, our actors should play their own point of view on the fairy tale, their irony, and their smile, directed at the "tragic" content of the fairy tale. This smile is merged with their love for the fairy tale. This is what must emerge as the new content of the performance. Vakhtangov wants to permeate the performance with a loving and gentle Vakhtangovian irony. It is evoked by the content of the ancient Italian theatrical novella. Who needs to see the real China on the stage today, in 1920? Who needs to see Peking, be it even a fairy-tale, fantastical Peking? Who needs a real palace to be erected on the stage—be it even a real *fairy-tale* palace? Who needs a palace where, screened off from the audience by the fourth wall of the psychological naturalism, Prince Calaf would suffer from his love pangs, wearing a magnificent costume a real prince would wear?

A *theatrical* world should emerge on the stage, not a fairy-tale world. A *performance* of the fairy tale must emerge on the stage ...

We have the right, said Vakhtangov, to play our performance as "presentational." We have this right, because we will manage, if we so want it, to also give a pure "experiencing" onstage. We know the methods and techniques of the Stanislavsky school. An actor who can "experience" the role, has the right to search for the theatrical form of expression, or "to present": he will be convincing, he will manage to fill the form with content and discover the right justification for his behavior on the stage. This justification might have to be discovered in the theatrical layer of the performance rather than in the psychological layer. As for the actors who "present" their roles, their performances are often not convincing, deprived of content and stilted. They do not know what "the feeling of truth" is, let alone "the truth of the emotional experience."

Vakhtangov is fantasizing. He imagines that this is exactly how it would happen in the faraway Italy of the seventeenth century ... He dreams of the kind of performance where the actor would shed the "ultra-real tears" while acting his tragic monologue. The purpose behind these tears, however, would be larger than simply evoking the audience's compassion for the suffering character. The actor's purpose would be carrying his tears to the footlights and laying himself open to the audience's applause. Such an actor would joyfully smile to the audience through tears, still wet on his cheeks. Then he would act some more, for as long as he feels like acting, and when he does not feel like acting anymore he would not act at all, having left this job to his partners. He would sit on the stage with perfect calm and chew oranges—his reward from the audience for the tears he just shed, and a well-performed monologue.

Improvisation: Gozzi's *Turandot*

Everything in this performance must sound like an improvisation, said Vakhtangov. The "actors' sweat," or effort and labor of the actors, who work onstage, should not be felt. In order to achieve this, a lot of "effort" should be spent in rehearsals. The improvisational nature of the contemporary performance does not imply an actual improvisation onstage. It implies that everything be made in advance, forged into a precise, definite, deliberate, and singular form that has been discovered through work. At the same time, this form should be delivered in such a way that the audience would perceive everything in the performance as if created on the spot—accidentally, spontaneously, subconsciously, entirely involuntarily. The very text of the play must sound as if it had not been committed to memory but rather created by the actor before the audience's eyes. The main goal has been determined thus: to act as if it was an improvisation.[7] This resulted in the demand of "ease." Ease must become the major force of the performance. In order to achieve this, every actor must become a "master." The performance of *Turandot* must revolve around the axle of *mastery of acting*. As far as rehearsals are concerned, the fairy tale of Princess Turandot is only a pretext for the performance, a pretext for training to be a master. As far as performances are concerned, it is a pretext for expressing the actors' mastery.

If this is achieved, then the very content of the fairy tale will imperceptibly become interesting and begin to excite the audience. This will happen, because everything in theatre that is presented theatrically inevitably excites the audience and arouses their interest.

Thus Vakhtangov defined the goals of the *Princess Turandot* production, and soon the work was in full swing ...

According to the new plan, it was decided to stage the play based on Gozzi, rather than Schiller.

Vakhtangov's Principles of Improvisation/Theatrical Communication

What methods did Vakhtangov use to help his actors achieve the above-mentioned goals?

The Studio began rehearsing the first scene: the meeting between Calaf and Barak. What is happening in this scene? Calaf and Barak tell what happened prior to the start of the play. Why are they telling this? So that the audience would know. Why does the audience need to

---

7   A more advanced principle of improvisation was outlined by Vakhtangov during his work on the second variant of *The Miracle of Saint Anthony*. It redefined the actor's treatment of "fixed form" in performance. See the Glossary for Boris Zakhava's definition of Vakhtangov's term, "feeling of the stage."

know? So that they would understand the events to follow. Therefore, this is an exposition. As such, it should be performed accordingly: as an open address to the audience. Each of the two actors should address the audience rather than his partner and tell the story in such a way that the audience would understand and remember. This means that both the emotional element and the psychological justification should be banned. If this is an exposition, then so be it. We must search for the means to convey it. Vakhtangov suggests that the performers listen to how the circus clowns speak. They know how to bring a thought home for the audience. They continue explaining a thought to the audience until they are sure that every audience member has understood and digested it well. They don't move on until this happens. They are also used to feeding the lines to the audience over a long distance; they are not investing the text with anything except for its content. This is exactly what is needed. So, the performers begin to train in speaking like clowns. This is being done so that the thought contained in the text would be expressed not through the text alone but also through the intonation that perfectly matches the thought. Vakhtangov assigns to Calaf and Barak the task of analyzing the text of their roles according to the methods and rules devised by Sergei Volkonsky.[8]

The next step is to achieve the ease and improvisational quality of line feeding. In order to do so, Vakhtangov suggests that the performers, instead of playing Calaf and Barak, play the Italian actors who perform these roles. These actors, without any prior agreement, improvise lines neither of them anticipates, right on the spot. Out of mischief, they create different obstacles for each other, compete with one another in wit, resourcefulness, inventiveness, etc. When the performers managed to achieve the suggested task, suddenly the text that was committed to memory acquired the necessary ease and began to sound like an improvisation.

Simultaneously, they searched for the ease in movement, primitive theatrical gesture, the manner of walking (strutting instead of walking), etc.

Having sketched, in general, the first scene, Vakhtangov assigns the fulfillment and consolidation of what was sketched to Boris Zakhava. In the meantime, Vakhtangov himself set to work on the female (third) scene, having skipped the second scene in view of its magnitude (being an ensemble scene).

---

8 Volkonsky's theatrical speech principles are outlined in Volkonsky 1913.

In the third scene Vakhtangov used the same means: he suggested that Anna Orochko, instead of playing Adelma, play an Italian actress who *plays* Adelma. [See Figure 20.] His fantasy made her the wife of the troupe manager and the leading man's lover. In Vakhtangov's imagination, she wore torn shoes, too big for her feet. As she walked, the shoes lagged behind her and dragged on the floor. She liked to play *awfully tragic* roles, and, no matter what character she played, she always held a dagger in her hand (so as to make her acting even more terrifying and tragic). An actress playing Zelima turned out to be a lazybones; she did not want to act, and she did not hide this from the audience (she really felt like taking a nap). All these ways of working were only necessary in order to find the ironic style and the right tech-

Figure 20
Anna Orochko as Adelma in
Princess Turandot, 1922. ©
Vakhtangov Theatre's Museum.

nique of acting, to achieve the necessary ease and create an impression of improvisation.

Improvisation of the *Commedia* Masks

Having sketched the female scene in general, Vakhtangov passed it to Kseniya Kotlubai for further work. Vakhtangov himself began working with the masks. This task was complex; the improvisational *style* of acting did not suffice here. True improvisation had to be achieved, including the improvised text, *lazzi*,[9] etc. The performers had to guess the improvisational style for the lines as well as the nature of the *lazzi* humor. At the same time, they had to develop their skill at feeding improvised lines to the audience and carrying out the conceived *lazzi* with ease and dexterity, etc. In short, a difficult and lengthy work lay ahead of the actors.

The first task Vakhtangov assigned to the performers was discovering the inner experience of the improvisers. Vakhtangov defined this experience as one of feeling extremely courageous and constantly being ready to take a risk. The actors should be prepared to face failure, or a flop. They should remain calm when the audience does not receive their jokes, in order to win it over in the end. "To lose shame," to feel confidence in oneself, to acquire complete inner calm which, coupled with the sensation of inner elation, produces courage—those were the tasks to be achieved by the actors playing the Italian *commedia* masks. To be able to survive failure with courage is the guarantee of the improviser's success, Vakhtangov used to say. The actors who played the masks had to spend one rehearsal after another courageously talking nonsense onstage. They had to do this for hours at a time, boring those studio members who sat in the audience—all in order to learn how to evoke an inner experience required for the improvisation.

Improvised Costumes

Turandot costumes conformed to the same principle of improvisation; they were improvised out of fabrics and objects that happened to be at hand. These costumes conformed to the principle of masking and making up a regular contemporary costume.

---

9   The comedic routine of the *commedia dell'arte*; the word comes from the Italian *lazzo*, which means a joke or witticism.

Costumes were created in rehearsals by actors. Vakhtangov suggests that the performers dress for rehearsals. Everything that could be found in the theatre wardrobe is put to use: Calaf winds up a towel for a turban; he uses a coat that belonged to one of the female studio members as a cape; he sticks a foil, used for fencing lessons, under his sash—and the fairy-tale prince is good to go [see Plate 10]. Barak puts on wide trousers borrowed from some vaudeville skit. Having tied the sleeves of a woman's knitted jacket on his chest, he fancies a splendid cape fluttering behind his back. An ivory book knife, to be used in subsequent scenes by both Calaf and Adelma, serves Barak as a dagger. Timur ties up a scarf on his head, instead of a beard. For his cape, he uses a canvas backdrop from the Studio's chamber stage. One of the wise men ties up a clothes brush as his beard and solemnly holds a wig head. One of the slave women substitutes a headscarf with wide pants and holds a handbag, etc. Finally, the basket is emptied, and poor Brigella is left with nothing. What is to be done? Without a second thought, the actor Glazunov, who plays Brigella, picks up the empty basket and ties it to his stomach, feeling himself incredibly fat [see Figure 21].

Commedia masks were later excluded from the general principle [of costuming]; it was decided to dress the actors who played the masks in the authentic traditional costumes of the Italian *commedia dell'arte*. The designer Ignaty Nivinsky altered their historic appearance somewhat to reflect his individuality as a contemporary designer. Nevertheless, he made sure that the Vakhtangov Studio masks could still be recognized as the historic Italian *commedia* masks. [See Plates 6 and 8.]

Naturally a question came up: what should serve as a "background" for these "maskings" the Studio actors put on in front of the audience? What kind of costume should be chosen as an everyday actor's attire? If each actor were to appear in front of the audience wearing the costume he usually wears in everyday life, these costumes would not be celebratory enough, and they would not harmonize with the festive theatrical performance. It was decided to invent a special "actor's working attire." All the proposals to this regard seemed far-fetched, deliberate, and unconvincing, because they were untrue—insofar as actors were not using any special attire in their everyday work. This is why Vakhtangov eventually decided to favor tailcoats for men and evening gowns for women—the kind of attire historically used by actors for their recitals. After the revolution, tailcoats gradually disappeared from common use and, therefore, became an exclusive attribute of an actor.

Figure 21
Osvald Glazunov as
Brigella in *Princess
Turandot*, 1922. ©
Vakhtangov Theatre's
Museum.

It was decided to commission women's gowns from one of the best
Moscow dressmakers. The Studio soon came to an arrangement with
Nadezhda Lamanova, who executed this commission.

Nivinsky invented wide and comfortable costumes for the *zanni*, or
the "servants of the proscenium." These costumes allowed the *zanni*,
who worked as skillful stagehands, their quick movements in scene
changes.

In the long run, Nivinsky's costume designs merely finalized the
costumes discovered by the actors throughout the rehearsal period.
Actors discovered the kind of costumes that allowed them to feel
as their character with the utmost freedom and ease. Nivinsky is a
constant participant in the rehearsals. He searches together with the
actors. Instead of searching in the privacy of his studio, he does so
right here, in rehearsals, intuitively discovering and improvising the

images he later formalized and fixed in his sketches. Thus, in full harmony with the mission of the performance, Nivinsky discovered the headwear for the wise men, created from the most unexpected objects: bread baskets, soup spoons, photography trays, napkins and random pieces of fabric. Khan Altoum's headwear, for example, was made out of a desk-lamp lampshade; a football served him as an orb, a tennis racket as a scepter; during his conversation with his daughter, Altoum wore a pince-nez, bathrobe, and a stocking pulled over his head, and he carried an issue of *Izvestiya*,[10] etc.

Stage Platform as "Improvised" Set

A universal "studio" must be created on the stage, [Vakhtangov demands,] where one could comfortably and easily train any theatrical exercise, or perform any kind of play. The main, functional platform must be built, with many small platforms. One should be able to build any configuration out of these platforms, as required by a given exercise, or a given play. The "studio" should feature doors for entrances and exits, a balcony, a trapdoor and an arch, a trapeze, the rings, and ladders for exercises in gymnastics. These elements can serve to hang the sets during the performance. An idea was born to build a large glass window, like the ones found in painters' studios, with a set behind it, depicting Arbat Street in winter. May the audience, transported into the sunny atmosphere of the joyful Italian *commedia*, nevertheless remember where they are. May the snowflakes falling behind the window remind them that this is just a performance, and they are only at the Vakhtangov Studio on Arbat Street. If, however, for the duration of the performance, they do suspend their disbelief, they would owe this exclusively to the magic of theatre art and the mastery of the actor, who managed to create a new life onstage. The window idea was later abandoned strictly because of the technical limitations (the small size of the stage).

The Initial Concept of the Prologue

The original idea for the prologue was thus: while the audience gathers in the auditorium, the actors train behind the curtain—it may be gymnastics today, rhythm tomorrow. Some performances will be preceded by a

10 Popular Russian newspaper, established in 1917.

singing lesson for actors led by Mitrofan Pyatnitsky, others by a speech class led by Sergei Volkonsky. In short, a regular class would take place on the stage, as per the Studio schedule. The curtain would yet be closed. When the audience gathers, four Italian masks would walk up the foyer stairs to the auditorium. They would enter the auditorium. From their dialogue, the audience would learn that that they have been traveling the world since the time when Goldoni claimed his victory over the author of fairy tales Gozzi, and his faithful Sacchi,[11] and the *commedia dell'arte* disappeared from the stage. The masks travel the world in order to remind people about the true theatre and true comedy. They traveled through the centuries from their beautiful sunny Italy and arrived in snowy Moscow. Searching for refuge, and a shelter from the winter cold, they wandered inside the Vakhtangov Studio's Arbat Street mansion. The masks would ask the audience where they find themselves now. When they learn that they were in a theatre, the masks would decide to organize a performance at once, employing the actors at hand. They would part the curtain. Having discovered actors engaged in their training on the stage (a teacher conducting the class would also be present), the masks would suggest to the actors organizing an improvised performance at once. A fairy tale about the princess of China, Turandot, would be proposed for its theme. The actors would consent, and immediately—since the audience is here—set to work. The roles would be distributed and bales of fabric brought from the Studio storage room. *Zanni* (i.e. servants), in the rhythm of the music, would dress the stage with these fabrics. A basket with all possible "rags" would be brought from the wardrobe. Actors would contrive their costumes in front of the audience, out of these rags. When everything is finally ready, the performance would begin. This initial plan of the prologue kept transforming in the course of rehearsals, until it reached the audience in its final form.

The Stage Platform

The theatre designer Nivinsky (invited by Vakhtangov immediately following their collaboration on the production of *Erik XIV* at the First Studio of the MAT) proposed to implement the following stage design: the functional stage platform must resemble a circus arena, confined by a back wall. The wall would form a spherical surface

---

11 Both Gozzi and Goldoni were affiliated with the Sacchi *commedia dell'arte* company, founded by the Italian actor Antonio Sacchi (Sacco) (1708–1788). In his talk, Vakhtangov suggests that Gozzi, as a true proponent of the *commedia dell'arte* tradition, was closer to the Sacchi Company.

around the platform; a gate, balcony, and a trapdoor below the balcony—all this would be incorporated into the wall. An arch (it was later substituted by a column) would be built in the middle of the main platform. Nivinsky also proposed that the platform be raked, rather than horizontal, with a steep rise from the proscenium to the upstage area. This was done in order to impart maximum expressiveness to the actor's body and give plenty of space for the director's fantasy, as he builds his *mises-en-scène*. Both the platform and the wall would be of gray neutral color. So, if today you wanted to use this platform, essentially suitable for any play, to perform *Princess Turandot*, all you had to do is make it up, or costume it, just as the actors would be costuming themselves. How should the stage platform be costumed? It should be costumed in anything that can be found in the Studio storehouse. [See Plates 5, 7 and 9.]

"Improvised" Music for *Turandot*

The work on *Turandot* was coming to an end. In the meantime, the rehearsals were still accompanied by improvised waltzes, polkas, and gallops, performed on a piano by a female studio member.[12]

At that point Kseniya Kotlubai proposed to organize an orchestra from among the students of the Studio School, who possessed even a modest knowledge of music, or, at the very least, had a good ear. A Studio associate, Aleksandr Kozlovsky, was delegated to organize the orchestra. The instruments were found: violins, mandolins, balalaikas, flutes, timpani, castanets, a drum, and even a dulcimer. The orchestra mainly consisted of the "musicians" playing ordinary hair combs, wrapped in cigarette paper. The improvised orchestra soon continued to play the same waltzes and polkas, previously performed on the piano. Then Aleksandr Kozlovsky attracted composer Nikolai Sizov, a student of Medtner,[13] to the Studio. Inspired by Vakhtangov's assignments, Sizov created the *Princess Turandot* music in collaboration with Kozlovsky.

---

12 Vakhtangov's attempt to commission the music for *Turandot* from the Italian composer Eugenio Esposito (1863–1935), who served as a conductor for the Moscow Circus orchestra, did not materialize. Esposito was perplexed by Vakhtangov's concept of an "improvised" orchestra. At the same time, Esposito played an indirect, yet important, role in the creation of *Princess Turandot*. His reminiscences of the popular Italian performers he witnessed in his childhood were so lively that Vakhtangov pronounced him "the soul of the *commedia*," and called his actors to absorb Esposito's childish and festive spirit.

13 Nikolai Medtner (1880–1951), Russian composer and concert pianist.

The Skill of Handling Theatre Accessories

By the end of the 1920–1921 theatre season, rough drafts of scenes 1, 3, 4, and 6 were completed at the Studio's chamber stage, and a contract agreement was signed with the designer.

When the season was over, Vakhtangov went to recuperate at a health rehabilitation resort, while the Studio went on a tour along the Volga and Kama riverbanks.

In fall 1921, the Studio returned from its tour to find the set and costume designs completed. They were created by Nivinsky in the course of the entire summer in collaboration with Vakhtangov. Nivinsky kept in close touch with him throughout the summer.

The work resumed. Vakhtangov challenged the Studio with a new slogan: the skill of handling theatre accessories. The actors started learning to handle their costumes, fabrics, and stage props. This had to be done rhythmically, in the rhythm of the music. Vakhtangov himself possessed an exceptional skill in this area. Anyone who saw a "dead" piece of fabric come to life in his sinewy hands—deft, soft, and agile hands—could not look at this spectacle without amazement and delight. Thrown up by Vakhtangov, the piece of fabric flew in the air, creating the most unexpected shapes. Moreover, it flew in such a way that it immediately revealed all the qualities present in this particular piece of fabric: the richness of its texture, colors, and movements. Vakhtangov would catch the fabric in the air, and it would begin to coil in his hands, like a living creature. He made one believe that his hands and fingers did not move the fabric but that the fabric strove to escape from his grasp. Such was Vakhtangov's skill of submitting a mere piece of fabric to his creative will and bringing it to life by the power of his mastery.

Vakhtangov spent long hours striving to cultivate in his students a seemingly simple skill of picking up a piece of fabric from the floor while expending minimal energy. This meant that the piece of fabric should be picked up with precision and spontaneity and a full consideration of the particular fabric's weight. The Studio spent long hours in these exercises, learning to "pick up" and "put down" objects. The actors were supposed to first pick up an object (a chair, for example) noiselessly, with freedom and ease, and then put it down exactly where it belonged—equally noiselessly, and with equal freedom and ease. Thus Vakhtangov developed in his students theatrical dexterity, precision and economy of movement, a faultless eye, and the feeling of the object.

Vakhtangov strove to achieve the kind of performance where no "dead" objects would be present onstage at the moment of acting. Living souls, and lively existence, should be present everywhere onstage; anything dead should come to life at the first theatrical touch—any fabric can be turned into a theatrical costume, and any object can be transformed into a stage property. Alas, the opposite is also true: any theatre costume can be made soulless, and any prop can be turned into a dead object.

Having outlined the main principles behind exercises, Vakhtangov designated Ruben Simonov, his most able student in the field, to conduct movement classes in his stead. [See Figure 22.]

While Vakhtangov conducted exercises and worked to revive the scenes started during the previous season, Kseniya Kotlubai prepared a rough draft of Scenes 2 and 7, not yet touched by Vakhtangov.

Figure 22
Ruben Simonov
as Trufaldino in
Princess Turandot,
1922. © Vakhtangov
Theatre's Museum.

Walking the Raked Platform

The construction of the *Turandot* platform was completed on the main stage in mid-December 1921. The results of the preliminary work conducted on the chamber stage were now moved to the main stage. Vakhtangov came up with a new slogan: training to "walk the platform." The platform was raked so an actor could not walk on it as they would on a flat surface; it was necessary to learn to walk and stand so as to fully utilize the rake for the most expressive *modeling* of the actor's body. New exercises were born out of this slogan: to step onto the platform, to jump off the platform, to walk across the platform from the upstage to the downstage, or from the downstage to the upstage, to come to a stop, to run across the platform, etc.

The Feeling of Today

As Vakhtangov rehearsed the scene of the riddles, someone came up with the idea of substituting for Turandot's riddles some other—more pointed, contemporary, or even topical—riddles. Vakhtangov imagined that it might be good if the audience, along with Calaf, was solving the Princess's riddles. This way the audience would appreciate the brilliant and unpredictable answers the Studio might create. Thus, Vakhtangov proposed to create riddles with answers such as "Konstantin Stanislavsky," or "Moscow Art Theatre," etc. An experiment, however, soon revealed that this should not be done, as this scene is supposed to make the audience care about Calaf's fate and the development of the plot—not about the content of the riddles. The riddles as such are unimportant. What is important is whether Calaf finds the answers. Topical riddles would distract the audience to the point that it would be difficult to restore their interest in the play's action. Finally, the theatre limited itself to substituting the third riddle (Venetian Lion) with one of Schiller's riddles (Rainbow); Gozzi's riddle was not accessible to a non-Italian audience [see Figure 23].

A larger question arose in connection with the scene of the riddles and the masks' improvised lines: is it permissible to introduce a topical and contemporary element into the performance, and where does one draw a line? Vakhtangov finally resolved the question thus: the contemporary nature of the performance should not express itself through a topical text or jokes on contemporary themes. It should show itself instead in the very *form of the performance*, which would be in harmony with the spirit of the times. Vakhtangov contrasted the feeling of the contemporary with the topical aspect. The feeling

Figure 23 Scene from Act 2 of Princess Turandot, 1922 (scene of the riddles). © Bakhrushin State Central Theatre Museum.

of the contemporary in the performance was the goal to be achieved; the topical aspect was to be avoided. Vakhtangov allowed the topical element in the masks' jokes and witticisms with great care and only in those cases when it was not done for a cheap effect. Vakhtangov only allowed the topical element when it was introduced delicately, not crudely, and in good measure.

The New Year's Eve Rehearsal

On New Year's Eve, the entire play was presented for Vakhtangov's approval in front of the Studio and its school. Also present were the guests invited to celebrate the New Year at the Studio, including Michael Chekhov. The presentation continued into the morning hours, ending at 8 A.M. This New Year rehearsal was very helpful in discovering the improvisational creative state; it significantly advanced the work on the play. A series of New Year-related tricks and jokes, as well as Studio-related witticisms, were incorporated into the play. The masks created a special text for the New Year. It was for this occasion that Yuri Zavadsky devised the servants' pantomime mocking the plot of the play. This pantomime was later featured in the performance, as an interlude between the fifth and the sixth scenes. During the New Year rehearsal, the character of Skirina appeared in Calaf's bedroom with a typewriter under her arm, instead of pen and ink; Calaf, during the same scene, dreamed of wise men, who courted the female slaves. This *Turandot* rehearsal also featured characters from Anton Chekhov's play *The Wedding*, as well as the outcry of the doctor's assistant (a character from Chekhov's *The Thieves*) whose horse was stolen. Calaf was preparing to flee Peking with a slew of bales and suitcases, etc. All these tricks were later scratched, but, nevertheless, they played a significant part by freeing the actors. It is with the help of these tricks that the actors discovered the appropriate creative state. It moved the remaining work along at a much faster pace.

The Medical Council's Verdict

After the New Year, the *Princess Turandot* rehearsals were temporarily stopped. Vakhtangov needed to dedicate himself entirely to the Habima Studio, where he was about to open *The Dybbuk*. After the opening of *The Dybbuk*, Vakhtangov went to the health rehabilitation resort for a period of ten days. This time, however, a ten-day vacation did not improve Vakhtangov's health—he came back from the resort feeling worse than he did when he left. Nevertheless, he immediately got back to work.

The Studio, concerned with the state of Vakhtangov's health, decided to call a council of physicians. The outcome of the council was devastating: it revealed that Vakhtangov's days were numbered: he had cancer. The doctor's verdict became known to the Studio's central group.[14] The central group went to great pains to conceal this verdict from the rest of the collective so as not to create an atmosphere of panic and depression around Vakhtangov.

Vakhtangov's Final Rehearsals

An interval in Vakhtangov's work, the entire month of January, was taken up predominantly by the production work, led by Nikolai Gorchakov. All the drapes decorating the stage platforms were sewn and embroidered by the Studio's female members. The work was in full swing—day and night, with needle in hand, the female Studio members, guided by Nivinsky, carried out their elaborate work. When all sets were ready, the *zanni* began learning to make fast set transitions in the rhythm of the music. They carefully learned every movement, as the slightest mistake could ruin the entire transition—one cannot catch up on a missed musical bar. Ruben Simonov and Boris Zakhava worked with the *zanni*. Simultaneously, Yuri Zavadsky oversaw the vigorous work of the masks.

Vakhtangov, who came back from the health rehabilitation resort in February, devoted himself entirely to the work. All of the work done during his absence, including the minuscule production details, was examined, corrected, completed, and approved by Vakhtangov himself. Separate scenes were elaborated and perfected, *mise-en-scène* finalized, and the musical composition created by Sizov and Kozlovsky approved.

The survey of all costumes was scheduled for February 20th.

The lighting for the first part of the play was set on February 22nd.

At the same time, Vakhtangov searched for the form of the "parade" meant to open the performance.

According to the initial concept, the actors were to be present in the audience, prior to the opening of the curtain. They would greet the arriving audiences; they would speak with their friends and, in general, carry on as if they are not involved in the night's performance. In the meantime, the orchestra would strike the march, and all actors would

---

14 The Vakhtangov Studio's central group consisted of his oldest and most experienced students.

head from the audience to the stage; they would quickly line up on along the proscenium and greet the audience. The curtain would open, the actors would put on their "maskings," in the rhythm of the music, and the performance would begin. This plan was later altered. The newly discovered form limited the parade to the stage.

The Last Rehearsal of *Turandot*

The entire performance was assembled by Vakhtangov into one single whole and completed in the course of ten days, from February 13th to 22nd.

Vakhtangov's rehearsals usually began between 10 at night and 12 midnight, and they often lasted until the morning hours. Vakhtangov divided his nights between *The Dybbuk* and *Princess Turandot*, as both plays were worked simultaneously. His days were occupied by his work at the First Studio of the MAT.

Vakhtangov's night rehearsals will forever remain in his students' memory as the happiest hours of their life although, more and more frequently they were interrupted by Vakhtangov's aggravated condition. More and more often Vakhtangov had to stop the rehearsal to rest for a short while on a leather couch in his Studio office. Again and again, with renewed energy, Vakhtangov would get back to work, until pain and exhaustion said their final word: "enough for today."

On February 24th Vakhtangov's work was finished. It was Vakhtangov's last *Turandot* rehearsal—the last rehearsal in his life— the night straddling February 23rd and February 24th, 1922.

Vakhtangov started the rehearsal by setting the lights for the second half of the play. The work with lights lasted long past midnight. Vakhtangov was not well, he was running a fever of 102.2 degrees Fahrenheit. He is sitting in his fur coat, his head tightly wrapped in a wet towel. His eyes ache from the constant flickering of the lights, but Vakhtangov is tireless and persistent: *he must finish today.* It was already four in the morning when the lights were set, and a command was heard: "The entire play—from start to finish." The entire play was "marked" in costumes, makeup, with orchestra and set transitions. When Vakhtangov finished the rehearsal, he went to his study and lay down on the coach. It took him a long time to gather his strength so that he could get home. It was full daylight when Vakhtangov was taken in a cab to his Denezhny Lane flat.

Never again did Vakhtangov get up from his bed; never again did he come to his Studio.

Turandot Dress Rehearsals

The first public dress rehearsal took place on February 23rd for the Studio members' friends and relatives. The success of the production did not yet become evident at that rehearsal.

On Monday, February 27th, a dress rehearsal was held for the entire MAT company and staff, headed by Stanislavsky, as well as for MAT First and Second Studios, and the Habima Studio. It is impossible to express the actors' agitation before the rehearsal. No one knew if Stanislavsky, the MAT, and all three studios would accept the performance. In the meantime, a few blocks away from the Studio, at No. 12, Denezhny Lane, Vakhtangov lay ill. He suffered from the thought that he could not come to the dress rehearsal and cheer up his students. During the "parade," Yuri Zavadsky read the following letter, written by Vakhtangov, in which he addressed the audience with a brief summary of the performance goals: "Our teachers, our senior and junior friends!"[15]

The first act alone brought the kind of success no one at the Studio could have anticipated. During the first intermission, Stanislavsky appeased Vakhtangov via telephone, informing him of the audience's impression of the first act. Finding the telephone conversation insufficient, Stanislavsky decided to go to Vakhtangov and share his impression in person. The audience in the house, and actors onstage and backstage, waited for Stanislavsky's return. The success grew throughout the rest of the performance. Every moment of the production, every witty situation and word, found live response in this exclusive audience—an audience imposing heavy responsibility on every performer. The applause went on and on after the end of the performance. "Bravo, Vakhtangov," proclaimed Michael Chekhov; by doing so he created a storm in the audience. A phoned telegram addressed to Vakhtangov was composed at once on behalf of everyone present. Stanislavsky expressed his wish to see the orchestra, and all instruments were brought onto the stage. Several musical numbers were performed in front of the audience. Then Stanislavsky addressed the actors, who gathered on the stage, with a short speech in which he expressed his joy at the victory achieved by Vakhtangov and his Studio. "In the twenty-three year history of the Moscow Art Theatre such victories were few," Stanislavsky said. "You found what many theatre companies sought in vain." After the performance, Stanislavsky continued talking with the

---

15 See p. 145 for Vakhtangov's address to the audience of the dress rehearsal for *Princess Turandot*.

Studio members for a long time, warning the Studio against getting too absorbed in their own success. He advised that they don't stick up their noses, don't stop at the victory achieved, and continue to work ceaselessly, perfecting and moving ahead. The next dress rehearsal for the press and theatre community took place on February 28th; it received a moderate response from the audience. Only the following performances made it evident that *Turandot* was enjoying definite success. Vakhtangov was not destined to see his last work—he had to be content with his students' and friends' accounts of the *Turandot* run. He constantly demanded that one of the directors who assisted him on the show visit him after each performance. Vakhtangov made detailed inquiries, gave instructions, encouraged and guided his Studio until his illness deprived him even of this last small pleasure.

Vakhtangov is no longer, but the memory of his creative work, of the inspiring days and nights, will live on. That memory will forever live in the souls of those whose training and work were governed by Vakhtangov's masterful hand—cruel at times, but also soft and gentle. Their best hours on this earth were captured in these memories.

Those who lived through such hours, do not dare reproach their destiny, however brutal the trials it may send them in the future [see Figure 24].

Figure 24 Finale of *Princess Turandot*, 1922. © Vakhtangov Theatre's Museum.

Part IX

Correspondence with Colleagues

32 First Studio of the MAT Letters

Letter to Leopold Sulerzhitsky[1]

August 4, 1912, Moscow

My dear, my precious Leopold Antonovich, yesterday Konstantin Sergeyevich told me that all last season I was improper ...

This is how he summed up my work, this is how he defined and characterized all of my work at the theatre.

All night through I searched my memory for ways in which I might have exhibited my impropriety.

I could not have been improper toward the theatre, even if I wanted to, since the place I occupy there is too insignificant. It is impossible to even invent a situation where an extra could be improper toward the entire organization—the organization where he stands in the lowest ranks and where his work outside of ensemble scenes is completely ignored.

Not once have I been improper toward actors, directors, or my peers, because according to my nature I cannot be rude and insensitive toward people in general.

I could not be improper toward you, because my respect, devotion, and love for you as my teacher, as a human being and as an artist, are too great.

Konstantin Sergeyevich is the only one left ...

I abandoned everything that could constitute my earthly prosperity; I left my family; I left the university when I was only one exam short of graduation; I resolved to subject myself to a semi-starving existence (as it was at the start of the year). This is enough evidence that in my soul I treat the object of my sacrifices as sacred. Is it possible to be improper

---

1 This is the first English-language publication of the letter.

toward what you love so much and with such joy? I have not insulted Konstantin Sergeyevich in word, thought, or deed. Not in his presence, not behind his back. If not for his presence at the theatre I would not have entered it to begin with, and, secondly, I would have left it the moment I felt that the theatre lost its link with its great creator and follows some path of its own, which is not to my liking.

People cannot and don't know how to be improper toward what they worship. And I cannot be an exception, as this would be against my very nature.

So, what are the signs of my year-long impropriety? I am lost, my dear, kind man. I understand nothing. Do help me figure it out.

Now, about my work.

I worked with the youth for a little more than four months. And here is what I did:

Prepared the youth so far that Konstantin Sergeyevich's language is no longer foreign to them.

Submitted my work to you, as it was required by Konstantin Sergeyevich's instructions.

This is it. What else could I have done?

It is true that, after a five-month break, I refuse, decidedly refuse, to demonstrate before Konstantin Sergeyevich my students' abilities to use his system's methods. This is because I firmly believe and know that the results of the exercises are only perceptible when they are conducted frequently. In two months' time (this is, on average, how long I trained each of the groups) one cannot master his creative self. And after a six-month break, one can no longer demonstrate even what was still fresh immediately after classes.

I don't know how one can ask more of me. I fulfilled everything that was required, as far as the time allowed me. I submitted my work to you. For five months I have not met with any of the students as far as training is concerned. They have been doing something—performed somewhere, learned something—so how can I show Konstantin Sergeyevich the ballast they perceived during these five months? How can I be so naive as to think that two months' work took such deep root that my students spent the following five months in daily exercises and assimilated what they just more or less began understanding and feeling?

When I, having just entered the theatre, began working with the people who have been at this theatre long before myself, I saw how wrongly they understand everything, or understand nothing at all, and how they laugh at everything that is dear to you and Konstantin Sergeyevich. At that time I understood that my predecessors had failed to cultivate love for the system in these people. This is why yesterday I took upon myself the courage to declare that Mister Mardzhanov's[2] classes brought the youth less good than mine. One can only cultivate love when he himself loves. I am not being improper if I maintain the fact that Mardzhanov's classes did less than mine. If I state the fact that at the theatre I found people who understood absolutely nothing prior to my classes, who now feel something, are excited, and do not mock [the system] (with few exceptions). I am speaking of the associates, a fraction of the school, and a fraction of the affiliate group.

What else can I do but point to that fact at the moment when such a heavy, significant reproach is cast upon me?

If I deserve this reproach, I will suffer an appropriate punishment. I am asking to be freed from all classes.

If I did not deserve it, it is a great sin: repaying me with a reproach of impropriety for my love, ardor, youth, faith, and boundless devotion.

As for the money, I wanted to have 1,200 [rubles per year] based on some comparative data, and this question is more a question of pride than of self-interest: I am ashamed to receive less than such and such for the work that is not a single bit easier. I don't like money, and it is finally of no difference to me how much I will get: what I need I will earn on the side.

The conversation that took place yesterday affected me so greatly that I was unable to come to work today; for that I apologize before you, and I ask you to convey it to Konstantin Sergeyevich.

I will digest everything, calm down, and come back tomorrow.

I am writing so that you won't think badly of me.

Loving you,

Ye. Vakhtangov

From Vendrovskaya and Kaptereva 1984

Letter to Aleksandr Cheban

AUGUST 3, 1917

... At the Studio they are rushing with the sets for *The Twelfth Night*. Stanislavsky concocted something awful. It will be beautiful, rich, unnecessary, and expensive. Up till this point it already cost 6,000. There goes the principle of simplicity! "Nothing superfluous, so that the audience does not demand expensive and visually striking productions ..."

---

2 Konstantin Mardzhanov (Kote Mardzhanishvili) (1872–1933), Georgian director. From 1911 to 1913 Mardzhanov worked at the MAT.

What a strange man Stanislavsky is! Why he needs this exterior—I fail to understand this. Acting in this setting will be difficult. I believe that this production will be very interesting externally, and that it will have success, but it will produce no step forward in the internal aspect. And the system will not win from it. And the creative individuality of the Studio will be polluted. Not transformed, mind you, but polluted. All of my hopes lie with you, my Rosmersholmers,[3] my brothers and sisters. We must bring to this work our pure, unembellished, true souls and a genuine awareness of each other. We must bring our fully preserved and untouched individualities, an almost spiritual, not theatrical, passion; an art of the finest embroidery of the delicate curves of the human soul, and a complete unity with the author's feelings. Through these means we must all unite with the atmosphere of the "white horses" and convince others that this kind of art, however complex, is the most precious, most exciting, and top-notch art.

This is a step toward mystery plays. External characterization is an amusing art, but on our way toward mystery plays we must step over its "attractive" corpse. Perhaps the very reason I like the way you play the doctor in *The Incurable*[4] is that you keep your own voice and your own intonations. One must approach character while proceeding from oneself, by asserting oneself. Our actors often proceed from their own individuality, taking the word "proceed" literally—they proceed *away* from their individuality [into their character].

I love theatre in all its incarnations, but I am mostly drawn to such moments in theatre that don't merely depict everyday life (although I love them too, if they hide humor or tragedy in a humorous mask), but to moments when human spirit is at its liveliest.

Reconciliation and quarrel by the Christmas tree—in *The Festival of Peace*. Scenes from the second act of *The Deluge*. The moment of silent panic from *The Deluge*. All of *Rosmersholm*. The second part of the fourth act of *The Cricket*. The scene with Toby at the bell tower from *The Chimes* and *Wandering Minstrels*. I find nothing of this nature in *The Wreck of Hope*. And since most of *The Twelfth Night* is nothing but magnificent buffoonery (not my kind of humor!), I don't see any possibility of stepping into the spiritual realm of theatre (vs. the realm of artistic spectacle) in *The Twelfth Night*.

---

3 Vakhtangov addressed the cast members of his production of Ibsen's *Rosmersholm* as "Rosmersholmers." Cheban rehearsed the character of Mortensgard in this production.
4 Vakhtangov is referring to the First Studio of the MAT's performance evening that featured an adaptation of the 1875 short story *Incurable* by the Russian author Gleb Uspensky (1843–1902).

Letter to Oleg Leonidov (Shimansky)[5]

OCTOBER 23, 1918

... If you look at my daily schedule, and do it carefully, with your heart—only then will you see and believe how inhumanly busy I am. Take yesterday, for example (all of my days are the same, really):

> From 12 noon to 3: the Habima
> From 3 to 5:30: a private lesson
> From 6 to 10: *The Festival of Peace*
> From 10:30 to 1 at night: rehearsals for the anniversary performance.[6]

One day, when you visit Nadezhda Mikhailovna,[7] do take a look at my calendar, and you will see this wretched schedule, made up ten or twelve days ahead. I don't even have time to eat; during fifteen minutes I am allowed for my lunch break I manage to receive someone.

When I go to work, or come back from work, I am almost always accompanied by someone who needs to talk business with me.

1 The First Studio
2. The Second Studio
3 My Studio
4 The Habima
5 Gunst Studio
6 The Popular Theatre
7 Proletkult
8 Art Theatre
9 a private lesson
10 November anniversary performance

5   Oleg Leonidov (Shimansky) (1894–1951), Russian writer and playwright, a friend of Vakhtangov's.
6   On October 22, 1918, Vakhtangov accepted the Popular Theatre commission to stage a performance featuring two one-act plays (*Thief*, based on Mirbeau's play *Scrupules*, and Lady Gregory's *The Rising of the Moon*). This production was meant to open on November 7th, to commemorate the one-year anniversary of the Bolshevik Revolution.
7   Nadezhda Vakhtangova (1885–1968), Vakhtangov's wife. After her husband's death, Nadezhda Vakhtangova published two collections of Vakhtangov's writings and headed the Vakhtangov Theatre museum.

This is the list of ten institutions, so to speak, that tear me apart.[8]
Tell me, where is that minute I can spend on myself?

It has been a month since I could carry out a simple desire to play my mandolin ...

I drag this colossal weight, doubled over from my illness ... And I cannot, I don't have a right, to say no to even one of these tasks—I need to give what I know, I need to have time to give what I have (if I have it).

I am so closely tied, morally, with each of the organizations that leaving even one of them is a crime. In the meantime, new organizations keep calling me, and, on top of it all, they tell me that I am supposed to create them ... Thank God that there is only twenty-four hours in a day, so, at least, I can refuse them on this basis.

Can you imagine? I earn almost no money, that is every month I accumulate a debt, and it keeps growing from month to month ... This is because I charge everyone who hires me so little. Why? I don't know, I simply don't know why ... My only hope is for my director's royalties—when the Popular Theatre's productions commence ...[9] Lots of negotiations, sums of money flicker in my eyes, even counting such sums feels scary—and it all comes to nothing in the end. Perhaps, I simply lack the skills ... Perhaps, I simply lack life skills.

So, I keep banging my head against a brick wall.

Letter to the First Studio of the MAT

NOVEMBER 26, 1918

Rosmersholmers!

My heart is with you.

I am excited for you, and I know that you will win. I kiss you, I bow to you, and I love you.

Well, everything we went through with *Rosmersholm* is now over.

How long was our road ...

May there be joy, joy.

Yours,

Ye. Vakhtangov

---

8   On October 29, 1918, Vakhtangov wrote in his diary: "Today's issue of *Teatral'nyi Kurier* (*Theatre Courier*) magazine printed the list of registered studios. There is a typographical error in this list that reads: "Vakhtangov's 9th Studio" (Vakhtangova et al. 1939: 125) The error would become a reality in less than three years. By 1921 Vakhtangov would be the head and/or lead teacher in about nine theatrical schools and studios.

9   This hope did not immediately come true: Vakhtangov's illness prevented him from personally directing the Popular Theatre's inaugural production.

Letter to Vladimir Nemirovich-Danchenko

JANUARY 17, 1919

… You do not know how inquisitively I seek the answers from you to many theatrical questions, and always find them. The first conversation on *Rosmersholm* energized me for the entire period of work, and when the work was performed for your approval, a lot was revealed to me. Soul and spirit,[10] nerve and thought,[11] the quality of temperament, "seconds [in the performance] that everything else is meant to serve." Clarity of bits, subtext, temperament, and the psychology of the author, searching for the *mise-en-scène*, directorial composition of bits that differ in density and yet much more, significant and beautiful, astonishing in its simplicity and clarity, became so familiar and filled me with the joy of persuasion. I won't have another chance to express all the gratitude I feel for you, and, perhaps, many years will pass in quiet and modest work before life sends me another real chance of associating with you. This is why I hasten to express at least some of my feelings and offer you the words, however humble, of admiration, faith, gratitude, and love—genuine human love.

With deep respect and esteem,
Ye. Vakhtangov

10 See p. 192, B, Parts 4 and 5. Nemirovich's concept of "soul and spirit" is not featured in his published works. The director might have referred to the process of an actor's transformation into character. Nikolai Demidov, for example, considered that while the actor's "soul" transforms into character, his "spirit" of the creator-artist remains unchanged. This concept seems to be in line with Vakhtangov's ideas, as outlined in his Plan of the (Stanislavsky) System, as well as Vakhtangov's overall creative beliefs.
11 During the rehearsal for Pushkin's *Feast During the Plague* Vakhtangov told his actors, "Nerve without the thought is drunk. Give the right thought to the nerve— you will get the correct feeling—this is what Vladimir Ivanovich Nemirovich-Danchenko says." See p. 285.

33 Letters to the Vakhtangov and Habima Studios

Letter to Konstantin Stanislavsky

MARCH 29, 1919, ZAKHARYINO REHABILITATION CENTER, NEAR KHIMKI RAILROAD STATION

Dear Konstantin Sergeyevich,

I beg you to forgive me for bothering you with my letters, but I am so miserable and having such a hard time that I can't help but appeal to you. I will write of what I never told you out loud. I know that my earthly days are short. I know calmly that I won't live long, and I need you to know, at last, how I feel about you, about the art of theatre, and about myself.

Ever since I got to know you, you became the one I came to love fully, whom I believed fully, by whom I began to live, and by whom I started measuring my life. This love and admiration I passed, intentionally or unintentionally, onto everyone who was deprived of knowing you personally. I thank life for giving me the chance of seeing you closely and even allowing me, from time to time, to associate with the world-class artist that you are. And I will die with this love for you, even if you would turn away from me. I know nothing higher than you.

In art I only love the truth you speak and teach. This truth permeates not only that modest part of me that expresses itself in theatre but also the part called "man." This truth breaks down the old me, day after day. If at the end of the day I don't have time to become better, it is only because there is so much in me I have to defeat. This truth, day after day, guides my attitude toward people, my self-discipline, my path in life, and my attitude toward art. I consider, thanks to this truth I received from you, that art is our service to the highest in everything. The art cannot and should not be a property of a group, property of certain individuals—it is a national heritage. Service to art is service to the people. An artist is not a treasure that belongs to only one group—he is a national treasure. You once said, "The Moscow Art Theatre is my civil service to Russia." This is what entices me; me—a little man. It entices me even if I am not destined to do anything and if I do nothing in the end. In this phrase of yours is every artist's Nicene Creed.

As for my attitude toward myself, I do not believe in myself; I like nothing about myself, never dare to think of anything bold, and consider myself the least of your students. I feel ashamed before you for my every step, and I always consider myself unworthy to show my work to you, the One and the Unreachable.

This is, in short, what I have in me.

Presently the young people I worked with, and whom I taught to love what I learned from you and Leopold Antonovich,[1] are coming to you. These young people stopped believing me. I do not know what they tell you, and how they tell it. I don't know what they say about me and my feelings for you.

I write to you now so that you will know the truth, so that you can see that I "don't have a swelled head," so that you can receive an impression about me directly from me. If you trust me, if you believe that one has no need to act against one's conscience when his days are numbered, if you believe that I am disinterested in my appeal to you, then you will also believe in what I say next. My every step and my every deed, connected with you, are illuminated with an indispensable and unchanging demand of purity, modesty, and regard for your name, from myself and the others alike. I was against showing you the excerpts, and now I am against showing you other works, as they are not worth your attention. I ask you to give me two years' time to create the face of my group. Please allow me to bring you a performance (not excerpts, not the accounts of work), in which both the spiritual and artistic entity of the group will reveal itself. I ask these two years, providing I am capable of working, in order to show you my true love for you, my true admiration for you, and my boundless devotion to you. I ask you to believe that I don't have any thoughts whatsoever—of career, desire to serve some important role, or of any kind of daring.

All I need from you is a little trust—not in my abilities, no, but in the purity of my intentions.

Loving you,
Ye. Vakhtangov

---

1 In 1919, twelve of Vakhtangov's most experienced actors left his Studio and joined the Second Studio of the MAT.

Letter to Vsevolod Meyerhold

NOVEMBER 10, 1920, ALL SAINTS' REHABILITATION RESORT

Esteemed Vsevolod Emilyevich,

I am seriously ill, and cannot come to you in person, although I have an immense desire to spend even a brief moment in your company; you are so busy. I ask you to receive my young friends—students, members of the Studio council of what is now the Third Studio of the Moscow Art Theatre. I have loved you as an artist for a long time. I loved your work in *The Puppet Booth*, *The Strange Woman*, and *Columbine's Scarf*. I have long sought an opportunity for a communication, and so, in case you might be interested, this communication is possible via the Third Studio. The people here are young, wonderful, and unspoiled by any "theatrical" traditions. Our people know how to be enthusiastic, and they know how to be excited in a good way. Perhaps, you will want to stage something with such people; perhaps, sometime you will come to talk to us ...

Please accept my greetings,

With feeling of sincere respect for you.

Ye. Vakhtangov

From Vendrovskaya 1959

Letter to Serafima Birman

AUGUST 8, 1921

Dear Simochka,

Your note at the Habima Studio touched me to tears. Do understand it literally. I believe you; I believe you and thank you. I too want everything to be well.

I wish that next year we would all be friendly and attentive, and tolerant of each other's shortcomings, and extraordinarily demanding of each other and of our theatre ethics—especially where we meet—onstage and in rehearsals.

I crave—yes, this is the word—crave working to the point of utter exhaustion. I foresee new theatrical horizons.

I imagine that in *Hamlet*[2] I will again discover a new form. I find it important, most important, that the Studio cherishes its mistakes and deviations from its course, as without these nothing can be discovered.

---

2   Vakhtangov planned to stage Shakespeare's *Hamlet* simultaneously in two different theatres: the First Studio of the MAT and the Vakhtangov Studio. See Introduction, p. 83, and also p. 320.

For as long as we walked along the well-trodden Art Theatre road, we did so peacefully and comfortably, without the slightest notion of what it means to stage and perform a play. From the same type of dough we baked a doughnut today, a pretzel tomorrow, then a bun, and then a tart, but the taste was the same. So, we walked along this road and reached a luxurious cemetery.

Now we know what we should do.

Without contempt for the elders; on the contrary, with even greater respect for them, we should do our *own* work.

And we will ...

We should update the old repertoire with the new form, with the new contemporary principles of the theatrical acting. So, if I have my health—together with those who would want to help me, I undertake to restage all our plays in such a way that they would sound contemporary. Without infringing upon the characters.

From Vendrovskaya 1959

Letter to Nadezhda Bromley[3]

To N. N. Bromley, on her saint's day [September 30, 1921]

Wondrous Nadya!

You have been particularly dear to me lately, and I am moved with enthusiasm, because you are such a talented author. I know that your play [*Archangel Michael*] is an event in the realm of theatrical form, and in the field of theatre literature.

Greetings on your saint's day.

Please excuse my paper and pencil.

Ye. Vakhtangov

From Vendrovskaya 1959

Letter to Nikolai Yanovsky[4]

[January 1922]

Dear Nikolai Pavlovich!

These are my days:

From 2 p.m. on: *Archangel Michael* [rehearsals] until 4:30 p.m.

---

3 This is the first English-language publication of the letter.
4 Nikolai Yanovsky (1894–1968), Russian actor, a student at the Vakhtangov Studio from 1920, later an actor at the Vakhtangov Theatre.

5 P.M.: working with Stanislavsky until 8 P.M. or 7:30 P.M.[5]
8 P.M.: Third Studio, or Habima, or else I am acting.
Following the performance, I rehearse at one of these two places.
I go to bed every day at 6—7 A.M. (until 1 P.M.).
You see, my dear, that I don't have a free minute, literally.
Do believe me that I want to see you very much. Do get better soon, very soon. I embrace you affectionately. May Vera Vasilyevna[6] forgive me—when I find a half hour window, I will come to introduce myself to her.
Yours,
Ye. Vakhtangov

Vsevolod Meyerhold's Message to Vakhtangov

JANUARY 3, 1922, 11:25 P.M.

My dear *collega*, in your quiet office I spoke (and relaxed) with the soldiers of your army. I lived through some pleasant moments and only regret that you were not there.[7] I would very much like to see you. Will you show us *Turandot* soon? Will you soon speak to the students at GVYRM?[8] The soldiers of my army eagerly await you. Greetings.
V. Meyerhold.

From Vendrovskaya 1959

Letter to Vsevolod Meyerhold

JANUARY 17, 1922

My dear, beloved Master!
Eternally grateful to you for everything you do in theatre, I thank you for every moment when you touch us, your enthusiastic admirers. I regret that I did not meet you back then—I have long wanted to glance at you.[9] I know that you are cross with me; but I am ill, very ill, and

---

5   Vakhtangov worked with Konstantin Stanislavsky on the role of Salieri from Pushkin's play *Mozart and Salieri*; see Introduction, p. 31.
6   Yanovsky's wife.
7   During his visit to the Vakhtangov Studio on January 3, 1922, Meyerhold left this written message for Vakhtangov.
8   Gosudarstvennyh Vysshih Rezhisserskih Masterskih, the State Advanced Theatre Directors' Workshop—a theatre school affiliated with Meyerhold's theatre in Moscow.
9   See the preceding document.

I walk hunched over, and my eyes are lackluster. One more thing—on January 23 I show *The Dybbuk* (invitation to you and Bebutov, and Aksyonov[10] will be mailed), and on January 30, *Turandot*. Frail as I am, I work day and night.

You won't like either: the first lacks definiteness, and the second is unworthy of your attention, because it is too subjective.[11] It is an honest confession of the Third Studio: "This is what we are doing so far. Scold us, if you can't wait for our consequent steps."

Forgive me, Grand One! Sometime—just give me a chance to catch my breath a bit—I will redeem myself. Do tell the soldiers of your army that I am extremely ill (I have had a recurrence of a gastric ulcer—endless bouts). I would embrace you warmly, if you would allow me. I would like to hear that you absolve me from my guilty feeling.

Loving you,

Ye. Vakhtangov

From Vendrovskaya 1959

Letter to Konstantin Stanislavsky[12]

JANUARY 21, 1922

Dear Konstantin Sergeyevich,

I have fallen quite ill, so that the last few days I have taken to my bed.

This is why I don't seek you for *Mozart*;[13] this is why I cannot come to you to speak about the "consolidation"; this is why I cannot be at the board meeting today. Now I need to open *Dybbuk* (Monday the 23rd) and *Turandot* (on the 30th, I assume), and then I will go to the rehabilitation center to take some rest.

Several times I was told that you are accusing me and Misha Chekhov of separatism.[14] Dear Konstantin Sergeyevich, this is a mistake. Let my studio comrades say how hotly I defend the project of consolidating

---

10 Ivan Aksyonov (1884–1935), Russian poet and theatre critic. In 1922 Aksyonov served as a rector at the GVYRM.

11 Subject to the Vakhtangov's Studio individuality.

12 This is the first English-language publication of the letter.

13 Vakhtangov is referring to Pushkin's play *Mozart and Salieri*; see p. 31 of the Introduction.

14 Vakhtangov, who worked in numerous Moscow theatrical organizations throughout his MAT career, was continually accused of separatism from the First Studio of the MAT by Stanislavsky. He is answering some of these concerns in this letter.

for the sake of the pantheon performances.[15] Misha does sin with the Third Studio a little.[16] This is a new flame of his.

The Third Studio is a small laboratory, and it cannot stand in anyone's way; it has no such plans as Misha speaks of. This was just a flash in Misha's mind; this flash is now all gone.

Loving you,

Ye. Vakhtangov

15 In 1918 Stanislavsky developed a plan for the Pantheon of the Russian Theatre, a permanent theatrical establishment that would feature the best performances of the MAT and its several studios.
16 Michael Chekhov was a constant presence at the Third Studio of the MAT, also known as the Vakhtangov Studio. Chekhov even taught there for a relatively short time, in fall 1915. The informal relationship between Michael Chekhov and the Vakhtangov Studio continued well beyond this point.

34 Three Final Letters

Letter to Nadezhda Bromley

MARCH 1922

Nadyenka, the doctor said that I definitely have pneumonia of the left lung. He said that it will pass very soon. Imagine that I, while also performing, can, let us say, rehearse well, let us say, from 2 P.M. on. What then?

Then very very carefully, we can begin some rehearsals at 12 noon. What then?

Why should [Michael] Chekhov rehearse?[1]

I swear that if a rehearsal was called today, my work would satisfy you considerably.

Please, take the hope away from Misha, especially since he sees it himself [that he does not have a hope of performing the role of Master Pierre]. Otherwise, it is very wrong. Drop me a couple of lines—how are the rehearsals of *Archangel* going, and what is being done at this time?

I am sending you two of Sergei's sketches for *Archangel*, for the ensemble.[2]

This is just in principle, of course.

Your Yevgeny.

It is so difficult writing while in fever.

---

1 Vakhtangov is referring to his role of Master Pierre in Bromley's play *Archangel Michael*. Vakhtangov rehearsed it until mid-February 1922. Vakhtangov remained bedridden from February 24th. At that point, Michael Chekhov, who rehearsed the role of Master Pierre in turn with Vakhtangov, assumed the role as a sole performer.
2 Vakhtangov is referring to his son, Sergei Vakhtangov (1907–1987), a noted Russian architect, who, in the 1930s co-designed the new building for the Meyerhold Theatre in Moscow (currently Tchaikovsky Concert Hall). The letter included Sergei Vakhtangov's makeup design.

Letter to Vladimir Nemirovich-Danchenko

APRIL 8, 1922

Dear Vladimir Ivanovich, yesterday after every act of *Turandot* they telephoned me to share how you received the performance. After your talk with the students, at night, four of them came to me and told me in detail what you said. I was extremely moved, and so was my Studio.

Now they bring me a package from you. Your photograph with such an inscription ... [3]

What can I say! I regret that I am so very weak and ill that I cannot come to you immediately and thank you for the joy; I regret that I am having difficulty writing and cannot gather my thoughts in order to say everything that fills me at this moment.

January of last year marked ten years since the greatest event in my life: I was accepted by you to the Art Theatre. "What would you like to give us, and what would you like to receive from us?" you asked in our conversation. "I want to learn," I replied.

And since then, to this very day, I learn. I learn from you and Konstantin Sergeyevich. You do not know how greedily I absorbed everything you said in the rehearsals of *Hamlet*, *Thought*, *Rosmersholm*, in general talks. I learned to understand the difference between your feeling of theatre and Konstantin Sergeyevich's. I learned to combine yours and Konstantin Sergeyevich's [approaches]. You revealed to me concepts such as "theatricality," and "the mastery of acting." I saw that in addition to "emotional experience" (you did not like this term), you demanded something else from an actor. I learned to understand what it means to "speak of feeling" onstage and what it means to feel. And many, many other things I learned from you; I told you about this once, however briefly.

My gratitude is deep and inexpressible. Your inscription on the photo is an act of recognition—there cannot be a greater joy for me, since recognition is the only thing an artist strives for in the arts.

To be recognized by you and Konstantin Sergeyevich, even if others do not recognize, is the top achievement. I am now afraid of the future: what if my next work does not justify the gift I was given!

---

3   Nemirovich-Danchenko's inscription read: "To Yevgeny Bogrationovich Vakhtangov, on the night of *Princess Turandot*. In gratitude for the lofty artistic joy, for marvelous achievements, for noble courage in resolving theatrical problems, and for beautifying the name of the Moscow Art Theatre. Vl. Nemirovich-Danchenko. April 7, 1922" (Vendrovskaya and Kaptereva 1984: 427).

Thank you, thank you for everything you did for me, perhaps, without even knowing it, and for giving me such a joy these days.

I would like you to take on the labor of watching *The Dybbuk* at the Habima. This work cost me my health. Firstly, I had to find a theatrical, contemporary treatment for [depicting] the mundane onstage, and, secondly, I had to "make actors." I had to act the entire play myself—all of the roles, down to the slightest details, down to every gesture, down to intonations and timbre of voice. I had to make every line, since the Habima troupe was so weak from the standpoint of acting and its mastery. I had to organize special, separate classes. Don't scold me, if you don't like it—this is an experiment, the search for form. It is an investigation; it is material for future works, if I am destined to work further.

Do forgive me for the long letter. I am very excited, and I am holding myself back.

Yesterday was one of the most festive days of my life, and I will never forget it, dear Vladimir Ivanovich. I bow to you, with the feeling of deep gratitude.

Please give the kind Ekaterina Nikolayevna,[4] who showed me so much kindness, my reverential greeting.

With deep and sincere respect,

Yevg. Vakhtangov.

I beg you to forgive my pencil—I am in bed, and I could not manage writing in ink while lying down.

Ye. V.

Letter to Boris Sushkevich

MAY 24, 1922[5]

Dear Boris Mikhailovich!

I embrace you, and through you, send my greetings to the male part of the troupe.

I recognize the significance of this day. I am excited for the Studio, for the play, for every performer (it is a good excitement), and I have

---

4   Ekaterina Nikolayevna Nemirovich-Danchenko (née Baroness Korf) (1858–1938), Nemirovich's wife.
5   This is Vakhtangov's last letter that he wrote five days before his passing. It was written on the day of the first dress rehearsal for the performance of *Archangel Michael* at the First Studio of the MAT.

an agonizing desire for the victory—now. If it comes today—it will be a miracle, but I do not doubt "tomorrow's" victory.

Archangel Michael is a phenomenon in theatre, a prime event. I doubt we can hope for a quick appreciation [of the majority] in a case like this. As for all the actors performing splendidly—I have been hearing it for a while. And if the form and content of the play do not reach the audience right away, this is only natural.

May God help the Studio, may God help you all. I embrace you. I love you. I shake everyone's hand. This is the first battle. Whatever the outcome may be—saving victory—it is not significant. Courage, courage, my dear, close, beloved friends.

Loving you, Yevg. Vakhtangov.

Glossary of Terms

action (*deistviye*)   In the Stanislavsky method, a process of an actor's psycho-physical influence upon their partner (or upon their own self), aimed at the fulfillment of an actor's creative task. According to Vakhtangov, a true motivation for an actor's actions comes from their ability to perceive the festive essence of the stage circumstances and events. (*See* "task," "festivity" and "creative passion that arises from perceiving the essence.") What follows is an actor's *creative process*, or *act* that involves the audience—a crucial recipient and co-participant in the creative action. (See Introduction, pp. 26–7.)

actor cultivation (*vospitaniye aktyora*)   "Actor cultivation must consist of enriching the actor's subconscious with varied abilities: freedom, concentration, seriousness, stage intelligence, artistry, activity, expressiveness, gift of observation, quickness to adapt, etc ... The subconscious, equipped with such a supply of means, will forge a near perfect creation from the material it receives.

"[Common] actor cultivation ... allows an actor to merge with the collective; its absence creates a division between the actor and the troupe" (p. 87).

actors' performance (*aktyorskoye predstavleniye*)   The type of performance, characteristic of the method of fantastic realism. In Vakhtangov's practice, actors' performance was fully realized in his final production of *Princess Turandot*. In this production, the audience was invited "into the midst of actors, doing their theatre work." The creative life of a *Turandot* actor was the one of a skilful master *performing* their character. Although each of Vakhtangov's performers played a role of a presentational Italian master-actor, Vakhtangov's performer, nevertheless, did so according to the laws of the organic creative life onstage (according to the School of Experiencing.)

adaptation (*prisposobleniye*)   An actor's unique way of resolving their creative task (*see* "task"). Vakhtangov considered an actor's creative *how* (an expression of their creative individuality) the leading component of the creative task and a reason that brought the audience to the theatre.

According to Vakhtangov, actors should improvise their adaptations anew at every rehearsal or performance. "Emotion can be expressed externally. This expression is called 'adaptation'; adaptations are characterized by the performer's talent; the more talented the actor, the more different forms of adaptation he gives, the more varied the fulfillment of tasks" (see p. 252).

affective emotions/sensations (*affektivnyie chustva, oschuscheniya*) In Vakhtangov's understanding, an actor's creative passions, born out of the sensation of joy and festivity, are grounded in an actor's self-awareness as a creative artist. This awareness allows an actor to recreate and amplify, without external motivation, any of the feelings they have ever experienced in their everyday life. Vakhtangov's concept of affective emotions and sensation is discussed at length in the Introduction.

appraisal of the fact, shifting point of view on the fact (*otsenka fakta, peremena otnosheniya k faktu*) An actor's ability to take in a new fact, or an event occurring onstage, according to the given circumstances of the play, or accidentally. As any other element of the system, the process of appraisal can be conscious, or subconscious. With subconscious appraisal, an actor spontaneously receives the essence of the event, or fact; this arouses an actor's creative passion and causes them to react to the event spontaneously. An actor can also strive to grasp the essence of what just occurred consciously, by the method of analysis. Analytical technique might allow them to *approach* the essence of the fact, but it won't allow them to permeate it. The depth of the appraisal and the richness of the reaction (adaptation) depend on the nature of perception. An intuitive perception allows an actor to react out of their creative individuality. Conscious perception causes them to intellectually manufacture their response; this type of perception produces a response that is logical but not necessarily original and unpredictable. At the same time, subconscious appraisal, or perception, does not guarantee an intuitive, creative reaction, as an actor may choose to put a brake on the perceived impulse, and react "intellectually." (*See also* "point of view.")

artistry, a desire to act (*artistichnost'*) Artistry is an actor's ability to sense himself or herself as creative artist with their individual artistic mission, or theme. A sense of artistic mission ("what for") begets an actor's desire to create. All elements of the Vakhtangov system are harmoniously connected with each other. The reader will sense the coalition between artistry and creative passion that arises from perceiving the essence, festivity, "what for," etc.

atmosphere (*atmosfera*) The actual term "atmosphere" was rarely used by Vakhtangov. According to the MAT practice, Vakhtangov used the term "mood." In contemporary theatrical vocabulary, however, "mood," or "emotional mood" has been substituted by "atmosphere." A certain psychological sensation or overtone that conveys from the stage to the audience through multiple expressive means—such is the contemporary definition of atmosphere. This is why, throughout the sourcebook, the term "mood" is translated as "atmosphere." This translation also helps distinguish atmosphere from the emotional life of the characters. (According to Michael Chekhov, characters in a given scene can live with different moods or emotions and nevertheless be united by a common atmosphere. This atmosphere, as it conveys to the audience, becomes a common "mood" uniting the actors with the audience.)

Vakhtangov denied the presence of artistic atmosphere in the MAT naturalistic productions. During his final discussions with the students, Vakhtangov insisted that naturalistic works produced by the MAT affected the audience with their bare content, or plot. Presented in the forms of life, these productions broke out of the artistic realm, turning an audience member into a witness to actual events. These events, presented as actually happening events, could depress, horrify, gladden the audience, but they could not radiate an artistic atmosphere. In Vakhtangov's view, festivity should substitute atmosphere in a theatrical performance, while the MAT's interpretation of atmosphere as "emotional mood" was incorrect. Vakhtangov exclaimed, "Only joy should exist in the theatre, and no atmospheres." (*See* "festivity.")

attention, concentration of attention (*vnimaniye*) "The second prerequisite of the creative state is concentrated attention, in brief—concentration" (see p. 176). (*See also* "muscular freedom.")

attention of the audience (*vnimaniye publiki*) A theatre artist's knowledge of the laws of audience perception that allows the artist to focus and guide their audience's attention throughout the performance. A director, who possesses the skill of manipulating the attention of the audience, can make the audience look at the stage reality from the theatrical collective's point of view. (*See* "directorial bit.")

audience (*publika*) A prerequisite for the specific (public) creative process of a theatre artist. In Vakhtangov's view, audience serves both as a source of artistic impulses for the actor as well as a creative collaborator in the formation of the performance's image.

Vakhtangov was asked how his suggestions as a director were embodied in the play in a manner that was inevitably "conveyed" to the audience. His answer was, "I never direct before an empty audience room. From the first rehearsal, I imagine the theatre filled with the audience. When giving my suggestions or demonstrating to the actor this or that passage, I 'hear' and 'see' clearly the reaction of the imaginary audience and reckon with it. Very often I quarrel with the imaginary audience and insist upon my point of view" (Chekhov 1991: 21). (*See also* "image," "character," and "circle of attention.")

breath (*dykhaniye*) Breath is the prototype of the musical measure, the ancestor of rhythm. Breath implies an ability to transform time and impart our soul with a sensation of rest, of the stoppage in time (Lussy 1884: 3; cited in Volkonsky 1912: 148).

No evidence of Vakhtangov's concepts of breath survive. Sergei Volkonsky, who worked with the Vakhtangov Studio students on movement and speech, had the following philosophy of breath:

> To receive and to give: these are the two life functions that belong to everything living on this earth. Breath continually repeats these two functions—from a newborn's first breath that begins the human's process of accumulation, to the "last breath," in which man returns to nature what he no longer needs. Inhale and exhale is a microcosm of our existence: inhale—birth, exhale—death … The principle of polarity that acts in this world, with all its manifestations—height and depth, strength and weakness, darkness and light, woe and joy—finds its expression in the rising and lowering of the chest. With this movement, a man takes from nature and gives back the air he took from her.
> (Volkonsky 1913: 32)

> Breath consists of two movements—inhale and exhale. The first movement is an action, while the second is rest. Because of this, the psychological meaning of both functions, as well as the general character of the spoken word, is determined by the stress placed on each of the functions. Inhale is heard in excitement, and exhale—in calm. All emotions can be divided into "inhaling" and "exhaling"; the first group is the one of suffering, the second group is the one of joy.
> (Volkonsky 1912: 148)

Breath exercises offered by Volkonsky were based in deep observation of life and nature; nevertheless, these exercises were external, or mechanical. When it came to mechanical exercises, Vakhtangov always advised his students to dive deeper into an exercise, in order to penetrate the very soul, or the essence of the technique. In other words, Vakhtangov insisted that his students use intuition to internalize external technique. By doing so, a student could gain a deep experiential understanding of breathing—the one inherent in the essential principles, as described in Volkonsky's philosophy of breath.

Both masters Vakhtangov employed at his Studio as voice teachers, Volkonsky and Pyatnitsky, insisted on the so-called "diaphragmal" breathing. Pyatnitsky, a self-taught man, practiced a more organic approach than Volkonsky. Here is an example of a Pyatnitsky approach to diaphragmal breathing that leads to a genuine emotional experience, as described by Nikolai Demidov:

> Speak a monologue, or a verse and, instead of following the lines, follow the stomach walls as they rise (with inhale) and fall; at the same time, he [Pyatnitsky] recommended not to inhale until all of the air was used up (until all of the air was squeezed out). And, instead of breathing with one's chest, to breath with one's stomach [diaphragm]!
>   With time, less and less concentration will be needed for the mechanical work per se, and the spare concentration will move onto the lines.

Little by little, the lines will begin to captivate and then emotionally move the actor.

(Demidov 2009: 252)

character, image of the character (*obraz*)   The word *obraz* in Russian has multiple meanings. In the artistic vocabulary, it means two things: image and character. Vakhtangov's approach toward character was essentially the same as in music, visual art, and literature. Theatrical character, according to Vakhtangov, is not a living, breathing human being but *an image of the character*, created by the living, breathing creative artist. Vakhtangov's concept of the character image is similar to his concept of theatrical reality. The artistic image of the theatrical production cannot equal life; it is a new artistic reality that does not duplicate nature and everyday life. At the same time, this reality is governed by the essential creative rules present in life and nature.

characterization (*kharakternost'*)   *See* "kernel" and "transformation."

circle of attention (*krug vnimaniya*)   "The circle of attention is a concentrated state, distinguished by free muscles and faith in the importance of what happens onstage. This circle can be expanded or contracted. An ability to swiftly shift the boundaries of the circle is one of an actor's very important qualities" (see p. 180).

In a "fourth wall"-type production, an actor's artistic world is "restricted by the circle of the stage characters" (see p. 247). During an actor's performance, in those cases when actors communicate directly with the audience, the actor's circle of attention (or artistic world) includes the audience.

clarity (*chyotkost'*)   An intrinsic quality belonging to every great work of art. Everything a theatre artist does onstage should be done with clarity and distinction. Vakhtangov speaks of the distinction of character drawing, distinction of bits in the role and the play, etc. He insisted that even "blurring" of movements, qualities, bits, and textures onstage should be done with clarity.

cliché, cliché acting (*klishe*)   Any spiritually and psychologically void theatrical form, be it character form, character adaptations, or the overall form of the performance. Theatrical form, deprived of creative impulse and literally copied from life or art, is called a cliché. Actors who repeat or borrow character forms and adaptations, mechanically reproducing them performance after performance, resort to clichés.

communication (*obscheniye*)   "We act upon our partner with the strength of our entire self—not just with our words and appearance, but with our whole being. This influence of my self on the self of my partner we will call 'communication.' During such communication with my partner, his spiritual experiences become an object of my attention. We shall also call it a partner's living spirit" (see p. 187).

concentration of attention   *See* "attention."

condensed form/condensed characterization (*ostraya forma/ostraya kharakternost'*)   A transitional form between physical characterization and grotesque; it implies defamiliarization of a realistic physical characterization.

contemporary form (*sovremennaya forma*)   The contemporary form, discovered by Vakhtangov for his final productions, was the form of grotesque (*see* "grotesque"). In Vakhtangov's views, this form was harmonious with the rhythms and forms of the revolutionary life. In fact, such a form can be contemporary to any period of a historic cataclysm. Contemporary form, according to Vakhtangov, requires a periodic renewal—throughout the life of the performance—in order to stay contemporary. Following his experiments with the contemporary form, or the form of grotesque, Vakhtangov was planning to work on discovering the eternal form (*see* "eternal form.")

creative individuality (*tvorcheskaya individual'nost'*)   A unique creative mission of an artist constitutes their creative individuality (*see* "what for," "festivity.") Full expression of an actor's creative individuality implies an actor's ability to live onstage as an improviser and "fantasize" their adaptations. Therefore, according to Vakhtangov, an actor can only practice their individuality by the means of spontaneous subconscious creativity. No matter how "stage savvy" or experienced an actor might be, intellectual expressive means and choices do not distinguish their creative individuality. Any other actor could arrive at the same choices, and the skill of manipulating the audience's attention onstage can be learned by anyone. "One can learn the means; as for the form—it should be created, it should be fantasized" (see p. 158).

creative passion that arises from perceiving the essence (*temperament ot suschnosti/volneniye ot suschnosti*)   An actor's ability (conscience, or subconscious) to condense the stage circumstances to their very essence and spontaneously react to this essence onstage. This term of the Vakhtangov method is closely connected with another aspect of his technique: festivity. In Vakhtangov's mind, festivity (an acute sense of living and dead tendencies present in every phenomenon) constitutes the essence of every stage event, character, circumstance, object, etc. For any theatre artist, the essence of the stage object (event or circumstance) is connected with this universal theme. Each artist's creative individuality responds to it in its inimitable way. According to Vakhtangov, it is this theme (and not the actual object) that inspires an artist's creative passion.

creative spirit (*tvorcheskiy dukh*)   In Vakhtangov's philosophy, the highest force obtainable by human beings on earth. Evoking the creative spirit is the ultimate goal of Vakhtangov's method and theatre.

creative state (*tvorcheskoye samochustviye*)   An actor's self-experience, grounded in festivity. According to Vakhtangov, the creative experience of every artist is based in festive joy, but it also varies, based on the creative individuality and the artistic laws of the given performance. In other words, there is no "generic" creative stage, as there is no "generic" theatrical truth. Both the creative state and the feeling of truth need to be rediscovered anew in every production and in every role.

desire (*khoteniye*) "An actor's every step is justified by a certain desire. While living in character, an actor, at any given moment, wants something; an action is born out of this desire and is followed by the feeling that comes last" (see p. 252).

"An action and the desire to implement it, i.e. artistry—such is the essence of the stage task" (see p. 182).

Vakhtangov considered artistry an actor's desire to fulfill his or her artistic mission, the only true desire fueling an actor's creative life onstage. (*See also* "task.")

directorial architecture (*rezhissyorskaya arkhitektura*) Directorial architecture, or composition, is based in the concept of stage rhythm. It implies harmony of the separate parts of the performance that arises from the director's ability to embrace the entirety of the production. Many of the expressive means outlined in the glossary are used as means of directorial composition.

directorial bit (*rezhissyorskiy kusok*) A section of the performance, in which the creative collective communicates a particular aspect of their overall creative task to the audience.

discipline (*distsiplina*) An actor's sense of responsibility for the form of the performance. When engaged in a performance, based in the contemporary form, or in the form of grotesque, an actor is supposed to discover a special kind of creative freedom, based in the rigid discipline of the pre-established form. In Vakhtangov's philosophy, the category of discipline is closely connected with the actor's feeling of the stage. (*See also* "freedom.")

dynamics (*dinamika*) The laws of movement and gesture, outlined by François Delsarte (*see* "gesture"). In Vakhtangov's philosophy: continuous inner (psychological) movement of the performance, accompanied by alternations between external (physical) movement and stillness. (*See* "rhythm" and "statuary immobility.")

essence (*suschnost'*) In Vakhtangov's philosophy, essence is the creative spirit, invested by the artist-creator into the creation. Out of this spirit, the play and the role can grow organically. As long as a theatre artist preserves the sense of the play's, or the character's essence, the artist is able to live creatively onstage—from the essence. The essence of an artistic work resides within the subconscious realm, and, therefore, it cannot be fully intellectually defined. The essence of the artistic work is absorbed as the artist receives their first spontaneous (intuitive) impression from the work. (*See* "spirit," "creative passion that arises from perceiving the essence," "subconscious perception.")

eternal mask, eternal form (*vechnaya maska, vechnaya forma*) The form of theatre that always remains contemporary, as it evolves and renews itself in *every* performance.

étude In theatre training practice, an *étude* is an improvisational exercise with a simple plot.

everyday life/the mundane (*byt*)   "Resolving the mundane elements of life artistically onstage," according to Vakhtangov, is one of the most difficult theatrical tasks. In his letter to Nemirovich-Danchenko, Vakhtangov wrote that in his production of *The Dybbuk* he "had to find a theatrical, contemporary treatment for [depicting] the mundane onstage" (see p. 327).

eye (*glaz*)   According to Vakhtangov, an actor's eyes are their most powerful means of expression and a source of continuous spiritual radiation.

faith/gaining faith (*vera*)   An actor's belief in the seriousness of their artistic mission awakens their creative passions and allows them to "gain faith" in the artistic reality of the stage. The truth of passions begets faith. "The moment of passion within the theatrical creative state, when an actor almost forgets that he or she is onstage, is the moment of faith, the moment of truth" (see p. 92).

fantasizing (*fantazirovaniye*)   An *active* psycho-physical life of a theatre artist's imagination, instrumental to the theatre artist's creative process at all of its stages—in development and execution of a theatre work.

fantasizing about the role (*fantazirovaniye o roli*)   An actor's ability to vividly recreate and *allow inside* elements of his or her character's imaginary environment (the events of characters' lives, their likes and dislikes, the people that surround them in life, etc). The homework of fantasizing about the character leads an actor to the subconscious, improvisational fantasizing in rehearsal and performance. (*See* "saturating yourself for the role.")

fantastic realism (*fantasticheskiy realizm*)   A creative method, formulated by Vakhtangov and utilized in the creation of Vakhtangov's final productions, such as *The Miracle of Saint Anthony*, *Erik XIV*, *The Wedding*, *The Dybbuk*, and *Princess Turandot*.

"Naturalism in theatre should not exist, and neither should realism. Only fantastic realism should exist. Rightly discovered theatrical means give an author a true life onstage. One can master the means; as for the form, it should be created, it should be fantasized" (see p. 158). (*See also* "actors' performance.")

feeling of the stage (*stsenizm*)   An actor's ability to experience his or her body and psychology as an instrument for creating stage forms and theatrical textures; his or her movements and voice are an expressive means within the space and time of the performance.

Vakhtangov's close colleague, Michael Chekhov, had this to say about the feeling of the stage:

> The sense of stage space is ... unfamiliar to the actor. He does not distinguish the right side from the left, he does not distinguish in all its fullness the proscenium from the back of the stage, the straight and curved lines in which he is walking ... An actor's eyes are his means of maximum expressiveness, although they will only be truly expressive when the whole of the actor's body, imbued with will, is drawing

forms and lines in the stage space ... The body in space and rhythms in time—these are the means of an actor's expressiveness.

(Chekhov 2005: 59–60)

Zakhava (1930: 130) described this principle thus:

Only when everything [the form of the performance] was prepared, has the actor *regained* his right to improvise (movements, gestures, intonations), according to those requirements dictating the form of the performance. Thus the actors received their right to improvise "adaptations" only when there was a guarantee that they became so firmly grounded in the principles of acting in a given performance that their improvisation won't leave the boundaries established by these principles. The actors' ability to improvise "adaptations" while sensing full responsibility for these adaptations, i.e. subjecting adaptations to the requirements of the form and mastery of acting, is called by Vakhtangov "feeling of the stage."

The "feeling of the stage" is an actor's ability to live and act in the environment of "stage air." Vakhtangov taught that the "stage air" differs from the one we usually breathe. Just as one cannot feel and act the same in water as on earth, one also cannot feel the same on the stage as in everyday life. As one finds himself in water, one ought to adapt to the new environment. He becomes responsible for his behavior, and he ought to subject his every movement to the environment's demands. In order to stay in the water, one must learn to *swim*. So must the actor adapt. As he finds himself on the stage, he must learn how to "swim" in the stage environment. Without such ability he will "drown." The slightest movement on the stage does not equal its life equivalent; the slightest movement on the stage is of great consequence, as *the audience sees it*.

Vakhtangov scholar Natalia Smirnova (1982: 33) provides the following definition of Vakhtangov's term:

Vakhtangov staged a production and simultaneously taught his actors how to model a blocking; he developed in them a skill of seeing themselves from the side, being able to sense themselves in the space, drawn in a blocking. This cannot be achieved without developing "in an actor the sense of his own material, as well as the sense of the stage air as a condensed environment. According to Vakhtangov, an actor was supposed to feel himself in this environment, like in water. He had to develop a different way of calculating his movements, and a special sense of responsibility for every movement he makes."

(Zakhava 1930: 130)

festival/festivity, joy (*prazdnik, rados't'*)   The essence of the theatre process, every theatrical situation, as well as the essence of creativity.

There are moments in a man's life when he wants to live more than ever and when he joyfully feels himself belonging to everything living.

He becomes vigorous, and both his good and bad seeds express themselves with special vividness.

In such moments a man becomes inspired, his eyes light up festively, and he fills up with vigorous desires and a thirst for activity. This is a festive moment.

It is the same for an actor.

(see p. 108)

first reading (*pervoye chteniye*)　A crucial stage of a theatre artist's creative process when the first spontaneous impression is formed and the creative spirit of the work is absorbed by a theatre artist. (*See also* "essence," "spirit" and "subconscious perception.")

first spontaneous impression (*pervoye neposredstvennoye vpechatleniye*) The essence of the artistic work is absorbed as artists receive the first spontaneous (intuitive) impression from the work. (*See also* "essence," "spirit," "first reading," and "subconscious perception.")

freedom (*svoboda*)　An actor's ability to freely follow their creative impulses onstage. (*See* "organic technique" and "crossing the creative threshold".) "The entire teaching is a device, the means to achieve something. This 'something' is an absolute freedom!" (see p. 99).

full stop (*tochka*)　An expressive device used to prepare and sustain rhythmical bits in performance. A full stop usually comes at the end of a play/ role bit, to separate one bit from another and, thus, achieve definition and clarity of rhythmical division. (*See* "statuary immobility" and "clarity.")

gesture/laws of the gesture (*zhest*)　If rhythm is meant to transform and organize space and time, then gesture is the most powerful device an actor has at their disposal in order to execute their rhythmical patterns and create the image of character, or performance. A man's relationship to space and to self is expressed in gesture.

"Gesture is an expression of a human being's inner self by the means of his external self. Gesture is a process of self-modeling that constantly evolves both in terms of a man's relationship to self and to his surrounding world. Each human being is a center of his own cosmos, and his every movement causes a shift of all the relationships. An arm is a beginning of an endless radius; its end touches an invisible and seemingly nonexistent periphery of the universe" (Volkonsky 1912: 16).

The size of the glossary does not allow outlining all laws of gesture. Here are a few of those especially important for Vakhtangov:

- Gesture is connected with the thought behind the words, rather than with the literal meaning of the words.
- The spirit of the gesture should permeate an actor's entire being and affect their psychology, body and speech.
- The gesture will only be theatrical and beautiful, when it is inwardly purposeful.
- Theatrical gesture requires a physical and esthetic balance. Delsarte's

law of opposition in gesture implies interdependent positions and responsive movements of the different parts of the human body. "When the limbs follow the same direction, they cannot be simultaneous without injury to the law of opposition. Therefore, direct movements should be successive and opposite movements simultaneous" (Delsarte; quoted in Stebbins 1902: 262).

Theatrical gesture must be fully executed. "A gesture, when discovered, should be executed *in its completeness* (except for those cases when the psychology of the character requires the gesture to be incomplete)" (Volkonsky 1912: 34–35).

According to Delsarte, "There are nine laws that govern the significance of motion in the human body, namely: 1. Attitude; 2. Force; 3. Motion; 4. Sequence; 5. Direction; 6. Form; 7. Velocity; 8. Reaction; 9. Extension" (Stebbins 1902: 257). Other fundamental laws of gesture and movement outlined by Delsarte are the laws of trinity, evolution, and correspondence.

The types of gesture used in theatre are numerous. We distinguish between historical gesture, national gesture, descriptive gesture, "automatic," or reflexive gesture, gesture of the individual characteristic, archetypal gesture, psychological gesture, etc. Vakhtangov used all of the following gestures as his acting and directorial expressive means. For example, in Vakhtangov's production of *The Dybbuk*, several characters had their own gestural "*leitmotif*," a repeated gesture that expressed their psychological and social essence. According to Vakhtangov, a gesture he observed from a Jewish accountant, his ward mate at the health rehabilitation resort, served him as an inspiration for the form of *The Dybbuk*.

grimace (*grimassa*)   A physical mask of the character. Vakhtangov utilized it for those characters, executed in the manner of condensed characterization, or grotesque. Vakhtangov the actor used the grimace for the facial mask of his character of Tackleton from the First Studio of the MAT production of *The Cricket on the Hearth*. Tackleton's facial mask featured lips pursed in disgust and one eye permanently screwed.

grotesque (*grotesk*)   A form of the theatrical art that allows an artist to create a form that expresses the quintessence of the object being depicted or to emphasize its particular aspects. Several definitions of grotesque exist in Russian theatrical practices, given by such different artists as Meyerhold and Stanislavsky. Vakhtangov's definition of grotesque is featured in Nikolai Gorchakov's book *Vakhtangov's Directorial Lessons*:

> Grotesque is a method that allows an actor and director to inwardly justify the content of the given play in a dramatic and condensed way. Grotesque is the limit of expressiveness, a rightly discovered form that manifests the deepest, innermost essence of the play's content. In the art of the director, grotesque is the conclusion of his creative

search expressed through the harmonious, organic combination of the performance's form and content.

(Gorchakov 1957: 41)

Another definition of Vakhtangov's art of grotesque is given by the Vakhtangov scholar Natalia Smirnova. In her book on Vakhtangov (Smirnova 1982), she writes of Vakhtangov's tendency to introduce satirical elements to a character after it has been thoroughly developed by an actor, in accordance with the school of psychological realism. In other words, after such an actor "justified" his or her character, Vakhtangov asked them to condense some of their character's psychological or social traits to the form of the tragic-comic grotesque: "From the collision and struggle of two opposing forces—lyricism and satire, psychological element and a tendency toward 'mask-like characterization'—an entirely new quality was born, endowed with sudden tragic overtones" (Smirnova 1982: 32).

hands (*ruki*) "Hands are the eyes of the body" (Ivanov vol. II 2011: 532). Vakhtangov considered hands the most expressive part of an actor's body. In his productions, such as *The Miracle of Saint Anthony* and *The Dybbuk*, the expression of the actor's inner life culminated in their hands.

In terms of expressiveness, legs and feet play a supporting part, while arms and hands play the leading part; legs and feet bind us to the earth while arms and hands lift us up from the earth. The unbendable law of gravity acts upon our legs and feet. Our arms and hands are permeated with an upward striving; our legs and feet ground us, while our arms and hands free us from the earth and lift us up (Volkonsky 1912: 155).

image (*obraz*) In the Vakhtangov method, an archetypal (symbolic, grotesque) image is behind the entirety of the performance. The original source of the archetypal imagery, according to Vakhtangov, is myth—a creation of popular consciousness. The image of the performance is formed gradually, throughout the entire performance. It is formed within the audience's subconscious mind and does not reveal itself to the audience in its entirety until after the performance is over.

image of the character *See* character.

instantaneous grasp of the whole (*mgnovennyi vsestoronniy okhvat*) An actor's ability to instantly permeate the essence of a play, character, or theatrical situation, thus being able to conceive (and consecutively recreate) their subconscious creative intentions. (*See* "subconscious perception" and "essence.")

joy (*rados't*) *See* "festivity."

justification (*opravdaniye*) "What should one do in order to gain … faith? In order to do it, one should discover a justification, that is the cause of every given action, situation, sensation, etc." (see p. 177).

Vakhtangov distinguished between the Stanislavskian psychological justification that originates from the private life of an actor and *artistic* justification. When Stanislavsky justified theatre according to everyday life (What would I do, how would I behave if, in my real life, I was put in a similar situation?), Vakhtangov justified theatre according to the creative life of an actor. The question Vakhtangov actors asked of themselves differed from Stanislavsky's formula. According to Lee Strasberg (1988: 85), this question was, "The circumstances of the scene indicate that the character must behave in a particular way; what would motivate you, the actor, to behave in that particular way?" Overall, Vakhtangov's take on justification is closely connected with an actor's ability to sense the seriousness of their mission, as well as the festivity, artistry, and passion that arises from perceiving the essence, and other concepts of the Vakhtangov technique featured in this glossary. (*See also* "theatrical justification.")

kernel (*zerno*) An inner sensation that causes actors to assume the character's external characterization and express themselves as characters, both physically and psychologically. Realistic characterization, as one of the theatrical textures, and as one of the techniques of drawing the image of the character, was preserved by Vakhtangov. Vakhtangov did, however, abandon the inner technique of the "kernel." The image of the character, according to Vakhtangov, does not originate from the character's kernel. It is conceived when the creative spirit of the author fertilizes an actor's (theatre artist's) creative spirit. (*See* "transformation.")

mastery (*masterstvo*) An actors' ability to *consciously* express themselves onstage according to the requirements of the external technique, as dictated by the form of a particular performance. (Vakhtangov's master also inwardly justifies the fixed form of the performance, however complex it might be.) An actor who possesses the feeling of the stage, however, can subconsciously improvise according to the *principles* of the required form. (*See* "subconscious expression.")

modeling (*lepka*) An actor's ability to model their body, speech, and psychology. (On modeling, see Vakhtangov's rehearsals of Pushkin's *Feast During the Plague* in Part VII of the sourcebook. *See also* "sculptural expressiveness," "plasticity," and "feeling of the stage.")

motivation/motive (*tsel'*) In the realm of the play's circumstances, a pretext that motivates a character to enter the stage and engage in their actions. Since these pretexts are fictional in a theatre performance, Vakhtangov believed that true motives of an actor's creative passions lie in his or her subconscious artistic mission.

mouth (*rot*) According to Vakhtangov's student Boris Vershilov, in the summer of 1920 Vakhtangov confessed to him, "I am now creating a new method, the method of presentation ... I am now interested in the mouths" (Vershilov 1959: 392). Vershilov also noted that, when the following year he watched Vakhtangov's production of Anton Chekhov's *The Wedding*, he was reminded of this confession of Vakhtangov's:

> In this performance, the mouths acted onstage in an unexpected, unusual way. At times they were round and wide-open mouths,

stupidly yelling the ridiculous "hooray." At other times, they were stiff and pursed angry mouths, appalled by the unworthy behavior of "the general" … As we watched this production, we were reminded of Goya's etchings; Goya was one of Vakhtangov's favorite artists.

(Vershilov 1959: 392)

mundane, the   *See* "everyday life."

muscular freedom and control (*muskul'naya svoboda i kontrol'*)   An actor's ability to spend a *sufficient* amount of muscular energy for every activity. Overspending or underspending muscular energy would lead to physical tension and interfere with an actor's creative process. Therefore, Vakhtangov called muscular freedom the first prerequisite of an actor's creative state.

"Muscular freedom and concentration closely depend on each other. When you are concentrated, you are necessarily free, however, a lack of muscular freedom won't allow you to concentrate your attention. This is why, first of all, you must destroy tension, as far as possible, and then discover an object for your attention. The remaining trace of tension will then disappear" (see p. 176).

mystery (*misteriya*)   In Vakhtangov's philosophy, the Theatre of Mystery evokes the presence of a higher force, or a higher being, and unites the audience and the actors in this act. Vakhtangov's final productions achieved the synthesis of the Theatre of Mystery and the Popular Theatre, thus signifying a new type of performance. In Vakhtangov's theatre, the audience and the actors united in evoking the creative spirit.

naivety (*naivnost'*)   "Applying my faith to the task before me causes me to become *naive*. This notion should be set apart from its usual interpretation. My faith does not come as a result of my naivety; rather, I become naive as a result of my faith. *Faith, achieved through justification, causes naivety*" (see p. 178). In other words, creative faith makes an actor "naive" and allows them to create new points of view on the stage. (*See* "point of view" and "seriousness.")

object of attention (*obyekt vnimaniya*)   "By sending our attention in some direction we are going to create a center of attention. It is clear that we cannot have two centers of attention at the same time; one cannot at the same time be reading a book and listening to a conversation in the next room. At any given moment, you can only concentrate your interest upon one object. Such an object we call *an object of attention*. A sound, a physical object, a thought, an action, your own emotion or your partner's emotion can all become an object of your attention.

"How can we attract our interest to one particular object? We can concentrate our five senses either on some object, or on a sound (hearing), our thought power upon some thought, and inner feelings upon a feeling, be it our own feeling or our partner's. *Every second of his existence on the stage an actor must have an object of attention*. Otherwise, an actor won't be able to experience the required feelings at his own will" (see p. 176). (*See also* "attention" and "muscular freedom.")

observation (*nabliudeniye*)   A character study technique where an actor is asked to observe a person in everyday life and bring to class the results of their observation. Instead of narrating their observations, actors are asked to perform them. The school of experiencing requires that actors don't stop at incorporating the external aspects of people's behavior but inwardly justify their observations. According to Vakhtangov Studio class records, in February 1915 Vakhtangov introduced a new principle of observation (see pp. 106–8), Fyodorov (1993) described it thus:

> Vakhtangov's students observe objects [imaginary characters] inside of themselves; they imagine these objects as they appear to them—these objects are born of the students' imagination and, therefore, represent a part of them. This changes a person. People who train this way are no longer reduced to the plane of *extractors*, grasping to the forms of the external world. These people transform into artists, who, through their own experience, gain an essential knowledge of the world's unity. These people sense all things, learn to know themselves and the others from inside, and they possess an infinite inner space. They are also aware of this [inner] space, and they express it in the forms of art. People who train this way become transformed into people-creators; Vakhtangov put all of his efforts into cultivating such people.

organic technique, crossing the creative threshold   Practicing organic technique requires an actor's courage to trust that whatever he or she actually experiences while crossing the threshold of the stage will apply to the fulfillment of his or her creative task. According to Vakhtangov, an actor does not need to alter his or her experience upon entering the stage; it is individual and unique, and, therefore, valuable. An actor's creative nature will incorporate this experience into the equation of the creative task; this subconscious nature will eventually create the needed artistic effect out of the actor's initial experience. An actor's job is not to interfere with his or her creative impulses and yield to them fully onstage. In other words, an actor should allow himself or herself full freedom to do what he or she truly feels like doing onstage. The creative subconscious will take care of the "required" artistic result.

passion that arises from perceiving the essence   *See* "creative passion that arises from perceiving the essence."

perspective (*perspektiva*)   There are several kinds of perspective that belong to the art of theatre. Vakhtangov introduced the perspective of varying expressive means, or theatrical textures, utilized by the actor. This issue is thoroughly discussed in the Introduction. The overall perspective of the performance is mentioned in Vakhtangov's directorial plan for the production of Ibsen's *Rosmersholm*. It is achieved through the composition of main and auxiliary bits. In his letters to Nemirovich-Danchenko, Vakhtangov mentions quotes from Nemirovich's lessons in the realm of perspective, such as "seconds [in the performance] that everything else is meant to serve" and "composition of bits that differ in density." Finally, the issue of speech perspective is approached by Vakhtangov through such terms of his technique as thought (perspective of thought) and voice-leading (word-leading).

plasticity (*plastichnos't*)   An essential artistic quality that implies complete physical and psychological freedom, harmony, flexibility, and naturalness. According to Vakhtangov, plasticity is a natural phenomenon, and, therefore, a theatre artist must absorb it from nature. (*See* Vakhtangov's notes on plasticity, p. 120.)

"Actors should engage in long and diligent work to consciously *cultivate* the habit of plasticity, so that later they can unconsciously *express* themselves in a plastic way. This applies to their ability to wear a costume, adjust the volume of their voice, achieve physical transfiguration (through a visible external form) into the form of the character they portray, allocate their muscular energy efficiently, and model themselves into anything in gesture, voice, or musical speech. Actors should also be able to achieve plasticity in the logic of their feelings" (see p. 120).

point of view (*otnosheniye*)   A property of the theatre artist's imagination, capable of creating a new artistic, or creative reality of the performance. Vakhtangov had this to say about the point of view in theatre: "Creative play in theatre is a play of the new points of view. One cannot believe literally. One must have an ability to take lies for truth, using the power of one's creative imagination; one must know how to instigate a new point of view on what happens onstage ...

"Adults lose the naivety of a child. When a child is tired of play, it means that he is tired of creating new points of view. A child is naive, which is why he creates new points of view so seriously.

"To be serious means to know that I am doing an important work. An actor, creating new points of view seriously, becomes naive" (see p. 89).

Vakhtangov distinguished between the creative point of view of the author and that of the theatrical collective. (This collective includes the director, actor, designers, composer, etc.). Many productions staged by Vakhtangov presented reality from a particular character's point of view—usually from the point of view of those characters possessing the popular consciousness or those who transgressed their social masks.

As a teacher of theatre, and director, Vakhtangov utilized the technique of shifting an actor's point of view on object, place, partner, and fact. On Vakhtangov's use of these techniques, see rehearsal records for *The Lanin Estate* (p. 248) (*see also* "appraising the fact").

Popular Theatre (*narodnyi teatr*)   The kind of theatre where the reality is presented through the prism of the popular consciousness. (*See also* "mystery.")

Presentational Theatre/School of Acting (also known as Theatre of Symbolism, Expressionism, Futurism and the Fantastic; School/Theatre of Presenting the Part, Non-Psychological Theatre) (*Predstavleniye*)   A trend of theatre where the theatrical collective copies the form of the role and the performance night after night. This form of theatre does not imply a creative emotional experience, transformation, as well as the working of the subconscious "creative nature." It relies on highly polished external technique (voice, speech, movement, gesture) to copy, or approximate the portrayed reality. In opposition to it, the School of the Emotional Experience calls for the stage reality to be recreated anew in every performance.

Vakhtangov is often credited with marrying the presentational school of acting with the school of experiencing. The reason Vakhtangov was able to achieve this merger is that he significantly redefined Stanislavsky's concept of experiencing. By doing so, he was able to place the numerous expressive means, usually associated with the presentational art, in the hands of the "experiencing" creative artist.

proceeding from oneself (*idti ot sebya*) *See* "transformation."

public solitude (*publichnoye odinochestvo*) According to Vakhtangov, a circle of attention, assumed in front of the audience, constitutes public solitude. This process, when executed right, creates the following sensation in an actor: "In front of an audience I (we) am (are) busy with what is important, necessary and interesting to me (us)" (Ivanov vol. II 2011: 359).

rhythm (*ritm*) In a work of art, rhythm signifies harmony of its separate parts that arises from of an artist's ability to embrace the entirety of the work. The idea of stage rhythm also implies uninterrupted internal movement of the performance. On the performance external side, it is paralleled by an alteration between movement and stillness. (*See* "statuary immobility," "dynamics," and "full stop.")

Vakhtangov applied his concept of rhythm to every aspect of the performance, be it actor's movement (gesture) and speech, character development, or the overall composition of the performance. Vakhtangov approached rhythm as the life stream of an artistic creation. If in life, rhythms can be arbitrary, in theatre they need to be harmonious. In theatre, as in other forms of art, rhythm serves as a force that organizes a performance. It is also the essential creative means of an actor. The artistic image, and the overall artistic reality of the performance, according to Vakhtangov, is created through the use of rhythm.

In his letter to the Gunst Studio movement class, Vakhtangov refers his students to Sergei Volkonsky's book *A Man on the Stage* (1912). To follow are the guiding principles of rhythm outlined in the Volkonsky's book:

"Space and time are the forever present conditions a man is placed under; they cannot be escaped. Physical conditions of space and time affect every single perception and action, and every single creation, spiritual or physical. He, who wants to create, must place space and time under his command; in order to do so, he must develop appropriate skills—the physical means of perception and expression that allow him to act within the boundaries of space and time.

"The means of perceiving the space is vision; the means of perceiving time is hearing.

"The means of expression in space is body, in time—voice.

"The method of training the actor for the space is plasticity of movement, for the time—speech.

"The means of merging the two is rhythm—correspondence of image and sound, of plasticity of movement and speech, of the categories of space and time.

"Only through such a merger will the entire, complete human (actor) be able to affect the entire, complete human (spectator)" (Volkonsky 1912: 179–180).

According to Vakhtangov, every nation, every character, every activity or action has its own rhythm that belongs to them by nature. An actor must be able to assume this rhythm.

saturating yourself for the role (*nasyschatsa dlya roli*)   "Keep reading the play informally; try to feel it, to dream, to fantasize about it, and some part of you will become captivated. This is called *saturating yourself for the role*. If you saturate yourself for the role, this will appear onstage unconsciously. Today I dreamed some [about my role], and tomorrow it will act itself out beyond my will" (see p. 260).

sculptural expressiveness, sculptural form (*skul'pturnost'*)   An actor's ability to create a visually expressive and meaningful combination between his or her own body, partners, and objects surrounding him or her on the stage. Distinct, sculptured, graphically outlined forms of imagery created by director and actor. Sculptural form implies the expressive, sculptural treatment of characters and stage compositions. (*See also* "modeling" and "plasticity.")

sculptural modeling (*skul'pturnaya lepka*)   *See* "modeling" and "sculptural expressiveness."

seriousness/being serious (*seryoz, byt' seryoznym*)   "Laughter that does not come from the essence of what happens onstage is caused by an actor's inability to take the given situation seriously. The theatrical lie should not interfere with seriousness; it should not distract …

"To be serious means to know that I am doing an important work. An actor, creating new points of view seriously, becomes naive. Onstage, it is unpleasant to speak a naturalistic truth; it ruins artistic fiction, as it is not a creative moment. The audience believes everything an actor believes" (see p. 89). (*See also* "faith/gaining faith.")

soul (*dusha*)   The emotional life of the actor-character and the emotional core of the play constitute the soul of the theatrical performance.

spirit (*dukh*)   An artistic spirit of the character, play, or performance is the creative spark, invested in it by the artist-creator. It is this spirit of the work of art (play, character) a theatre artist must perceive from the author. When the spirit of the artistic work "inseminates" the spirit of the theatre artist, it is then that a theatrical work of art is born. (*See* "essence.")

stage intelligence (*stsenichnost'*) An actor's ability to adapt his or her behavior to the conditions of the stage. It implies a number of automatic skills, including such basic skills as adjusting the volume of voice, based on location on the stage, as well as other speeches, noises, and sounds. Stage intelligence also implies a habit of not blocking the partner from the audience and not staying blocked by the partner if this occurs. Not repeating a partner's gestures and position of their body, if located in close proximity to the partner, is another one of these skills. Another habit to develop, as part of the stage intelligence skill, is the habit of filling the stage evenly in an ensemble scene. For a member of an ensemble, this implies not grouping in one place of the stage (unless required), while leaving the rest of the stage unoccupied.

stage platform, a place of (theatrical) action (*stsenicheskaya ploschadka*) Physical organization of theatre space is essential to the theatrical nature of the given production. A stage platform creates a necessary environment that supports the method of acting and the nature of communication with the audience utilized in the given performance. In addition to that, the stage platform contributes to the performance imagery. In his 1921 diary entry, Vakhtangov points out that "every kind of performance calls for its own form of stage platform." He continues by naming four theatrical personalities, whose names signified an epoch in the development of theatre: Shakespeare, Molière, Gozzi, Ostrovsky. Vakhtangov's thought is easy to transcribe: every great theatrical epoch introduced a new principle of the stage platform that did not change from one performance to the next. It might have been "dressed" differently for a different production, but its overall architecture remained the same.

Vakhtangov's concept of a stage platform that can serve several performances of the same type contradicted the "progressive" principles of stage design, introduced by his contemporary directors and designers. For example, the MAT prided itself in creating a unique set for every new performance. Vakhtangov, on the contrary, put the emphasis on discovering a *new method of actors' existence onstage* for every type of theatre. As for the overall architecture of the stage platform, he considered that a contemporary version of the stage platform should be discovered for every type of theatre, once and for all. On Vakhtangov's principle of stage platform for the contemporary version of the *commedia dell'arte*, see accounts of *Princess Turandot* rehearsals published in Part VII of the sourcebook.

statuary immobility (*statuarnost'*) A stopping in the physical movement of the performance that implies continuous inner movement. Interrupted movement is a powerful means of attracting the audience's attention to the essence of the stage bit, character, etc. Vakhtangov's principle of statuary immobility develops Delsarte's principles, such as the law of opposition, harmonic poise, and statue-posing. (*See* "gesture.")

subconscious expression (*podsoznatel'noye vyiavleniye*) "He who consciously feeds his subconscious and expresses the results of its work in a subconscious way is a talent.

"He who subconsciously feeds his subconscious and engages in a subconscious expression is a genius.

"He who expresses consciously is a master" (see p. 112).

subconscious perception (*podsoznatel'noye vospriyatiye*) An actor's ability to instantaneously grasp the essence, or the entirety of an artistic phenomenon—be it an object of observation, a character, a play, a theatrical situation, etc. "A couple of empty hints" (see p. 131) or details of the phenomenon coming to such an artist's attention allow the artist to synthesize the phenomenon at hand.

"A genius actor ... immediately, at once, embraces the character in its entirety, thus finding himself instantly at its apex. It is from this place that he perceives the details" (see p. 105). (*See also* "first spontaneous impression," "essence," "spirit," "first reading," and "subconscious expression.")

super task/super objective (*sverkh-zadacha*) "Every work [of art] contains the zest that compelled the poet to write it. With Chekhov—it is yearning for a beautiful life, with Tolstoy—self-perfection. This zest is the super task ...

"There may be a small task. And what if I deepen it? Then my 'I am' will be heard in a more complex, significant way.

"The deeper you dig into the task, the closer you come to its center, which *is* the super task.

"An actor must reach the deepest spiritual super center that includes everything in it. True acting results from the fulfillment of this deepest task" (see p. 101).

task, creative task (*zadacha, tvorcheskaya zadacha*) In every particular instance of the performance, be it plot, artistic form, or character psychology, a theatre artist is meant to resolve a particular creative task. The way by which the task is resolved (creative means, or actors' adaptations) constitutes the aspect of the performance perceived by the audience. Through these means or adaptations the audience receives the overall image of the performance. Therefore, if the task is resolved consciously, and adaptations are calculated, the image of the performance will not affect the audience's creative core. In order to do so, according to Vakhtangov, the resolution of the task should be fulfilled creatively: in other words, it should be spontaneous, improvisational, and imaginative.

According to Vakhtangov, a stage task consists of five elements:

	1	Action, Physical and Verbal (What do I do?)
Task	2	Motive (Why do I enter the stage?)
	3	Desire (Why do I want to fulfill my motive?)
	4	Adaptation (How do I fulfill my motive?)
	5	Subtext (What do I truly mean by what I say?)

The fourth element of task, adaptation, is its leading element, a measure of the actor's talent and his or her ability to affect the audience's creative nature.

temperament (*Temperament*) Creative passion, or emotional individuality of an artist. "Temperament is an ability to flare up, to react to circumstances. Temperament differs, depending on a person. An actor must learn to always arrive at the degree of temperament, as required by the given moment." (Vakhtangov) (Ivanov vol II 2011: 50). (*See* "creative passion that arises from perceiving the essence.")

texture *See* "theatrical texture."

Theatre of Experiencing/School of Experiencing (also known as Experiencing, School of Living the Part, Theatre of the Emotional Experience, Psychological Theatre, Theatre of Psychological Realism, Representational Theatre/Acting) (*Perezhivaniye*) A school of theatre that develops an actor's ability to awaken emotional experience at every performance. Experiencing is tightly connected with the process of an actor's transformation; in fact, one cannot happen without the other.

For Vakhtangov, experiencing signified an actor's ability to relive an emotional experience onstage without any external motivation. In Stanislavsky's opinion, the emotional life of the actor is motivated by the actor's faith in his or her character's given circumstances. Vakhtangov considered it both impossible and anti-artistic for an actor to literally believe in the fictitious circumstances. In Vakhtangov's opinion, such a literal belief would either be a sign of naivety or sick hallucination. According to Vakhtangov, an actor's faith was motivated by their imagination as well as their self-realization as a creative artist.

"An actor must awaken his passion *without any external motivation* for creative passion; to achieve this, an actor must work in rehearsals chiefly to make everything that surrounds him, according to the play, his own atmosphere and to make his role's tasks his own; this will cause his passion to speak 'from the essence'" (see p. 141).

In other words, every creative individual, according to Vakhtangov, needs to discover a unique atmosphere and the essence of every stage event, situation or object. This unique atmosphere is the atmosphere of this particular artist's private artistic mission or theme; it awakens in them a sense of creative festivity. Only this individual creative mission, as refracted in the events, objects, and situations on the stage, is capable of arousing this individual's creative passion. In many instances, an actor's very realization, or a sensation of having such a theme, or mission, is sufficient to produce the desired effect.

Theatre of Mystery *See* "mystery."

theatrical communication (*teatral'noye obsheniye*) By "theatrical communion" Vakhtangov implies the type of communion he developed during his final years and utilized in his work on his final productions, specifically in *Princess Turandot*. Vakhtangov distinguished between several types of theatrical communion, including an actor's direct communion with the audience, indirect communion with the audience, via a partner, as well as communion between the two partners in rhythm and movement. Vakhtangov's concept of theatrical communion also included direct and indirect communion between the actors outside of the "character mask," or by the means of the "character mask."

theatrical form and theatrical content (*teatral'naya forma i teatral'noye soderzhaniye*)   The two were inseparable for Vakhtangov, as, to his mind, a theatre artist is supposed to fantasize a form that would fully express (or exhaust) the performance's content.

theatrical justification (*teatral'noye opravdaniye*)   A term (and device) used by Vakhtangov during his work on *Princess Turandot*. According to this device, the life of *Turandot* characters received justification in a specific reality of a theatrical performance—as opposed to the everyday reality.

theatrical texture (*teatral'naya faktura*)   The method of an actor's life onstage and their choice of means of expressiveness in creating a stage image. Vakhtangov's concept of theatrical textures is discussed in the Introduction.

theatricality (*teatral'nost'*)   Each element of the performance can only be theatrical when it is essential to the unique world of the theatre production and to the essence of theatre at large. In Vakhtangov's mind, any object, blocking, character, set, etc., either "acts," or it does not, based on how fitting and meaningful it is in the artistic word of the given performance. A play, or a literary work, may be theatrical if it contains in it the essence of theatricality. For Vakhtangov, this essence was expressed in his concept of festivity. (*See* "festivity.")

thought (*mysl'*)   Vakhtangov's concept of thought is thoroughly explained in his October 11, 1917, talk (pp. 117–18), as well as in his rehearsals for Maeterlinck's *The Miracle of Saint Anthony* (see October 9, 1916, rehearsal record on p. 262) and for Pushkin's *Feast During the Plague* (see rehearsal records on pp. 284).

According to various aims behind a question, the thoughts that lie underneath the text of the question ("What time is it?") will differ, while never concurring with the literal meaning of the text. To follow are the thoughts that could lie underneath the question "What time is it?" "Why are you late?" or "why are you still here?" or "My God, what tedium!" or "Am I late?," etc.

In accordance with various thoughts, lying under the given bit of text, its intonations and gestures would also differ. This is easy to prove by asking the question "What time is it?" while investing it with one or the other of the thoughts indicated above.

This is why Vakhtangov demanded that his students do not speak the words but thoughts. He called an actor's work of discovering the thoughts underneath the words of the text "unsealing the text" (p. 193).

Thus, in order to "make the author's ... words his own" (see p. 90), an actor must make his own "the thoughts" his character lives with (Zakhava 1930: 59). (*See also* "perspective" and "word-leading.")

through action (*skvoznoye deistviye*)   "The execution of the super task is the through action" (see p. 101).

through line of the theatrical performance (*skvoznoye deistviye teatral'nogo predstavleniya*)   In Vakhtangov's understanding, the through line of the performance is created by varied expressive means; unlike the through action, it does not pertain solely to the psychological realm but also to the director's and actor's use of composition. A visual, rhythmic, musical, and/or atmospheric leitmotif constitutes the through line of the theatrical performance.

transformation/transfiguration   (*perevoploscheniye*)   Vakhtangov's   actor organically transforms as a creative individual. Transformation makes a creative individual out of the actor's everyday self. Such a creative individual reveals the hidden aspects of his or her inner world to the audience. With such a transformation an actor remains free to use a variety of expressive means, both physical and vocal, using them to create the artistic image of the character.

Between 1913 and 1918, Vakhtangov explored the Theatre of Mystery. At that stage of his work, Vakhtangov denied the art of characterization and insisted that actors must preserve their "God-given face" and "God-given voice." This phase of Vakhtangov's creative search, however, did not signify his denial of the creative transformation. Vakhtangov demanded that an actor must transform "by the power of the inner impulse," or by proceeding from oneself. Between 1918 and 1922, Vakhtangov created his method of fantastic realism, synthesizing the Theatre of Mystery with the Popular Theatre. This innovation, as well as the spirit of revolutionary times, caused Vakhtangov to arrive at a new logical conclusion on transformation. Vakhtangov concluded that an actor who transforms and lives onstage as a creative individual is free to use any theatrical texture (characterization, grotesque, symbolism, futurism, etc.), as long as this texture remains true to the spirit of the work and of the contemporary times.

voice-leading/word-leading (*golosovedeniye/slovovedeniye*)   This is the arrangement and movement of voices in musical composition. Vakhtangov insisted that his actors master the art of voice-leading in order to make their speech expressive, artistically varied, and dynamic. The term "word-leading" is similar to voice-leading; it indicates an actor's ability to lead the main thought through a text bit. Word-leading uses many of the same devices utilized in voice-leading in order to create a perspective of thought in the bit. According to Vladislav Ivanov (1999: 90), the use of voice-leading was instrumental to Vakhtangov's concept of ecstatic (or festive) composition—such as the one achieved in the production of *The Dybbuk*. In the first act of *The Dybbuk* (synagogue scene), a woman praying for her dying son began her prayer with an "everyday patter," gradually "elevating" it to rhythmic chanting, and, finally, to singing.

The following terms and devices, used by Vakhtangov, constitute the variables of the voice-leading:

1   Sound (*zvuk*): Some of the variable qualities of the sound in dramatic speech are loudness, pitch, vibration, intensity, and distance of sending the voice, etc.

2   Timbre (*tembr*): A distinguishing characteristic of voice, its color and quality.

3   Accent (*aktsent*): There are many ways of accentuating a particular sound, word, or group of words in dramatic speech. Almost any element of "voice-leading" can be utilized as the means of accent.

4   Overtone (*oberton*): An ability of the human voice to produce a number of tones, along with the fundamental tone.

5   Degree (*gradus*): Gradual increase, or lessening, of the inner intensity of speech.

6   Apostrophe (*apostrof*): An exclamatory rhetorical figure of speech. An apostrophe occurs when a speaker interrupts the flow of their speech and addresses an imaginary person or abstract quality, or idea. In dramatic works and poetry, an apostrophe often begins with the word "Oh."

7   Motif/delivery of the leitmotif (*motiv, peredacha leitmotiva*): A recurring theme, associated with particular character, place, idea, etc. (*See* "rhythm" and "through line of the theatrical performance".)

8   Articulation (*artikulyatsyia*): The following is an account of Vakhtangov's articulation in the role of Master Pierre from Nadezhda Bromley's play *The Archangel Michael*. According to the memoir of the actor Nal',[1] Vakhtangov pronounced his lines "with special modeling, and extremely hard consonants. The text was delivered with great sharpness, in a striking and graphically vivid way" (Nal' 1984: 368).

9   Melody (*melodiya*).

10   Musical rest (*ostanovka*): An interval of silence in music.

11   *Legato*.

12   *Staccato*.

13   Syncopation (*sinkopa*): A deviation from the regular flow of rhythm.

14   Tone (*zvychnost'*).

"what for" (*radi chego*)   The unique artistic theme or mission belonging to the theatre artist's creative individuality. According to Vakhtangov, every creative individual, or creative formation (theatrical collective) has their unique artistic theme and mission that distinguishes them from any other creative individual and creative formation. It is this individual theme, and nothing else, that they need to express in their every role and every performance in order to remain creative and true to their own artist.

---

1   Anatoly Nal' (1905–1970), the Vakhtangov Studio and Theatre actor from 1921 to 1949.

Bibliography

Amaspiuriants, Abri (1996) *Turandot-63*, Moscow: Folio.

Apollonskaya (Stravinskaya), Inna (1910) *Teatr Ibsena* [*Ibsen's Theatre*]: *"Rosmershol'm,"* St. Petersburg: Tipografia tovarischestva "Obschestvennaya pol'za."

Bakhtin, Mikhail (1984) *Rabelais and His World*, trans. Helene Iswolsky, Bloomington, IN: Indiana University Press.

Barba, Eugenio (1995) *The Paper Canoe: A Guide to Theatre Anthropology*, London and New York: Routledge.

Barba, Eugenio and Savarese, Nicola (2005) *A Dictionary of Theatre Anthropology: The Secret Art of the Performer*, London and New York: Routledge.

Bely, Andrei (1934) *Mezhdu dvukh revoliutsyi*, Leningrad: Izdatel'stvo Pisatelei.

Ben-Ari, Raikin (1957) *Habima*, London and New York: Thomas Yoselof.

Bericht des Gewerkschaftsbundes der Angestellten: Bericht über das Arbeitsjahr 1930, Berlin-Zehlendorf: Verlag des GDA, 1931.

Black, Lendley C. (1987) *Mikhail Chekhov as Actor, Director and Teacher*, Ann Arbor, MI: UMI Research Press.

Brecht, Bertolt (1964) *Brecht on Theatre: The Development of an Aesthetic*, ed. and trans. John Willett, New York: Hill & Wang.

Brestoff, Richard (1995) *Great Acting Teachers and Their Methods*, Lyme, NH: Smith and Kraus.

Bromley, Nadezhda (1923) *"Turandot Vakhtangova"* in *Printsessa Turandot* ["Vakhtangov's *Turandot*" in *Princess Turandot*], Moscow-Petrograd: Gosudarstvennoie Izdatel'stvo.

—— (1959) "Put' iskatelia [Seeker's Path]," in Lyubov Vendrovskaya (ed.), *Yevg. Vakhtangov, Materialy i statyi* [*Yevgeny Vakhtangov, Materials and Articles*], Moscow: VTO, pp. 322–330.

Brook, Peter (1996) *The Empty Space*, New York: Touchstone.

Chamberlain, Franc (2004) *Michael Chekhov*, London and New York: Routledge.

Chekhov, Michael (1984) *Michael Chekhov's To the Director and Playwright*, New York: Limelight Editions.

Chekhov, Michael (1991) *On the Technique of Acting*, New York: HarperCollins.
—— (1995) *Literaturnoie nasledie* [*Literary Heritage*], 2nd edn, vol. II, Moscow: Iskusstvo.
—— (2002) *To the Actor*, London and New York: Routledge.
—— (2005) *The Path of the Actor*, London and New York: Routledge.
Clurman, Harold (1997) *On Directing*, New York: Fireside.
Craig, Gordon (1939) "Habima's Achievement," in *Habima*, English Publication of *Bama*, Theatre Art Journal of Habima Circle in Palestine, Tel-Aviv, August.
Demidov, Nikolai (2004a) *Tvorcheskoie nasledie* [*Creative Heritage*], vol. I, book 1: *Iskusstvo aktyora v ego nastoyaschem i buduschem* [*The Art of the Actor: Its Present and Future*] and book 2: *Tipy aktyora* [*Actor Types*], St. Petersburg: Giperion.
—— (2004b) *Tvorcheskoie nasledie* [*Creative Heritage*], vol. II, book 3: *Iskusstvo zhit' na stsene* [*The Art of Living Onstage*], St. Petersburg: Giperion.
—— (2009) *Tvorcheskoie nasledie* [*Creative Heritage*], vol. IV, book 5: *Teoria i psikhologia aktyora affektivnogo tipa* [*Theory and Psychology of the Affective Type Actor*], St. Petersburg: Baltiyskie Sezony.
Dennis, Rabbi Geoffrey W. (2007) *Encyclopedia of Jewish Myth, Magic and Mysticism*, Woodbury, MN: Llewellyn Publications.
Deykun, Lidiya (1984) "Iz vospominaniy [From Memoirs]," in Vendrovskaya and Kaptereva (eds.), *Yevgeny Vakhtangov*, Moscow: VTO, pp. 355–356.
Fydorov, Pyotr (1993) *Nerazgadannyi Vakhtangov?* [*Undiscovered Vakhtangov?*] Online. Available http:<mutabor.land.ru/fors/fant_vah.htm> (accessed November 22, 2010).
Gorchakov, Nikolai (1957) *The Theater in Soviet Russia*, New York: Columbia University Press.
Gorchakov, Nikolai Mikhailovich (1957) *Rezhissyorskiye uroki Vakhtangova* [*Vakhtangov's Directorial Lessons*], Moscow: Iskusstvo.
—— (1959 probable year) *The Vakhtangov School of Stage Art*, Moscow: Foreign Languages Publishing House.
Gordon, Mel (1987) *The Stanislavsky Technique: Russia*, New York: Applause Theater Book Publishers.
Hethmon, Robert H. (ed.) (1991) *Strasberg at the Actors Studio: Tape-Recorded Sessions*, New York: Theatre Communications Group.
Hodge, Alison (ed.) (2000) *Twentieth Century Actor Training*, London and New York: Routledge.
Ivanov, Vladislav (1999) *Russkiye Sezony Teatra Gabima* [*The Russian Seasons of the Habima Theatre*], Moscow: Artist. Rezhissyor Teatr
—— (ed.) (2011) *Yevgeny Vakhtangov, Dokumenty i svidetel'stva* [*Yevgeny Vakhtangov, Documents and Evidence*], vols I, II, Moscow: Indrik.
Karev (Prudkin), Aleksandr (1959) "Vesyolyi, neuyomnyi khudozhnik [Merry, Persistent Artist]," in Lyubov Vendrovskaya (ed.), *Yevg. Vakhtangov, Materialy i statyi* [*Yevgeny Vakhtangov, Materials and Articles*], Moscow: VTO, pp. 416–422.

Khersonsky, Khrisanf (ed.) (1940) *Besedy o Vakhtangove* [*Conversations About Vakhtangov*], Moscow-Leningrad: VTO.

Komissarzhevsky, Fyodor (1916) *Tvorchestvo aktyora i teoriya Stanislavskogo* [*An Actor's Creativity and Stanislavsky's Theory*], Petrograd: Svobodnoe Iskusstvo.

Leach, Robert and Borovsky, Victor (eds.) (2006) *A History of Russian Theatre*, Cambridge: Cambridge University Press.

Levy, Emanuel (1979) *The Habima: Israel's National Theater, 1917–1977*, New York: Columbia University Press.

Lussy, Mathis (1884) *Le Rythme musical*, Paris: Heugel.

Maikov, L. (1896) "Schepkin o Rasheli [Schepkin on Rachel]," *Ezhegodnik Imperatorskikh teatrov* [*The Annual of the Imperial Theatres*], Season 1894/5, Supplement, St. Petersburg: Izdanie Direktsii Imperatorskikh teatrov.

Malaev-Babel, Andrei (forthcoming) *Yevgeny Vakhtangov*, London and New York: Routledge.

Marowitz, Charles (2004) *The Other Chekhov*, New York: Applause Theater Book Publishers.

Meyerhold, Vsevolod (1913) *O teatre* [*On Theatre*], St. Petersburg: Knigoizdatel'skoe tovarischestvo "Prosvieschenie".

—— (1998) *Nasledie* [*Heritage*], vol. I, Moscow: OGI.

—— (2001) *Lektsii 1918–1919* [*Lectures 1918–1919*], Moscow: OGI.

Moore, Sonia (1984) *The Stanislavski System: The Professional Training of an Actor*, London: Penguin.

Nal', Anatoly (1984) "Iz vospominaniy [From Memoirs]" in Vendrovskaya and Kaptereva (eds.), *Yevgeny Vakhtangov*, Moscow: VTO.

Norman, Itzhak (ed.) (1966) *Be-reshit Habimah* [*The Birth of Habima*], Jerusalem: ha-Sifriyah ha-Tsiyonit.

Parke, Lawrence (1985) *Since Stanislavski and Vakhtangov: The Method as a System for Today's Actor*, Hollywood, CA: Acting World Books.

Polyakova, Yelena (ed.) (1970) *Leopold Antonovich Sulerzhitsky*, Moscow: Iskusstvo.

Printsessa Turandot [*Princess Turandot*] (1923) Moscow-Petrograd: Gosudarstvennoie Izdatel'stvo.

Rafalovich, Sergei (1908) "Evol'utsia teatra (Kratkii istoricheskii sintez) [The Evolution of Theatre (Concise Historic Synthesis)," in *"Teatr" Kniga o novom teatre* [*"Theatre" Book on the New Theatre*], St. Petersburg. Reprinted in 2008 by GITIS (Moscow).

Ramacharaka, Yogi (Atkinson, William Walker) (1904) *Hatha Yoga; or the Yogi Philosophy of Physical Well-Being*, Chicago, IL: Yogi Publication Society.

Rolland, Romain (1919) *Narodnyi teatr* [*Popular Theatre*], intro. by Predislovie Viacheslava Ivanova, Petrograd: Izdatel'stvo Teatral'nogo otdela Narodnogo komissariata po prosveshcheniiu.

Rudnitsky, Konstantin (2000) *Russian and Soviet Theatre: Tradition and the Avant-Garde*, London: Thames & Hudson.

Rybakova, Yu (1994) *V. F. Komissarzhevskaya: Letopis' zhizni i tvorchestva* [*Chronicle of Vera Komissarzhevskaya Life and Art*], St. Petersburg: Institut istorii iskusstv.

Rzhevsky, Nicholas (ed.) (1999) *The Cambridge Companion to Modern Russian Culture*, Cambridge: Cambridge University Press.

Schmidt, Paul (ed.) (1996) *Meyerhold at Work*, New York: Applause Theatre & Cinema Book Publishers.

Shikhmatov, Leonid (1970) *Ot studii k teatru* [*From Studio to Theatre*], Moscow: VTO.

Simonov, Ruben (1969) *Stanislavsky's Protégé: Eugene Vakhtangov*, trans. Miriam Goldina, New York: DBS Publications.

Slonim, Mark (1961) *Russian Theater: From the Empire to the Soviets*, Cleveland, OH: The World Publishing Company.

Smirnova, Natalia (1982) *Yevgeny Vakhtangov*, Moscow: Znanie.

Sobolev, Yuri (1922) "Den' Vakhtangova [Vakhtangov's Day]," *Teatr i muzyka*, December 5.

Stanislavsky, Konstantin (1991) *Sobranie sochineniy v devyati tomakh* [*Collected Works in 9 Volumes*], vol. IV: *Rabota aktyora nad roliu* [*Actor's Work on the Role*], Moscow: Iskusstvo.

—— (1993) *Sobranie sochineniy v devyati tomakh* [*Collected Works in 9 Volumes*], vol. V: *Statyi. Rechi. Vospominaniya. Khudozhestvennye zapisi* [*Articles. Speeches. Memoirs. Notes on Art*], Moscow: Iskusstvo.

—— (1996) *My Life in Art*, London and New York: Routledge/Theatre Arts Books.

—— (1999) *Sobranie sochineniy v devyati tomakh* [*Collective Works in 9 Volumes*], vol. IX: *Pis'ma 1918–1938* [*Letters 1918–1939*], Moscow: Iskusstvo.

—— (2008) *An Actor's Work*, London and New York: Routledge.

Strasberg, Lee (1988) *A Dream of Passion: The Development of the Method*, New York and Scarborough, Ontario: Plume.

Stebbins, Genevieve (1902) *Delsarte System of Expression*, New York: E. S. Werner.

Sulerzhitsky, Leopold (1970) *O vzaimootnoshenii akyora i rezhissyora* in *Leopold Antonovich Sulerzhitsky* [*On the Relationship Between the Actor and the Director* in *Leopold Antonovich Sulerzhitsky*], ed. E. I. Polyakova, Moscow: Iskusstvo.

Tartakovskaya, Yelena (2007) "Dibuk, vyidi!—Ne vyidu! [Dybbuk, Exit!—I won't!]," *L'Chaim*, 178 (2): 39–43.

Vakhtangov, Yevgeny (1947) *Preparing for the Role: From the Diary of E. Vakhtangov* in Cole, Toby (ed.) *Acting: A Handbook of the Stanislavski Method*, New York: Lear Publishers, pp. 116–124.

—— (1953) *Fantastic Realism [Two Final Discussions with Students]* in Cole, Toby and Chinoy, Helen Krich (eds.) *Directing the Play*, Indianapolis, IN: Bobbs-Merrill, pp. 160–165.

—— (1987) "Vsekhsvyatskie zapisi [All Saints' Notes]," *Teatr*, no. 12.

Vakhtangova, Nadezhda (1959) "Vladikavkaz i Moskva [Vladikavkaz and Moscow]," in Lyubov Vendrovskaya (ed.), *Yevg. Vakhtangov, Materialy i statyi* [*Yevgeny Vakhtangov, Materials and Articles*], Moscow: VTO, pp. 331–343.

Vakhtangova, Nadezhda, Vendrovskaya, Lyubov and Zakhava, Boris (eds.) (1939) *Vakhtangov: Zapiski. Pis'ma. Statyi* [*Vakhtangov: Notes. Letters. Articles*], Moscow and Leningrad: Iskusstvo.

Vendrovskaya, Lyubov (ed.) (1959) *Yevg. Vakhtangov, Materialy i statyi* [*Yevgeny Vakhtangov, Materials and Articles*], Moscow: VTO.

Vendrovskaya, Lyubov and Kaptereva, Galina (eds.) (1982) *Evgeny Vakhtangov*, Moscow: Progress Publishers.

—— (eds.) (1984) *Yevgeny Vakhtangov*, Moscow: VTO.

Vershilov, Boris (1959) "Stranitsy vospominaniy [Merry, Pages from the Memoirs]," in Lyubov Vendrovskaya (ed.), *Yevg. Vakhtangov, Materialy i statyi* [*Yevgeny Vakhtangov, Materials and Articles*], Moscow: VTO, pp. 372–395.

Volkonsky, Sergei (1912) *Chelovek na stsene* [*A Man on the Stage*], St. Petersburg: Izdanie "Apollona".

—— (1913) *Vyrazitel'noe slovo* [*Expressive Word*], St. Petersburg: Tipografia Sirius.

Volkov, Nikolai (1922) *Vakhtangov*, Moscow: Korabl'.

Worrall, Nick (1989) *Modernism to Realism on the Soviet Stage: Tairov–Vakhtangov–Okhlopkov*, Cambridge: Cambridge University Press.

Yzraely, Yosef (1970) "Vakhtangov Directing *The Dybbuk*," unpublished doctoral dissertation, Carnegie-Mellon University's Department of Drama.

Zagorsky, Mikhail (1922) "*Gadibuk* (Studia Gabima) [*The Dybbuk* (The Habima Studio)]," *Teatral'naya Moskva*, no. 25.

Zakhava, Boris (1927) *Vakhtangov i ego studia* [*Vakhtangov and His Studio*], Leningrad: Academia.

—— (1930) *Vakhtangov i ego studia* [*Vakhtangov and His Studio*], 2nd edn, Moscow: Teakinopechat'.

—— (1935) *Vzaimodeistvie mezhdu aktyorom i rezhissyorom* [*Interaction Between Actor and Director*], Moscow: TS K RABIS.

—— (2010) *Vakhtangov i ego studia* [*Vakhtangov and His Studio*], 3rd edn, Moscow: Arsis Books.

Zavadsky, Yuri (1959) "Oderzhimost' tvorchestvom [Creative Possession]," in Lyubov Vendrovskaya (ed.), *Yevg. Vakhtangov, Materialy i statyi* [*Yevgeny Vakhtangov, Materials and Articles*], Moscow: VTO, pp. 278–305.

—— (1975) *Uchitelia i ucheniki* [*Masters and Students*], Moscow: Iskusstvo.

Index